Race, Culture, and Identities in Second Language Education

D0937515

"…a pioneering collection of groundbreaking studies that interrogate how race operates overtly and covertly in contexts of second language learning."

Angela Reyes, Hunter College, City University of New York

The concept and construct of race is often implicitly yet profoundly connected to issues of culture and identity. Meeting an urgent need for empirical and conceptual research that specifically explores critical issues of race, culture, and identities in second language education, the key questions addressed in this groundbreaking volume are these:

- How are issues of race relevant to second language education?
- How does whiteness influence students' and teachers' sense of self and instructional practices?
- How do discourses of racialization influence the construction of student identities and subjectivities?
- How do discourses on race, such as colorblindness, influence classroom practices, educational interventions, and parental involvement?
- How can teachers transform the status quo?

Each chapter is grounded in theory and provides implications for engaged practice. Topics cover a wide range of themes that emerge from various pedagogical contexts, including ESL and bilingual programs in primary and secondary education in the U.S. and Canada, post-secondary ESL programs in Australia and the U.S., second/foreign language teacher education in the U.S., Canada, and Venezuela, and EFL settings such as Brazil and South Korea. Authors from diverse racial/ethnic/cultural backgrounds and geopolitical locations include both established and beginning scholars in the field, making the content vibrant and stimulating. Pre-reading Questions and Discussion Questions in each chapter facilitate comprehension and invite dialogue.

Ryuko Kubota is Professor in the Department of Language and Literacy Education at the University of British Columbia, Canada.

Angel Lin is Associate Professor in the Department of English, City University of Hong Kong.

Race, Culture, and Identities in Second Language Education

Exploring Critically Engaged Practice

Edited by
Ryuko Kubota
University of British Columbia

Angel Lin
City University of Hong Kong

Routledge
Taylor & Francis Group

NEW YORK AND LONDON

First published 2009
by Routledge
270 Madison Ave, New York, NY 10016

Simultaneously published in the UK
by Routledge
2 Park Square, Milton Park, Abingdon, Oxon OX14 4RN

Routledge is an imprint of the Taylor & Francis Group, an informa business

Transferred to Digital Printing 2010

Typeset in Minion by Wearset Ltd, Boldon, Tyne and Wear

Library of Congress Cataloging-in-Publication Data
Race, culture, and identities in second language education : exploring critically engaged practice / edited by Ryuko Kubota, Angel Lin.

p. cm.

1. English language–Study and teaching–Foreign speakers–Social aspects.
2. Second language acquisition–Social aspects. 3. Discrimination in education.
4. Ethnicity. I. Kubota, Ryuko. II. Lin, Angel, 1962–

PE1128.A2R23 2009

428.0'4089–dc22   2008050959

ISBN10: 0-415-99506-X (hbk)
ISBN10: 0-415-99507-8 (pbk)
ISBN10: 0-203-87665-2 (ebk)

ISBN13: 978-0-415-99506-1 (hbk)
ISBN13: 978-0-415-99507-8 (pbk)
ISBN13: 978-0-203-87665-7 (ebk)

Contents

PART II
Racializing Discourses and Identity Construction in Educational
Settings

PART III
Toward a Dialectic of Critically Engaged Praxis

Preface

In this groundbreaking collection of research-based scholarly works on issues of race and their intersection with culture and identities in second language education, each chapter presents data-based research or conceptual inquiry and provides both theoretical and practical insights into second language teaching and learning. The research sites range from the United States to Australia, Brazil, Canada, South Korea, and Venezuela and the racial and ethnic backgrounds of the teachers and students in these studies represent further diversity. The topics include: construction of racialized identities for culturally and linguistically diverse students in primary, secondary, and higher education; manifestations of racism in relation to culturally and linguistically diverse students; ESL/EFL teachers' views of race, racism, culture, and language; and critically engaged pedagogies that affirm the racial heritage of students and challenge racism in language learning and teaching.

The idea for this book emerged from our experiences of difficulties in discussing issues of racism with colleagues in second language education. For many years, the field of teaching English to speakers of other languages has attempted to solve pedagogical challenges by exploring cultural differences between the sociolinguistic conventions that English-language learners grew up with and the perceived expectations of the target language and society. In the academic literature in this area, ESL/EFL learners are often constructed as the Other or as members of traditional cultures conditioned by collectivism and respect for authorities, which is contrasted by individualism and critical thinking of the West. We critiqued that this cultural dichotomy parallels discourses of colonialism in which racism lies at its core (Kubota, 2001; Lin & Luk, 2002). The critique by one of us (Kubota, 2001) evoked a defending response and a rebuttal (Atkinson, 2002; Kubota, 2002). In this exchange, the critique of racism embedded in discourses of colonialism and cultural difference was unfortunately interpreted as a personal criticism of the author as racist, rather than a critique of structural and epistemological forces that legitimate power hierarchies. A similar incident happened a few years later at a major conference, and this time it was a face-to-face confrontation. One of us (Kubota) was informally conversing with friends in a hotel lobby late at night. A researcher whose approach to culture had been critiqued approached and abruptly said, "You called me racist and I am upset." These exchanges illuminate the sensitive and treacherous nature of discussing racism in our academic inquiry, which inhibits scholars and teachers from confronting critical issues of racialization and racism in second language teaching and learning.

In the field of education, Gloria Ladson-Billings (1999) states that discussing racism is an uncomfortable and unpopular position when many teachers and teacher educators believe that they are "permanent residents in a *nice* field like education" (p. 27). Specialists in second language education would identify their field as even *nicer* than the general field of education because the field constantly deals with intercultural and multilingual encounters. Perhaps because of this, second language education has not extensively engaged in academic exploration of racialization and racism, even though the field has made a critical turn since the 1990s. More and more books and articles have been published, addressing and critiquing socially and ideologically contentious issues from neo-Marxist, postmodernist, poststructuralist, and postcolonial perspectives. While issues of gender, culture, and identities have been popular topics to explore, issues of racialization and racism have been underexplored in academic discussions and especially in rigorous scholarly inquiry. Yet, ideas of race constitute a significant part of our knowledge of culture and identities. They indeed underlie teaching and learning in a second language classroom that creates contact zones for teachers, students, and imagined speakers of the target language from various racial backgrounds.

This book is an attempt to fill this gap. We hope that it will serve as a springboard for further academic inquiry and pedagogical innovations to problematize racialization and racism in many facets of educational practice, affirm racial and cultural diversity, and promote equity and social justice among groups of teachers and learners from diverse backgrounds. As a resource that provides useful knowledge and insight into theory, research, and practice, the book is suited for undergraduate and graduate students of TESL/TEFL, bilingual education, foreign-language teaching, applied linguistics, intercultural communication, or related fields, teacher educators who are preparing teachers to work with culturally and linguistically diverse students, and researchers who wish to explore issues of race in language, culture, and identities.

Overview

The book is divided into three parts: Part I, Interrogating Whiteness; Part II, Racializing Discourses and Identity Construction in Educational Settings; and Part III, Toward a Dialectic of Critically Engaged Praxis. Following Chapter 1, which introduces key concepts and theories, Part I presents chapters that critically address and analyze Whiteness, a privileged position in the global racial hierarchy. Part II contains chapters that explore how racializing discourses construct teacher and student identities. Finally, Part III addresses pedagogical issues that incorporate critical engagement in racialization and racism. We introduce each part with a brief summary of each chapter. Each chapter begins with a set of pre-reading questions to orient the readers to the topic and issues addressed in the chapter. Discussion questions that follow each chapter can be used for classroom discussions or assignments.

The publication of this book was made possible by the chapter authors' hard work, patience, and commitment to the project. We thank Jennifer Drolet, Terry Osborn, and anonymous reviewers of the manuscripts for their careful reading of the manuscripts. We also thank Naomi Silverman at Routledge for her support of this publication and the University Research Council at the University of North Carolina at Chapel Hill for its financial support.

References

Atkinson, D. (2002). Comments on Ryuko Kubota's "Discursive construction of the images of U.S. classrooms": A reader reacts ... *TESOL Quarterly, 36,* 79–84.

Kubota, R. (2001). Discursive construction of the images of U.S. classrooms. *TESOL Quarterly, 35,* 9–38.

Kubota, R. (2002). The author responds: (Un)Raveling racism in a nice field like TESOL. *TESOL Quarterly, 36,* 84–92.

Ladson-Billings, G. (1999). Just what is critical race theory, and what's it doing in a *nice* field like education? In L. Parker, D. Deyhle, & S. Villenas (Eds.), *Race is—race isn't: Critical race theory and qualitative studies in education* (pp. 7–30). Boulder, CO: Westview Press.

Lin, A. M. Y., & Luk, J. (2002). Beyond progressive liberalism and cultural relativism: Towards critical postmodernist and sociohistorically situated perspectives in ethnographic classroom studies. *Canadian Modern Language Review, 59,* 97–124.

1 Race, Culture, and Identities in Second Language Education

Introduction to Research and Practice[1]

Ryuko Kubota and Angel Lin

Pre-reading Questions

This introductory chapter presents basic concepts such as race, ethnicity, culture, racialization, and racism. It also introduces theoretical and pedagogical frameworks that can be used to address issues of race. Some possible inquiry themes are discussed to stimulate further explorations of race, culture, and identities. Before reading this chapter, think about the following questions:

*   How would you define race?
*   Why are explorations of race, culture, and identities important in second language education?
*   What kind of research projects on race, culture, and identities can be developed?

Introduction

Second language education, including teaching the host society's majority language to immigrants, bilingual education, and teaching foreign languages involves direct and virtual interactions among many groups of people who are often perceived as racially and culturally distinct. Through teaching and learning a second language, racialized images of the teacher, students, and people that appear in teaching materials get produced and reproduced. Nonetheless, inquiry into ideas of race has not yet earned significant visibility in second language scholarship, unlike other related fields such as sociology, anthropology, education, and composition studies (see Amin, 1997; Ibrahim, 2000; Willett, 1996). The lack of discussion could stem from the stigma attached to the term race. It evokes racism which is often interpreted as overt forms of bigotry, rather than structural or institutional inequalities, and this undertone tends to prevent open dialogs. However, issues of race have recently begun to be addressed especially in the field of teaching English to speakers of other languages (TESOL), as seen in a collection of essays by racial-minority scholars in TESOL (Curtis & Romney, 2006) and a special-topic issue of *TESOL Quarterly* (Kubota & Lin, 2006). Together with the recent inquiries into critical issues in second language education, such as gender (Davis & Skilton-Sylvester, 2004; Langman, 2004), sexual identities (Nelson, 1999, 2006, 2008), and class (Vandrick, 1995, 2007), issues of race address power, identity, subjectivity, and social (in)justice, which are vital to all aspects of second language education. At the same time, racial difference is often discussed as equivalent to cultural difference in the contemporary discourse of racism. In this sense, critical investigations of cultural differences could contribute to revealing the mechanism of racialization and racism.

This book presents scholarly investigations of the intersection between race, culture, and identities in second language education. We consider this inquiry essential, as our field creates numerous contact zones for diverse groups of people from all over the world, zones in which questions and tensions related to the idea of race are inescapable and constitute valid topics for critical exploration. In this introduction, we survey some of the concepts and theories about the idea of race as defined and debated in various fields and make connections between them and second language education. The amount of scholarly discussion on race is immense in the fields outside second language studies, such as sociology, anthropology, and education. To provide a comprehensive summary of theories, views, and research methodologies is beyond our scope here. Rather, the main purpose of this introduction is to provide second language professionals with a springboard for future exploration of the topic.

Race, Ethnicity, and Culture

Race

In everyday discourse, the word race invokes phenotypical features such as skin color, eye shape, hair texture, facial features, and so on. However, scientists generally agree that race is not a concept determined by biological evidence. In other words, categorization of different races cannot be verified by biological constructs such as genetic characteristics. Arguing that any differentiation of races, if they exist at all, depends on relative, rather than absolute, constancy of genes and raising a problem of classifying the human species in racial terms, Goldberg (1993) states:

> Human beings possess a far larger proportion of genes in common than they do genes that are supposed to differentiate them racially. Not surprisingly, we are much more like each other than we are different. It has been estimated that, genetically speaking, the difference in difference—the percentage of our genes that determines our purportedly racial or primarily morphological difference—is 0.5 percent.
>
> (p. 67)

More recently, the Human Genome Project has shown that 99.9% of human genes are shared in common, leaving only 0.1% for potential racial difference in a biological sense (Hutchinson, 2005).

In the sense that racial categories are not biologically determined, races do not exist. However, the recent approval of BiDil in the United States, a cardiovascular drug targeted for African Americans or the first racial drug (Duster, 2005), represents sustained scientific interest in grouping people according to race in investigating the relationship between genetics and diseases. In such explorations, the category of race has been replaced by the concept of *population* identified by genetic characteristics (St. Louis, 2005). According to St. Louis, particular populations are identified through certain objective genetic distinctions which may only partially correspond to socially conceived racial categories. He argues that, nonetheless, the concept of population tends to slide back into the existing social category of race, making biological racialization, for instance, in the discourse that supports the relationship between a racial group, identified as *special* or *target* population, and greater health risks.[2]

The above slippage signifies the conceptual basis of race as a socially constructed discursive category and the pervasiveness of the idea of race used for legitimating divisions of human beings and forming our judgment of where people belong based on phenotypical characteristics. According to Omi and Winant (1994), "race is a concept which signifies and symbolizes social conflicts and interests by referring to different types of human bodies" (p. 55). As a social construct, racial representations are always in flux and situated in social and historical processes. Race is socially and historically constructed and shaped by discourses that give specific meanings to the ways we see the world, rather than reflecting the illusive notion of objective, stable, and transcendent truths. Put differently, race parallels the nation as "imagined community" (Anderson, 1983). Miles (1987) argues:

> Like "nations," "races" too are imagined, in the dual sense that they have no real biological foundation and that all those included by the signification can never know each other, and are imagined as communities in the sense of a common feeling of fellowship. Moreover, they are also imagined as limited in the sense that a boundary is perceived, beyond which lie other "races."
>
> (pp. 26–27)

Furthermore, that race is a social construction raises the question of whether the term *race* can be used as an analytical category for scholarly investigation and discussion. Some sociologists with neo-Marxist perspectives, especially those in the United Kingdom, have argued that using *race* as a descriptive and/or analytical category assumes its existence as a reality that divides groups of people into different races, contradicting the notion that race is a social construct rather than an ontologically determined category. It further legitimates the process of racialization, which leads to racism when a negative view of the Other as inferior is attached (see Miles, 1993; Darder & Torres, 2004). These scholars advocate abandoning *race* as an analytical category and focusing instead on racialization and racism (see more discussion below). Yet others argue that while race is a historical, cultural, and political construction rather than a homogeneous, unitary, and static category, it can politically and strategically mobilize racially oppressed groups to create solidarity and resistance (see Solomos, 2003). These contested meanings of *race* indicate the need for us to continue theorizing and clarifying our focus of investigation.

Ethnicity

A concept related to race is ethnicity, which is sometimes used as a politically correct code word for race (Miles & Brown, 2003). It is often used as a category to distinguish groups based on sociocultural characteristics, such as ancestry, language, religion, custom, and lifestyle (Thompson & Hickey, 1994). However, like race, ethnicity is an equally contentious term with definition and boundary problems (Miles & Brown, 2003). If it denotes sociocultural characteristics, how do we, for instance, define culture? Where can cultural boundaries be drawn in order to distinguish unique ethnic groups? How are diasporic groups categorized? Take, for instance, Asians who immigrated to Peru and other Latin American countries generations ago but have recently moved to Los Angeles (see Darder & Torres, 2004). Which ethnic group do they belong to? If they enroll in ESL classes, will they be perceived as Asian or Latin American? What assumptions would their teachers and peers have in interacting with them? Thus, although the notion of ethnicity appears to be concrete and easy to conceptualize because it is closely connected to a familiar and ordinary notion of culture, the concept is as elusive as race given the tremendous variability within a group and similarity among groups. Just as race is not a biologically determined construct, ethnicity does not denote innate or inherent attributes of human beings. Rather, it is a relational concept that sets one group of people apart from another—a process of constructing differences. In discussing ethnicization and racialization, Lewis and Phoenix (2004) argue:

> "Ethnicity" and "race" are about the process of marking differences between people on the basis of assumptions about human physical or cultural variations and the meanings of these variations. This is what we mean when we say that individuals and groups are racialized or ethnicised … [such] identities are about setting and maintaining boundaries between groups.
>
> (p. 125)

Culture

The above discussions underscore the importance of scrutinizing the notion of culture in relation to race and ethnicity. One significant question to be posed is this: Is exploring or examining issues of culture in English-language teaching and learning (e.g., cultural difference in linguistic and non-linguistic practices, construction and performance of cultural identities) equivalent to or part of scholarly inquiry into the idea of race? We grappled with this important question at many levels in editing this volume. This question also reflects a characteristic of contemporary discourse about race. Historically, the European expansion to various parts of the world prompted Europeans to categorize the Other that they encountered into savages or cannibals, while they identified themselves as civilized (see Spack, 2002, 2006). The development of science in the late 18th century created a discourse in which *race* referred to biological categories of human beings and it was exploited to perpetuate a hierarchy of superiority/ inferiority (Miles & Brown, 2003). In our postcolonial society, a scholarly consensus considers race not as a biologically determined concept, as mentioned earlier. However, the human will to differentiate and draw boundaries between groups of people has not disappeared. Thus, in our contemporary world, racial difference has increasingly been replaced by the notion of cultural difference, a more benign and acceptable signifier than *race*, yet used as a means to exclude the experiences of certain racial/ethnic groups as Other and undesirable (Anthias & Yuval-Davis, 1992; Bonilla-Silva, 2003; May, 1999; van Dijk, 1993). Thus, religion, for example, as part of culture can become a means for racialization as demonstrated by Rich and Troudi (2006) who discussed how Saudi Arabian students of ESL in the United Kingdom are affected by Islamophobia. Sharing the same function with the idea of race, cultural difference is conveniently used to differentiate, exclude, or privilege certain groups of people. Therefore, issues of culture can be investigated with the understanding that they are often implicitly and yet profoundly connected to the idea of *race*.

Racialization and Racisms

We have argued that race, ethnicity, and culture are ideas that sort and divide human beings based on perceived or discursively constructed phenotypical and cultural characteristics. This leads to the notions of racialization and racism, both of which are not easy terms to define and involve a great deal of argument. Racialization can be simply defined as racial categorization, "a dialectical process by which meaning is attributed to particular biological features of human beings, as a result of which individuals may be assigned to a general category of persons that reproduces itself biologically" (Miles & Brown, 2003, p. 102). In other words, it is "a core concept in the analysis of racial phenomena, particularly to signal the processes by which ideas about race are constructed, come to be regarded as meaningful, and are acted upon" (Murji & Solomos, 2005, p. 1). Racialization is also similar to what Omi and Winant (1994) call racial formation, which is "the sociohistorical process by which racial categories are created, inhabited, transformed, and destroyed" (p. 55). Thus, racialization produces and legitimates difference among social groups based on perceived biological characteristics, yet it is a dynamic and historically situated process in which racial significations are always shifting. However, racialization per se does not necessarily lead to racism (see below), partly because the agent involved in the process of racialization is not always the socially powerful or dominant group. For instance, a minority and subordinate group can racialize themselves to construct their own identity in positive terms for the purpose of resistance (e.g., the strategic essentialism discussed by postcolonial critics; see Spivak, 1988, 1993).

Racialization or the categorization of people carries a legacy of colonialism and often contains value judgments of the categories, although a scientific discourse masks such judgments with a neutral, objective, and even liberal humanistic tone. Underlying the categorization is the discourse supported by a specific power dynamic that excludes certain racialized groups as the inferior Other while maintaining the status quo of the Self. Such discourse can be identified as racism. Despite the familiarity of the term, the definition of racism is not straightforward. Various scholars have given definitions: "racism excludes racially defined others, or promotes, or secures, or sustains such exclusion" (Goldberg, 1993, p. 101), racism is "a fundamental characteristic of social projects which create or reproduce structures of domination based on essentialist categories of race" (Omi & Winant, 1994, p. 162), and racism is "a discourse and practice of inferiorizing ethnic groups ... racism can also use the notion of the undesirability of groups ... this may lead to attempts to assimilate, exterminate or exclude" (Anthias & Yuval-Davis, 1992, p. 12). Miles and Brown (2003) concisely define racism as ideology, arguing that "racism is ... a representational form which, by designating discrete human collectivities, necessarily functions as an ideology of inclusion and exclusion" (p. 104).

The term ideology has also been widely used in the field of second language teaching, as seen in scholarly inquiries into linguistic imperialism, critical discourse analysis, language ideologies and so on (e.g., Phillipson, 1992; Rogers, 2004; Woolard, 1998). However, echoing the concern expressed by Anthias and Yuval-Davis (1992) about the connotation of false consciousness inherent in the Marxist usage of the term ideology, the poststructuralist discourse in applied linguistics cautions against the implication that ideology is juxtaposed with something else that represents truth (Pennycook, 2001). In this perspective, racism can be viewed as both discourse and social practice which construct and perpetuate unequal relations of power through inferiorization, a process in which the Other is rendered inferior to the Self.

Kinds of Racisms

Despite such complexity in the definition of the term, racism in everyday life usually evokes only overt forms of prejudice and personal discrimination. Thus, when the term racism or racist is used in public discourse, the listener/reader often concludes that the group of people referred to are implicitly identified as racist and defends that he/she is absolutely not. Worse yet, individuals that critically analyze race and racism or write about the topic are sometimes accused of promoting racial divisions and thus being racists (Bonilla-Silva, 2003). This may well be a natural reaction given the negative connotation of the term in contemporary society. However, the notion that racism is a discourse allows us to understand that most individuals are not racist; what is racist are the structured ideas that shape social reality. Thus, a statement, "I am not a racist, but ..." (expressing xenophobic ideas about immigrants of color, for instance) reflects the nature of this contemporary discourse of racism. In order to scrutinize racism, it is necessary to move beyond the understanding of racism at the level of individual beliefs and prejudices and instead examine various forms of racism or racisms (Goldberg, 1993; Omi & Winant, 1994).

For instance, racism conceptualized as a discourse permeates every corner of society and shapes social relations, practices, and institutional structures. This is what is often called institutional or structural racism. In the field of teaching English, this type of racism is embodied in various ways. One example is hiring practices of English-language teachers worldwide. It has been pointed out that native speakers of English have a privileged status in employment, a privilege that is increased by having white skin (Amin, 1999, 2004; Golombek & Jordan, 2005; Lee, in press; Leung, Harris, & Rampton, 1997; Rampton, 1990). Such practices are sometimes implicit, masked by a liberal discourse of racial and ethnic equality (Mahboob, Uhrig, Newman, & Hartford, 2004), or could be quite explicit in job advertisements in some "expanding circle" countries. Another example is how students of color in schools in North America are often labeled as lacking culturally, socially, linguistically, or academically (e.g., Lee, 2005; Willett, 1996; see also Scheurich, 1997; Solórzano & Yosso, 2002) and often excluded from having mainstream educational experiences because of the gate-keeping and tracking function that ESL has as an institutional label and because of the unwillingness among mainstream teachers and students to socially engage with ESL students in a meaningful way (Harklau, 2000; Lee, 2005; Valdés, 1998; Valenzuela, 1999).

Another level of racism can be called epistemological racism (see Kubota, 2002).

Scheurich (1997) argues that it is based on the epistemologies, knowledges, and practices that privilege the European modernist white civilization. Referring to influential philosophers, social scientists, and educators, who have been virtually all white males, Scheurich argues that the world ontological categories and epistemologies that we use to think, analyze, socialize, and educate have been largely developed within this racial and cultural tradition, including "the legitimated ways of knowing (for example, positivism, neo-realism, postpositivisms, interpretivisms, constructivism, the critical tradition, and postmodernisms/poststructuralisms) that we use" (p. 140).

Epistemological racism is reflected in North American textbooks for various disciplines, such as biology, history, and English, which construct and perpetuate racial stereotypes and the hegemony of whiteness stemming from Western imperialism (Willinsky, 1998). Hegemony of whiteness is also reflected in ESL/EFL textbooks, constructing the norm with regard to what is legitimate linguistic and cultural knowledge (cf. Matsuda, 2002).

Another consequence of epistemological racism constructs what counts as more academically valuable or scholarly rigorous. One example is a comment one of us heard from a teacher educator from New York: "Teacher education programs should recruit undergraduate students majoring in Latino/Chicano studies because such a degree is useless for them. A degree in education would give them better career opportunities." While this view emphasizes practicality, it blatantly devalues knowledge of the specific discipline. Such thinking discourages many scholars of color from using non-mainstream race-based ways of thinking and writing in their research. Scheurich (1997) argues that even creating race-oriented journals, such as *The Journal of Negro Education*, would still marginalize scholars of color because these journals are less respected than mainstream ones and negatively affect tenure and promotion of the faculty of color, which feeds into institutional racism.

Intersection of Racism with Other Injustices

Just as the idea of race interacts with gender and sexuality in identity construction and negotiation, racisms can also intersect with other types of injustices such as sexism, classism, homophobia, linguicism, ageism, and so on. The combination is not manifested in a zero-sum fashion, but in a complex way. For instance, in a situation of hiring teachers, we can think of multiple types of candidates: white female English native speaker in her 60s; white gay male English native speaker in his 40s; black female English native speaker from Uganda in her 50s; Asian female English native speaker in her 20s; white female nonnative English speaker from Russia in her 20s; Asian male nonnative English speaker in his 30s; and so on. Who gets hired would be influenced by the complex interplay of multiple factors, not just racialized images or any one factor, although one factor might eventually carry a significant weight in each individual case. In other words, the perceived profiles of the candidates based on race, gender, nationality, age, sexual identity, and language background would complicatedly interact with who the employer is, what the program goal is, what the institutional mission is, who the students are, and so on.

Another example is how racism produces assumptions about someone's language proficiency. Using a matched guise test, Rubin (1992) investigated how racial images (e.g., Asian face versus Caucasian face) would affect listening comprehension and perception of accent in an instructional setting. The result showed the superiority of the white face. This experiment confirms the image of Asian Americans who are native speakers of English as perpetual foreigners regardless of their ability in English, as reflected in a question sometimes posed to them, "Your English is excellent. How long have you been in this country?" (Takaki, 1993). This intersection of race and language raises an important question with regard to native/nonnative issues which have gained increased attention in the field of TESOL and deserves some discussion here.

Racialized (Non)native Speakers

Various facets of the native-speaker construct—dominance and norm as the linguistic model for students—have been problematized in TESOL in recent years (e.g., Amin, 1997; Braine, 1999; Kamhi-Stein, 2004; Mawhinney & Xu, 1997; Leung et al., 1997; Lin, Wang, Akamatsu, & Riazi, 2002; Rampton, 1990). Critics have discussed how the myth of the native speaker influences hiring practices and the construction of students' view of the ideal speaker of English. However, as Lee (in press) points out, the discussions on native/nonnative issues have tended to address the linguistic aspect only (e.g., accent, standard/nonstandard use of language) without sufficient attention paid to the racialized aspect of native/nonnative speakers. The problem lies in the tendency to equate the native speaker with white and the nonnative speaker with nonwhite. These equations certainly explain discrimination against nonnative professionals, many of whom are people of color. Unfortunately, this essentialized dichotomy (i.e., *native speaker = Standard English speaker = white* versus *nonnative speaker = non-Standard English speaker = nonwhite*) has tended to blind us to the discrimination experienced by teachers who do not fit this formula (e.g., Asian or black native speaker of English, white native speaker with southern U.S. accent). As Nero (2006) argues, the paradigm of native/nonnative speakers indeed perpetuates racist assumptions about language and overlooks the complex linguistic landscape of the world.

Focusing on nonnativeness in employment discrimination is absolutely necessary to engage in activism for seeking social justice in the globalized era when an increased number of English-language teachers are recruited in many communities around the world. However, it is equally important to question the above essentialized dichotomy that racializes (non)native speakers, acknowledge the voices and experiences of teachers of color who are native speakers of English, and address racial discrimination at the same time. This approach enables TESOL professionals to establish solidarity among these two marginalized groups.

Theoretical Orientations for Investigating Issues of Race in Teaching and Learning English

Issues of race, racism, and racialization have been theorized in North America, influencing practice in disciplines such as legal studies and education. In this section, we will review basic tenets of Critical Race Theory (CRT), Critical White Studies or Whiteness Studies, critical pedagogies, and critical multicultural education.

Critical Race Theory

Issues of race and racisms have been proactively taken up and investigated in CRT (see Marx and Michael-Luna in this book and Taylor, 2006). Originating in critical scrutiny of the U.S. legal system, which claims to be objective and yet favors the racially and economically privileged, CRT investigates and transforms the relationship between race ideas, racism, and power (Delgado & Stefancic, 2001). Delgado and Stefancic (2001) delineate the following basic tenets of CRT: (1) racism is deeply ingrained in the ordinary ways in which everyday life in our society operates and thus it cannot be fixed by colorblind policies of superficial equality; (2) because racism benefits "both white elites (materially) and working-class people (psychically), large segments of society have little incentive to eradicate it" (p. 7); (3) "races are categories that society invents, manipulates, or retires when convenient" (p. 7); (4) the forms of racialization or racial discrimination are in flux, influenced by socioeconomic needs of the dominant society; (5) anti-essentialist understandings of racialized groups (i.e., recognizing various kinds of diversity that exist within a racialized group rather than viewing it as homogeneous or static) are vitally important; and (6) coexisting with the previous point, the unique voice of the people of color about their experiences can be communicated to white people through storytelling which exposes and challenges hidden forms of racism in everyday interactions (see Ladson-Billings, 1999 for a more detailed summary of these points). The last point is referred to as counter-storytelling (Delgado, 2000) or counter-story (Solórzano & Yosso, 2002), which is defined as:

> a method of telling the stories of those people whose experiences are not often told (e.g., those on the margins of society). The counter-story is also a tool for exposing, analyzing, and challenging the majoritarian stories of racial privilege.
>
> (Solórzano & Yosso, 2002, p. 32)

CRT has been introduced in the field of education. Various scholars have critically examined how educational policies, including curriculum, instruction, and funding, are related to racial inequity and relations of power (e.g., Ladson-Billings, 1999; Ladson-Billings & Tate, 1995; Parker, 2003). Issues related to nonnative English speakers (e.g., use of their native language in the workplace, schools, and government offices, discrimination based on nonstandard accents) create great concern, especially to immigrant populations, and thus constitute another area of inquiry within CRT (Delgado & Stefancic, 2001). In addition to language, intersectionality among race, gender, class, national origin, and sexual identity is taken into account as an important factor in shaping and interpreting racial discrimination.

Critical White Studies

Related to CRT is the critical inquiry into issues of whiteness called Whiteness Studies or Critical White Studies (e.g., Delgado & Stefancic, 1997, 2001; Fine, Weis, Powell, & Wong, 1997; Frankenberg, 1993; McLaren & Muñoz, 2000; Leonardo, 2002). Whiteness Studies investigates the social construction of whiteness (e.g., how Irish, Jewish, and Italian people came to be labeled as white), white privilege (see oft-cited article by

McIntosh, 1997), and the normative yet invisible nature of whiteness observed in everyday practices and discourse. It has been argued that whiteness exerts its power as an invisible and unmarked norm against which all Others are racially and culturally defined, marked, and made inferior. The invisibility of whiteness also allows whites to evade responsibility for taking part in eradicating racism. Frankenberg (1993), for instance, demonstrated that white women in her study tended to evade references to race, racial difference, and individual complicity with power and privilege. Such power evasion confirms and reinforces a colorblind or difference-blind discourse (Larson & Ovando, 2001), which denies the existence of differences among groups and consequently the need to scrutinize the roots of social inequalities and to generate ethically situated social and educational interventions.

In scrutinizing whiteness, the anti-essentialist approach again becomes important. It is necessary to explore how whiteness intersects other social categories such as gender, class, age, sexual identities, religious identities, and so on (Fine & Weis, 1993). Another cautionary point is an oft-used analogical strategy to use sexism, for instance, to raise awareness among white people about racial discrimination. Grillo and Wildman (1997) argue that such an analogy obscures and marginalizes the actual experiences of racism and instead white people's concern tends to take the center stage. Despite its good intention, this approach could reinforce colorblindness (see Hammond, 2006 on diversion to analogy observed among EFL students in a simulation activity conducted to raise their awareness of racism). It is important to note that whiteness is not a biological category but discursively constructed (McLaren & Muñoz, 2000) and that "whiteness as a privileged signifier has become global" (Leonardo, 2002, p. 30). Whiteness in the globalization discourse has particular significance for TESOL, which confronts the challenge of the global spread of English and English-language teaching.

Criticisms of CRT and Critical White Studies

Although both CRT and Critical White Studies have paid explicit attention to race ideas and provided useful analytical lenses, there are some criticisms. Delgado and Stefancic (2001) discuss various criticisms from both outside and within. Among them, one is the use of counter-storytelling as a method. From the mainstream scholarship influenced by the Enlightenment, the narrative approach is criticized as lacking analytical rigor and objectivity. Conversely, from a critical perspective, the narrative approach is criticized for inadvertently romanticizing the experiences of the marginalized or creating a racial dichotomy between whites and people of color, supporting and reinforcing the mainstream capitalist discourse of individualism and liberal multiculturalism (Darder & Torres, 2004).[3]

One self-criticism discussed by Delgado and Stefancic (2001) is a need for more focus on material conditions and poverty in relation to racism. This point has been raised from a Marxist point of view as well. Darder and Torres (2004) argue that CRT, by isolating race as the main unit of analysis, may run the risk of downplaying issues of class which reflect the economic aspects of domination and subordination. They further argue that the emphasis on intersectionality among race and other social categories, such as gender, class, and sexual identities, tend to give an equal analytical and explanatory power to these categories, even though "class is located within production relations and represents a very different and unique structural feature in a capitalist political economy" (p. 117). These authors cite Wood (1995) and point out a distinct feature of class, arguing that whereas racial, cultural, gender, and sexual differences as group or individual identities can be celebrated in a true democracy, celebrating class difference is a nebulous concept in relation to democracy (see also Kubota, 2003). Thus, instead of treating race as an equal unit of analysis that intersects with gender, class, and so on, they emphasize a focus on how race ideas, racial differences, and racism are entrenched in the political economy of capitalism, producing racialized class relations.

Some potential problems of Critical Whiteness Studies have also been raised. As one of us discussed elsewhere (Kubota, 2004), it could place whites at center stage and impose on people of color the role of helpers who serve the interest of whites in their pursuit of becoming change agents (Sheets, 2000). These criticisms address a need for TESOL professionals to be cognizant of the conceptual diversity, complexity, and potential problems in critical inquiries such as CRT or Critical White Studies despite their radical thrust for antiracism and social justice.

Capital, Habitus, and Field

A theory that is rarely used in analyzing issues of race in second language education is Pierre Bourdieu's concepts of *habitus, capital,* and *field.* As a socially constructed category, race constitutes an integral part of individual and group identity that shapes the ways people think, believe, and act, which is habitus or "a system of dispositions" and cognitive structures which generate perceptions, appreciations, and actions (Bourdieu, 1984, p. 6). It is a set of embodied dispositions that shapes individuals' and groups' ways of viewing the world and living their lives. A certain habitus gains power in a particular social space called a *field,* which creates hierarchical positions of power. Habitus then becomes a resource or *cultural capital,* which refers to knowledge and skills that constitute resources or power that one is endowed with by virtue of socialization and education in one's family and community.

For instance, children of the white socioeconomic elite are bestowed by their familial socialization with both more and the right kind of cultural capital for school success (i.e., their habitus is turned into cultural capital). A recurrent theme in Bourdieu's works is that children from socioeconomically disadvantaged groups come to school as a social field with habitus incompatible with that displayed by the children of the socioeconomic elite. The unequal amount of cultural capital between the two groups leads to the reproduction of social stratification (see Lin, 1999 for an analysis of such reproduction in some schools in Hong Kong). Although Bourdieu's analysis is mostly focused on social class, his concepts can be applied to the social category of race (cf. May, 2001 for application of habitus to ethnicity).

Another recurrent theme in Bourdieu's writings concerns how the disadvantaging effect of the schooling system is masked, legitimized, or naturalized in people's consciousness. School failure can be conveniently attributed to individual cognitive deficit or lack of effort and not to the unequal initial shares of the cultural capital both valued and legitimized in school:

> the dominated classes allow [the struggle] to be imposed on them when they accept the stakes offered by the dominant classes. It is an integrative struggle and,

by virtue of the initial handicaps, a reproductive struggle, since those who enter this chase, in which they are beaten before they start … implicitly recognize the legitimacy of the goals pursued by those whom they pursue, by the mere fact of taking part.

(Bourdieu, 1984, p. 165)

Symbolic violence, according to Bourdieu, is the imposition of representations of the world and social meanings upon groups in such a way that they are experienced as legitimate. This is achieved through a process of *misrecognition*. For instance, the superiority of whiteness among teachers of ESL/EFL create a common belief among white as well as nonwhite teachers and students as to who is the legitimate English-language teacher.

While literacy educators have drawn on Bourdieu's concepts to analyze home–school (mis)match of habitus and capital (e.g., Luke, 1996), few have used Bourdieu's theory to analyze *race* as a form of embodied habitus that gains different currencies in different social and cultural fields governed by different rules of exchange (see Luke, this volume). Seen from Bourdieu's theoretical lens, race and language are integrally connected to cultural capital, the value of which never has absolute, universal, or guaranteed value but depends on particular social and cultural fields and the rules of exchange in those fields. Race and language are, thus, readable and interpretable elements of habitus brought to social fields of educational institutions, as Allan Luke argues in this volume.

Critical Pedagogies and Critical Multicultural Education

Critical pedagogies and critical multicultural education are interrelated approaches to education that share similar social, cultural, and educational visions: promoting social justice and equity through critical examinations of power and politics that produce and maintain domination and subordination in various dimensions of local and global society (e.g., Freire, 1998; Freire & Macedo, 1987; Kanpol & McLaren, 1995; Kincheloe, 2004; Kincheloe & Steinberg, 1997; Nieto, 1999, 2004; Ovando & McLaren, 2000; Sleeter, 1996; May, 1999; Sleeter & McLaren, 1995). As such, they explicitly engage teachers and students in dialogues on relations of power with regard to race, gender, class, and other social categories.

One of the core tenets of critical pedagogies is a critique of knowledge-transmission-oriented and fact-focused approaches to teaching which serve to perpetuate the dominant ways of interpreting the world. Along with the conception that knowledge constructed in the classroom is always political rather than objective or neutral, critical pedagogies provide analytical tools in examining ideas of race, racialization, and racism. Because knowledge that privileges the dominant white male middle-class heterosexual culture is deeply ingrained in curricula and instruction, critical pedagogies would help students identify and analyze hidden racialized and racist discourses that shape our social structures and world-view. In critical pedagogies, raising critical consciousness always interacts with actual experiences, "producing a synergy that elevates both scholarship and transformative action" (Kincheloe, 2004, p. 16). This naturally leads to antiracist education, which can take the shape of an antidiscrimination leadership program or a simulation activity in the classroom, as reported by Taylor (2006) and Hammond (2006).

Similarly, critical multicultural education questions normative knowledge of the white dominant society often constructed in a liberal approach to multiculturalism—namely, a difference-blind egalitarian vision about diverse cultures and peoples, perpetuation of the exotic and romanticized Other through celebrating superficial aspects of cultural difference (i.e., the *heroes and holidays* approach), and evasion of the power and privilege of whiteness (Kubota, 2004). It encourages students and teachers to confront racism and other kinds of social injustice not only individually but also collectively. It is therefore a form of antiracist education (Kailin, 2002; Nieto, 1999, 2004).

Both critical pedagogies and critical multicultural education have been extensively discussed and applied to teaching ESL/EFL (e.g., Auerbach, 1995; Benesch, 2001; Canagarajah, 1999; Hoosain & Salili, 2005; Lin, 1999; Norton & Toohey, 2004; Pennycook, 2001; Morgan, 1998). Issues of race can be further investigated within this inquiry framework.

Inquiry Themes for Second Language Education

The topics addressed in this volume expand the emerging discussions on race and related issues of culture and identity which have appeared in the field of second language education during the last decade. Possible themes of inquiry and some of the previous studies are presented below. Although these themes are in no way exhaustive, they demonstrate that issues of race, culture, and identities can be addressed from multiple angles. One general issue that applies to research on all themes is the racial relation between the researcher and the researched and its implications for the process and product of research. As Lee and Simon-Maeda (2006) discuss, the relation between the researcher and the researched—whether they share the same racial background or not—poses a number of questions such as: How could a white female researcher, for instance, obtain emic perspectives of the lived experiences of women of color? Would studying people whose racial background is the same as the researcher's necessarily resolve the problem? What are the responsibilities of a researcher who studies people of color who suffer from racism? These questions become even more complex when issues of class, sexual identities, and other social categories intersect with race. These questions need to be taken into consideration in critically investigating racialization and racism.

Learner/Teacher Identities and Race

Race gets constructed as a visible attribute of individuals. The process of racialization plays a significant role in (co)construction of identities and subjectivities among students and teachers. Identity and subjectivity—a poststructuralist concept that signifies the self as both discursive construction and agency—have become important topics of investigation in multilingual contexts and second language teaching and learning (e.g., Kanno, 2003; Norton, 2000; Pavlenko & Blackledge, 2004). Some studies in TESOL have explicitly focused on race. Ibrahim (1999), for instance, illustrated how racial and gender expectations influenced English-language learning and identity construction ("becoming black") of French-speaking black immigrant youths from Africa who were learning English in Canada. The study demonstrates how racial discourses influence the formation of identity and language learning. In a context of U.S. secondary schools, Bashir-Ali (2006) observed a Mexican female immigrant student's desire to acquire African American Vernacular English to become part of the majority social group while resisting the school culture that privileges Standard American English. Identity formation of students with mixed racial heritage and the effects of language acquisition is another area for investigation. Through interviewing racially mixed-heritage adults, Pao, Wong, and Teuben-Rowe (1997) found some differences between bilinguals and monolinguals in their outlook toward their own identities. Teachers' racial positionalities in U.S. schools shape and are shaped through their daily interactions with ESL students of color (Motha, 2006). Their educational practices are further influenced by larger discourses that assign racialized meanings to legitimate forms of English.

Issues of race and/or ethnicity emerge in other studies investigating how identities are discursively constructed and how students or teachers actively construct their identities in discourses in transition (e.g., Harklau, 2000; McKay & Wong, 1996; Motha, 2006; Simon-Maeda, 2004; Taylor, 2006; Thesen, 1997). Future research could further link existing theories on race with the role that race plays in constructing and negotiating identities in various settings including primary, secondary, and postsecondary education, training for international teaching assistants, pre-service and in-service teacher education, and so on.

Manifestations of Race in Pedagogy, Curriculum, Materials, and Technology

The notion of race and racialization as discourses would encourage second language professionals to examine in what ways racialization, white norms, racism, and other racial meanings are reproduced in local and global educational practices or how they are challenged by antiracist pedagogies. The analytical foci could include classroom instruction, curriculum, teaching materials, and technology.

As discussed earlier, contemporary textbooks of various school subjects in North America, for instance, reflect legacies of colonialism and imperialism which privilege white European knowledge and epistemologies (Willinsky, 1998). Such legacies are reflected in the dominance of Inner Circle English standards as well as white Anglo linguistic and cultural norms in various aspects of education (Canagarajah, 1999; Pennycook, 1998). Inquiries into these topics can be pursued through focusing on race-based epistemologies and asking questions such as: What teaching methodologies are deemed more legitimate and what epistemologies are they based on? What aspects of culture and society are or are not taught in a second/foreign-language course? Are any particular racial groups represented more than others? What racial images are projected in second/foreign-language textbooks and how do they influence the learners' view of the target language, target-language-speaking world, and their identities? In this respect, a high school textbook analysis by Herman (2007) has revealed that materials for teaching Spanish as a foreign language in the United States tends to paint the Spanish-speaking world with only light-skinned middle-class people.

While curriculum, materials, and instructions tend to reflect the white norm, the growing use of technology could either exacerbate inequalities among racial groups

(Murray, 2000) or offer new possibility for literacies that interconnect with race (Warschauer, 1998; see also Bangou and Wong in this book). The hegemonic ideologies and racism are also resisted by antiracist education. Taylor (2006), for example, reports the impact of an antidiscrimination leadership program in Canada on immigrant students' understanding of their own experiences, identities, and kinds of racism that surrounded them. Hammond (2006) reports an overall effectiveness of an antiracist simulation exercise conducted in a Japanese college classroom and yet points out students' tendency to avoid explicit engagement in racism. These studies suggest further need for implementing and improving antiracist education.

Language Policy, Language Ideology, and Race

As discussed, race and racism are embedded in the legacy of (neo)colonialism which is closely related to the past and present global spread of English as well as English monolingualism promoted domestically in English-speaking countries (see Spack, 2002, 2006). Discourses of colonialism not only legitimated racial distinctions and discrimination in the past but have also continued into the present to perpetuate racism and unequal racial relations of power (Pennycook, 1998). Race is indeed an important aspect of inquiry in postcolonial studies, which analyze the colonial discursive construction of racial categories and hierarchies (Said, 1978), the post- and neocolonial relations of power, ambivalence of simultaneous collusion and resistance, strategic essentialism, and subaltern agencies (Spivak, 1988, 1993). Postcolonial studies also destabilize the boundaries of racial and ethnic identities (Radhakrishnan, 1996). The field of second language education has begun to engage in postcolonial inquiry into teaching and learning English globally (Lin & Luke, 2006). In this investigation, race becomes an important focus.

Related to this direction, our field has paid increased attention to various types of ideologies including the contested notion of linguistic imperialism (Brutt-Griffler, 2002; Phillipson, 1992), ideologies of Standard English accent and discriminations (Lippi-Green, 1997, 2002), the English-only movement in the United States (Wiley, 2004; Wiley & Lukes, 1996), Ebonics and other non-Standard Englishes (Adger, Christian, & Taylor, 1999; Ramirez, Wiley, de Klerk, Lee, & Wright, 2005), and so on. Moreover, language ideology (or linguistic ideologies or ideologies of language) is another area that examines how ideologies influence not just linguistic forms and use but also individual and collective identities as well as social institutions (Woolard, 1998).

Race could certainly be a focus of analysis in investigating language-related ideologies. For instance, critics of the English-only anti-bilingual education movement in the United States have pointed out that racism, xenophobia, and ethnocentrism against Hispanic immigrants are hidden behind such political and educational initiatives (e.g., Crawford, 2000; Cummins, 2000).

Hill (2001) further argues that English-only policies in public institutions including schools are not strictly about language but about race—that is "they are part of the discourse system of racist culture, with a principal function to produce 'racial subjects' (Goldberg, 1993)" (p. 249). The field of teaching ESL/EFL could focus explicitly on race and ask a question such as: What significance do racism and other racial meanings have for linguistic imperialism, English-only, Standard English, and other hegemonic ideologies?

Critical (Classroom) Discourse Analysis and Race

Racial representations are disseminated and contested through written and spoken discourses at both micro and macro levels. One of the topics of inquiry in critical discourse analysis is to unpack the discursive mechanism of racism (Reisigl & Wodak, 2000). This approach can be applied to various facets of second language education. Critical classroom discourse analysis proposed by Kumaravadivelu (1997), which pays close attention to sociopolitical dimensions of classroom discourse, provides another tool for investigating how domination, subordination, and resistance in relation to race and racial hierarchies manifest themselves in classroom discourses.

Beyond the classroom, racialization and racisms related to language policy and language ideology permeate public spaces as mentioned earlier. The English-only anti-bilingual education initiatives in the United States in recent years, for instance, was promoted under the slogan of "English for the children" which emphasized the benefit of teaching and learning English and only English for bilingual immigrant children (Crawford, 2000; Wiley, 2004). In the discourse of elite racism, this rhetoric can be called "Apparent Altruism" or "for their own good" paternalistic discourse about immigrants which in turn perpetuates positive self-representation of the dominant group (van Dijk, 1993, p. 95). Critical discourse analysis can be a useful analytic tool to reveal the discursive mechanism that creates and sustains subtle and hidden forms of racism and racialization in the classroom and beyond.

Conclusion

The idea of race, racialization, and racism are factors that shape social, cultural, and political dimensions of language teaching and learning. Teaching second or foreign languages entails complex relations of power fueled by differences created by racialization. The relative silence in our field on topics about racialization and racism is peculiar given the tremendous amount of racialized diversity manifested in second language education. It is vitally important for the field to move beyond the colorblind vision of imagining that it is inherently filled with understanding and sensitivity of diverse cultures and people.

In exploring the idea of race, racialization, and racism, a danger of essentialism needs to be recognized. For instance, although whiteness as a social norm and privilege has been scrutinized in recent scholarship, imagined racial difference, which generates racial identities and racism, is relational—it is not a static or essentialized notion across groups or situations. As Memmi (2000) notes, "difference cannot be considered an end in and of itself" and "the real stakes against racism ... do not concern difference itself but the use of difference as a weapon against its victim, to the advantage of the victimizer" (p. 51). This follows that second language education, the field in which teachers and students are racialized across the globe, needs to address hegemonic racialized norms not only in relation to whiteness but also from multiple racial/ethnic relations which are dynamic and situational. Thus, racism is not restricted to inferiorization of people of color in the white dominant society but is observed in, for instance, Japanese discrimination against nonwhite people including other Asians. Just as race ideas and racism cannot be reduced to white versus nonwhite issues, theories on them should not solely rely on Anglo-European scholarship. It is necessary to overcome epistemological racism particularly in a field that encourages collaboration between scholars from all over the world.

As second language practitioners, we should engage in daily critical reflections of how our ideas of race influence what we teach, how we teach it, and how we understand our students. This should be followed by committed action to confront and eradicate overt and covert racisms with an understanding that they are intricately connected with other injustices and that the commitment for action always requires the awareness of our own racial and other privileges that are both relational and situated.

Discussion Questions

1. Think about your own background. What is your racial identity? How is your racial identity viewed by others? How does such racialized identification affect your private and public life?
2. One type of racism is institutional or structural in nature. Think of some concrete examples of how such racism is manifested in your daily life. Think about how a group of people might be differentially treated or positioned in schools, companies, or other public domains.
3. Another type of racism is epistemological. It is manifested in the white-European dominance of knowledge. Yet, there are other kinds of racial relations of power in the world. Describe epistemological racism involving other racialized groups. Is there any resistance to this type of racism?
4. The authors discuss some themes and topics of inquiry within second language education that address racialization and racism. Think of other research themes and topics to explore in relation to issues of race.

Notes

1. Parts of this chapter have appeared in Kubota and Lin (2006). Race and TESOL: Concepts, research, and future directions. *TESOL Quarterly, 40,* 471–493.
2. An example of using the notion of population is seen in the human DNA research study called the International HapMap Project (see Takezawa, 2006). The guidelines of this project warn against the equation of geography and race and use such labels as YRI, JPT, CHB, and CEU to denote Yoruba in Ibadan, Nigeria; Japanese in Tokyo; Han Chinese in Beijing; and Utah residents with ancestry from northern and western Europe. However, this warning might not be faithfully followed when others interpret the data.
3. A similar argument has been made in the field of composition studies. Expressivism, which became a popular approach in the 1970s and 1980s to expressing one's authentic voice in a narrative mode, has been criticized. Berlin (1988) pointed out that this approach could be co-opted by the ideology of individualism and undermine the collective struggle against social injustice and transformation.

References

Adger, C. T., Christian, D., & Taylor, O. (1999). *Making the connection: Language and academic achievement among African American students.* McHenry, IL: Center for Applied Linguistics and Delta Systems.

Amin, N. (1997). Race and the identity of the nonnative ESL teacher. *TESOL Quarterly, 31*, 581–583.

Amin, N. (1999). Minority women teachers of ESL: Negotiating White English. In G. Braine (Ed.), *Non-native educators in English language teaching* (pp. 93–104). Mahwah, NJ: Erlbaum.

Amin, N. (2004). Nativism, the native speaker construct, and minority immigrant women teachers of English as a second language. In L. Kamhi-Stein (Ed.), *Learning and teaching from experience: Perspectives on nonnative English-speaking professionals* (pp. 61–80). Ann Arbor, MI: University of Michigan Press.

Anderson, B. (1983). *Imagined communities: Reflections on the origin and spread of nationalism.* London: Verso.

Anthias, F., & Yuval-Davis, N. (1992). *Racialized boundaries: Race, nation, gender, colour and class and the anti-racist struggle.* London: Routledge.

Auerbach, E. R. (1995). The politics of the ESL classroom: Issues of power in pedagogical choices. In J. Tollefson (Ed.), *Power and inequality in language education* (pp. 9–33). New York: Cambridge University Press.

Bashir-Ali, K. (2006). Language learning and the definition of one's social, cultural, and racial identity. *TESOL Quarterly, 40*, 628–639.

Benesch, S. (2001). *Critical English for academic purposes: Theory, politics, and practice.* Mahwah, NJ: Lawrence Erlbaum Associates.

Berlin, J. (1988). Rhetoric and ideology in the writing class. *College English, 50*, 477–494.

Bonilla-Silva, E. (2003). *Racism without racists: Color-blind racism and the persistence of racial inequality in the United States.* Lanham, MD: Rowman & Littlefield.

Bourdieu, P. (1984). *Distinction: A social critique of the judgment of taste.* Cambridge: MA: Harvard University Press.

Braine, G. (Ed.). (1999). *Non-native educators in English language teaching.* Mahwah, NJ: Lawrence Erlbaum Associates.

Brutt-Griffler, J. (2002). *World English: A study of its development.* Clevedon, UK: Multilingual Matters.

Canagarajah, A. S. (1999). *Resisting linguistic imperialism in English teaching.* Oxford: Oxford University Press.

Crawford, J. (2000). *At war with diversity: US language policy in an age of anxiety.* Clevedon, UK: Multilingual Matters.

Cummins, J. (2000). *Language, power and pedagogy: Bilingual children in the crossfire.* Clevedon, UK: Multilingual Matters.

Curtis, A., & Romney, M. (Eds.). (2006). *Color, race, and English language teaching: Shades of meaning.* Mahwah, NJ: Lawrence Erlbaum Associates.

Darder, A., & Torres, R. D. (2004). *After race: Racism after multiculturalism.* New York: New York University Press.

Davis, K. A., & Skilton-Sylvester, E. (2004). Looking back, taking stock, moving forward: Investigating gender in TESOL. *TESOL Quarterly, 38*, 381–404.

Delgado, R. (2000). Storytelling for oppositionists and others: A plea for narrative. In R. Delgado & J. Stefancic (Eds.), *Critical race theory: The cutting edge* (pp. 60–70). Philadelphia, PA: Temple University Press.

Delgado, R., & Stefancic, J. (Eds.). (1997). *Critical white studies: Looking behind the mirror.* Philadelphia, PA: Temple University Press.

Delgado, R., & Stefancic, J. (2001). *Critical race theory: An introduction.* New York: New York University Press.

Duster, T. (2005). Race and reification in science. *Science, 307*, 1050–1051.

Fine, M., & Weis, L. (1993). *Beyond silenced voices: Class, race and gender in United States schools.* Albany, NY: State University of New York Press.

Fine, M., Weis, L., Powell, L. C., & Wong, L. M. (Eds.). (1997). *Off white: Readings on race, power, and society*. New York: Routledge.

Frankenberg, R. (1993). *White women, race matters: The social construction of whiteness*. Minneapolis, MN: University of Minnesota Press.

Freire, P. (1998). *Pedagogy of the oppressed*. New York: Continuum.

Freire, P., & Macedo, D. (1987). *Literacy: Reading the word and the world*. South Hadley, MA: Bergin & Garvey.

Goldberg, D. T. (1993). *Racist culture: Philosophy and the politics of meaning*. Oxford: Blackwell.

Golombek, P., & Jordan, S. R. (2005). Becoming "black lambs" not "parrots": A poststructuralist orientation to intelligibility and identity. *TESOL Quarterly, 39*, 513–533.

Grillo, T., & Wildman, S. M. (1997). Obscuring the importance of race: The implications of making comparison between racism and sexism (or other isms). In R. Delgado & J. Stefancic (Eds.), *Critical white studies: Looking behind the mirror* (pp. 619–629). Philadelphia, PA: Temple University Press.

Hammond, K. (2006). More than a game: A critical discourse analysis of a racial inequality exercise in Japan. *TESOL Quarterly, 40*, 545–571.

Harklau, L. (2000). From the "good kids" to the "worst": Representations of English language learners across educational settings. *TESOL Quarterly, 34*, 35–67.

Herman, D. M. (2007). It's a small world after all: From stereotypes to invented worlds in secondary school Spanish textbooks. *Critical Inquiry in Language Studies, 4*, 117–150.

Hill, J. H. (2001). The racializing function of language panics. In R. D. González & I. Melis (Eds.), *Language ideologies: Critical perspectives on the official English movement* (pp. 245–267). Mahwah, NJ: Lawrence Erlbaum Associates.

Hoosain, R., & Salili, F. (Eds.). (2005). *Language in multicultural education*. Greenwich, CT: Information Age Publishing.

Hutchinson, J. F. (2005). The past, present and future of race and health. *Anthropology News, 46*(8), 13.

Ibrahim, A. (1999). Becoming Black: Rap and hip-hop, race, gender, identity and the politics of ESL learning. *TESOL Quarterly, 33*, 349–369.

Ibrahim, A. (2000). Identity or identification? A response to some objections. *TESOL Quarterly, 34*, 741–744.

Kailin, J. (2002). *Antiracist education: From theory to practice*. Lanham, MD: Rowman & Littlefield Publishers.

Kamhi-Stein, L. D. (Ed.). (2004). *Learning and teaching from experience: Perspectives on nonnative English-speaking professionals*. Ann Arbor, MI: The University of Michigan Press.

Kanno, Y. (2003). *Negotiating bilingual and bicultural identities: Japanese returnees betwixt two worlds*. Mahwah, NJ: Lawrence Erlbaum Associates.

Kanpol, B., & McLaren, P. (Eds.) (1995). *Critical multiculturalism: Uncommon voices in a common struggle*. Westport, CT: Bergin & Garvey.

Kincheloe, J. L. (2004). *Critical pedagogy*. New York: Peter Lang.

Kincheloe, J. L., & Steinberg, S. R. (1997). *Changing multiculturalism*. Buckingham: Open University Press.

Kubota, R. (2002). The author responds: (Un)Raveling racism in a nice field like TESOL. *TESOL Quarterly, 36*(1), 84–92.

Kubota, R. (2003). New approaches to gender, class, and race in second language writing. *Journal of Second Language Writing, 12*, 31–47.

Kubota, R. (2004). Critical multiculturalism and second language education. In B. Norton & K. Toohey (Eds.), *Critical pedagogies and language learning* (pp. 30–52). Cambridge: Cambridge University Press.

Kubota, R., & Lin, A. (Eds.). (2006). Race and TESOL [special topic issue]. *TESOL Quarterly, 40*(3).

Kumaravadivelu, B. (1997). Critical classroom discourse analysis. *TESOL Quarterly, 33,* 453–484.

Ladson-Billings, G. (1999). Just what is critical race theory, and what's it doing in a *nice* field like education? In L. Parker, D. Deyhle, & S. Villenas (Eds.), *Race is—race isn't: Critical race theory and qualitative studies in education* (pp. 7–30). Boulder, CO: Westview Press.

Ladson-Billings, G., & Tate, W. F., IV (1995). Toward a critical race theory of education. *Teachers College Record, 97,* 47–68.

Langman, J. (Ed.). (2004). (Re)Constructing gender in a new voice [special issue]. *Journal of Language, Identity, and Education, 3*(4).

Larson, C. L., & Ovando, C. J. (2001). *The color of bureaucracy: The politics of equity in multicultural school communities.* Belmont, CA: Wadsworth/Thomson Learning.

Lee, E. (in press). Race: A third voice in the native/nonnative speaker debate. *TESOL Quarterly.*

Lee, E., & Simon-Maeda, A. (2006). Racialized research identities in ESL/EFL research. *TESOL Quarterly, 40,* 573–594.

Lee, S. J. (2005). *Up against whiteness: Race, school, and immigrant youth.* New York: Teachers College Press.

Leonardo, Z. (2002). The souls of white folk: Critical pedagogy, whiteness studies, and globalization discourse. *Race Ethnicity and Education, 5,* 29–50.

Leung, C., Harris, R., & Rampton, B. (1997). The idealised native speaker, reified ethnicities, and classroom realities. *TESOL Quarterly, 31,* 543–560.

Lewis, G., & Phoenix. A. (2004). "Race", "ethnicity" and identity. In K. Woodward (Ed.), *Questioning identity: Gender, class, ethnicity* (2nd ed., pp. 115–150). London: Routledge.

Lin, A. M. Y. (1999). Doing-English-lessons in the reproduction or transformation of social worlds? *TESOL Quarterly, 33,* 393–412.

Lin, A. M. Y., & Luke, A. (Eds.). (2006). Coloniality, postcoloniality, and TESOL. *Critical Inquiry in Language Studies, 3*(2–3).

Lin, A. M. Y., Wang, W., Akamatsu, N., & Riazi, A. M. (2002). Appropriating English, expanding identities, and re-visioning the field: From TESOL to Teaching English for Glocalized Communication (TEGCOM). *Journal of Language, Identity, and Education, 1,* 295–316.

Lippi-Green, R. (1997). *English with an accent.* London and New York: Routledge.

Lippi-Green, R. (2002). Language ideology and language prejudice. In E. Finegan & J. R. Rickford (Eds.), *Language in the USA: Perspectives for the twenty-first century* (pp. 289–304). Cambridge: Cambridge University Press.

Luke, A. (1996). Genre of power? Literacy education and the production of capital. In R. Hasan & G. Williams (Eds.), *Literacy in society* (pp. 308–338). New York: Addison Wesley Longman.

Mahboob, A., Uhrig, K., Newman, K. L., & Hartford, B. S. (2004). Children of a lesser English: Nonnative English speakers as ESL teachers in English language programs in the United States. In L. Kamhi-Stein (Ed.), *Learning and teaching from experience: Perspectives on nonnative English-speaking professionals* (pp. 100–120). Ann Arbor, MI: University of Michigan Press.

Matsuda, A. (2002). Representation of users and uses of English in beginning Japanese EFL textbooks. *JALT Journal, 24,* 80–98.

Mawhinney, H. B., & Xu, F. (1997). Reconstructing the professional identity of foreign-trained teachers in Ontario schools. *TESOL Quarterly, 31,* 632–637.

May, S. (1999). Critical multiculturalism and cultural difference: Avoiding essentialism. In S. May (Ed.), *Critical multiculturalism: Rethinking multicultural and antiracist education* (pp. 11–41). London: Falmer Press.

May, S. (2001). *Language and minority rights: Ethnicity, nationalism and the politics of language.* Harlow, UK: Pearson Education Limited.

McIntosh, P. (1997). White privilege and male privilege: A personal account of coming to see correspondences through work in women's studies. In R. Delgado & J. Stefancic (Eds.), *Critical white studies: Looking behind the mirror* (pp. 291–299). Philadelphia, PA: Temple University Press.

McKay, S., & Wong, S.-L. (1996). Multiple discourses, multiple identities: Investment and agency in second language learning among Chinese adolescent immigrant students. *Harvard Educational Review, 66,* 577–608.

McLaren, P., & Muñoz, J. (2000). Contesting whiteness: Critical perspectives on the struggle for social justice. In C. J. Ovando & P. McLaren (Eds.), *Multiculturalism and bilingual education: Students and teachers caught in the cross fire* (pp. 22–29). Boston, MA: McGraw Hill.

Memmi, A. (2000). *Racism.* Minneapolis, MN: University of Minnesota Press.

Miles, R. (1987). Recent Marxist theories of nationalism and the issues of racism. *British Journal of Sociology, 38,* 24–43.

Miles, R. (1993). *Racism after "race relations."* London: Routledge.

Miles, R., & Brown, M. (2003). *Racism* (2nd ed.). London: Routledge.

Morgan, B. (1998). *The ESL classroom: Teaching, critical practice, and community development.* Toronto: University of Toronto Press.

Motha, S. (2006). Racializing ESOL teacher identities in U.S. K-12 public schools. *TESOL Quarterly, 40,* 495–518.

Murji, K., & Solomos, J. (2005). Introduction: Racialization in theory and practice. In K. Murji & J. Solomos (Eds.), *Racialization: Studies in theory and practice* (pp. 1–27). New York: Oxford University Press.

Murray, D. E. (2000). Protean communication: The language of computer-mediated communication. *TESOL Quarterly, 34,* 397–421.

Nelson, C. (1999). Sexual identities in ESL: Queer theory and classroom inquiry. *TESOL Quarterly, 33,* 371–391.

Nelson, C. (2006). Queer inquiry in language education. *Journal of Language, Identity, and Education, 5,* 1–9.

Nelson, C. (2008). *Sexual identities in English language education: Classroom conversations.* New York: Routledge.

Nero, S. (2006). An exceptional voice: Working as a TESOL professional of color. In A. Curtis & M. Romney (Eds.), *Color, race, and English language teaching: Shades of meaning* (pp. 23–36). Mahwah, NJ: Lawrence Erlbaum Associates.

Nieto, S. (1999). *The light in their eyes: Creating multicultural learning communities.* New York; London: Teachers College Press.

Nieto, S. (2004). *Affirming diversity: The sociopolitical context of multicultural education* (4th ed.). New York: Addison Wesley Longman.

Norton, B. (2000). *Identity and language learning: Gender, ethnicity and educational change.* Harlow, Essex: Pearson Education.

Norton, B., & Toohey, K. (Eds.). (2004). *Critical pedagogies and language learning.* Cambridge: Cambridge University Press.

Omi, M., & Winant, H. (1994). *Racial formation in the United States: From the 1970s to the 1990s* (2nd ed.). New York: Routledge.

Ovando, C. J., & McLaren, P. (2000). *Multiculturalism and bilingual education: Students and teachers caught in the cross fire.* Boston, MA: McGraw Hill.

Pao, D. L., Wong, S. D., & Teuben-Rowe, S. (1997). Identity formation for mixed-heritage adults and implications for educators. *TESOL Quarterly, 31,* 622–631.

Parker, L. (2003). Critical race theory and its implications for methodology and policy analysis in higher education desegregation. In G. R. Lópex & L. Parker (Eds.), *Interrogating racism in qualitative research methodology* (pp. 145–180). New York: Peter Lang.

Pavlenko, A., & Blackledge, A. (2004). *Negotiating identities in multilingual contexts.* Clevedon, UK: Multilingual Matters.

Pennycook, A. (1998). *English and the discourses of colonialism.* New York; London: Routledge.

Pennycook, A. (2001). *Critical applied linguistics: A critical introduction.* Mahwah, NJ: Lawrence Erlbaum Associates.

Phillipson, R. (1992). *Linguistic imperialism.* Oxford: Oxford University Press.

Radhakrishnan, R. (1996). *Diasporic mediations.* Minneapolis, MN: University of Minnesota Press.

Ramirez, J. D., Wiley, T. G., de Klerk, G., Lee, E., & Wright, W. E. (2005). *Ebonics: The urban education debate* (2nd ed.). Clevedon, UK: Multilingual Matters.

Rampton, M. B. H. (1990). Displacing the "native speaker": Expertise, affiliation and inheritance. *ELT Journal, 44*(2), 97–101.

Reisigl, M., & Wodak, R. (2000). *The semiotics of racism: Approaches in critical discourse analysis.* Wien: Passagen.

Rich, S., & Troudi, S. (2006). Hard times: Arab TESOL students' experiences of racialization and othering in the United Kingdom. *TESOL Quarterly, 40,* 615–627.

Rogers, R. (Ed.) (2004). *An introduction to critical discourse analysis in education.* Mahwah, NJ: Lawrence Erlbaum Associates.

Rubin, D. A. (1992). Nonlanguage factors affecting undergraduates' judgments of nonnative English-speaking teaching assistants. *Research in Higher Education, 33,* 511–531.

Said, E. (1978). *Orientalism.* New York: Pantheon Books.

Scheurich, J. J. (1997). *Research method in the postmodern.* London; Washington, DC: Falmer Press.

Sheets, R. H. (2000). Advancing the field or taking center stage: The white movement in multicultural education. *Educational Researcher, 29*(9), 15–21.

Simon-Maeda, A. (2004). The complex construction of professional identities: Female EFL educators in Japan speak out. *TESOL Quarterly, 38,* 405–434.

Sleeter, C. E. (1996). *Multicultural education as social activism.* Albany, NY: State University of New York Press.

Sleeter, C. E., & McLaren, P. L. (Eds.). (1995). *Multicultural education, critical pedagogy, and the politics of difference.* Albany, NY: State University of New York Press.

Solomos, J. (2003). *Race and racism in Britain* (3rd ed.). Basingstoke: Palgrave Macmillan.

Solórzano, D. G., & Yosso, T. J. (2002). Critical race methodology: Counter-story telling as an analytical framework for education research. *Qualitative Inquiry, 8,* 23–44.

Spack, R. (2002). *America's second tongue: American Indian education and the ownership of English, 1860–1900.* Lincoln, NE: University of Nebraska Press.

Spack, R. (2006). English lessons. *TESOL Quarterly, 40,* 595–604.

Spivak, G. (1988). Can the subaltern speak? In C. Nelson & L. Grossberg (Eds.), *Marxism and the interpretation of culture* (pp. 271–313). London: Macmillan.

Spivak, G. (1993). *Outside in the teaching machine.* New York: Routledge.

St. Louis, B. (2005). Racialization in the "zone of ambiguity." In K. Murji & J. Solomos (Eds.), *Racialization: Studies in theory and practice* (pp. 29–50). New York: Oxford University Press.

Takaki, R. (1993). *A different mirror: A history of multicultural America.* Boston, MA: Little, Brown & Co.

Takezawa, Y. (2006). Race should be discussed and understood across the globe. *Anthropology News, 47*(3), 6–7.

Taylor, L. (2006). Wrestling with race: Implications of integrative antiracism education for immigrant ESL youth. *TESOL Quarterly, 40,* 519–544.

Thesen, L. (1997). Voices, discourse, and transition: In search of new categories in EAP. *TESOL Quarterly, 31,* 487–511.

Thompson, W. E., & Hickey, J. V. (1994). *Society in focus: An Introduction to sociology.* New York: HarperCollins College Publishers.

Valdés, G. (1998). The world outside and inside schools: Language and immigrant children. *Educational Researcher, 27*(6), 4–18.

Valenzuela, A. (1999). *Subtractive schooling: U.S.-Mexican youth and the politics of caring.* Albany, NY: State University of New York Press.

Van Dijk, T. (1993). *Elite discourse and racism.* London: Sage Publications.

Vandrick, S. (1995). Privileged ESL university students. *TESOL Quarterly, 29,* 375–380.

Vandrick, S. (2007, April). Understanding students of the new global elite. Paper presented at the meeting of the International Society for Language Studies, Honolulu, Hawaii.

Warschauer, M. (1998). Researching technology in TESOL: Determinist, instrumental, and critical approaches. *TESOL Quarterly, 32,* 757–761.

Wiley, T. G. (2004). Language policy and English-only. In E. Finegan & J. R. Rickford (Eds.), *Language in the USA: Perspectives for the twenty-first century* (pp. 319–338). Cambridge: Cambridge University Press.

Wiley, T. G., & Lukes, M. (1996). English-only and standard English ideologies in the U.S. *TESOL Quarterly, 30,* 511–535.

Willett, J. (1996). Research as gendered practice. *TESOL Quarterly, 30,* 344–347.

Willinsky, J. (1998). *Learning to divide the world: Education at empire's end.* Minneapolis, MN: University of Minnesota Press.

Wood, E. M. (1995). *Democracy against capitalism: Renewing historical materialism.* New York: Cambridge University Press.

Woolard, K. A. (1998). Introduction: Language ideology as a field of inquiry. In B. B. Schieffelin, K. A. Woolard, & P. V. Kroskrity (Eds.), *Language ideologies: Practice and theory* (pp. 3–47). New York: Oxford University Press.

Part I

Interrogating Whiteness

Whiteness occupies a privileged position in a racial hierarchy of power. Whiteness refers to not only skin color but also cultural knowledge constructed in Western colonial histories. Like other socially dominant categories such as native speakerness, middle-class status, and heterosexuality, Whiteness constitutes an invisible taken-for-granted social norm, while exercising coercive power of both assimilation and alienation. The chapters in Part I make visible the invisible Whiteness observed in various educational settings and geographical locations. At the same time, they provide researchers and practitioners with conceptual and methodological tools to problematize Whiteness.

In Chapter 2, "Unpacking White Racial Identity in English Language Teacher Education," Tonda Liggett addresses the role of White racial identity in the teaching and pedagogy of beginning English as a second language (ESL) teachers in the United States. She focuses on White racial identity and cultural positionality, and investigates how a lack of racial awareness on the part of White teachers of ESL could negatively affect how they interpret the academic work of students. Analyzing interview and observation transcripts of six public school ESL teachers in both urban and rural settings, Liggett demonstrates how the participants conceptualize and articulate their notions of race in general and Whiteness in particular. She argues that in order for ESL teachers to appropriately serve multiracial and multicultural students, ESL teacher education needs to incorporate a critical multicultural education stance that explicitly addresses issues of race and White privilege.

Chapter 3, "The Ideal English Speaker: A Juxtaposition of Globalization and Language Policy in South Korea and Racialized Language Attitudes in the United States," frames the historic underpinnings for the ideal English speaker with respect to speakers of African American Vernacular English (AAVE) and individuals learning English in South Korea. Drawing on distinctions that include race, language variety, class, and power, Grant and Lee analyze, across two national contexts, perspectives that contribute to theory building around race, identity, and class in language education, and social practice. The authors convincingly show that the globalization discourses that dominate language policies in South Korea, in fact, share much of the racialized language attitudes that underpinned the historical and present discrimination of AAVE in the United States.

Chapter 4, "Construction of Racial Stereotypes in English as a Foreign Language (EFL) Textbooks: Images as Discourse" by Cosette Taylor-Mendes explores how the images which represent English-speaking cultures in EFL textbooks shaped Brazilian students' and teachers' impressions of the target second language culture. Taylor-Mendes finds that the United States is consistently represented as a peaceful land of the social and political elite, all of whom are White. The second major finding is that Blacks are consistently represented as poor or powerless, while Whites are represented as rich and powerful. Finally, the perceived images divide race by continent with Whites living in North America, Asians living in Asia, and Blacks living in Africa. As a result, the images reflect and reinforce pre-existing stereotypes about race. The author concludes by offering some suggestions on how EFL teachers can engage students in critical analysis of their textbook images and ideologies.

Returning to the United States, Sherry Marx presents Chapter 5, "'It's Not Them; It's Not Their Fault': Manifestations of Racism in the Schooling of Latinas/os and ELLs," in which she demonstrates how colorblindness and ethnic stereotypes prevent teachers from confronting the hidden racism against English-Language Learners (ELLs) and Latina/o students. Drawing on critical race theory and critical Whiteness studies, Marx identifies deficit thinking and White racial superiority concealed in the comments made by schoolteachers, many of whom are well-meaning. Marx points out the lack of White teachers' understanding of the students' backgrounds and lived experiences, which is exacerbated by the physical distance between these two groups in the community. The pervasive stereotypes about Latina/o students and parents prevent White teachers from gaining a new understanding. Marx argues that persistent high Latino dropout rates indicate perpetual racial disparity in education, which cannot be fixed without our awareness that the fault of racial inequality lies with us.

2 Unpacking White Racial Identity in English Language Teacher Education

Tonda Liggett

Pre-reading Questions

The meaning of being white is not usually discussed in a white dominant society. Focusing on white racial identity among ESL teachers at primary and secondary schools in the United States, Tonda Liggett explores six white teachers' experiences and beliefs about race and whiteness.

- How would you characterize whiteness?
- How do people with different racialized identities, including whites, talk about their own identities? Are there any differences in the ways different groups of people discuss their own racial identities?

Introduction

The racial make-up of the majority of the American teacher-education students in my methods course on English-language learners (ELLs) in the United States share a white-European heritage. I draw upon this background to initiate our analysis of racial and cultural identity, not of the ELLs they are learning to teach, but rather of the teachers themselves, turning the gaze inward in a way that most have not been pressed to do. It is my belief that by reflecting on white racial identity and dominant culture membership, these pre-service and in-service English-language teacher (ELT) candidates will recognize the extent to which these two factors influence their perspectives and values about everyday life as well as the decisions they make about what to teach and what to leave unexamined. I argue that by examining the assumptions and perspectives that they hold based on being a member of the dominant group, teachers begin a process-oriented form of inquiry that is often new and fundamentally unsettling. Being challenged to take on such inquiry initiates a self-reflective process that impels teachers to rethink not only their individual beliefs, but the ways in which these beliefs play out in their teaching and assessment of diverse students. Analysis of racial identity allows teacher candidates to understand that there are alternative conceptions that guide students' values and perspectives—that these conceptualizations are seen in student writing, in responses to teacher questions, and in understandings of classroom readings. This broadened awareness can ultimately contribute to better understandings of how race and ethnicity inform student learning.

While race has several complex intersections with other social categories such as class and gender, I have found that the particular way that racial discourse has been constructed over time and linked to political and economic gain, lends to inquiry into underlying power structures and relations of domination in U.S. society. Analyzing the power relations involved in the intersection of social categories then reveals the hierarchical structures that inform individual notions of racial identity. Looking through the lens of race is a way to broaden teacher candidates' conceptions of the connections with class, ethnicity, culture, gender, and other social categories.

I come to this inquiry as a white, middle-class woman with an ongoing attempt to recognize the ways in which my race and class influence how I teach and what I choose to emphasize in my own curriculum. That I went through my undergraduate and Master's degree programs without ever having touched upon aspects of race or whiteness impels me to incorporate such material in the teacher-education programs that I now teach in order to counteract the inequality in society and institutions of schooling. Recognizing the benefits and privileges one receives because of one's skin color and dominant-class membership takes constant vigilance. This recognition enables me to catch the assumptions I make about the people I come in contact with throughout my day, the students I teach in my classes, and the colleagues with whom I work. By creating curricula that work to dismantle unexamined stereotypes and racial hierarchy, I hope to raise awareness for my students so that they may enter their classrooms with broadened perspectives on how racial identity influences the ways they approach their teaching and understand their diverse student population.

This chapter is divided into three sections. In the first section, I discuss how racial discourse has been conceptualized in a socially and historically specific American context that determines the expressibility of race. Examining the social construction of race and racial discourse highlights the influence that such constructions have on shaping individual values and beliefs. In the second section, I analyze the avoidance behaviors that emerged from my research data in order to emphasize the difficulty that the white English-language teachers (ELTs) in my study had when discussing issues of race and white racial identity (Liggett, 2005). This section highlights how such avoidance could impact ELLs' identity development by obscuring the centrality that race may have in their lives. The third section discusses ways for ELT educators to address issues of race and white racial identity to differentiate, yet connect, the individual, cultural, and institutional levels of racial discourse so that students can better understand how personal beliefs are influenced by cultural membership and, in turn, reinforced and maintained by institutions of schooling. In my experience, to facilitate open and reflective dialogue when taking up issues of race and whiteness with ELT candidates, addressing these issues through such differentiation enables a means of connection to students' lives in multiple ways. Distinguishing these three levels are important to such discussions with students because of the resistance and avoidance that white students often display when confronted with material on white racial identity (Kailin, 2002; McIntyre, 1997).

Terms and Definitions

I use the term ELL to represent students who are learning English as their nonnative language. I realize, however, that the widespread use of the terms ESL (English as a

Second Language), ESOL (English to Speakers of Other Languages), nonnative English speakers, English learners, and second language learners are often used synonymously.

I use the term race in its socially constructed sense to refer to the imposed racial categories usually based on differences in skin color and physical characteristics (Kailin, 2002). While there is only one race, the human race, the concept of race as an ideology was developed with the expansion of Europe to justify the African slave trade and European colonialism (McIntyre, 1997). Being mindful of the historical influences that slavery has had on conceptions of race in the United States is important because existing notions of racial hierarchy are reflected in discourse on race. Goldberg (1993) emphasizes the changing nature of meanings assigned to race and maintains that these conceptions are "a fluid, transforming, historically specific concept parasitic on theoretic and social discourses for the meaning it assumes at any historical moment" (p. 90). Speaking of race as a dynamic "historically specific concept" enables an analysis of racial discourse that considers the conditions under which American teachers have been socialized.

I use the term culture to refer to a dynamic system of social values, cognitive codes, behavioral standards, world-views, and beliefs used to give order and meaning to people's lives (Delgado-Gaitan & Trueba, 1991). In this sense, one's culture is developed as a dynamic process through which everyday practices and events are interpreted, coded, and assigned value (Spindler & Spindler, 1990). While culture is often used synonymously with one's racial category, there are key distinctions that necessitate a specific targeting of racial discourse in order to address issues of racial advantage (white privilege) and relational domination (Howard, 1999; Kailin, 2002; McIntyre, 1997).

The term racial identity refers to "a sense of group or collective identity based on one's *perceptions* that he or she shares a common racial heritage with a particular racial group" (Helms, 1993, p. 3). While racial identity refers to how one perceives oneself within a racial group, the term whiteness refers to "a system and ideology of white dominance that marginalizes and oppresses people of color, ensuring existing privileges for white people in [this country]" (McIntyre, 1997, p. 3). The term white privilege is a concept that specifically addresses systemic-level advantages that benefit Euro-American culture. The driving concepts of white privilege consist of two elements: the characteristics of the privileged group to define the societal norm, which often benefits the members of this group, and second, members of this group can rely on their privilege to avoid objecting to oppressive outcomes (Wildman & Davis, 2002).

The Social Construction of Racialized Discourse and its Expressibility

In this section, I articulate how racial discourse has been conceptualized and expressed in an American context and examine how such articulations have merged material and conceptual conditions over time to result in a socially and historically specific discourse that has determined the expressibility of race. It is important, in teacher-education courses, to discuss how knowledge is created over time to be deemed valid or worthy, so that notions of race and racial differentiation can be seen as shaped by popular societal beliefs as well as by America's history of slavery, rather than as natural or normal categorizations of humankind. By examining how racial discourse has been expressed over time, the preconceptual and presumptive aspects underlying such discourse indicate the macrosocial conditions that pervade social and personal identity in ways that influence how teachers think about their diverse students as well as what they choose to discuss and emphasize in curricula. Inquiry into the construction of racialized discourse then is a key component in highlighting the confinement of it within certain parameters determined by societal notions of acceptability. For white teacher candidates, expanding these boundaries to explore what it means to be white and to belong to the dominant culture, translates into an exploration of power, its connection to knowledge, and how this knowledge influences one's perspectives, beliefs, and values. In my experience, this exploration is an emotional one, often met with resistance, defensiveness, and at times, moments of deep self-reflection.

Uncovering the complex nature of how our perceptions of race and culture are formed begins with trying to deconstruct the multiple ways we are influenced by overt and covert messages in society. The gradual and subtle practices, the repeated performance of specific acts that become so ingrained in people's lives that, without notice, they are taken for granted to become a part of the normal and natural (Foucault, 1977). Foucault describes these unnoticed acts as being of eternal importance, for these small details can emerge as a set of techniques, methods, plans, and eventually knowledge.

There are various social conditions that make possible the expressibility of racialized discourse as well as conceptual conditions that enable such discourse to emerge (Goldberg, 1993). While school culture is a significantly influential factor in how racialized discourse is revealed, history has determined the extent to which this discourse can change by setting parameters wherein certain school localities can modify a shift. Such modifications, however, are only able to transgress the already predetermined formations of racialized discourse, which maintain verbalizations of race that specifically reflect the sociohistorical context of America. As Goldberg (1993) argues,

> racialized discourse does not consist simply in descriptive representations of others. It includes a set of hypothetical premises about human kinds (e.g., the great chain of being, classificatory hierarchies, etc.) and about the differences between them (both mental and physical). It involves a class of ethical choices (e.g., domination and subjugation, entitlement and restriction, disrespect and abuse). And it incorporates a set of institutional regulations, directions, and pedagogic models (e.g., apartheid, separate development, educational institutions, choice of educational and bureaucratic language, etc.).
>
> (p. 47)

The underlying set of factors that directly generate the discursive field take place at what Foucault (1972) calls the preconceptual level. Goldberg (1993) describes this preconceptual level as "manifestations of power relations vested in and between historically located subjects, and they are effects of a determinate social history. ... They generate the concepts and categories in terms of which racism is actually expressed and comprehended" (p. 48). One consequence of such ordering is the establishment of a hierarchy of humankind where racial classification—the ordering of human groups on the basis of inherited or environmental differences—implies that certain races are superior to others (Goldberg, 1993). While hierarchy may not be conceptually implicit in the notion of racial classification, the concept of difference is borne out by the synonym racial differentiation ... [where] Difference and identity inhere in the concept of race, furnishing whatever grounds can be claimed for racial classification ... It is then that racial differentiation begins to define otherness, and discrimination against the racially defined other becomes at once exclusion of the different.

(Goldberg, 1993, p. 51)

Goldberg argues that differential exclusion is the most fundamental base underlying racist expression where racist desires, dispositions, beliefs, hypotheses, and assertions (including acts, laws, and institutions) establish entitlement and restriction, endowment and appropriation (1993). As such, racial exclusion serves, first, as a *presumption* for which rules and rationalizations may be formulated and second, as the *outcome* of deliberation in such domains as pedagogy or legislation (Goldberg, 1993). Racial exclusion as an outcome of deliberations can be seen in the ongoing focus on diversity and multiculturalism in teacher education that excludes inquiry into underlying power structures and social stratification. With this exclusion, efforts toward multicultural inclusion and awareness remain on a superficial level and the differential treatment that students of color experience is unknown, and thus, unchanged. To dismantle the notion of racial hierarchy that pervades white teachers' thinking about race, it is imperative for ELT education to include examinations of America's history of race relations, the ways that race has been constructed, and the responsibility that white teachers have in counteracting the socially constructed notions of racial advantage (Liggett, 2007). Until white educators take on the task of interrupting the status quo, racial differentiation will be the outcome of diversity initiatives.

To counteract this existing racial hierarchy, it is necessary to identify the connection between teacher conceptualizations of race and racial identity and the ways that these conceptions actually link to teaching practice. In order to explore this connection, I used a qualitative research methodology to interview and observe six white ELTs who received their Master's degrees and had been teaching for less than 3 years. I conducted structured interviews for participants to share their experiences, beliefs, and assumptions about race and whiteness. In addition, I conducted classroom observations of each participant, keeping notes on the class subject, number of students and country of origin, classroom arrangement, students' response to the material, and teachers' responses to the class. I tape-recorded the interviews and observations, and these transcriptions, along with my notes, constitute the data used for analysis. I observed the rural participants' one-on-one and small-group (three to four students) tutoring sessions in reading, writing, history, grammar, and vocabulary building. The urban participants had an average of eight students per class and I observed classes in language arts, reading, writing, social studies, and math. In the next section, I describe the background information of the participants in this study as a way to contextualize the school and societal influences that informed how these teachers approached their teaching.

The Urban Setting and Participants

Three teachers, Maureen, Hannah, and Bridget, taught within one mile of each other in an urban[1] New England city that I call Milltown. With a total population of 107,006,

Milltown's racial breakdown according to the 2000 U.S. Census figures and terms was as follows: White 91.7%, Hispanic 4.6%, Asian 2.3%, Black or African American 2.1%, and some other race 1.2%. Of the total population, 80.4% of the households spoke English only, compared to 91.7% in the state and 82.1% in the country. In Milltown, 13.3% spoke Indo-European languages, 4% Spanish, 1.7% Asian and Pacific Island languages, and 0.6% other languages. According to the school district data, 7.3% of the student population was considered limited English proficient (LEP) and enrolled in programs that provided specific English-language assistance.

Maureen

During this study, Maureen was in her third year of teaching ELLs at Mountain View High School, a magnet school serving students in grades 9–12, in the heart of Milltown's large working-class neighborhood. This school had 2,381 students, of which 85.4% were White, non-Hispanic, 7.5% Hispanic, 4.2% Black non-Hispanic, 2.3% Asian, and 0.5% Native American. Of the total school population, 9.6% were considered limited English proficient and 12% were eligible for free or reduced-cost lunch. As a magnet school, the 9.6% of LEP students was above the district average of 7.6% and well above the state average of 1.6%.

Maureen, a native-English-speaking woman in her early 50s, grew up on Long Island in an all-white neighborhood with mixed ethnicities and religions, most notably Italian, Irish, and Jewish. She identified most strongly with her father's Italian side and was saddened by the fact that she had not continued to speak and study Italian. Maureen taught ESL1, the lowest of four levels in her strict and orderly classroom, which she felt was most appropriate for the refugee students from Bosnia, Sudan, Somalia, Egypt, and Afghanistan. For many of these students, English was learned in refugee camps or through sporadic school attendance in their war-torn countries.

Hannah

Hannah was in her third year of teaching ELLs at Pine Ridge Middle School when I began my data collection. This school was about one mile from Mountain View High School and was similarly designated as a magnet for ELLs. Pine Ridge had an enrollment of 1,070 students, of which 84% were White, non-Hispanic, 9.9% Hispanic, 3.8% Black, non-Hispanic, 2.2% Asian, and 0.1% Native American. Of the total school population, 6.6% were limited English proficient and 29.3% were eligible for free or reduced-cost lunch, well above the state average of 16.4%.

Hannah, a native-English-speaking woman in her mid-20s, grew up in a small town that was mostly white. Hannah remembers there were "two black kids in my school, possibly." She tried hard to get her students to focus on their studies and not waste time because, as she reminded them, they had a lot of catching up to do in order to reach the level of work that their mainstream peers were doing. She taught level one and two social studies, math, and language arts to students from Puerto Rico, El Salvador, Honduras, Mexico, and Columbia. She also had immigrant students from Korea and China, and refugee students from Bosnia, Sudan, and Somalia, some of whom came to her class with no educational experience or English-language background.

Bridget

Bridget was in her second year as an ELT at the time of my data collection, teaching ELL kindergarteners at Milltown Elementary School. The population of Milltown Elementary was 422, including 99 kindergarten students. Of these, 67.6% were White, non-Hispanic, 23.6% Hispanic, 6.3% Black, non-Hispanic, 2.3% Asian, and 0.2% Native American. The large Hispanic population at this school stood in stark contrast to the state average of 2.2%, as did the relatively small percentage of White students, which was far below the state average of 94.6%. ELLs comprised 17.1% of the total school population and 70.4% of the students at Milltown Elementary were eligible for free or reduced-cost lunch, well above the district average of 28.9% and the state average of 17.3%.

Bridget, an energetic, native-English-speaking woman in her early 20s, grew up in white, middle-class towns that had very little diversity in comparison to the setting in which she taught. She focused on creating a relaxed, polite, and fun setting in her small classroom. She wanted her young students to feel comfortable so that they would begin to participate in the ongoing dialogue that was at the center of her instruction. Many of the students were Hispanic, from Puerto Rico and the Dominican Republic; others were from Albania, Russia, and Liberia.

Rural Setting and Participants

Three participants in this study, Carly, Allie, and Beth, taught in rural school districts within the state.[2] In these rural school settings, these teachers most often supported the curriculum of the mainstream teacher and traveled from school to school depending on where the ELLs were located. The demographics of each school district and details about each teacher are addressed below.

Carly

Carly taught in the university town of Rockfield. During this study, she was in her third year as an ELT at Rockfield High School where 738 students were enrolled, of whom 97% were White, non-Hispanic, 1.2% Asian, 1.1% Hispanic, and 0.7% Black, non-Hispanic. Of the total school population, 1.8% were considered limited English proficient and 2% were eligible for free or reduced-cost lunch; unlike other schools in this study, this was far below the state average of 16.4%.

When I asked Carly, a native-English-speaking woman in her early 50s, where she grew up, she laughed and replied "honkyville" then further described it as "a heavily Caucasian environment" in a large suburb of New England. She was a strong advocate for her students and tried hard to get them involved in the social fabric of the school so that they felt like they belonged.

Allie

Allie was in her second year as an ELT in her district with a student enrollment of 2,088. Of this number, 96.7% were White, non-Hispanic, 1.3% Native American, 1.1%

Hispanic, 0.7% Asian, and 0.3% Black, non-Hispanic. Within the total district population, 0.4% were considered limited English proficient and 10.4% were eligible for free or reduced-cost lunch, below the state average of 16.4%. The median household income in the county that Allie taught in was $48,875, slightly below the state median of $49,830.

Allie, a native Spanish speaker in her late 40s, was born in Cuba and immigrated to the United States when she was 11. While living in Cuba, she attended American schools so that she could learn English. She went to private schools most of her life that were "mostly white" with "some Black students and some white students and the Hispanic students were mostly Cubans, so there was some diversity, but not a whole lot." Her students were mostly Spanish speakers from Latin America and Puerto Rico. Allie spent about 1 hour "on the road" each day traveling to three elementary schools and one high school to provide English-language services to 12 students.

Beth

Beth, the other rural teacher, was in her third year of teaching K–12 ELLs during this study. Her school district had an enrollment of 2,846 students, of which 98.6% were White, non-Hispanic, 0.7% Black, non-Hispanic, 0.4% Asian, and 0.3% Hispanic. Within the total district population, 0.3% were considered limited English proficient and 24.3% were eligible for free or reduced-cost lunch, significantly higher than the 2% in Carly's high school, the 11.7% in Allie's district, and the state average of 16.4%. The median household income in the county where Beth taught was $40,792, the lowest of all participants in this study and below the state median of $49,830.

Beth, a native-English-speaking woman in her mid-40s, grew up in a small town on Long Island where many people commuted to New York City to work. When asked the racial make-up of her town, she laughed, "Oh, white, white, and white." She knew of two African Americans in her school throughout her K–12 years. Beth was a very conscientious teacher who strove to maximize her time with her students through detailed planning and frequent short meetings with their mainstream teachers. As with Allie, Beth taught K–12 in a rural district with few ELLs. At the time of my data collection, she worked with two students regularly and monitored five others in the district.

The teachers in this study had an array of background experiences that informed the ways they approached their teaching and curriculum. In the next section, I analyze how socially constructed notions of race factored into the tendency of these teachers to resist addressing race or their own racial identity. By illustrating these avoidance tendencies, I explicate how to speak to these issues in ELT education courses as well as to highlight the implications that stem from such avoidance.

White Teacher Identity in a Diverse Classroom: Avoidance and Negativity

From the transcript data of the interviews with teacher participants in my study, avoidance behaviors emerged in negative discourse about whiteness and in participants' efforts to distance themselves from their white heritage. An example of this distancing was apparent when Hannah, an urban middle school ELL teacher, described her racial and cultural background,

I'm about as … Anglo-American as you can get. I often laugh because I feel like I don't have much to be proud of in my heritage because it goes back to the English and the German, which is [sic] like the major oppressors in the world [laugh] … I'm not very proud of saying that of my English [laugh] heritage … if I was to get really specific about my cultural identity it would be more in terms of being a teacher, mother, and identifying with groups of people who would identify with that.

Shunning her Anglo-American heritage, Hannah focuses on other identity groups that she feels more connected to, thus distancing herself from the "major oppressors in the world." In addition, Maureen, an urban high school ELL teacher, speaks negatively and distances herself from her whiteness, but does so by embracing her Italian culture. She states:

when I tell [my students] that my grandparents were from Italy, I become a much more … I don't know, they can relate to me better. I suddenly become less of a white American to them and I become a part of their world … I had kids say to me —tell me that that made a difference in the way they felt about me … I have a heritage I can go back and find people overseas … It just makes them feel a little bit more connected to me than just being this person who has always been a white American.

Distinguishing herself by being able to trace her heritage overseas, Maureen sees herself as "less of a white American." Katz and Ivey (1977) note that

when faced with the question of their racial identification, Whites merely deny that they are White … Ask a White person what he or she is racially and you may get the answer Italian, English, Catholic, or Jewish. White people do not see themselves as White.

(p. 486)

Not seeing white as a race results from being in a position where other races and cultures are held up to the standard of whiteness (McIntosh, 2002; Rothenberg, 2002). McIntosh (2002) believes that "whites are carefully taught not to recognize white privilege" and that "many, perhaps most, of our students in the United States think that racism doesn't affect them because they are not people of color; they do not see whiteness as a racial identity" (p. 79).

By not recognizing white as a race, it is easier to dismiss or minimize the importance of racial identity and members can rely on their privilege to choose whether to object to oppression or ignore it (Jensen, 2002; McIntosh, 2002; Wildman & Davis, 2002). Dismissing racial identity as insignificant or unimportant to one's identity construction implies that alternative perspectives stemming from a minority position run counter to normalized standards. Doing so implies that one's knowledge system is right, while the Other is wrong. Howard (1999) states:

Dominant groups tend to claim truth as their private domain. For the most part, hegemonic groups do not consider their beliefs, attitudes, and actions to be determined by cultural conditioning or the influences of group membership. As Whites, we usually don't even think of ourselves as having culture; we're simply right.

(p. 50)

The assumption of rightness has been a powerful force in establishing relations of domination by whites (Howard, 1999). In the ELL classroom, this could translate to negative student evaluations based on nonconformity to dominant culture standards rather than recognition that these standards are culturally nuanced and thus determined by teacher racial and cultural identity.

While the participants in this study avoided talk of their own white racial identity or spoke of it negatively, they became aware of their racialized identities by referencing other groups, in particular the social standing of blacks and whites in terms of slavery and socioeconomic class. In so doing, they illustrated the extent to which the notion of racial hierarchy pervades the thinking about race relations in a U.S. context. For example, Carly, a rural high school ELL teacher, addressed her racial identity with reference to the presence of Africans in her life. She stated,

I did not realize to what a huge extent the African slaves and their descendants played on the population demographics of the early United States [laugh]. HUGE percentage of this country were slaves or descendants of slaves—HUGE! … So, its … resonates particularly, when you see all these … really terrific young kids that are from Africa who could have been slaves [laugh] had they, you know … the fact that this country is built … on stolen land and slave labor … never really hit me to such an extent until just recently. And, that's from wandering through a variety of history courses with my kids and having people from Africa in my life.

By looking at group identity and stratification, Carly became aware of her own racial identity. Similarly, Bridget defined her racial identity through group distinctions in socioeconomic status. She stated,

I never really had thought about [racial and cultural identity] growing up until I started working in [Milltown], especially with ESL, then I did obviously, you just see the background you're from … not just ESL … the schools I'd been working in because they were low income, tough areas … I don't think I stood out to the children, in my mind I stood out just coming from a completely different background, you know, I had a really great home life. I always had the comforts I needed, so in that respect I felt, you know, being white and having like a really great experience … you feel different in that regard.

Teaching ELLs in a "low income, tough area" made her more aware of not only her own racial identity, but also the advantage that often exists between racial membership and socioeconomic class, "being white and having … a really great experience."

In my examination of racial identity, there were no examples of positive associations related to being white. Helms (1993) states,

Because White racism in the United States seems to have developed as a means of justifying the enslavement of Black Americans during the slavery eras of the 1700s and 1800s ... most Whites may have no consistent conception of a positive White identity or consciousness. As a consequence, Whites may feel threatened by the actual or presupposed presence of racial consciousness in non-White racial groups.

(pp. 49–50)

Given that white racial identity is inextricably tied to the social, political, and historical context of America (Goldberg, 1993; Morrison, 1992), negative connotations of whiteness along with the discomfort of developing a racial consciousness could account for the reasons why these participants spoke of their racial identity in the ways described above.

As members of the dominant white majority, these teachers do not consider their beliefs, attitudes, and actions to be determined by cultural conditioning or the influences of racial membership (Howard, 1999). They have been socialized to downplay issues of race (Goldberg, 1993). As such, their responses about racial identity reflect the peripheral role that race has in their own identity construction. This peripheral placement could be problematic by obscuring the centrality that race may have in the lives of their ELLs, making it more difficult for them to understand or negotiate their racial identities within a new school context (Canagarajah, 1999; Kubota, 2001). In addition, it could cause these teachers to inaccurately evaluate student work by not being aware of how alternative perspectives inform approaches and interpretations of academic work. The following examples illustrate how this could play out in the classroom.

Maureen's class had just finished reading a short article when she began to ask questions about the two separate American wedding pictures illustrated below it. In the pictures, one couple sat side-by-side in wedding attire from the 1920s and another couple sat in a similar pose, but in more casual dress from the 1980s. The point of the lesson was to develop reading comprehension skills by learning about traditional and modern American wedding customs. When Maureen asked her first question about what the students noticed in the two photos, one Black student from Rwanda immediately responded with "A man who is white." Maureen's response came slowly, "OOOOkkkaayyyy," in a tone that indicated this was not the answer she was expecting or thought relevant. After a few more questions to refocus the students on the book's distinction between formal and informal, Maureen asked, "But, the groom over here [the 1980s couple] looks, what?" A student said, "Poor." Maureen replied, "Poor? You think he looks poor? [laughter] O.K., well, that's—that's, if you think that that's fine." As they compared the brides' dresses, the students commented back and forth making a case for whether and why one was rich and the other poor, and were much more interested in discerning this distinction than the formal/informal one.

Being white went unnoticed for Maureen as it was the norm in the city and school where she taught, yet race was the first aspect that the African student noticed. When she tried to redirect the students' attention, they focused on socioeconomic status. The topics of race and class were not taken up or given consideration. In this situation, Maureen did not seem to register the importance of the racial aspect of the couples in the wedding pictures because they were all white. By not recognizing the role of race in individual identity construction, the student's response regarding the man's whiteness could translate to not understanding the focus of the reading passage.

Another example of how teachers could inaccurately evaluate student responses based on differential placement of racial identity occurred as Bridget read *A Day at the Beach*, a book with elaborate color pencil drawings that include a diverse mix of people and families with various shades of skin and hair color enjoying a beach habitat. As she read, she asked detailed questions about the color, shape, length, and size of the shells and sea animals in the pictures: "[this sea animal is] the same shape isn't it? But, this is not a shell, right? But it looks the same ... Look at the picture, *look at this one carefully and then this one*. Are they the same?" Bridget tried to get her students to understand the concept of similarities and differences between sea animals and shells. However, when she asked about the people in the pictures, her questions were fewer and less specific, asking about the number of people, not their physical characteristics. "What do you see on the cover? Do you see something [Marina]?" [Marina] pointed to the people and Bridget replied, "The people, yeah. Are there just some or are there many?" While she may have focused on the distinction between "some" and "many" in previous lessons, she did not ask about marine life in this truncated way. The people in the pictures were not examined in such detail and the focus shifted from similarities and differences of the shells and sea animals to quantities of "some" or "many" for the people. By limiting the expansions that students can make on topics of race, their ability to draw on background knowledge decreases. For ELLs, this knowledge is a key factor as they attempt to make meaning of their academic coursework.

Racial Discourse in ELT Education

Educational institutions play a significant role in limiting inquiry into racial issues because of the ways control is maintained over the presentation and reinforcement of certain forms of inquiry (Lesko & Bloom, 2000; Popkewitz & Brennan, 1998). This plays out on the individual level in what teachers feel is important to address as well as what they dismiss as unimportant. In my experience teaching both pre-service and in-service ELT candidates, inquiry into whiteness and white racial identity is often met with skepticism and defensiveness. Indeed, my research indicated that white racial discourse involved talk that served to distract from an examination of individual and collective white identities (Liggett, 2005). Because of this tendency toward resistance and avoidance, there is an imperative need for teacher educators to explicate the contextual factors that bind and determine how race and whiteness are discussed in course material. I have found that by highlighting the differences between individual acts of racism, cultural aspects that influence racist behavior, and institutional constructs that maintain racial hierarchy, teacher candidates are better able to differentiate the varying contexts wherein race is discussed (see Appendix 1). In making a distinction between the individual, cultural, and institutional realms wherein racial discourse occurs, the scope, purpose, and power located at each level becomes visible because the relationship between the formation of personal beliefs can be linked to cultural values, which in turn are connected to and influenced by institutional systems of governance.

Talking about race on the individual level involves discussion that focuses on choices one makes and the ways one conforms (or not) to the social pressures that surround life choices. At this level, examining personal choice in relation to societal pressure to conform allows for an expansion to the broader cultural level, illustrating the dynamic interaction between cultural and individual conceptions of the good. For example, asking about the identity groups to which teacher candidates belong helps them focus on personal identity such as race, ethnicity, native language, sexual orientation, physical ability, gender, religion, previous education, and work experience. In addition, I ask students to list their affinity-group memberships such as sports/exercise groups, organizations, and clubs as well as free-time activities. Such focus allows teacher candidates to see that their individual identity has cultural orientations that shape the ways they think about values, beliefs, communication styles (models of politeness/formality), historical perspectives, art, music, family, rituals (graduations, sports-team rallies), rites of passage (notable birthdays), and other social-group activities.

For white ELT candidates to recognize that they are, indeed, "cultural beings" (Sleeter, 1996) is important to becoming aware of differential status, positionality, and stratification in the broader realm of society. When discussing dominant-culture values and beliefs, such as individualism and meritocracy, it is necessary to make historical connections that reveal how ideologies are constructed by political and social influences.

At the institutional level, the focus turns to discussion of entities beyond any one individual or group of individuals to include systems or structures that have the power to enforce (government, education, religious structures) that are firmly established in societal governance frameworks. Describing the extent to which knowledge is socially constructed is often a challenge. I have found that videos/DVDs such as *Race: The Power of Illusion* (2003) or *The Eye of the Storm* (1970) enable teacher candidates to identify links between all levels of racialized discourse discussed above. In addition, readings from critical race theorists help reveal the power behind institutional structures to influence individuals. Such an orientation inherently looks through a lens that considers institutional-level inequity. This includes other social categories such as socioeconomic status, gender, and ability, among others, while acknowledging that issues of race are often obscured because of the political and economic relationship that has been tied to the construction of race in America. Material from scholars such as Jane Bolgatz (2005), Ruth Frankenberg (1997), Gary Howard (1999), Julie Kailin (2002), Gloria Ladson-Billings (2001), Peggy McIntosh (2002), Paula Rothenburg (2002), and Christine Sleeter (1996), are helpful in highlighting the connections between these social categories. Particularly, these works challenge definitions of racism located in individual acts and view racism as a system of privileged discourses and discriminatory institutionalized practices that act upon individual perceptions of reality (Greene & Abt-Perkins, 2003).

In order to expand beyond the individual and facilitate connections to the institutional, the inclusion of a cultural analysis as a mediating link enables better understandings of identity-group dynamics as well as explanations about how racial matters are defined and historically constructed. Examining the shared element of experiencing racial construction in an American context assists ELT candidates to move beyond the sense of personalization that can limit or shut down discourse on race. A study of race that begins with an analysis of what it means to have a racial identity, along with the presence of a racial hierarchy that benefits one group over another, presses teacher candidates to analyze their personal assumptions in ways that can cause a fundamental rethinking of approaches to teaching, designing curricula, and evaluating a diverse classroom of ELLs.

Conclusion

Avoiding talk about race and racial advantage is what Alice McIntyre (1997) refers to as "white talk," "talk that serves to insulate white people from examining their/our individual and collective role(s) in the perpetuation of racism" (p. 45). In McIntyre's (1997) study of white, undergraduate, middle-class, female pre-service teachers, speech tactics were used to create a "culture of niceness" that worked to distance individuals from the difficult task of addressing racism and white privilege.

> The language of the participants' white talk, whether it was intentional or not, consciously articulated or unconsciously spoken, resisted interrogation. Interruptions, silences, switching topics, tacitly accepting racist assumptions, talking over one another, joining in collective laughter that served to ease the tension, hiding under the canopy of camaraderie – these maneuverings repelled critical conversations.
>
> (McIntyre, 1997, p. 47)

Discourse among these participants focused on maintaining a sense of camaraderie in order to maneuver around more critical analysis of white racial identity and the ways in which white participants may have benefited from it. Given the importance of racial identity in McIntyre's study, it seems likely that there would also be implications for white ELTs similarly socialized in the context of American education.

For white ELTs with students from various racial, ethnic, and cultural backgrounds, it is essential to be exposed to material in ELT programs that problematize relations of domination and the influence that white racial membership has on teaching and pedagogy. This entails including curricular materials that reflect a critical multicultural and antiracist perspective as well as an activist component that connects curriculum to lived experience. Without fostering critical awareness, ELTs run the risk of negatively evaluating their students' work because they are unaware of the influence that alternative knowledge systems may have on their students' approaches to academic work (Liggett, 2007).

In addition, addressing avoidance behaviors in discourse about white privilege enables ELTs to be more aware of their own avoidance tendencies in the classroom when discussing perspectives that run counter to their dominant-culture beliefs. When ELLs talk about their belief systems, ELTs may be more apt to explore these beliefs so that students can more easily understand connections between home culture and dominant culture. Not addressing issues of racial privilege in ELT education keeps notions of equality on a superficial level due to the inability to conceptualize whiteness and its advantages while failing to see how these advantages come at the expense of the marginalized.

Discussion Questions

1. Why do white teachers tend to avoid discussing race and racism? How would this avoidance influence teaching both white and non-white students?

2. The author states, "Racial exclusion as an outcome of deliberations can be seen in the ongoing focus on diversity and multiculturalism in teacher education that excludes inquiry into underlying power structures and social stratification." In multicultural education (e.g., addressing cultural diversity in the classroom), how can issues of race, power structures, and social stratification be addressed? Think about some concrete activities.

3. The author encourages white educators to take on the task of problematizing racial differentiation and discrimination. What challenges would be involved in this task? What can be done to remove these obstacles?

4. The author lists useful activities for discussing issues of race. How can they apply to your own situation? In addition, think about more activities that would help teachers become aware of the racialized identities of others and their own.

Appendix 1: Differentiating contexts of racial discourse in ELT education

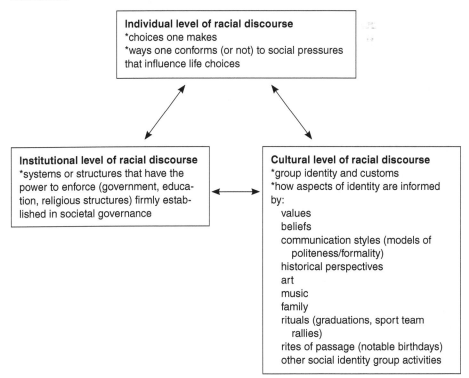

Individual level of racial discourse
*choices one makes
*ways one conforms (or not) to social pressures that influence life choices

Institutional level of racial discourse
*systems or structures that have the power to enforce (government, education, religious structures) firmly established in societal governance

Cultural level of racial discourse
*group identity and customs
*how aspects of identity are informed by:
    values
    beliefs
    communication styles (models of politeness/formality)
    historical perspectives
    art
    music
    family
    rituals (graduations, sport team rallies)
    rites of passage (notable birthdays)
    other social identity group activities

Notes

1. Urban is defined as "All territory, population and housing units in urbanized areas and in places of more than 2,500 persons outside of urbanized area. 'Urban' classification cuts across other hierarchies and can be in metropolitan or non-metropolitan areas." See Glossary in the U.S. Census website at www.census.gov/dmd/www/glossary/glossary_u.html.
2. Rural is defined as "Territory, population and housing units not classified as urban. 'Rural' classification cuts across other hierarchies and can be in metropolitan or non-metropolitan areas." See the above U.S. Census website.

References

Bolgatz, J. (2005). *Talking race in the classroom*. New York: Teachers College Press.

California Newsreel. (2003). *Race: The power of an illusion* [video-recording]. San Francisco, CA: Independent Television Service.

Canagarajah, A. (1999). *Resisting linguistic imperialism in English teaching*. Oxford: Oxford University Press.

Delgado-Gaitan, C., & Trueba, H. (1991). *Crossing cultural borders: Education for immigrant families in America*. New York: Falmer Press.

Foucault, M. (1972). *The archaeology of knowledge*. New York: Pantheon.

Foucault, M. (1977). *Discipline and punish: The birth of the prison*. New York: Random House.

Frankenberg, R. (Ed.). (1997). *Displacing whiteness: Essays in social and cultural criticism*. Durham, NC: Duke University Press.

Goldberg, D. (1993). *Racist culture: Philosophy and the politics of meaning*. Oxford: Blackwell.

Greene, S., & Abt-Perkins, D. (2003). *Making race visible: Literacy research for cultural understanding*. New York: Teachers College Press.

Helms, J. E. (1993). *Black and white racial identity: Theory, research and practice*. Westport, CT: Praeger.

Howard, G. (1999). *We can't teach what we don't know: White teachers, multiracial schools*. New York: Teachers College Press.

Jensen, R. (2002). White privilege shapes the U.S. In P. S. Rothenberg (Ed.), *White privilege: Essential readings on the other side of racism* (pp. 103–106). New York: Worth Publishers.

Kailin, J. (2002). *Antiracist education*. Lanham, NJ: Rowman & Littlefield.

Katz, J., & Ivey, A. (1977). White awareness: The frontier of racism awareness training. *The Personnel and Guidance Journal, 55*, 485–489.

Kubota, R. (2001). Discursive construction of the images of U.S. classrooms. *TESOL Quarterly, 35*, 9–38.

Ladson-Billings, G. (2001). *Crossing over to Canaan: The journey of new teachers in diverse classrooms*. San Francisco, CA: Jossey-Bass.

Lesko, N., & Bloom, L. (2000). The haunting of multicultural epistemology and pedagogy. In C. McCarthy & G. Dimitriadis (Eds.), *Multicultural curriculum: New directions for social theory, practice, and policy* (pp. 242–260). London: Routledge.

Liggett, T. (2005). *Visualizing the invisible: The role of white racial identity in the teaching and pedagogy of new ESOL teachers*. Unpublished dissertation, University of New Hampshire, Durham, NH.

Liggett, T. (2007). The alchemy of identity: The role of white racial identity in the teaching and pedagogy of new ESOL teachers. In M. Mantero (Ed.), *Identity and second language learning: Culture, inquiry, and dialogic activity in educational contexts* (pp. 45–70). Greenwich, CT: Information Age Publishing.

McIntosh, P. (2002). White privilege: Unpacking the invisible knapsack. In P. Rothenberg (Ed.), *White privilege: Essential readings on the other side of racism* (pp. 97–102). New York: Worth Publishers.

McIntyre, A. (1997). *Making meaning of whiteness.* Albany, NY: State University of New York Press.

Morrison, T. (1992). *Playing in the dark: Whiteness and the literary imagination.* New York: Vintage Books.

Peters, William (1970). *The eye of the storm* [motion picture]. Columbus, OH: Xerox Films.

Popkewitz, T., & Brennan, M. (Eds.). (1998). *Foucault's challenge: Discourse, knowledge, and power in education.* New York: Teachers College Press.

Rothenberg, P. (Ed.). (2002). *White privilege: Essential readings on the other side of racism.* New York: Worth Publishers.

Sleeter, C. (1996). *Multicultural education as social activism.* Albany, NY: State University of New York Press.

Spindler, G., & Spindler, L. (1990). *The American cultural dialogue and its transmission.* Philadelphia, PA: Falmer Press.

Wildman, S., & Davis, A. (2002). Making systems of privilege visible. In P. Rothenberg (Ed.), *White privilege: Essential readings on the other side of racism* (pp. 89–96). New York: Worth Publishers.

3 The Ideal English Speaker

A Juxtaposition of Globalization and Language Policy in South Korea and Racialized Language Attitudes in the United States

Rachel A. Grant and Incho Lee

Pre-reading Questions

Historical attitudes of racial bias and language discrimination are seldom examined across international borders. Rachel Grant and Incho Lee reveal ways in which our global connections sustain systems of racial, class, and linguistic privilege in the United States and South Korea.

- Consider the issue of language policies in your own community. What are the burning issues of language policies in your community? What languages enjoy high status in your community?
- What have been your experiences with speakers of African American Vernacular English or speakers of other English varieties?

Introduction

This chapter discusses the intersections of race and social class with respect to language and power in the United States and South Korea. We focus on the teaching of English and its status in South Korean society and offer a juxtaposition with the unique situation of African Americans relative to standard, mainstream English ideals. Within the U.S. context we frame the historical attitudes toward native languages and English speech of the descendants of African slaves. The first author, Rachel Grant, is of African American heritage and a bidialectal speaker of mainstream English and African American Vernacular English (AAVE). The second author, Incho Lee, is from South Korea and is bilingual and biliterate in Korean and English. The approach to the chapter reflects our shared identities as critical scholars in literacy and language education and women of color. The perspectives presented here also attempt to make clear the position that interdependent world systems based on global capitalism and access to symbolic resources reproduce exploitation of historically oppressed groups. We will argue that the spread of English serves as a unifying tool for exploiting local realities regarding race/ethnicity, class, and power, thereby reinforcing the mythic norm of the White ideal English speaker.

There are two lines of argument here. First, hegemonic ideologies of language and of the relationships between language, race, and social class have played an important role in official constructions of difference. We find that these differences sustain White middle-class privilege within the United States and solidify U.S. political, military, and material economy worldwide. We contend that the political economy of language pivots around commodification and global capitalism. This is to say, language (i.e., English) has come to represent capital and power and symbolizes a kind of dividing rod of class and racial disparity within the United States and around the world.

The second point of our argument here is that the crafting of English as economic and cultural commodity means that hegemonic constructions of identity around language often situate people of color in competing, and frequently hostile, positions relative to one another. Specifically, in the case of South Koreans and African Americans, as the United States forges friendships with governments around the world, nationals and those who immigrated to the United States have usually accepted U.S. racialized discourses around language and social worth. As a result, the evolving hegemonic notions of race and language continue to subjugate, marginalize, and oppress speakers of African American Vernacular English, marginalized varieties of English, and indigenous and heritage languages.

Attitudes toward and treatment of African Americans, who have often been characterized as nonstandard, deficient speakers of English, are perpetuated because of their former slave status, racial segregation, economic discrimination, and the continuing poor-quality education afforded to many African American children (Grant & Asimeng-Boahene, 2006). This situation is part and parcel of the racialized language apartheid reproduced by notions of the ideal English speaker/listener that also accompanies the teaching of English worldwide (Edge, 2003). In this chapter, we draw from broad, complementing theoretical perspectives including the critical pedagogies of sociocultural theory, womanism/feminism, critical race theory, and critical sociology. We articulate a range of approaches such as critical multiculturalism, anti-oppressive education, and culturally substantive teaching. We unpack the interrelated and complex workings of racism, classism, and language discrimination reflected in the hegemony of traditional Western epistemology and political theory that perpetuate ideology and policy to maintain a certain kind of English as a status marker and basis for a new kind of social division and polarization in society.

To illustrate these various tensions, we focus the first section on a historical framework for examining the development of English usage by people of African heritage and trace the social and educational positioning of African Americans with respect to language, literacy achievement, and power in the racialized United States. Following this section we discuss situated globalization in South Korea and commodification of the English language in South Korea's globalization efforts. The internalization of globalization ideology and influence this has on social stratification, racial attitudes, and language policy in South Korea are then discussed. Particularly, we explore multifaceted and unique interactions among South Koreans' perception of White, middle-class English as Standard English, their discrimination against certain racialized groups, and the widespread belief in English as a personal and national commodity in an era of globalization. In doing so, we scrutinize South Korea's historical and political ties with the United States which have paved the way for reciprocal import and export of racial discrimination. And finally, we suggest areas where more analysis is needed to reduce cleavages among those who are most exposed to English and those who are least exposed to it and among those who speak a standard variety of English and those who speak other varieties. In our final thoughts we offer perspectives that contribute to theory building around race, identity, and class in language teaching and social practice.

Roots of a Linguistic Past

> I now saw myself deprived of all chance of returning to my native country, or even the least glimpse of hope of gaining the shore, ... I now wished for the last friend, death, to relieve me ... In a little time after, amongst the poor chained men, I found some of my own nation, which in a small degree gave ease to my mind. I inquired of these what was to be done with us; they gave me to understand we were to be carried to these white people's country to work for them (From the Interesting Narrative of the Life of Olaudah Equiano, or Gustavus Vassa, the African, Written by Himself, 1789).

> (cited in Gates & McKay, 1997, p. 157)

Without doubt, the capture and exportation of Africans to the Caribbean and the Americas fueled one of the first global economies contributing to prosperity for Europe and, later, the United States. For European traders, settlers of the "new" land, and their governments, slavery was the odious reality of capitalism and Africans were the prized resource for their economic institution.

If Africans managed to survive the "Middle Passage" after captivity, they had few tools to help them make sense of their lives as captives and slaves. Subsequently, through contact with other enslaved Africans as well as Europeans (free and indentured), the voice that Africans developed to make sense of the world is one variously labeled Negro English, Black Speech, Black English, AAVE, and Ebonics. In this chapter the terms AAVE and Ebonics are taken as rough equivalents to reference the language spoken by most Americans who are the descendants of the first African slaves. In the next section we offer explanation of the origins of AAVE.

Theorizing the Origins of African American Speech

Rickford (1999) provided a widely accepted explanation of three theoretical perspectives that inform possible origins of the variety of English spoken by the descendants of African slaves living in the United States. According to Rickford, "Arriving in an American milieu in which English was dominant, the slaves learned English. But how quickly and completely they did so and how much influence from their African languages are matters of dispute among linguists" (p. 324). The Afrocentric or Ebonics (taken literally to mean "ebony speech") view recognizes the Niger–Congo roots of African American speech and holds that the most distinctive features represent imports from Africa. A second view, the Eurocentric or dialectologist, stresses the English origin of African American speech with little trace of their African languages remaining. A third view, Creolist, holds that in acquiring English, African slaves "developed a pidgin language— a simplified fusion of English and African languages—from which Ebonics evolved"

(Rickford, 1999, p. 326). We acknowledge that both the Afrocentric and Creolist views influenced our points of view and inform the interpretations expressed herein.

African Americans have long understood the function of language and how it is uniquely used by people of African heritage. Literary luminaries such as James Baldwin and Toni Morrison acknowledged the power of language in conveying the African experience in America. James Baldwin publicly described Black English as "this passion, this skill … this incredible music," and in his eloquent essay, "If Black English isn't language, then tell me what is," he wrote,

> The argument concerning the use, or the status, or the reality, of [B]lack English is rooted in American history and has absolutely nothing to do with the question the argument supposes itself to be posing … People evolve a language in order to describe and thus control their circumstances or in order not to be submerged by a situation that they cannot articulate. (And if they cannot articulate it, they are submerged.)
>
> (Baldwin, 1985, p. 649)

Nobel laureate Toni Morrison insists that a critical ingredient of her writing was: "the language, only the language … it is the thing that [B]lack people love so much—the saying of words, holding them on the tongue, experimenting with them, playing with them" (cited in Rickford & Rickford, 2000, pp. 4–5). For speakers of AAVE, the interplay of race and slavery is inexorably linked to racial and linguistic disadvantage.

Racialized Linguicism

For newly arriving Africans, slave owners realized the potential threat that shared-heritage languages posed. In the brutal system of trans-Atlantic slavery, the ability of slaves to communicate in languages unknown to Europeans posed a dangerous uncertainty. Throughout U.S. history most immigrants were able to continue speaking their ancestral language in ethnic communities. However, African slaves were not merely torn from their native communities and transported thousands of miles, they also suffered linguistic isolation and silencing (Baugh, 1999).

During colonial times the very first language policies forbade, under threat of severe punishments, African peoples from using their native languages and from teaching those languages to their children. The dimensions of this act of silencing African ancestral languages continue to have consequences for many AAVE speakers today. Throughout slavery and, later, during the era of Black Codes and Jim Crow laws, Whites established power and sustained domination. Their tactics were consistent with Bourdieu's notion of symbolic violence in which dominant groups utilize *officializing* strategies making it possible to reproduce the relations of domination even in the absence of physical violence (Bourdieu, 1977). However, slavery, unlike any other system, has had an enduring influence ensuring that blacks have less social, economic, and cultural capital than all other immigrant groups. However, violence inflicted by slaveholders did not take place in a vacuum: it was accompanied by and mediated through other acts to restrict access.

With the arrival of enslaved Africans, Whites imposed compulsory illiteracy laws: i.e., laws that outlawed the teaching of reading and writing to African slaves. These measures meant that blacks "learned English through pidginization and creolization rather than through a gradual bilingual transition to English, as did other immigrants" (Baugh, 2005, p. 236). Later, as blacks were able to attend schools, it was done so within an atmosphere where *linguicism* (language discrimination) was functionally parallel to racial discrimination. Baugh (1999) noted that, "the linguistic consequences of American slavery are unlike the linguistic heritage of those whose American ancestors were never enslaved or subjected to the inferior social circumstances of racial segregation and educational apartheid" (p. xiv).

As African slaves learned English and later as former slaves were afforded an education, the system of linguistic bias evolved from one of denying access to one that devalued the dialect and variety of English used by African Americans. In schools and through other institutions, Whites quickly emphasized that the speech of African Americans was different, nonstandard, *less than* the speech of Whites. The branding of black speech as underdeveloped, inferior, or lacking in formal properties led to calls for eradication of this *underdeveloped* version of English. Today images of the ideal English speaker are still more closely associated with Whites of European ancestry than people of color. In the next section we explore how racializing language influences relationships between Blacks and Whites and among people of color across national and group identities.

Constructing Racial Divide

Perceptions of African Americans and AAVE are directly linked to the legacy of racialized slavery and U.S. racialized social stratification. Using the notion of a *tri-racial system* sociologist Bonilla-Silva (2004) redefines the racial system in the United States as a system comprised of Whites, Honorary Whites, and the Collective Blacks who occupy various positions within the racialized system. Whites occupy the highest standing as Honorary Whites, who in turn have a higher position than members of the Collective Black in this hierarchy. Income, education, wealth, occupation, and social prestige, in addition to skin color, determine the standing of groups within the stratification order.

The emergence of the Honorary White group is the result of White elites' strategies to whiten their population and preserve racial power. Whites hope that an intermediate group can act as a *buffer zone* for racial conflict. Therefore, in spite of historically shared experiences (colonialism, exploitation, and oppression), those positioned as Honorary Whites and Collective Blacks usually differ in social and economic status, resulting in a racial divide between these two groups. This buffer zone has served to deflect attention from Whites as Blacks and other groups vie for positioning relative to each other and not Whites. This effectively leaves Whites unchallenged.

Linguicism, Education, and Policy

Over time, less violent measures were taken in shaping a racialized, monolingual nation and impose a Standard English ideology. Social, political, and economic agencies have always served as official gatekeepers for American culture, linguistic tradition, and division. Public policy has defined language and literacy requirements, creating educational, social, political, and economic barriers for speakers of AAVE, indigenous languages, and other linguistic varieties (Phillipson, 1992; Tollefson, 1995). Literacy has always been a critical weapon used in denying African Americans voting rights and preventing immigrants from gaining citizenship or employment. Ownership of literacy along with language supremacy work in tandem and historically have been manipulated to deny and control access to people of color, women, and the poor.

Throughout the schooling of African American children, attention has focused on relations between their language variety and literacy performance. However, Baugh (2005) notes,

> But these differences are not significant enough to account for the failure of many African American students to develop advanced literacy skills. Speaking a nonstandard dialect is not the primary reason for these students' difficulties in school ... in the United States, however, because of the unique history of African Americans, there is little understanding of the linguistic and educational issues that face these students, and they are often stigmatized for speaking nonstandard English, which is far too often made the primary reason for their school failure.
>
> (p. 237)

The historical failure of American schools to fully address the educational and literacy needs of African American children is certainly a matter of racial discrimination, but also characterizes the linguicism within the education system that promotes the supremacy of Standard English.

Ramirez, Wiley, de Klerk, Lee, and Wright (2005) identified a language policy framework that presents six orientations: promotion-oriented, expediency-oriented, tolerance-oriented, restriction-oriented, null policies, and repression-oriented. Today, language-oriented policy that favors mainstream English reinforces historic attitudes about race, class, and privilege ensuring that institutions, including schools, are part and parcel in sustaining systems of discrimination and exclusion. In the next section we demonstrate how language and social policy act in tandem to prevent local systems from taking action deemed appropriate to remove barriers to educating speakers of AAVE.

Crafting English Teaching

In 1996, controversy that so often accompanies discussion about the AAVE was renewed. The catalyst creating this firestorm involved the efforts of Oakland Unified School Board in California to address the academic achievement gap between African American students and their White counterparts by recognizing Ebonics as the primary language of African American students and utilizing it in teaching to facilitate their mastery of English. The deliberate *spin* generated by corporate media deflected attention away from the real issue at hand: i.e., how to provide for the educational needs of those speakers of AAVE/Ebonics who experienced difficulties with reading and writing in Standard English. In reality the resolution was a policy statement stressing that the superintendent of school devises a program to improve the English-language acquisition and application skills of African American students. Instead, the media constructed

Ebonics as a legitimate language deserving tax dollars for education programs, which inevitably invited public outrage.

The Oakland controversy reminds us that, as violence diminishes and legal barriers to social and material resources disappear, dominant groups devise other tactics to sustain hegemonic systems. African Americans have a longstanding belief that education would be the great equalizer in the fight to win their freedom and gain their rightful place in American society. However, Blacks remain disproportionately represented among the poor, incarcerated, poorly educated, underemployed and unemployed, and hopeless in America. In many cases, instead of providing critical tools needed for academic success, schools have become the breeding ground for failure and despair for far too many African American and other children of color.

African American historian, Carter G. Woodson (1933) cautioned that education could be a tool for Whites in continuing their domination over Blacks:

> The same education process which inspires and stimulates the oppressor with the thought that he is everything and has accomplished everything worthwhile, depresses and crushes at the same time the spark of genius in the Negro by making him feel that his race does not amount to much and never will measure up to the standards of other peoples.
>
> (p. xiii)

Research has shown that overall the teachers, instruction, facilities, and administrations are inferior in schools where the majority attending are children of color as compared to schools where majority middle-class and White students are in attendance (Anyon, 1997; Kozol, 2005).

The speech of African Americans is "an inescapable vessel of American history, literature, society, and popular culture" (Rickford & Rickford, 2000, p. 4). Yet the status of this beloved and beleaguered language has been a convenient basis for marking differences among us in the media, in society, and in schools; and provides a means for positioning people as being dominant or subordinate, native or nonnative, standard or nonstandard, ideal or unacceptable. "Once these differences are labeled, social rewards, privileges, and penalties are easily justified by those who have the power to impose their own standards as if they were universal" (Ramirez et al., 2005, p. xi). For the descendants of slaves and other oppressed people, language has provided the acceptable camouflage, surrogate for more racism and other forms of social and class prejudice. Without doubt, as English increases its popularity as an international language of development and globalization, it fortifies and exports historic distinctions of race, class, and linguistic privilege that will influence countries around the world (Edge, 2003).

Spreading English and Linguistic Anglo-Americanization

On the world front, as the United States engages the tools of empire (imperialism, militarism, and capital), English has swiftly become the language of modernization and globalization. Writing on racialized and privileged identities as ESOL teachers in the United States, Motha (2006) notes that, "Racialization is inevitably salient in English language teaching. Because the spread of the English language across the globe was historically connected to the international political power of White people, English and Whiteness are thornily intertwined" (p. 496).

As this process of linguistic domination widens, it is not surprising that notions of the ideal English-language speaker are still largely determined by one's race, cultural and economic capital, and access to English. In a discussion of globalization that focuses on the pros and cons of English spread in Europe, Modiano (2004) pointed out that, "While the spread of English is beneficial in some respects, Anglo-Americanization is seen as threatening to the social and cultural integrity of non-native speakers of English" (p. 215).

The status of the United States as the last super power, with its enormous military and economic holdings and democratic initiatives, ensures that other countries, even those with vastly different social, historical, political, economic, and religious complexities, look westward for resources, modernization, and leadership. The global integration of English, however, turns attention to the ontological impact of language learning and transfer of ideological characteristics of English, especially American culture and social practices. Writing on the emerging nexus between oil and English, Karmani (2005) suggests that it is economics within the Arabian Gulf, specifically oil, that "sustains certain social, economic, and political conditions for the expansion of English" (p. 87). The hegemonic reproduction of a series of social privilege (e.g., native-speaker privilege, White privilege, middle-class privilege, and American privilege) outside the United States mirrors the social privileges within its borders with respect to language, class, and race. In the next section we shall look at the reproduction of systems of privileging in South Korea through the mechanisms of globalization and English as a global commodity. In South Korea, ways in which reproduction of social privilege occur in relation to White middle-class English exhibits unique political, economic, and historic ties with the United States. The longstanding relationship between these two countries reveals the shaping of social and education policies in South Korea that in turn influence systematic reproduction of privilege for English speakers and reflects South Koreans' racial attitudes at home and elsewhere. We draw from South Korea sustaining examples of the impact that American English, a privileged language, has on social, political, and cultural systems around the world.

South Korea, Globalization, and the Spread of English

Globalization is a "process by which the experience of everyday life, marked by the diffusion of commodities and ideas, is becoming standardized around the world" (www. britannica.com/ebc/article-9365689?quer=globalization&ct=). This simple definition can be deceiving as researchers argue that globalization cannot be easily defined because of its very complexity. This complexity justifies examining globalization from not one single perspective but from diverse perspectives. For example, although globalization is frequently equated with Westernization, Americanization, and cultural imperialism of the United States (Barber, 1998), understanding globalization as sheer homogenization around U.S. culture fails to capture the complexity and subtlety of globalization (Luke & Luke, 2000).

In fact, globalization is interwoven into many fields and contexts, and cultures interact with many unique societal, historical, political, and economic aspects in multidirectional ways. Each society experiences globalization in its own way, so researchers need to view globalization through a dialectical lens. In other words, unique factors within each society influence the globalization process, and these distinct factors are crucial in understanding the nature of globalization. Emphasizing the importance of not defining globalization in linear and determinist ways, Luke and Luke (2000) argue for "situated, local and self-critical analyses" in order to see "the two-way, mutually constitutive dynamics of local-global flows of knowledge, power, and capital" (p. 276). This perspective of globalization is sometimes called "glocal" (Burbules & Torres, 2000), "hybridization," "creolization," or "reterritorialization" (Short & Kim, 1999), strongly suggesting that the unique features of a specific society or context play a crucial role in the globalization process. Thus, the analysis of the globalization process in a society should always be informed by the situated perspectives and local unique context.

Understanding Globalization in South Korea

Unique social, historical, and cultural factors have influenced the globalization process in South Korea. When the globalization policy officially began under the Kim Young Sam government (1993–1998), the policy was not unexpected to many South Koreans. Some discourses around globalization, such as those centering on the achievement of economic and political power, were already familiar. Historically, because of numerous invasions from China and occupation by Japan (1910–1945), South Koreans understood all too well the significance of economic and political power. Extreme poverty permeated everyday life under the Japanese occupation and during the Korean War (1950–1953). Following this conflict, the Park government (1963–1979) promoted modernization with the stated aim of eliminating poverty. It resulted in fast economic growth known as "the miracle on the Han."

The Kim Young Sam government then undertook the second wave of modernization, expanding the concept of economic growth to include the achievement of economic leadership globally. This second wave created and shifted discourses from *New Korea* (in 1993) to *internationalization* (in 1994), and finally, *globalization* (*segyehwa*, in 1995). These discourses envisioned South Korea as a *superpower nation* and a *central nation of world management* through achievement of economic and political power (Kang, 1998, 2000; Park, 1996).

To borrow Bourdieu's terms, globalization for the South Korean state represents efforts to gain social and economic capital to be acknowledged as a world-class nation. Bourdieu posits that people have access to use, produce, and reproduce power through different kinds of capital, such as economic and social capitals. Bourdieu understands economic capital as monetary power that can be converted into social or cultural power. He sees social capital as social networks and group memberships that provide access to other forms of capital. Social capital is a person's asset that provides a well-networked individual, families, or groups with substantial advantages. Such capital may have different values in different contexts, and does not necessarily mean what an individual owns (Bourdieu, 1994). In the South Korean context, globalization policy is understood as a way to achieve economic power (i.e., Bourdieu's economic capital) to be recognized as a legitimate member of the community of superpowers that can influence world economy and politics (i.e., Bourdieu's social capital).

The South Korean government has devised a number of strategies and implemented policies to accomplish this goal. The Globalization Promotion Committee (GPC), which consisted of a set of committees on educational reform, administrative reform, and policy planning, was established to oversee the globalization process (Gills & Gills, 2000; Shin, 2006). As a specific way to promote the core purpose of globalization and economic advancement, the government demanded patriotism among all South Koreans, including those abroad. The concept of national unity has been upheld because of the belief that South Koreans abroad are national assets in achieving higher economic and political standing for the nation. As Park (1996) asserts,

> Although segyehwa is the official term for "globalization," which in the U.S. denotes internationalization of economic relations, this phrase in Korea evokes strong nationalist sentiment, calling for national unity in order to survive and gain leadership in the international community. What segyehwa represents is a de-territorialized national community among Koreans.
>
> (p. 2)

In South Korea, those who emigrate to other countries are viewed as a critical economic force within the framework of globalization. However, this social capital is selectively accorded only to those who immigrated to Western countries, especially to the United States, the principal partner in South Korea's globalization process. The West, with the United States as its unquestioned leader, is believed to have already acquired social, cultural, and economic capital. South Koreans see the need to emulate the West as a way of becoming an economic power and global leader. Accordingly, a high status is accorded to the Westerners and Koreans who are associated with the West. For example, Korean-Americans enjoy a high status, while ethnic Koreans in non-Western countries such as China, Russia, or other Asian countries do not enjoy the same level of social capital. In fact, they have experienced prejudice (Kang, 1998; Park, 1996) as well as carefully and strategically planned legal discrimination (Shin, 2003). When President Kim Dae Jung (1998–2003) promulgated a special law to produce a new global South Korean network, ethnic Koreans in China and Russia were excluded in the law because the government was afraid of opening the door to unskilled ethnic Koreans from these countries.

Another reason for the higher status accorded to Korean Americans is that they possess a crucial tool for globalization, that is, their knowledge of English. South Koreans consider knowledge of English to be an important marker of linguistic capital and see that this capital enables closer positioning with the West, most notably the United States. This perception of the superiority of English, however, does not reflect the belief held by linguists and professionals in bilingual education who affirm that English, like any other languages, is a vehicle for people to become members of the international community, not just American society. On the contrary, this position is not reflected in the view held by those in business and the government; they promote the teaching of English because they believe that English competence is a critical tool that enables South Korea to position itself closer to the seat of power, the United States.

Conflict, Globalization, and English

The worldwide hunger for English historically arose as an inheritance of the British Empire and U.S. hegemony in the contemporary world (Edge, 2003). In the South Korean context, English began to gain a high status as early as the Korean War in 1950, long before globalization became a national policy. Since the war, South Koreans have regarded the United States as a valuable ally and protector with its military and economic aid. After the Korean War, U.S. aid played a crucial role in economic rehabilitation (Macdonald, 1996). To South Korea, the United States was a model for development because of its power and willingness to ensure South Korea a recovery from the armed conflict with communists in the north. However, along with its charitable acts, U.S. economic and military aid required ideological conformity that, in turn, reinforced American hegemony (Phillipson, 1992). According to Baik (1994), "the consequences [of the war and aid] were that American ideologies, values and culture, as well as the language itself, were portrayed as being superior to those of [South] Korea" (p. 123).

Competence in English, historically, has been highly valued in South Korea and this value increased with the implementation of globalization policies. In pursuit of a competitive and viable economy, South Koreans believed linguistic competence in English was needed. The demand for EFL education and teachers has drastically increased, and EFL education has become a critical part of the national agenda. In 1997, as the new millennium approached, a new committee for promoting English education, the Presidential Committee for Globalization Policy, was established as a part of the country's globalization policy. This committee heavily funded a national English-education curriculum, multimedia facilities for schools, and English-language materials development, including teachers' guidebooks and reference books (Jung & Norton, 2002). Under the new policy, English instruction has started in the third grade, whereas previously it began in the seventh grade. Currently in South Korea, discussion is under way to begin English education in the first grade (Hong, 2005). As of 2008, students receive 1–2 hours of instruction a week in grades 3–6, 2–4 hours a week in grades 7–9, and 4 hours a week in grades 10–12. These new policies are expected to improve English-language education, and ultimately, facilitate the nation's globalization effort.

English and Socioeconomic Status in South Korea

In addition to having education policy stressing the importance of English learning, the demand for English is strong throughout South Korean society and English competence heavily influences one's employment prospects and life chances. In fact, after many companies and the government declared that competence in English would be a promotion criterion, students and their families began spending considerable time and money on learning English (Koo, 2002). Large numbers of children and youths learn English through costly private *cram* schools. Some South Korean children even spend summer or winter vacations learning English, while other wealthy ones study in English-speaking countries. Affluent families living in major urban areas spend significantly more money on learning English than families living in rural areas (Chung, 2005). Because of the economic resources required to learn English, the connection

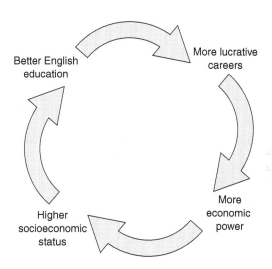

Figure 3.1 Knowledge of English as tool for socioeconomic advancement.

between knowledge of English and economic capital is obvious. Children whose parents have more economic capital receive better English education and these children can use English to obtain affluence in South Korean society. The cycle is clear and demonstrates how knowledge of English serves as a major tool for socioeconomic advancement (see Figure 3.1).

Varieties of English in South Korea

South Koreans consider English competence as the linguistic capital needed for securing social and economic power. However, proficiency in English is defined narrowly as competence in American English (Jeong, 2004). Mainstream American English enjoys especially high status in South Korea and this attitude facilitates the devaluing of non-American varieties of English, such as Australian, Irish, and Singaporean Englishes.

Just as many South Koreans devalue many World Englishes spoken outside the United States, they do not recognize the varieties/dialects of English spoken within U.S. borders, either. Standard English and mainstream English are coded phrases that connote *Whiteness*. In her study of ESOL teacher identities, Motha (2006) expressed, "I consider linguistic identities to be inextricable from racial identities because I believe Whiteness to be an intrinsic but veiled element of the construct of mainstream English" (p. 497). We would add that middle-class status is also endemic to *native speakerness*, along with Whiteness. In South Korea, and other countries where a fertile environment for learning English is present, the variety spoken by White Americans is considered to be standard or target. Linguists and others, however, argue that no one variety of English can be designated as standard (LeMoine, 2001). Rickford (1999) contends that AAVE is a systematic rule-governed language. Like other living languages, it has its own rules and regularities. The morphosyntax, phonology, lexicon, and pragmatics of AAVE also affirm that it is structurally self-contained in spite of what it shares with other

Englishes. Although AAVE is a historical and viable language system, for South Koreans, English spoken by Whites is considered representative of American English, while AAVE is not. This perception of *high language* reflects South Korean racial bias and reverence for *all things White* and the roots of South Koreans' prejudice against Blacks are deep.

Racism in South Korea

South Koreans' prejudice against Blacks had existed long before the globalization policy. South Koreans first became familiar with American values of democracy, Christianity, meritocracy, and individualism as South Korea underwent rapid industrialization and modernization following the Korean War. Since then, U.S. mass media, especially Hollywood movies and television shows, as well as American Forces Korea Network (AFKN) programs have been the primary tools for South Korean exposure to American values and racial attitudes. These media sources perpetuated stereotypical portrayals of Blacks, resulting in the exportation of racism (Chang, 1999; Lee, 1999).

South Koreans ridicule dark-skinned people in public places (Shin, 2003), and even the content of South Korean high school EFL textbooks frequently reveals prejudice against non-Whites (Lee, 2003). Among the non-White groups, Blacks are most often the target of negative attention and derogatory comments. For example, African Americans were characterized as "plunderers, drug addicts, and liars" in an editorial immediately following the 2005 Hurricane Katrina disaster in the United States (Jee, 2005). In a survey, Korean grade school students ranked Blacks the highest in categories such as laziness, dirtiness, and aggressiveness, while Whites were ranked highest in categories like diligence and cleanness (Kim, 2005). These pejorative attitudes are also expressed through South Korean television and newspapers (Moon, 2006; Shin, 2003; Yang, 2002).

South Koreans and Blacks in the United States

Prejudicial attitudes toward Blacks persist among not only Koreans but also Korean-Americans, especially among first-generation Korean-Americans (Chang, 1999). This is in part because their racial perceptions were already developed through South Korean societal beliefs and mass media well before their immigration to the United States. For years, portrayals of Blacks as criminals, drug dealers, and rapists dominated programs exported to South Korea (Chang, 1999; Lee, 1999; Lie & Abelmann, 1999). Unfortunately, South Koreans carry these negative portrayals with them to the United States and elsewhere.

Another factor contributing to Korean-Americans' bias toward Blacks is their lack of awareness that Blacks endured oppression and exploitation during the racial apartheid era and that discrimination against African Americans and other dark-skinned people still persists. Most South Koreans see the United States as the *land of opportunities* and think that personal incompetence and misfortune have caused the low social status of some Blacks. Many South Koreans fail to understand the link between systematic discrimination, inequality, and the legacy of slavery.

Negativity toward Blacks and a lack of deeper understanding of historical, social, and political factors surrounding current struggles contributed to the Black–South

Korean conflict in several urban communities during the 1990s and in recent years. In fact, second-generation Korean-Americans often single out the racism of their parents and other first-generation Korean-Americans as the cause of Black–Korean conflicts in the United States (Lie & Abelmann, 1999). Although racial prejudice alone did not produce Black–South Korean conflicts, racial bias has been cited as a contributing factor in the conflict (Norman, 1994; Park, 1999).

Intersections of Racism and Globalization

Racism experienced both in South Korea and the United States, and racial positioning as depicted in Bonilla-Silva's tri-racial system reflect South Koreans' view that Whites are an ideal globalized group. For most South Koreans globalization means economic advancement and achievement of global leadership. In turn, Whites symbolize power and privilege and all forms of capital. In contrast, individuals marked by race and linguistic difference, especially those who represent the Collective Black, in Bonilla-Silva's tri-racial system, are considered by South Koreans to have no real *capital* regardless of whether they live in the United States or other parts of the world. South Koreans, no matter where they settle in the world, attempt to distance themselves from other non-Whites, and work to maintain an economic and social trajectory to elevate themselves to the status of Whites. This behavior is consistent with Bourdieu's notion of positioning and provides a framework to understand this distancing phenomenon.

Within the social order, dominant groups legitimize the established order by "establishing distinctions (hierarchies) and legitimating these distinctions" (Bourdieu, 1994, p. 167), while subordinate groups define their positions within the social order by their distal or proximal positioning to the dominant group (Grant & Wong, 2008). Subordinate groups such as South Koreans desire positioning closer to Whites, and at the same time, wish to maintain distance from other subordinate groups, such as African Americans or other Collective Blacks. Within the global context, South Koreans identify more closely with Whites and Honorary Whites because they believe Whites represent the power and privilege they seek for themselves. With respect to English, this means that South Koreans at home and in the United States seek to acquire the standard/mainstream variety of English associated with upper-class White Americans.

Analysis

The complex convergence of diverse factors and local realities that are produced, shaped, and sustained by particular ideological and historical forces provides for an understanding of race and social status within the dynamics of linguistic hierarchies such as those of South Korea and the United States. A system of racialized slavery enforced through violence, both real and symbolic, legal apartheid and social discrimination, established U.S. capitalism and sustains U.S. economic dominance in the 21st century. Segregation and unequal access ensured that African Americans would have limited opportunities for acquiring official, mainstream language, and at the same time, they would be denied the right to utilize their own heritage languages and cultures. Over time, imposition of legal, social, and education limitations for the descendants of African slaves helped produce a society that differentially structures access to resources based on race, social class, and linguistic variety. Moreover, recent efforts to establish English as the official language, suggest that those who speak different varieties of English, speakers of indigenous languages of the Americas, and immigrants in the United States will remain *bankrupt*, having little linguistic or social capital of the kind accorded to standard mainstream speakers of English.

For South Korea, buoyed by years of U.S. military support and economic aid, knowledge of English remains critical linguistic capital that guarantees social status at home and economic advantage globally. In both the United States and South Korea notions of the ideal English speaker sustain disadvantage for groups without requisite racial, social, or linguistic capital. Importantly, inequality for those who do not speak American English or Standard English perpetuates *class divide* as a result of the myth of the ideal English speaker.

In the United States, privileged racial (White) and socioeconomic status (middle and upper class) are analogous to having standard mainstream-speaker status. In South Korea, linguistic capital (English) provides a mechanism for accessing social and economic resources for power. South Koreans who have immigrated to the United States often bring with them a national history, social attitudes, and mass-media images that perpetuate pejorative perceptions of Blacks. In both the United States and South Korea, factors including socioeconomic status, race, and linguistic orientation intersect to mediate access to power and privilege. As such, the inordinate workings of race, class, and the ever-rising global demand for English help recycle racism and classism, which further sustains linguicism and power differentials (see Figure 3.2).

In both countries, the forces of globalization and capitalism work in tandem to maintain the status quo by silencing and effacing racial and linguistic markedness. The result is that racism, classism, and linguicism sustain hegemonic systems of power and reproduce advantage and disadvantage. In the United States, the belief that there is an

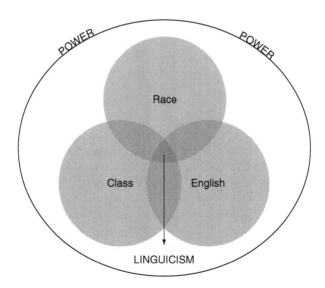

Figure 3.2 Race, class, linguicism, and power differentials.

ideal English speaker confirms the superiority of Whiteness and continues to marginalize members of historically disenfranchised groups such as African Americans. This is also the case for other peoples of color, speakers of other languages, and individuals who do not enjoy upper- or middle-class status. In South Korea, the spread of English and the Anglo-Americanization of English sustain U.S. imperialism and economic dominance. This enhances longstanding, international systems of privilege and power. The global market economy, in turn, sustains the demand for English because English has become a commodity with respect to globalization and economic development.

Around the world, socioeconomic and geopolitical dynamics help ensure U.S. domination and the spread of English. In the case of South Korea, dependence on U.S. economic and military aid as well as pursuit of global power drive the desire for English and Whiteness as currency for globalization. Moreover, because of their attitudes toward race and class and desire to mimic all things American, South Koreans have imported and now reproduce linguistic Anglo-Americanization and mono-culturalization that historically accompanies English-language learning.

Moving Forward

How can we begin to subvert or resist the hegemony and domination of U.S. standard/ mainstream English and Anglo-Americanization? We offer the following for consideration.

Research

Research is needed that problematizes traditional dichotomies of race and class and reflects the complexity of language learning and identity in South Korea. Of particular interest is research that investigates the ideological dimensions of second language learning and other dimensions of privilege and power. In South Korea, systematic research is needed to examine historical attitudes regarding various race groups, including biracial South Koreans, Blacks, and dark-skinned immigrants of other Asian countries. Research is also needed to help deconstruct the dynamic, context-specific relationships of African Americans and South Koreans living in the United States. Specifically, it would be desirable to explore generational differences in racial attitudes across African American and South Korean groups. This research would interrogate how such intersecting forces as capitalism and the corporate media work to maintain negative images and attitudes toward Blacks, Collective Blacks, and Honorary Whites. Finally, research should be conducted to explore the influence of globalization on the spread of English in South Korea and the effects this has on ethnic minority cultures and heritage languages.

Education

Teachers should be guided in learning about the characteristics of African American speech and cultural traditions as a means for using the *funds of knowledge* to improve education and life chances for AAVE speakers. Using perspectives guided by critical multiculturalism and culturally responsive practices, teachers would support bidialectalism, bilingualism, and biliteracy and provide opportunities for linguistic and cultural bridges to standard/mainstream English. This would promote an additive rather than subtractive approach to language learning and academic achievement. Moreover, research tools such as critical discourse analysis and methodological traditions associated with critical race theory can be used to encourage teachers and education researchers to explore attitudes about the *model minority* as well as *Others* to reduce essentializing around race/ethnicity, class, and language.

Social Context

Political coalitions and community partnerships among African Americans, South Koreans, and other Asian-American groups should be established to identify common ground for challenging and rethinking power relations in the United States and Korea. Such efforts would begin to debunk stereotypes and *us-versus-them* binaries that perpetuate the *divide-and-conquer* strategy practiced by dominant groups.

The challenges of racism, classism, and linguicism employ us to develop new combinations of research and pedagogic practices that will help in rethinking attitudes around privilege and power. Globalization and the spread of English contribute to a world that is more interconnected and, at the same time, we need to widen and deepen racial and class notions about the ideal English speaker. As we presented in this chapter, greater mobility across national and international borders means that formerly isolated groups frequently interact in ways that advance hegemonic ideologies and sustain systems of oppression. What we need is a counter-discourse that defends the integrity of language varieties such as AAVE and raises questions about the social and cultural impact of globalization on local communities and their linguistic traditions.

Discussion Questions

1. The authors argue that promotion of standard U.S. English (White, middle-class) contributes to the vicious cycle of discrimination and sustains linguistic, cultural, and economic capital for Whites and those who mimic so-called "white language" patterns. How can you begin to address the issues of race and class that so often accompany linguistic privilege?
2. How can you include the racial/ethnic and cultural perspectives of all linguistic groups?
3. What practices help facilitate cross-cultural communication within the classroom? How can these practices be used to inform policy and institutional change?
4. The authors call for rigorous research, culturally responsive teaching, and social consciousness in order to achieve a more just society. What specific teaching practices or resources can teachers in your specific contexts use to promote culturally responsive teaching and transform education to benefit racial and linguistic minority students?

References

Anyon, J. (1997). *Ghetto schooling: A political economy of urban educational reform.* New York: Teachers College Press.

Baik, M. J. (1994). *Language, ideology, and power: English textbooks of two Koreas*. Unpublished doctoral dissertation, University of Illinois, Urbana-Champaign.

Baldwin, J. (1985). If Black English isn't a language, then tell me, what is? In *The price of the ticket: Collected nonfiction 1948–1985* (pp. 649–652). New York: St. Martin's Press [Reprinted from the *New York Times*, July 29, 1979].

Barber, B. (1998). Democracy at risk: American cultures in a global culture. *World Policy Journal, 15*(2), 29–42.

Baugh, J. (1999). *Out of the mouths of slaves: African American language and educational malpractice*. Austin, TX: University of Texas Press.

Baugh, J. (2005). African American language and literacy. In Z. Fang (Ed.), *Literacy teaching and learning: Current issues and trends* (pp. 235–240). Upper Saddle River, NJ: Pearson Education Inc.

Bonilla-Silva, E. (2004). From bi-racial to tri-racial: Towards a new system of racial stratification in the USA. *Ethnic and Racial Studies, 27*, 931–950.

Bourdieu, P. (1977). *Outline of a theory of practice* (R. Nice, Trans.). Cambridge: Cambridge University Press.

Bourdieu, P. (1994). *Language and symbolic power*. Cambridge, MA: Harvard University Press.

Burbules, N., & Torres, C. (2000). Globalization and education: An introduction. In N. Burbules & C. Torres (Eds.), *Globalization and education: Critical perspectives* (pp. 1–26). New York: Routledge.

Chang, E. T. (1999). New urban crisis: Korean-African American relations. In K. C. Kim (Ed.), *Korean in the hood: Conflict with African Americans* (pp. 39–59). Baltimore, MD: Johns Hopkins University Press.

Chung, J. Y. (2005). Yeongo jalhaeya don jalbolgo, donyistoya yeongo jalgaleucheu [Better English leading to more money, more money leading back to better English]. *Chosun Ilbo*. Retrieved November 14, 2005 from www.chosun.com.

Edge, J. (2003). Imperial troopers and servants of the lord: A vision of TESOL for the 21st century. *TESOL Quarterly, 37*, 701–709.

Gates, H. L., & McKay, N. Y. (Eds.). (1997). *The Norton anthology of African American literature*. New York: W. W. Norton & Co.

Gills, B., & Gills, D. (2000). Globalization and strategic choice in South Korea: Economic reform and labor. In S. Kim (Ed.), *Korea's globalization* (pp. 29–53). Cambridge: Cambridge University Press.

Grant, R. A., & Asimeng-Boahene, L. (2006). Culturally responsive pedagogy in citizenship education: Using African proverbs as tools for teaching in urban schools. *Multicultural Perspectives, 8*, 17–24.

Grant, R. A., & Wong, S. D. (2008). Critical race perspectives, Bourdieu, and language education. In J. Albright & A. Luke (Eds.), *Pierre Bourdieu and literacy education* (pp. 163–184). London: Routledge.

Hong, S. C. (2005, October 21). Chodung haknyonbuto yongokyoyuk gomto [English education from first grade]. *Donga Ilbo*. Retrieved October 21, 2005 from www.donga.com.

Jee, M. W. (2005). Mikook huine daehan sogo [Thoughts on Blacks in the U.S.]. Retrieved November 3, 2005 from www.systemclub.co.kr.

Jeong, Y. K. (2004). A chapter of English teaching in Korea. *English Today, 20*(2), 40–46.

Jung, S. K., & Norton, B. (2002). Language planning in Korea: The new elementary English program. In J. Tollefson (Ed.), *Language policies in education* (pp. 245–265). Mahwah, NJ: Laurence Erlbaum Associates.

Kang, M. K. (1998). *A reconsideration of cultural imperialism theories: Globalization and nationalism*. Retrieved February 24, 2001 from www.prome.snu.ac.kr/~news/home/impe.html.

Kang, M. K. (2000). The second modernization failed: Discourse politics from "new Korea" to "globalization." In P. Gilroy, L. Grossberg, & A. McRobbie (Eds.), *Without guarantee: In honor of Stuart Hall* (pp. 181–192). New York: Verso.

Karmani, S. (2005). Petro-linguistic: The emerging nexus between oil, English, and Islam. *Journal of Language, Identity, and Education, 4*, 87–102.

Kim, W. B. (2005). Hwanginjongboda baekini choayo [We like whites, more than Asians]. *Hankook Ilbo.* Retrieved December 1, 2005 from http://sports.hankooki.com.

Koo, B. J. (2002, July 9). Jikjangin "yoekooko ggujunhi gongbu" 10% [Workers "steady study of foreign languages" 10%]. *Hankyoreh Shinmun.* Retrieved July 9, 2002 from www.hani.co.kr.

Kozol, J. (2005). *The shame of the nation: The restoration of apartheid schooling in America.* New York: Crown Publishers.

Lee, I. (2003). Intercultural competency and prejudice through the English language in South Korea. In L. Johanna & L. Lestinen (Eds.), *UNESCO Conference on Teaching and Learning for Intercultural Understanding, Human Rights, and a Culture of Peace.* Jyvaskyla, Finland. [CD ISBN 951-39-1531-X].

Lee, J. H. (1999). Conflict between Korean merchants and black customers: A structural analysis. In K. C. Kim (Ed.), *Korean in the hood: Conflict with African Americans* (pp. 113–130). Baltimore, MD: Johns Hopkins University Press.

LeMoine, N. R. (2001). Language variation and literacy acquisition in African American students. In J. L. Harris (Ed.), *Literacy in African American communities* (pp. 169–194). Mahwah, NJ: Lawrence Erlbaum Associates.

Lie, J., & Abelmann, N. (1999). The 1992 Los Angeles riots and the "Black-Korean conflict." In K. C. Kim (Ed.), *Korean in the hood: Conflict with African Americans* (pp. 75–87). Baltimore, MD: Johns Hopkins University Press.

Luke, A., & Luke, C. (2000). A situated perspective on cultural globalization. In N. Burbules & C. Torres (Eds.), *Globalization and education: Critical perspectives* (pp. 275–297). New York: Routledge.

Macdonald, D. S. (1996). *The Koreans: Contemporary politics and society* (3rd ed.). Boulder, CO: Westview Press.

Modiano, M. (2004). Monoculturalization and language dissemination. *Journal of Language, Identity, and Education, 3*, 215–227.

Moon, B. G. (2006, January 13). Baekingyenun gwaenchanjiman hukingyuenun jom … [Mixed with Whites are ok, but mixed with Blacks are…]. *Donga Ilbo.* Retrieved January 13, 2006 from www.donga.com.

Motha, S. (2006). Racializing ESOL teacher identities in US K-12 public schools. *TESOL Quarterly, 40*, 495–518.

Norman, A. J. (1994). Managing ethnic conflict within a community context: Black Korean relations in the American city. *Community Development Journal, 29*, 169–176.

Park, H. O. (1996). *Segyehwa: Globalization and nationalism in Korea.* Retrieved February 24, 2001 from www.umich.edu/~iinet/journal/vol. 4no1/segyeh.html.

Park, K. (1999). Use and abuse of race and culture: Black–Korean tension in America. In K. C. Kim (Ed.), *Korean in the hood: Conflict with African Americans* (pp. 60–74). Baltimore, MD: Johns Hopkins University Press.

Phillipson, R. (1992). *Linguistic imperialism.* Oxford: Oxford University Press.

Ramirez, J. D., Wiley, T. G., de Klerk, G., Lee, E., & Wright, W. E. (2005). *Ebonics: The urban education debate* (2nd ed.). Clevedon, UK: Multilingual Matters.

Rickford, J. R. (1999). *African American vernacular English: Features, evolution, educational implications.* Oxford: Blackwell.

Rickford, J. R., & Rickford, R. J. (2000). *Spoken soul: The story of Black English.* New York: John Wiley & Sons.

Shin, G. W. (2006). *Ethnic nationalism in Korea; Genealogy, Politics, and Legacy.* Stanford, CA: Stanford University Press.

Shin, J. (2003). Ugly Korean, yusaekinjong chabyolhana [Ugly Korean, discrimination against people of color]. *Chosun Ilbo.* Retrieved October 29, 2003 from www.chosun.com.

Short, J., & Kim, Y. (1999). *Globalization and the city.* London: Longman.

Tollefson, J. W. (Ed.). (1995). *Power and inequality in language education.* Cambridge: Cambridge University Press.

Woodson, C. G. (1933). *The mis-education of the Negro.* Asmara, Eritrea: African World Press, Inc.

Yang, S. A. (2002, August 16). Hotelseo umju, gosongbanga, gosaengchehom yetmal, bumodon hosa [Drinking at hotels, no more hardship, luxurious life on parents' money]. *Hankyoreh Shinmun.* Retrieved August 28, 2002 from www.hani.co.kr.

4 Construction of Racial Stereotypes in English as a Foreign Language (EFL) Textbooks
Images as Discourse

Cosette Taylor-Mendes

Pre-reading Questions

Recall any previous opinions or ideas that you or your students have had about the images in ESL/EFL textbooks. Certainly, many instructors and students informally discuss (or joke about) particular images in their textbooks. However, the busy reality of teaching and learning rarely allows ESL/EFL professionals and their students the opportunity to examine multiple textbook images in order to draw larger conclusions about the images used to teach English locally or internationally. Using the ESL/EFL textbook in a course you are presently teaching or have recently taught, consider:

- Which races are represented in the images, pictures, or cartoons? Which race is represented the most frequently?
- How many images include people from a variety of races or cultures within the same image?
- What situations, jobs, or roles are Whites portrayed in? What situations, jobs, or roles are Blacks or other visible minorities portrayed in?

Introduction

I see more White people than Black people. I saw ... when I saw Black people, I saw them in a poor situation. Here they don't put a rich Black man for example who have a job and have a happy family. To me this is ridiculous ... it's like they show the majority who have money is the White people, and who have this lifestyle is the majority of people who have money ... and they are White. I think the [English language] books ... This people who study in ... schools very expensive want to see themselves, and to see themselves is to see White people ... White people and happy situations, a car, a beautiful beach, beautiful things.

(Fatima)

Fatima was responding to a colour photograph which covers the majority of one page in her EFL textbook used in Brazil. The photographer's lens has captured a young shirtless Black boy sitting at a large table in a sparse dark room where he is studying from a thin book under a single faint light that hangs above him. The boy appears not to notice the photographer, or it is likely that he has been asked to pose in this fashion.

At the time of the research, Fatima was a business English student at the low–intermediate level who often relied on images to help her find meaning in her foreign English-language textbook. Fatima's response is illustrative of several opinions expressed by the business executive or student participants in this study who need English to enhance their career options. Her comment demonstrates that, whether or not the second language instruction includes explicit discussions about the images in EFL textbooks, students—consciously or unconsciously—use, absorb, and interpret the social, economic, and racial realities present in the photographs, cartoons, or pictures in their textbooks. Additionally, Fatima's comment shows that EFL students often have an opinion, critical or otherwise, about the presence of race (and its link to power) in images in their language textbook(s). Most importantly, Fatima's ideas contradict the commonly held notion that images in EFL textbooks are neutral, apolitical, or even an enjoyable part of learning English.

While few TESOL professionals would disagree that EFL students rely on textbooks to develop their knowledge about English-speaking nations, little research has been done on the effects of using mass-produced "English" images for instruction, particularly in developing nations with multiracial populations. Therefore, this study explored how the images (pictures) in textbooks, which represent English culture(s), shaped students' and teachers' impressions of the target foreign-language culture.

This collaborative study took place in the metropolis of São Paulo, Brazil, where English schools are abundant, but learning English for the purposes of business or travel is restricted to the privileged few. The purpose of this study was to examine how students and teachers explored issues of race, class, or gender in their English-language texts when asked to consider the images in their EFL textbooks. Although I was interested in critical enquiry, I had not anticipated that so many of the discussions with students and teachers would focus on race and the perceived (im)balances of power projected in the textbook images.

As an experienced EFL instructor who is a White woman from Canada, I am in a relative position of power in São Paulo. Some unemployed Brazilians look for work for months or years without success, but I received three job offers within the first week of my arrival. I am not naive about my advantaged role as a foreign researcher. In fact, my racial privileges were directly pointed out several times by the participants. Consequently, this study has led me to view EFL textbook images, my students, and my position in the world in an entirely new way.

The Ideologies of Textbooks

Long before I went to Brazil and learned to recognize my unearned White privilege, educators and parents had begun to pay attention to the impact of textbook images, for the images define who is included or excluded from an advantaged societal position based, at least in part, on race. In examining post-Second World War literacy instruction in public elementary schools in British Columbia, Canada, Luke (1988) explored the way in which text and images influence and even construct how youth view their society. Luke claimed that images like those in the *Dick and Jane* texts foster nostalgia for the clearly defined standards of behaviour and affluent standards of living which have been represented in Hollywood America since the Second World War. For instance, many movies and television reruns show "pristine lifestyles and social relations without visible minorities, economic injustice, English as a Second Language..." (Luke, 1988, p. 3).

More recent developments in adult literacy education in Brazil (Menendez de Souza, 2003) and media literacy in Malaysia (Belraj, 2001) confirm the argument made by Luke. However, as Menendez de Souza (2003) states, "no knowledge is value-free, nor is it acquired wholesale: it inevitably interacts with ... pre-existing knowledge in a particular culture" (p. 229). To put it in another way, teachers and students commonly bring different kinds of knowledge to the learning situation. However, texts and media can be used "as instruments for social development" (Belraj, 2001, p. 170), not social prejudice, if the teacher engages the students in ethical discussion and critical thought. In this chapter, I argue that the images in the EFL textbooks are a form of discourse that should be acknowledged and discussed in EFL classes for the purpose of countering racial stereotypes about English speakers and English-speaking nations.

Critical Perspectives

The idea that teachers and students can or should question race, class, and gender imbalances of power by asking who benefits from "the way things are" has its roots in Brazil. In the 1960s, Brazilian philosopher and educational theorist Paulo Freire developed a critical pedagogy which encouraged teachers, students, and intellectuals to critically examine the politics of unequal relations of power manifested in the everyday lives of people and to take actions for social transformation. This process, or praxis, involves both raising awareness about power inequality hidden behind taken-for-granted knowledge and transforming society so that the powerless become agents of change in their own world. Freire (1998) argued that questioning who benefits from the existing power structures is integral to change because if inequities in power are left unexamined in our teaching, we are apt to reproduce or legitimize unequal power relationships both in and outside our classrooms.

Since the late 1980s, ESL scholars such as Pennycook (1994, 1995), Fairclough (1989), and Phillipson (1992) have advocated a critical look at the assumed neutrality and benefits of the internationalization of English. Each author has argued that the lack of critical language instruction that problematizes English-language teaching in light of current power relations is related to the English teachers' belief that English/English-language teaching is mainly a technical matter of finding the best methodology of teaching.

Similarly, Widdowson (1993) cautioned TESOL professionals in "the designs we have on other people's worlds" for "English and English-language teaching are proper to the extent that they are appropriate, not to the extent that they are appropriated" (p. 389). In other words, helping students learn English to improve the circumstances of their lives is appropriate; however, dismissing or ignoring the sociopolitical reality in which EFL is taught is not appropriate. Furthermore, instilling unrealistic expectations for change within this reality is even more inappropriate in EFL teaching and learning. Finally, I extend Widdowson's statement to include taking advantage of EFL learners through instruction solely for material gain or profit. Teaching without consideration of methodology or consequence is *most* inappropriate because, inevitably, the inequities outside the classroom are reproduced within the classroom. In this case, learning is equated to consuming a commodity that further subjects the students who pay the often abhorrent fees to learn little and remain in similar/the same circumstances.

While extensive discussion exists on topics such as who owns English (Widdowson, 1993), who should teach English, what varieties of English should be taught (Warschauer, 2000), and under what circumstances English should be taught (Skutnabb-Kangas, 2000), the research thus far has not extended critical discussions to how the mass-produced "English" images in EFL textbooks are connected to the above debates.

Although Fairclough (2001), a key researcher in Critical Discourse Analysis (CDA), concedes that "visuals can be an accompaniment to talk which helps determine its meaning" (p. 23), I expanded the concept of discourse to include visuals, specifically the visuals in EFL/ESL textbooks. If discourse is defined as a social practice which can be determined by social structures, and if "language connects with the social through being the primary domain of ideology, and through being both the site of, and stake in, struggles for power," as Fairclough (2001) claims, then surely for a student who views images to find meaning where language may not be present, the image is discourse. In other words, even though the participants are separated over time and space, discourse takes place through the image as a social practice which evokes language for the purpose of negotiating one's space or place in the sociopolitical landscape. However, Fairclough (2001) himself noted that the separation of the participants of discourse is fraught with "hidden relations of power" (p. 41) for:

> media discourse is designed for mass audiences, and there is no way that producers can even know who is in the audience, let alone adapt to its diverse sections. And since discourse producers must produce with some interpreters in mind, what media producers do is address the ideal subject.
>
> (p. 41)

As both an instructor and researcher of English as a Foreign Language, I was interested in learning whom the students would identify as the "ideal subject," the English-speaking subject whom the students could/should take as a model. More specifically, I was interested in learning what racial and cultural characteristics the EFL learners and their educators would claim this ideal English speaker possessed. More importantly, I wanted to know if the participants would be able to recognize the subject as "ideal," for as long as we, in this case teachers and students, believe in or unthinkingly assume the roles we are playing and the positions we are holding, language will reinforce those roles and positions (Fairclough, 2001).

Giaschi is one of the few researchers of ESL teaching to have addressed the issue of images in EFL texts. Giaschi (2000) points out that the images in EFL texts that are "produced in or by one culture and in context-specific conditions" are "often used and absorbed in sometimes radically different contexts with different socio-political and cultural realities" (p. 33). His research examined "popular or successful" texts provided to him in teaching positions in Japan, Canada, and Italy (p. 38) in which there were images of men and women juxtaposed. Giaschi examined how physical positioning, body language, and clothing provided the impression that men were more powerful (or in more powerful positions) than women. Thus, I employed Giaschi's (2000) Critical

Image Analysis, an adaptation of Fairclough's (1989) CDA as the theoretical and analytical framework against which the teachers, students, and I examined the assumptions
and beliefs conveyed in the images.

I did not use Giaschi's methodology because his selection of texts was (loosely)
based on his own perception of "popular" or "successful" texts and because Giaschi
himself interpreted the textual images in his research without consulting professional
teachers in the field of TESOL or English-language students who consume the images.
Giaschi's work, while opening questions about EFL images, implied that teachers and
students passively accept and absorb the images presented to them in their texts.
Giaschi (2000) made the assumption that "students of ESL may find it difficult or
impossible to challenge the hidden meaning in the materials provided to them" and
given what he asserts are the immaturity of standards in English-language teaching,
teachers may not be "concerned with the integrity of the materials" (p. 34). My experiences as both an EFL teacher in Brazil and an ESL teacher in Canada prior to the
research led me to believe otherwise. I had not only encountered students and TESOL
professionals who were capable of critical discourse, but many of the teachers and
learners were more than willing to share their ideas about race and power in the images
in their textbooks.

Method

Research Questions

This exploratory study examined the following questions based on the work of Freire
(1995, 1998):[1]

- *What are we doing now?* How and to what extent are images used in an EFL context
  in Brazil? How and to what extent do teachers and students in an EFL context in
  Brazil interpret the images? I asked the students to choose and analyse dominant
  or influential images in their EFL texts.
- *Whose interests are being served by the way things are?* How are the images being
  absorbed or resisted? I asked the students to interpret representative images.
- *Is this how we want it to be and what are we going to do about it?* I asked the students and teachers if they wanted to do anything about the findings, and if they
  would develop recommendations for day-to-day teaching and learning practice.

Participants

There were 15 participants in the study: 11 students and four teachers, of whom eight
were men and seven were women, including (a) six students and two teachers from two
private, prestigious English-language schools in São Paulo, (b) four of my former English-language students, and (c) one student and two teachers by snowball sampling.

All student participants were in the two wealthiest social classes in Brazil, among the
wealthiest 20% of the population (Instituto Brasileiro do Geografia e Estatistica, 2002),
and the participants' social classes are representative of those who study English in
Brazil. All the executive participants had travelled outside Brazil, with the most

common destinations being New York, San Diego, or Miami. All the student participants expressed enthusiasm and concern about the importance of English in their work
or education; thus, they study English (a) to communicate with foreign management;
(b) to further their professional opportunities within their companies, or to apply for
positions which require one to communicate in English; and (c) as a personal interest.
However, the third reason was given by only three participants. Table 4.1 summarizes
the ages, professions, race, and conversational English proficiency of the participants at
the time of the research.[2]

The four teacher participants all work in private language schools and give private
lessons in São Paulo. All have either lived or travelled outside Brazil. All are bilingual
English–Portuguese speakers who began studying English at a young age. Glemerson's
first language is English, and Roberto Carlos was raised at home speaking both English
and Portuguese (see Table 4.2).

Procedure

The data collection with the 10 student participants took place in a series of two to
three individual interviews based on the images chosen by the students. The research

Table 4.1 Characteristics of Student Participants

Pseudonym	Profession	Age	Race	Conversational English Proficiency
Bia	Taxation lawyer for a Brazilian firm	29	White	Intermediate
Casia	Manager at an American multinational firm	30	Mulatto	Intermediate
Fatima	Lawyer with an Argentine firm	24	White	Low-intermediate
Kaka	Student and security guard	19	White	Beginner
Márcio	Manager at a Spanish bank	35	White	Upper-intermediate
Marcos	Manager at an American credit card firm	38	White	Advanced
Marta	Hospital administrator	37	Asian	Intermediate
Rivaldo	Investor for an American investment firm	30	White	Like native
Ronaldo	Manager at an American appliances firm	45	Black	Advanced
Vinícius	Financial manager at a Brazilian firm	32	White	Low-intermediate
Vera	Broker for a Brazilian brokerage firm	30	White	Upper-intermediate

Table 4.2 Characteristics of Teacher Participants

Pseudonym	Age	Race	Years teaching English
Glemerson	28	White	10
Glória	25	Mulatto[a]	5
Milene	26	White	2
Roberto Carlos	27	White	7

Note
a Mulatto, or Mulato/a in Portuguese, is a racial identity in which the individual has one White parent and
   one Black parent.

conversations were held at the participants' workplaces in a vacant conference room, in an empty classroom, and in two cases, at a coffee shop near their respective language schools. All the interviews were conducted in English over a period of 6 months.

My relationship with the Brazilian student participants was less formal than the relationships I had had with my former students at a university in Winnipeg, Canada. Although I had not met socially with any of the student (or teacher) participants, I had open discussions with the Brazilian participants, in part because the Brazilians I met were more open and direct in their communication than the majority of Canadians I knew. At the time of the research, I had lived in Brazil for over a year, and I spoke in a more direct manner; having lost what I suspected was my Canadian fear of offending someone (I had also stopped apologizing for no good reason, something I also discovered to be quite Canadian). Additionally, I think that the participants saw me as less of an outsider than the average foreigner living in Brazil because I was married to a Brazilian and I spoke fluent Portuguese in my daily interactions outside teaching or research. As a result, when the Brazilian participants spoke of situations in Brazil as "complicated," there was often an implied understanding that I had sufficient sociopolitical or cultural understanding to know what "complicado"[3] meant. Finally, I think the openness of the interactions was aided by the fact that all of the student participants met me individually; these participants did not risk offending or entering into a debate with a fellow Brazilian and could therefore speak relatively freely.

I asked student participants to bring the EFL textbook(s) that they were currently using or had most recently used in their English-language studies (see Table 4.3). In two cases, I asked the participants to choose a textbook that they found interesting from a library of EFL texts as the participants no longer owned any EFL book.

In the analysis, I refer to the individual participants, and not to the textbooks specifically. I found it interesting that the participants did not always choose a text that was appropriate to their language level; for instance, Fatima chose texts that were well beyond her language proficiency.

Table 4.3 Textbook Used in the Research Interviews

Participant	Textbook[a]
Bia	*The new interchange: Intermediate student's book*
Casia	*Making business decisions: Real cases from real companies*
Fatima	*Powerhouse: An intermediate business English course Headway: Upper intermediate student's book*
Kaka	*Northstar: Focus on reading and writing Powerhouse: An intermediate business English course*
Márcio	*Business opportunities Headway: Upper intermediate student's book*
Marcos	*Headway: Upper intermediate student's book*
Marta	*Workout advanced: Student's book*
Rivaldo	*Ship or sheep? Making sense of phrasal verbs*
Ronaldo	*Business opportunities*
Vinícius	*Insights into business*
Vera	*Headway: Upper intermediate student's book*

Note
a See Appendix for full references.

The first interview. I gave the students up to 15 minutes to examine the textbook with the following question in mind: What can you tell me about the pictures in general? Next, I posed the subsequent questions to discuss for a maximum of 30 minutes. Two questions were asked of teachers but not of students; they are shown in brackets in the order they were asked:

> Which images attract you? Which images do you like?
> Which pictures do you think represent American or British culture?
> What is it about the picture that makes it British or American?
> (Teachers: Does this message support or contradict what you teach your students about British or American culture?)
> What are you seeing in the pictures about life or lifestyle?
> Do the images help you learn English?
> What are the people doing? Who is acting? Who is not acting?
> What is the same about the pictures? What message(s) is/are communicated by these pictures in general?
> (Teachers: What do you think your students could learn from these pictures? Is the message positive or negative for Brazilian students?)

My role throughout the first interview was to listen, take notes, and allow the participants time if they required it. Consequently, I spent 45 to 60 minutes with each participant at the first interview.

The second interview. I met for 30 to 40 minutes with each individual student and the teacher groups (one group of two male teachers; one group of two female teachers) to discuss the critical analysis questions:[4]

> Who has power in the pictures? Who has status?
> What does the body language communicate to you? What do the eyes tell you?
> What does the clothing communicate to you?
> What do you think these pictures communicate about culture to Brazilian students of English?
> Do you think these pictures could influence Brazilian English students? How?
> (Teachers: Do you discuss pictures with your students? When? How?)

The third interview or correspondence. My intention was to then arrange a follow-up meeting with each participant or teacher group to find out how individuals had worked with the images or if they questioned them at all. However, a third interview was not possible with the majority of participants because of their time constraints (four participants cancelled their third interviews) and I left the country before they could be rescheduled. I conducted a third interview of 20 minutes with four students, but I did not ask further questions; in each case, the participants had a few follow-up ideas to share on previous questions, or they wanted to thank me for giving them the opportunity to practise their English. Five participants continued to correspond by email about the project and six ceased to participate further.

Stereotypical Images

Given that Brazil is more influenced by the United States than by any other English-speaking nation, it is unsurprising that the participants made very few references to England compared to the United States, even for textbooks produced in England. Among these perceptions of both the United States and "other" countries represented in the images in the texts, three common themes emerged: (a) the United States is portrayed as the land of the White elite; (b) Blacks are consistently represented as poor or powerless, while Whites are represented as wealthy and powerful; and (c) race is divided by continent.

The Land of the Successful Elite

> I have thought about pictures in English language books before. But I remember it was *before* I experienced my first travel to the USA. In that time, I thought about the organization, the education, and the clean pictures.
>
> (Marco)

Despite the fact that my conversations with the participants occurred in the 4 months before and the 6 months after the September 11th attacks, the student and teacher participants found that the images unswervingly represented the United States as a peaceful land of the social and political elite who are free from problems. Fatima, Vinícius, and Kaka told me that they *wanted* to see evidence of poverty and violence in the United States, as Fatima shared:

> I think it's better than Brazil, for example, because the pictures show the streets clean ... beautiful things, beautiful buildings. Show another things too, for example, I never read something like violence in America or England. When the books want to show violence, they show Afghanistan, show the war for example ... to me, it's ridiculous, this.

More specifically, the images equated American culture with economic and social success by including pictures of popular or successful social, business, or political figures that the students had labelled as American, although in a few cases, the person(s) in the image were not always American (see Table 4.4).

With the exception of one student, all of the participants pointed out the images of the rich and famous in their language books. Most recognized that American culture is exported through film, and the images "don't teach about lifestyles, but about movie-styles" (Bia). Similarly, the majority of student participants and all teacher participants commented on the presence of a privileged executive lifestyle, as the images "show the idea that you have many people talking on the phone, are on vacation, or shaking hands ... but making business all the time" (Vinícius). However, only two participants pointed out that none of the images of powerful or successful people were linked to stories explaining how they achieved their material, financial, or social power/influence. As Roberto Carlos pointed out,

Table 4.4 Summary of Popular or Successful Social, Business, or Political Figures

Entertainment	Politics	Business
Batman	Tony Blair*	Bill Gates
David Bowie*	Bill Clinton	James Hanson*
Marlon Brando	Princess Diana*	Nick Leeson*
Charlie Chaplin*	Queen Elizabeth*	Anita Roddick*
Sean Connery*	Martin Luther King	John Scully and Steve Jobs
Tom Cruise	Nelson Mandela*	Ted Turner
James Dean	Richard Nixon	
Danny Devito	Mother Teresa*	
Walt Disney		
Michael Douglas		
Richard Gere		
Tom Hanks		
Larry, Curley, and Moe		
George Lucas		
Madonna		
Marilyn Monroe		
Freddy Mercury*		
Demi Moore		
Elvis Presley		
Charlie Sheen		
Martin Sheen		
Wesley Snipes		
John Wayne		

Note
Individuals marked by * are non-American figures.

generally, the pictures market or sell a dream that you too can achieve, here in your poor country with all these problems, a standard of living like the United States. Only this is not the United States, and the culture is very different.

Nevertheless, this expectation is then tied to English as "English is the ticket to a better future" of "American dreams" (Milene).

Table 4.4 includes three images of Black men: (a) Wesley Snipes; (b) Nelson Mandela; and (c) Martin Luther King. Surely these three individuals alone do not sufficiently represent the diverse successful or popular social, political, and business figures who are (visible) minorities in English-speaking nations, or even the United States in particular. However, as the next section describes, not all the participants were able to recognize that the vast majority of the popular social, business, or political figures represented in their EFL texts were White.

Blacks Represented as Powerless and Whites Represented as Powerful

The White British school kids are posing in phoney well-behaved poses, arms at their sides in a row, while the Black school kids have their arms behind their backs and their heads bowed forward like they are waiting to be hit by a stick.

(Roberto Carlos)

Interestingly, it was the students and teachers who are themselves White who pointed out the lack of people of colour or minority status in the images: neither Ronaldo, who is black; nor Casia, who is mulatto; nor Marta who is of Japanese appearance and ethnicity, discussed colour or race as an issue in the images. However, the 10 White participants who did comment were critical about the predominance of Whites in the images; in particular they reacted to the lack of Blacks or minorities in the images. Comments from Vinícius and Kaka are illustrative of those given by the White participants of this study: "I think they should have more pictures of things that happen here in Brazil. They don't have any. Even the characters are not similar to Brazil. Everybody is white and you know … in a beautiful suit" (Vinícius), and "The majority of pictures are of Whites. The Blacks or Japanese in my English class do not find themselves represented in these books" (Kaka). Kaka mentioned that in his EFL class, of 15 students, two were Black and one was Japanese, but he communicated the injustice in their lack of representation in the EFL text.

Likewise, White participants discovered that the images often restricted status to White middle-aged men, who were most commonly in suits or positioned to imply that that they maintain political and social power in the presumed English-speaking context. For instance, when a teacher participant, Glória, looked at an image of the 3M Company Chart from a business-English text (Lannon, Tullis, & Trappe, 1999, p. 5) in which the president and four vice-presidents are all white middle-aged men dressed in suits, she commented "These are White men in power" (Glória). Additionally, a student participant, Márcio, talked at length about an image of an attractive older White couple. In the image the woman is dressed in a tailored jacket. She is wearing heavy eye makeup and a hairstyle similar to that of an American First Lady or news anchor woman. She is positioned in a chair under her husband who is standing behind the chair with one hand on the woman's shoulder and the other on the back of the chair. Both are smiling slightly but not enough to show their teeth:

> This picture where there is a man and a woman, a couple … probably they have a lot of money or a good position because it's a kind of picture that only who has money want to have, okay … the man standing behind the woman and using a suit and tie. And I don't like this kind of picture, really. Probably one day if I will be very, very rich I will not take one of these pictures. But I think they represent power, money and status.
>
> (Márcio)

In contrast, minorities, Blacks in particular, were represented as poor or powerless in the images as Fatima's comment at the beginning of this chapter suggests. For example, two teachers, Roberto Carlos and Glemerson, evaluated the physical positioning of a Black woman at a computer terminal, slouching slightly and looking bored. This image was labelled by the author of the textbook, Hollet (1997), as "using the mouse" (p. 47), what Roberto Carlos pointed out as "a pretty low level computer skill considering the year the text is published" (p. 9). The two teachers also discussed a Mulatto man gluing posters on the wall of an A&P grocery store (Lannon et al., 1999, p. 6) where "The white man is in command. The Puerto Rican is working" (Glemerson).

Reviewing a number of images in the textbooks, White students and teacher participants interpreted White men as the stakeholders or people with power and/or status. In other words, in a country where slavery had lasted 350 years, longer than any other slave nation in the Americas, the participants saw the colonization of Blacks or other minorities by powerful Whites in the images in their textbooks.

Race Divided by Continent

> I think the way those pictures can influence me is … at least teach me that a business person dressed in a suit works in boring places like they are not having a lot of fun. That American women use too much make up. Makes me think that, Indians are poor, Africans need food … not really different from the pictures we see in Brazil in terms of these countries but, it's enforces this kind of prejudice we have for other countries. It doesn't bring me another view of the country for example: some wealthy people in Africa. When I look at this with collection in my mind, I think that there is only poor people in Africa. In India, there is only guys meditating. It doesn't bring me a lot of things. I think the way it can influence Brazilians is kind of by reinforcing the feeling that we already had toward these countries. It doesn't bring news or a new way of viewing these countries.
>
> (Rivaldo)

The next major finding was that the images reinforce the limiting stereotype in which race and culture are divided by continent; in other words, the images implied that Whites live in North America, while Asians live in Asia, Arabs live in the Middle East, and Blacks live in Africa. The images did not explore the historical consequences of migration, immigration, and colonization or the intermixing of race and identity but rather:

> reinforce a stereotype of [White] American families eating hamburgers … And it hardly adds something to students' concepts of these situations and nationalities. The concept of "Japanese American" is not explored because it's continents not countries represented. You can't tell a Canadian from an American or the Mexican from [other] Latinos.
>
> (Roberto Carlos)

Examples from different texts confirm Roberto Carlos's point. An article that challenges you to discover the difference between Canadian and American social customs includes images of attractive white men and women of various ages, most of whom are smiling (Richards, 1998, IC-7). Asians, however, are shown posed with more serious expressions in traditional clothes, doing a traditional folk dance (Soars & Soars, 1987, p. 82) and being pushed into an overcrowded train (Lannon, Tullis, & Trappe, 1993, p. 54). Two student participants also identified two men as being from the Middle East because they are dressed in white robes and posed in discussion at a construction site with two White men whom the students presumed to be Westerners (Hollet, 1994, p. 74). Clearly, the image did not "bring a new way of viewing" (Rivaldo):

They show about the clothes. If you see the people dressing, different clothes all over the world. For example in Muslim, they dress totally different from us. The way Brazilians dress is what you are feeling. The Muslims are so closed, and here there is more freedom.

(Marta)

Finally, the single image that could potentially represent South America or Latin America is from a Hollywood film. The film makers have (re)created a tribal community in which most dark-skinned members are dressed only in grass skirts; the women wear their hair long, while the men have theirs cut in a bowl shape. In the image, a solemn, handsome White priest leads the tribal members towards the camera. Behind the White leader one tribesman carries a large wooden cross with a replica of Christ nailed to it. No cultural/historical explanation is provided; on the contrary, the authors ask the students to "write an appraisal of a book or film that you liked" (Soars & Soars, 1987, p. 36). Clearly only continents but not countries are represented. Furthermore, what is presented in the above image is both inappropriate and insensitive to the consumers of the images. As Vinícius put it, "They put the other peoples or cultures, but they present them in a way that is too aggressive."

Within the context of the interviews, the majority of the White participants posed the following questions: Where are representations of the people of the world of interracial heritage? Where are the immigrant and cultural communities present in almost every major city in the world today? Where is the Black Frenchman, the American Orthodox Jew, the Mexican-American in Texas, the Japanese-Brazilian, or the Indian-Englishman? How long has it been since (im)migration changed the world and altered what "an American" or any other nationality "looks like"? The images presented in the text are of a monocultural appearance divided neatly by continent. This kind of world has never existed.

Discussion

What does an English speaker look like? Although this question would appear biased, prejudiced, or even racist to just about anyone who lives or has lived in Canada, the United States, or the United Kingdom, for instance, and has experienced the rich social, cultural, and economic diversity that has accompanied immigration from all parts of the globe to these countries, the English-language textbook authors and editors ask questions such as "What does an American look like?" continually in and through the images in EFL texts. What does an American look like? The answer is simple: White, wealthy, powerful, isolated with members of their own race, and free of problems.

The most worrisome consequence is that images like those described in this chapter condone or even reinforce past and present racial biases. In other words, if the images and their layout chosen by the authors of textbooks do not challenge English-language students' perceptions of Americans, themselves, or "other" races, these images are apt to make participants of the discourse increasingly comfortable with or solidify their already entrenched racial stereotypes of the more economically powerful nation (White America), in contrast with the poorer nations with serious social problems (not America and not White).

Although the textbook publishers may attempt to neutralize EFL textbook images for a broader audience, most participants observed that the images did not represent the culture but rather seem to reinforce a made-in-Hollywood version of culture that does not exist (and likely never existed). In this case, the problem is that EFL images do not so much represent culture as construct cultural and racial identities. Most of the teachers and students in this study were critical consumers of the images, although it is significant that the most critical participants were White.

The White participants in this study appeared to connect their Whiteness with the White elitism represented in the images in their EFL textbooks. Some participants stated the connection as a matter of fact; Vera claimed "we [Whites] have more opportunities." Other participants, such as Fatima in her statement that opened this chapter, expressed this connection with sadness, while some students and teachers, such as Vinícius, Rivaldo, or Roberto Carlos in the previous sections, expressed this connection with anger. Therefore, the research interview did not necessarily heighten the participants' critical awareness of race, nor did the interview necessarily increase the participants' awareness of bias in the images in their textbooks; indeed, I had the impression that many of the participants were already aware of the stereotypes and inequities in the images. The interviews merely provided a space within which *some* of the participants could discuss the inequitable connections between race and power. I suspect the research interview allowed the White participants to speak more openly about Whites appearing most frequently with the most power in the images in the textbooks, largely because I, the researcher, am White also. Initially, I found this idea upsetting, as I realized that I might not be able to interact with all the participants in the same way. Today, I think I was naive to assume that everyone would want to treat me in the same way.

Furthermore, at the end of the study, nearly all of the participants felt that it was my responsibility as a researcher to take the necessary steps to improve the images in their EFL texts. Essentially, the participants' critical comments and interpretations became artefacts of the research interview, artefacts that I became responsible for displaying. It was a surprise to me, then, that I would need time to consider these findings before I was ready to write.

Implications for Praxis

The present study suggests that, while teachers may not always be able to choose the materials for their lessons, it is important for teachers to consider the images present in English-language textbooks prior to entering the classroom. In teacher-education programmes, teacher educators can ask teachers to consider questions such as those used in the interviews in this study to stimulate discussion, not only about EFL images, but also about White privilege, and towards antiracist education. While teachers may have clear opinions about the images in EFL textbooks, teachers may not have gone beyond asking their students to describe the images. In other words, teachers not only need to draw attention to the content of the image, but they also need to initiate discussions about the issues that the image implies. If teacher educators have not provoked thoughtful discussions with pre-service or practising professional teachers on the implicit meaning of images, one cannot expect that all teachers would know how to begin examining the race and power issues in an EFL image and handle these topics with sufficient sensitivity.

One way teacher educators can help teachers develop the professional and personal capabilities to decide how, when, or why to open discussions about race is to place pre-service and practising teachers in educational contexts or situations in which the teachers are the racial and/or linguistic minority, even if it is for a relatively brief period of time. In my experience as a teacher educator, very few teachers have been asked to consider how their lives would be different if they were of a different race. If a teacher is allowed the opportunity to develop a greater sensitivity to race and power, such experiences may lead this teacher to stimulate a number of useful discussions about the images in EFL textbooks.

While I can suggest that teachers engage students in discussions about the images, engage in projects redesigning images, or even write letters to textbook editors suggesting alternative images, the paradoxes of Paulo Freire's work are as alive today as ever before: if the students are uninterested or unwilling to engage in the discussions, redesign the images, or write to textbook editors, praxis becomes complicado. For this reason, the most effective means of improving the images in EFL textbooks in some contexts may be for teachers or EFL administrators to select and request textbooks with more equitable images of race and stop purchasing those textbooks that reproduce and reinforce the racial inequities of their community, their country, and the global community in which communication most often takes place in English (Crystal, 1997).

Implications for Future Research

The field of TESOL would benefit from further studies on the significance of race in the images in EFL and ESL textbooks. The findings of the present study are primarily limited by the relatively small sample size and the fact that the research was carried out in one location, São Paulo, with a relatively privileged group of participants. Further studies that replicate the line of questioning in this study, but compare student and teacher responses in diverse ESL and EFL contexts, would provide insight into how/if the images of race are viewed differently when the reader is part of or separate from the target-language culture. Moreover, future research might also explore questions from this study with different student populations, such as pre-teen or adolescent English-language learners, to discover if the depth or kind of response is linked to the maturity or media savvy of the English-language consumer/learner. Finally, a study in which teacher educators or teachers were the focus would also be useful in learning ways in which teachers can be better prepared to engage their students in discussions about race in the images in English-language textbooks.

Discussion Questions

1. In recalling your own students' comments about the images in an ESL/EFL textbook, to what extent have your students challenged the representation of race or culture in the images? Which images of people engaged or repelled your students? From your perspective, in what way(s) were your students' comments influenced by their cultural, social, or personal experiences with race?
2. One interesting result from the study was that the White students were most vocal about the oppressive images of Blacks or other visible minorities. What message(s)

might be implied if your students cannot find images of their own race in their EFL/ESL textbook? What kinds of messages are communicated if the images of your students' races are negative or degrading?

3. The author pointed out that many educators are not able to choose the textbook for their course. In the past, how have you responded to any student comments about the images? After reading the chapter about race in the images in EFL textbooks, would you alter your response? How? With whom? What strategies might you use to initiate discussions with your students about the images in the course textbook?

Notes

1. Freire's generic questions are in italic type and my reformulated questions follow in plain type.
2. The conversational English level was not determined by a test or any official/standard examination, but rather was based on my interpretation of their ability to communicate. This interpretation was based upon both my experiences as an EFL instructor and my knowledge of Brazilian Portuguese.
3. Complicated. Many of the Brazilians I met used this word to both summarize and dismiss the day-to-day realities of life in their country.
4. For the second interview, I transformed Giaschi's Critical Image Analysis questions (2000, p. 37) into my own questions.

References

Belraj, S. (2001). Media literacy in Malaysia: Making connections with critical awareness. In M. Kalantzis & A. Pandian (Eds.), *Literacy matters: Issues for new times* (pp. 161–172). Sydney: Common Ground Publishing.

Crystal, D. (1997). *English as a global language.* Cambridge: Cambridge University Press.

Fairclough, N. (1989). *Language and power.* London: Longman.

Fairclough, N. (2001). *Language and power.* London: Longman.

Freire, P. (1995). *The politics of education.* Boston, MA: Bergin and Garvey Publishers.

Freire, P. (1998). *Politics and education.* Los Angeles, CA: UCLA Latin American Center Publications.

Giaschi, P. (2000). Gender positioning in education: A critical image analysis of ESL texts. *TESL Canada Journal, 18,* 32–46.

Instituto Brasileiro do Geografia e Estatistica (IBGE) (1976). CENSO [CENSUS]. Retrieved February 26, 2002 from www.ibge.gov.br.

Lannon, M., Tullis, G., & Trappe, T. (1993). *Insights into business* (5th Edn). Harlow: Longman.

Lannon, M., Tullis, G., & Trappe, T. (1999). *Insights into business* (7th Edn). Harlow: Longman.

Luke, A. (1988). *Literacy, textbooks, and ideology: Postwar literacy instruction and the mythology of Dick and Jane.* New York: Falmer Press.

Menendez de Souza, L. M. T. (2003). Literacy and dreamspace: Multimodal texts in Brazilian indigenous community. In S. Goodman, T. Lillis, J. Maybin, & N. Mercer (Eds.), *Language, literacy and education: A reader* (pp. 221–230). Stoke on Trent: Trentham.

Pennycook, A. (1994). *The cultural politics of English as an international language.* New York: Longman.

Pennycook, A. (1995). English in the world/The world in English. In J. W. Tollefson (Ed.), *Power and inequality in language education* (pp. 34–58). Cambridge: Cambridge University Press.

Phillipson, R. (1992). *Linguistic imperialism.* Oxford: Oxford University Press.

Richards, J. (1998). *The new interchange: Intermediate student's book.* Cambridge: Cambridge University Press.

Skutnabb-Kangas, T. (2000). *Linguistic genocide in education or worldwide diversity and human rights?* Mahwah, NJ: Lawrence Erlbaum Associates.

Warschauer, M. (2000). The changing global economy and the future of English language teaching. *TESOL Quarterly, 34,* 511–24.

Widdowson, H. G. (1993). The ownership of English. *TESOL Quarterly, 28,* 377–389.

Appendix: Textbooks Evaluated in the Study

Baker, A. (1981). *Ship or sheep?* Cambridge: Cambridge University Press.

Boyd, F. (1994). *Making business decisions: Real cases from real companies.* New York: Addison Wesley Publishing Company, Inc.

Evans, D. (1998). *Powerhouse: An intermediate business English course.* New York: Addison Wesley Longman.

Frazier, L., & Robin, M. (1998). *Northstar: Focus on reading and writing.* New York: Longman.

Hollet, V. (1994). *Business opportunites.* London: Oxford University Press.

Lannon, M., Tullis, G., & Trappe, T. (1999). *Insights into business.* Harlow: Longman.

Radley, P., & Burke, K. (1997). *Workout Advanced: Student's book.* Harlow: Longman.

Richards, J. (1998). *The new interchange: Intermediate student's book.* Cambridge: Cambridge University Press.

Shovel, M. (1985). *Making sense of phrasal verbs.* New York: Prentice Hall.

Soars, J., & Soars, L. (1987). *Headway: Upper intermediate student's book.* London: Oxford University Press.

5 "It's Not Them; It's Not Their Fault"

Manifestations of Racism in the Schooling of Latinas/os and ELLs

Sherry Marx

Pre-reading Questions

In this chapter, Sherry Marx focuses on some ways racial inequality is evident in the public school educational experiences of ELLs and Latina/o children. Her focus is on the passive, institutional, and, often times, subtle ways that racism is maintained.

- What were your own experiences with race when you were a student?
- Did you think of yourself as a racialized person?
- If so, how and when did this come to your attention?
- If not, why do you think this is the case?
- If you have ever been a school teacher, how have race and racism in this milieu been evident to you?

Introduction

The United States is experiencing an immigration wave that has put more English-Language Learners (ELLs) in U.S. public school classrooms than ever before. In the year 2005, 20% of the U.S. school-age population spoke a language other than English at home (National Center for Education Statistics, 2007). The National Clearinghouse for English Language Acquisition (NCELA, 2006) reports that more than five million U.S. schoolchildren were considered "limited English proficient" in the 2004–2005 school year, although the number of children actually receiving language services is not clear. While it was reported that 8% of U.S. schoolchildren received English-language services during the 2000–2001 school year (NCES, 2003), that percentage has certainly grown by now. More recent data in California, the state with the highest number of speakers of other languages, show that 25% of its schoolchildren are in need of English-language services (California Department of Education, 2004).

These demographic shifts in American schools have not been without their challenges. English-language learners often struggle in their schooling. For example, NCES reports that,

> In 2005, the percentage of foreign-born 16-to-24 year-olds who were high school status[1] dropouts was twice the percentage of those born in the United States. For Hispanics of the same age group, the percentage of status dropouts among those

who were foreign-born (38%) was more than twice that of their native counterparts (13%).

(KewalRamani, Gilbertson, Fox, & Provasnik, 2007, p. 90)

Even more dramatic evidence is offered by Gándara, Maxwell-Jolly, and Driscoll (2005), who report that just 39% of English-language-learning students "were able to pass the English language arts portion of the California high school exit exam in 2004 compared to 81% of English speakers" (p. 2). In addition, "only 29% of [English learning] students in Los Angeles high schools are still in school 4 years after entering the ninth grade" (p. 2). That translates to an approximate status dropout rate of 70%. These numbers are even more distressing when considering the children who drop out of school before ninth grade and taking into account recent scholarship that suggests dropout rates are typically under-reported (Balfanz & Legters, 2004; Greene, 2002; Swanson, 2004).

As English-language learners struggle in schooling, so do their teachers. In 1993–1994, just 29.5% of public school teachers working with ELLs had either pre-service or in-service training regarding students with limited English proficiency (McCandless, Rossi, & Daugherty, 1996). Six years later, in 2000, the National Center for Education Statistics (NCES) found that just 26% of all public school teachers felt prepared to meet the needs of students with limited English skills (NCES, 2001). The same survey found that only 27% of teachers teaching English-language learners and 32% of teachers working with children from diverse cultural backgrounds felt very well-prepared to do so.

Due to the growing population of ELLs in schools, more and more school districts across the United States are requiring or strongly encouraging teachers to earn English as a second language (ESL) endorsements. Teacher education programs, too, are offering a wider range of ESL teacher-credential courses and they are more frequently requiring students to take multicultural and language-acquisition courses. Despite these admirable efforts, ELLs continue to struggle in schooling, as their high dropout rates attest. English-language acquisition is not the only challenge they face.

Challenges Beyond Language Skills

When examining the academic struggles of ELLs in the United States, attention must be given to Latinas/os as a multifaceted ethnic, racial, and cultural group simply because they account for 80% of U.S. children speaking another language at home (NCELA, 2006), 85% in California (Gándara et al., 2005). Overall, Latinas/os account for 19% of the U.S. public school population (NCES, 2006), with people of color making up 43%. Most students receiving English-language services in the United States are Latina/o. Because Latinas/os and Latina/o ELLs account for a substantial segment of children of color and ELLs in U.S. public schools, they are the focus of this chapter.

While the percentage of schoolchildren of color, including Latinas/os, continues to grow, the teaching population remains predominantly White. In fact, the teaching population has grown more homogeneous in the past decades as the student population has grown more diverse. More than 90% of teachers are White (National Education Association, 2003) and an estimated 97% speak only English (Darling-Hammond &

Sclan, 1996). In addition to these ethnic, racial, and linguistic differences between teachers and their students, just 53% of American teachers live in the school districts where they teach, with only 32% living "within the attendance areas of [their] school buildings" (NEA, 2003, p. 97). Great geographic and social distance separates most teachers from the lives of their Latina/o students. In fact, while most Latina/o students spend the majority of their school careers with White, monolingual teachers in schools dominated by White adults, these particular adults and students may never cross paths outside the school building.

Centering Race and Racism in the Discussion

I suggest that the racial differences between Latinas/os, ELLs, and the vast majority of the adults with whom they work in schools contribute to the racial/ethnic academic achievement gap in schooling at least as strongly as language issues. As I center race and racism in this discussion, it is important to define just what I am talking about. Regarding race, while some scholars assert the need to separate race from ethnicity (e.g., Kolchin, 2002), I purposely use the two terms interchangeably, as they are both social constructions that regularly overlap. Viewing race in this manner draws attention to its socially constructed nature, the way "its meaning changes over time," and its connections to "relations of power and processes of struggle" (Frankenberg, 1993, p. 11; see also Banks, 2003; Kincheloe, Steinberg, Rodriguez, & Chennault, 1998; Omi & Winant, 1994).

Regarding racism, I have adopted Wellman's (1977) definition of racism as "a system of advantage based on race" (Tatum, 1999, p. 7) that benefits Whites in the United States. This understanding of racism takes into account the U.S. history of slavery and racial inequality that has always privileged Whites as it has disadvantaged people of color. It gives attention to the everyday forms of racial inequality that are systematic, institutionalized, and often considered normal in our society. While systematic racism was clearly distinguishable in times of slavery and subsequent racial segregation, in contemporary times, racism is often passive and subtle, uneventful and ordinary. Those perpetrating and reproducing racism these days often do so unintentionally, without even the ability to articulate the racism within their beliefs and actions.

Colorblindness, the perspective that race has no influence on any aspect of one's life, experiences, or opportunities, makes a strong contribution to contemporary racism (e.g., Bonilla-Silva, 2003; Marx, 2006). In the U.S., we are presently living in an era of colorblindness, or as Frankenberg (1993, p. 145) terms it, "color-evasiveness." This post-civil rights discourse not only draws attention away from the relevance of race, but successfully prevents the topic from being considered as a contributing factor to a child's struggles in a classroom or a teacher's struggles with her or his students. At a more macro level, colorblindness prevents us from problematizing the fact that most cities and towns are divided into racial neighborhoods, ensuring that children go to racially segregated schools unequally affected by poverty, high dropout rates, and linguistic isolation (Balfanz & Legters, 2004; Orfield & Lee, 2004).

Critical Race Theory

Although I adopt a socially constructed understanding of race, I do not suggest that race does not exist. On the contrary, the ways that race affects the lives of all people living in the United States are real—all too real at times. In understanding the impact of race in the United States, it has been helpful for me to draw on a theoretical framework composed of both critical race theory (CRT) and critical studies in whiteness. CRT has a number of key tenets, including beliefs in the embedded, normal nature of racism; the permanence of racism; and the explicit goal of dismantling racism (DeCuir & Dixson, 2004; Delgado, 1995; Ladson-Billings & Tate, 1995). Adopting CRT as a theoretical perspective allows one to explicitly examine the effects of race and racism in all facets of society from institutions such as law, government, and schooling, to the related beliefs and actions of individuals.

Critical studies in whiteness, in concert, highlight whiteness as a fundamental characteristic of a racialized ethnic/cultural group that receives the benefits of racial inequality (e.g., Delgado & Stefancic, 1997; Frankenberg, 1993; Marx, 2006). Although Whites are as diverse as members of any other ethnic/racial/cultural group, they have in common racial privilege. These privileges can be as convenient as being able to find Band-Aids and pantyhose in the right skin color or as abstract as being perceived as trustworthy, smart, and appropriately clean. Peggy McIntosh compares these racial benefits to an "invisible weightless knapsack of special provisions, maps, passports, codebooks, visas, clothes, tools and blank checks" that enables Whites to negotiate the hidden rules of U.S. society (McIntosh, 1989, p. 10). Even if White people are aware of or against these unearned privileges, they nevertheless benefit from them and their whiteness (Scheurich, 1993). A theoretical framework of CRT and critical studies in whiteness, therefore, allows one to examine school achievement through the perspectives of systematic racial inequality and racial privileges.

While the focus of this chapter is race, I do not suggest that race is the only factor contributing to educational inequality. Race and economic status overlap in many ways and low-income communities are disproportionately affected by racial segregation and low-performing schools. Affluent communities and individuals of color do not experience the same barriers to education as those less well-off financially. However, people of color of all economic backgrounds still experience racism in the United States, as many personal stories on the topic have revealed (see, for example, Ladson-Billings, 1999; Singley, 2002). With these issues in mind, this chapter centers on race.

Manifestations of Racial Inequality in Schooling

As a White person growing up in the post-civil rights era, racial inequality has not always been obvious to me. Though the school district I attended in rural Kentucky was officially racially integrated, it was unofficially resegregated between and within the buildings, and few students of color attended my college track classes. I never really thought about this as a student. However, many years later, after living in Japan and on the U.S. East Coast as an adult, I went back to my old middle and high schools as a substitute teacher, pursuing my teaching credential in secondary education. It was then that I realized I had attended the almost all-White middle school as I found myself substitute teaching in the other middle school, the one that was almost entirely African American, with a growing population of Latinas/os. One day I passed out an absent teacher's report cards and noticed that every student in the class was failing. The "comments" section on each report card was blank. When I later asked the teacher about this, he simply responded, "Sometimes, you just don't have anything to say." While substitute teaching in my old high school, which was the only high school in the district, I finally found the classes where the students of color were assigned: special education and non-college-bound track classes such as home economics. There were few White students in these classes. These experiences stunned me as it was only then that I realized how different my own educational experiences had been from those of the children of color who grew up in my same school district.

As an adult with a little worldly experience and, by then, several years' experience teaching English as a foreign language (EFL) internationally and ESL to international students in the United States, I began to problematize the racial segregation I was now recognizing. After receiving my teaching credential in Kentucky, I went on to Texas to study racism in schooling in more depth. It was in Texas that I began drawing connections between the school experiences of ELLs and racism, a topic that had received almost no research attention at that point. Since then, I have examined racial disparities in schooling in Texas, California, and Utah. In particular, I have studied schools where Latina/o students have a strong presence, either by being the majority ethnic/racial group in the school or by being a rapidly growing minority. Because Latinas/os are the fastest growing ethnic/racial group in the United States, it is easy to find them as a presence in schools all around the country. Because most teachers are White and most Latinas/os and ELLs spend most of their school careers with White teachers, I have most often studied what these White teachers have to say about their Latina/o students.

In Texas, I conducted a qualitative study of White, English-only speaking pre-service teachers who tutored Mexican-American schoolchildren learning English (Marx, 2003, 2004, 2006). Over a four-month period, I interviewed these nine tutors three to 10 times each about the children they taught; I observed them tutoring; I collected their journals on the tutoring experience; and I tutored a fourth-grade ELL myself. A few years later, in California, I worked as a reading teacher in a school where 77% of the students were Latina/o and about half had been designated limited English proficient at some point in their school career. Every teacher in the school, including me, was White. At this school, I surveyed the students and conducted a qualitative study on the four teachers they felt they could "relate to" the best (Marx, 2008). All of these teachers were White women. After this experience, I moved to Utah, and have since been engaged in a longitudinal research and teacher-development project seeking to improve science education for Latina/o children, including ELLs, in middle school (Johnson & Marx, in press). In this mixed-method project, my colleague and I have been collecting life-history data, monthly teaching observations, and monthly focus-group workshop data from eight teachers, seven of whom are White. The other is Latino.

These research projects have revealed a number of ways that racial inequality is manifested in schooling. In this chapter, I analyze the three studies together to highlight some of these different manifestations. In all the settings, most discussions I have had about Latina/o students begin with grievances from pre-service teachers, teachers, and administrators about children who do not care about school and who are not motivated to succeed. Almost always, these grievances are extended to the children's parents, where they are entangled with feelings of concern, disappointment, and sometimes even disgust. Educators are often mystified as to why parents do not value education nor want their children to learn English. The parents of successful students are also criticized, as their lack of educational support is particularly mystifying. As the conversations continue, it is often revealed that the concerned teachers and administrators have never met the families they are discussing beyond the occasional parent–teacher conference.

This example alone reveals three manifestations of racism that are particularly damaging to Latina/o students and their families: (1) prevalent undercurrents of deficit thinking and White racial superiority in schooling; (2) ubiquitous misunderstandings that White teachers and administrators, hereafter referred to as "educators," have of their Latina/o students linked to their inability to relate to these students as language learners and members of cultural and racial groups different from their own; and (3) perceptions that White educators often have of successful or motivated Latinas/os as being exceptions to their cultural/racial/ethnic group. A fourth manifestation of racism presented in this chapter is related to policy rather than educator–student relationships. This manifestation concerns (4) the prevalence of unsuccessful school language-development programs across the United States. Each of these related manifestations is discussed below.

Undercurrents of Deficit Thinking and White Racial Superiority

When talking about Latinas/os with teachers and administrators, the children themselves are frequently described as "problems" and "challenges." Often well-intentioned, principals call me or my colleagues with requests for "help dealing with the Hispanic problem." At the same time, Latinas/os are often constructed by teacher-education students in multicultural and language-development courses as exceedingly pitiable. Usually well-intentioned, these future teachers cautiously admit that they have some negative beliefs about Latinas/os, immigration, and English-language policies they will need to "put aside" when teaching Latina/o children, including ELLs. "It's not them, it's not their fault," they say as a way to mitigate the negative constructions they share. While some teacher-education students take on paternal roles, sharing stories of the "hard-working" and "loyal" families who come to work on their parents' farms each summer, others laugh about Latinas/os, describing "them" as unintelligent, unclean, and uncaring about their appearance. Some White students even grumble that Latinas/os are unworthy of discussion in these classes, given that they hope to teach gifted and talented students some day, students they do not envision as Latina/o. Such comments are made without the usual good intentions.

All these comments reveal the reliance White educators and future educators have on deficit thinking for making sense of Latinas/os (Valencia, 1997). That is, rather than entering these discussions with no knowledge base or neutral beliefs, I suggest that most White educators bring quite negative views of Latinas/os with them into their teacher-education courses, as well as their own K–12 classrooms. As a result, Latinas/os enter their schooling experience with a dramatic handicap. They simply do not receive the benefit of the doubt when educators seek to make sense of them. Instead, educators often assume the worst.

Interviewing and otherwise studying White pre-service teachers tutoring Latina/o ELL children in Texas over the course of a university semester (Marx, 2006), I was able to tease out numerous ways that deficit thinking clouded their perceptions of the children they tutored. These misperceptions detracted from their obvious good intentions of wanting to work with children who needed extra help developing their English skills. In addition to having a generally deficit view of the children's native cultures, tutors described Spanish as less sophisticated than English, better suited for "the streets" than the classroom (Marx, 2006, p. 55). Spanish-accented English was also perceived negatively. One young woman lamented that the child she tutored had "the Mexican talk" (p. 55). This tutor was unable to recognize the child's strong English-language reading skills because she had a negative association with her Spanish accent. "See?" She told me, "Her English is so poor!" (p. 55).

Tutors also tended to judge children as having low self-esteem and low intelligence because of their Spanish accents and cultural backgrounds. They also assumed families were unsupportive and uncaring, characteristics that they felt exacerbated the children's low self-esteem. Several tutors were particularly drawn to the Latina/o children they tutored because they thought of themselves as much-needed surrogate parents. Throughout the tutoring experience, they never met the parents of the children. One young woman, however, told a story of Latina/o parents who had hired her to tutor their own child in the past. Her perception was that, "They basically wanted somebody else to do it" (Marx, 2006, p. 59). As she complained about the parents, she also revealed that they did not speak much English. While this tutor's concern for the child was genuine, her understanding of his parents was really a misunderstanding. Rather than commend them for hiring her to meet a need they could not, she criticized them as uninvolved and uncaring.

In my study of White teachers who could relate to their Latina/o students in California (Marx, 2008), I again found a strong reliance on deficit thinking. Although these teachers were highly qualified veterans who had caring relationships with their students, most nevertheless made sense of Latina/o students through deficit thinking. In particular, these teachers believed that Latinas/os did not value education and that Latina women and girls were disrespected due to a culture of *machismo*. Like the tutors discussed above, these teachers tended to blame students' families for holding children back and preventing them from succeeding in school.

In the longitudinal study in Utah (see Johnson & Marx, in press, for early findings), my colleague and I asked all participating teachers to conduct a home visit with a Latina/o student with the purpose of getting to know the children and their families better. Teachers were resistant to the idea and made numerous excuses for not making visits. As weeks went by, we finally offered to pay each teacher who conducted a visit $100. Most teachers subsequently visited a Latina/o family and all who did had wonderful, positive experiences that we talked about in detail during a focus-group session afterwards. During that meeting, teachers shared that their low expectations had not materialized in the visits. Rather, they had met intelligent, caring, funny, diverse individuals with all levels of educational backgrounds and clear goals for the future. We even had lunch that day at a taco stand owned by one of the families visited. I was tremendously pleased by the outcome of this experience as it seemed to abolish the deficit thoughts that had plagued our professional-development project. However, a few months later, when I asked teachers to revisit what they had learned from their home visits, they responded that one visit could not really tell them anything about the Latinas/os they had met, that these families could easily have hidden their true natures in one visit, and that it was possible they had met people who were exceptions to the general rule. They were not eager to conduct home visits again. Deficit thinking prevailed.

As these many deficit thoughts about Latina/o students are revealed, so are beliefs in White racial supremacy. While the notion of "supremacy" may call forth visions of the Ku Klux Klan and cross burnings, I use this term without such extremism in mind. Rather, I point to the "normalized and taken for granted White supremacy" (Gillborn, 2005, p. 486) revealed when the negative comments that signify deficit thinking about the Other are extricated. The silence that remains implies that Whites are not all those negative things that characterize Latinas/os. Rather than highlight the supremacy of whiteness by articulating its many unearned privileges, the denigration of the Other achieves this by default.

However, it is important to note that educators revealing deficit thinking and White racial supremacy do not necessarily—or even consciously—do this on purpose. Rather, they (and all people in the United States) are inhabitants of a racialized culture, breathing in and reproducing the values implicitly taught by our culture. Tatum (1999) compares this kind of racism to "a moving sidewalk at the airport" (p. 11). "Active racist behavior," she suggests,

> is equivalent to walking fast on the conveyor belt. The person engaged in active racist behavior has identified with the ideology of White supremacy and is moving with it. Passive racist behavior is equivalent to standing still on the walkway. No overt effort is being made, but the conveyor belt moves the bystanders along to the same destination as those who are actively walking. Some of the bystanders may feel the motion of the conveyor belt, see the active racists ahead of them, and choose to turn around, unwilling to go to the same destinations as the White supremacists. But unless they are walking actively in the opposite direction at a speed faster than the conveyor belt—unless they are actively antiracist—they'll find themselves carried along with the others.
>
> (pp. 11–12)

Even noticing the sidewalk requires conscious effort. Walking in the opposite direction or jumping off altogether requires a purposeful antiracist stance that few people in the United States find it necessary to take. The "business as usual" of racism that is maintained by deficit thinking and colorblindness is passive and easily denied; it is a normal pattern of discourse in U.S. society.

Ubiquitous Misunderstandings and Inability to Relate

Related to and contributing to deficit thinking are the ever-present misunderstandings between White educators and Latina/o students. As stated earlier, most teachers live outside the school boundaries where they teach and nearly half live outside their school districts (NEA, 2003). In our racially segregated society, White teachers are even more likely to live at a distance from their students of color, including Latinas/os (Donato, Menchaca, & Valencia, 1991). Orfield and Lee (2004) note that Latinas/os are highly segregated in their schooling and that "no substantial gains in segregated education for Latinos [occurred] even during the civil rights era" (p. 3). As a result, White educators tend not to see their Latina/o students in their neighborhoods, grocery stores, shopping centers, or places of worship. They tend not to know the families of their Latina/o students and they are often unfamiliar with their cultural backgrounds and experiences as bilinguals. Rather than knowing their students as holistic people with multiple dimensions, including many strengths and areas in which to grow, they know them only as students—many of whom are struggling in school.

In the California study (Marx, 2008), I found that the White teachers I got to know could relate well to Latina/o students who struggled academically through their own personal experiences of being shy, having unstable backgrounds, dealing with addictions, and even living through abuse. However, when I asked how they could *not* relate to Latina/o students, all of them brought up the topic of race. Most proceeded to describe the students in terms of stereotypes, explaining that they could not relate to such things as not valuing education, not respecting women, and encouraging teen pregnancy. One of these teachers, Ms. Starr, described Latinas/os as taking advantage of the welfare system and being either one or the other of "two different kinds of Hispanic people": "your gang banger-city type that I never like ... [and those who are] just really hard working people that don't earn high wages" (Marx, 2008, p. 44).

In the Utah study (Johnson & Marx, in press), one of the White teachers spoke as an expert on Mexican culture based on his experience in Mexico with the U.S. military many years previously. He informed the teachers in our professional-development meeting that day that the streets are long and straight in Guadalajara so drug runners can land airplanes on them; that most Mexican immigrants in his school district came to the United States to flee drug lords; and that festive parties celebrating a girl's 15th birthday, *quinceñeras*, were ways of advertising young women who were now sexually available to any man. The image he constructed of Mexico and Mexicans was truly frightening.

In contrast to such obvious deficit-fueled misunderstandings of students and their home cultures, some teachers have self-reflectively shared that their inability to personally relate to Latinas/os and ELLs has negatively affected their ability to teach. Ms. Alexander, one of the California teachers, shared these thoughts,

> They [ELLs] are probably the ones I relate to the least because I feel a deficiency in not being able to speak Spanish. And not understanding, again, not being able to relate to what that would be like, to be here and trying to go through school and not having a clear understanding of the language. It would be ... I can't even imagine. It is very, very hard. So that's probably where my biggest weakness is as far as — I wouldn't say relating to them on a personal level—but being able to really help them as much as I should, on the classroom level.
>
> (Marx, 2008, p. 48)

Notice that Ms. Alexander places the responsibility for better meeting the needs of her ELLs on her own shoulders, taking herself to task for not speaking Spanish and not having similar life experiences to many of her Latina/o students. The care she feels for her students comes through in this quotation. However, notice also that she separates the importance of relating to students "on a personal level" and "on the classroom level." Throughout our interviews, Ms. Alexander emphasized that relating to students on the personal level was not a necessary part of good teaching. In contrast, relating at the classroom level by being able to address academic challenges was very important to her.

Other California teachers made the same distinctions about relating to students. After talking about the "two different kinds of Hispanic people," for example, Ms. Starr said,

> The things that annoyed me in the [Latina/o] community were not things that I had to deal with in my classroom … In the classroom, it is just about skill level and what you can do to try and help this kid and what you can do to try and help that one, and yeah, language is an issue, but is just another skill level to try to help them with.
>
> (Marx, 2008, p. 44)

Ms. Starr went on to add that her feelings about Latinas/os were "not personal against my kids." If her "beefs" with Latinas/os in general ever entered her classroom, she said, "I would leave the profession because that would be grossly unfair to my kids and to me" (Marx, 2008, p. 44). Those educators and scholars who suggest that there is no inherent inequity when students of color and ELLs are taught predominantly by mono-lingual English-speaking Whites make the same points Ms. Alexander and Ms. Starr do here. Given the many misunderstandings and examples of deficit thinking shared by these and other pre-service and practicing teachers with whom I have taught, studied, and worked, I do not find these arguments to be particularly convincing.

Although the California teachers taught at a predominately Latina/o school, they rarely thought of it in those terms. In fact, they often emphasized how much race did not matter in the school. As Ms. Starr said, "[W]hen we are in my classroom, they're just kids and it doesn't really matter" (Marx, 2008, p. 45). As members of a colorblind society, teachers and administrators in the school did not problematize race as a possible factor in schooling, nor in their own constructions of the predominantly Latina/o students they taught. Latina/o students, also progeny of a colorblind era, rarely problematized race either. In fact, students regularly described the four teachers studied as "excellent" teachers who were trustworthy, kind, and even in possession of "huge heart(s)" (Marx, 2008, p. 45). Many students felt sufficiently cared for by these teachers. When initially studying these four popular teachers, I hoped to find ways in which they were bridging the racial/ethnic/cultural/language gap with their students. In fact, what I found was that the gap was largely ignored by the teachers and most of the students. Because race is so rarely problematized, it was not problematized in this setting either.

However, through interviews and observations at this California school for the year I taught there, it became clear that, with just a little pointed questioning, race was something that "really mattered" in the school. The many misunderstandings shared by Ms. Starr and other educators are largely due to ignorance and social and geographic distance; however, they are also fueled by systematic racism. Racism prevents these misunderstandings from being problematized and considered unacceptable. Rather than view Latina/o students and their families as complicated people with multiple dimensions and rich, complex, cultural backgrounds, White educators often reduce Latina/o peoples and cultures to simplistic stereotypes that do not even really make sense. Whites regularly believe that Latinas/os do not value education; they do not have a desire to learn English; their lives are fueled by drugs; and children's parents do not care about them. In contrast, Whites often cannot describe any markers of White culture or ethnicity, either pointing to immense complexity or denying that Whites have anything in common at all. Critical studies in whiteness offer much evidence for these two perspectives, one or the other of which is embraced by most Whites (Frankenberg, 1993; Marx, 2006; McIntyre, 1997; Rodriguez, 1998; Shome, 1999).

These misunderstandings and the related inability of most White educators to relate to their Latina/o students and their families remind me of the information-gap activity practiced in many ESL classrooms. In this popular language-learning game, students sit across from one another, one with a picture and the other with a blank paper and pencil. The students have a barrier between them so they cannot see each other's documents. The first student uses her second language skills to explain the picture to the other student, who tries to create a similar picture based on the spoken description alone. Without negotiating meaning with one another, the picture drawn by the second student is likely to have little in common with the picture explained by the first student. That seems to be just what is happening with White educators and Latina/o students. There is a barrier between them, yet educators try to make sense of what is going on with their students using very limited information—hardly any from students and their families. Meaning is rarely negotiated, but the re-created, mis-created pictures are shared with everyone and described as accurate portraits of reality.

Successful, Motivated Latinas/os as Exceptions to the Rule

While there is plenty of evidence that Latinas/os value education (e.g., Valencia & Black, 2002; San Miguel & Valencia, 1998), students who openly exhibit this value are often considered to be exceptions to their home cultures and families by White educators. It seems that no matter how often students flout this stereotype, the stereotype itself is not problematized or deconstructed. I suggest this is another way racism is experienced by Latinas/os in school.

In my study of teachers in California (Marx, 2008), teachers regularly described their Latina/o students as the most fun and likable students they had ever had. However, when talking about academic achievement, students were described as having to overcome many cultural and familial limitations. For example, when trying to explain complicated feelings about her Latina/o students and their goals and struggles with schooling, Ms. Alexander said that her own parents had created a very loving home environment with strong expectations of college attendance that made it difficult for her to relate to the lack of value Latinas/os placed on education. However, many of her Latina/o students clearly did value education and she admired them for it. As she said, "I think the kids find [education] more important and realize how much more important it is than their parents do" (Marx, 2008, p. 47).

This teacher also shared her belief that Latina/o cultures strongly valued *machismo* and consequently disrespected and disregarded females. She had learned from one of her colleagues that Latino males did not respect women in positions of authority and so would not respect female teachers, seek their guidance, nor follow their directions. Several White teachers in the school shared this belief. However, they also shared many stories that illustrated the respect their Latino students had for them. Ms. Alexander, in particular, shared that she pointedly got to know proud Latino gang members "with the attitude" (Marx, 2008, p. 47). As a result, she developed warm relationships with them that offered ample evidence of mutual respect. Similarly, Ms. Green shared that, "I can't relate to some of the Mexican heritage stuff, like the attitude of 'Well, you are a girl so you don't need to go to school'" (p. 40). However, many of her students were girls who put obvious efforts into improving their education. Despite many exceptions to this stereotype, it remained embedded in the teachers' beliefs about Latina/o students, their families, and their home cultures.

Another popular misperception of Latina/o families is that they do not care for their children. This belief exists despite the contradictory, well-known, positive stereotype that Latinas/os are very family-oriented. Teachers throughout the many districts I have studied and pre-service teachers in every state where I have taught offer this negative assessment of parents. As many scholars point out, parents who earn low wages are often forced to work multiple jobs or shifts that prevent them from attending many school functions (Delgado-Gaitan, 2004; Trueba, 1998). Parents may also feel a strong sense of disconnection from the schools their children attend due to social, cultural, and linguistic barriers (Delgado-Gaitan, 2004; Rose, 1989; Valenzuela, 1999). However, I have noticed in my own experiences that Latina/o parents who do attend parent–teacher conferences are not necessarily regarded as valuing education or caring about their children. Educators often dismiss them as someone they met just once during a conference. Again, the stereotype is reaffirmed rather than reassessed. It seems that Latina/o parents cannot do much to show schools the many ways they care about their children. Rarely are they granted the privilege of even being recognized as exceptions to this negative stereotype.

Prevalence of Poor Language-Support Services in Schools

It is beyond the scope of this chapter to thoroughly critique the educational opportunities offered to children in the United States who are not proficient in English. See the work of Krashen (e.g., Krashen, 1999; Krashen & McField, 2005), Hakuta, Goto-Butler, and Witt (2000), and others (e.g., Goto-Butler, Orr, Bousquet Gutierrez, & Hakuta, 2000) for closer examination of this topic. However, virtually no respected research in second language and bilingual education supports pullout ESL courses, likely the most common approach to meeting the needs of English-language learners in the United States today (Ovando, Combs, & Collier, 2006; Thomas & Collier, 1997). Students get little academic support in such courses and are often segregated from native English speakers in the school for most of the day. Thomas and Collier (1997) reported findings on the dismal achievement scores associated with traditional ESL programs more than 10 years ago. However, I have rarely visited a school that actually uses research-based information or curricula to support its English-language learners. In the aftermath of California's proposition 227 and similar efforts against bilingual education around the country, bilingual education has been scaled back to nothing or next to nothing in recent years. This has happened despite research that has shown late-exit bilingual education, which aims to develop bilingual and biliterate skills through at least the sixth-grade level, to be highly successful for the academic achievement of English-language learners (Collier, 1992; Genesee, Lindholm-Leary, Saunders, & Christian, 2006; Ramirez, Yuen, Ramey, Pasta, & Billings, 1991; Thomas & Collier, 1997).

Crawford (2000) describes U.S. language policy as a "war with diversity." I often wonder if "war" is the hidden curriculum behind the dismal schooling achievement of English-language learners, particularly Latinas/os, in the United States. In a recent study of dropout rates, Balfanz and Legters (2004) found that nearly 40% of Latina/o students in the United States attend (or, rather, do not attend) high schools where 60% or fewer freshmen go on to become seniors. That is, about 40% of students in these schools drop out before they graduate. Most of these schools have high populations of students of color and most are in large cities. These appallingly low graduation rates are not only the case in urban areas, however. The two school districts in the small Utah town where I live both report Latina/o dropout rates of 50% (Brown, 2005) and colleagues share similar stories around the country.

Latina/o children and their families are suffering. As a result, society suffers as well. Balfanz and Legters (2004) write that, "It is no coincidence that these locales [with failing schools for children of color] are gripped by high rates of unemployment, crime, ill health, and chronic despair" (p. 1). These areas tend to be racially segregated as well, with people of color bearing the burden of the challenges Balfanz and Legters describe. Systematic racism contributes to our society's reluctance to problematize this situation as anything out of the ordinary or—even more helpfully—to address this state of affairs with changes based on educational research that recommends bilingual education, improved funding, reduced class sizes, and dedicated efforts toward racial integration (e.g., Balfanz & Legters, 2004; Chamot & O'Malley, 1994; Orfield & Lee, 2004; Ovando et al., 2006; Samway & McKeon, 2007).

Conclusions

Discussing these aspects of education for Latina/o schoolchildren, including ELLs, as manifestations of racism is meant to call attention to the inequity experienced by these students in schools every day with teachers and other educators who are—and who are not—well-meaning. Despite frequent good intentions, these students are suffering. National dropout rates of 38% (as a minimum) (KewalRamani et al., 2007) and regional dropout rates as high as 70% (Gándara et al., 2005; Valenzuela, 1999) should be viewed by everyone as completely unacceptable. If White, native-English-speaking children were suffering the same poor relationships with educators, the same poor schools, poor programs, and poor results, there is no question that the education system would be dramatically overhauled.

Likely because of the manifestations of racism I have discussed in this chapter, deficit thinking, misunderstandings about Latinas/os and ELLs, and a tendency to view successful Latinas/os and ELLs as exceptions to the general rule of their race and culture, school difficulties and failure experienced by these students are often rationalized as problems of their own doing. Of course, their families and native cultures are named as sharing the blame. Because these children, their families, and their home cultures are viewed in these ways, schools often see little purpose in reassessing the academic services offered to them. Instead, Latinas/os are often described as not appreciating or making the most of the limited services that are offered. Changes that would implement comprehensive, research-backed bilingual education programs, and high expectations for Latinas/os are often dismissed as too radical, too expensive, and too upsetting to the status quo. Such changes are often viewed as unfairly geared toward a "minority" population, even when such populations make up the majority of the school (Kubota, 2004).

Viewing educator perspectives on Latina/o academic achievement as evidence of White privilege and racism advances a sense of responsibility to make changes for the better. Rather than blaming the students, educators and the education system are clearly responsible in this perspective. In this sense, what my teacher-education students have insisted over the years is true: "It's not them, it's not their fault."

While critical race theory and critical studies in whiteness create a lens through which racism is readily illuminated, it is the case that few educators indeed want to contribute to racial inequality. To the contrary, most educators care for their students and want them to succeed; many adamantly abhor racism. At the same time, however, racism persists. Carefully examining the ways racism is manifested in educators' relationships with Latina/o students and families, as well as at the education-policy level, can help improve the situation. As Balfanz and Legters (2004) state, "We must no longer tolerate the squandered potential, limited life chances, and social malaise that result from poorly educating our nation's youth" (p. vi). Acknowledging and examining the ways racism contributes to this intolerable situation is important work we can all do to bring about much-needed change.

Discussion Questions

1. Marx suggests that everyday racism is typically passive and subtle. Do you agree with her characterization of this issue? Why or why not?
2. Marx suggests that White K–12 educators typically misunderstand Latina/o students, including ELLs, viewing them through the skewed lens of deficit thinking. As a student or educator, have you ever experienced this misunderstanding?
3. Marx suggests that there are inherent issues of racial inequity in K–12 schooling when most teachers are White monolingual speakers of English and nearly half of all students are of color, with many speaking a language besides English at home. What are your own thoughts about this topic? Do these factors influence schooling?
4. How do you think a teacher population that more proportionately mirrored the diversity of the K–12 student population would affect U.S. schooling?
5. As an educator, what are some things you can do to actively work against racial inequality in school?

Note

1. "Status dropouts" are those students who are not enrolled in school and who lack a diploma or equivalent. For a critique of this measure and other ways of determining dropout rates, see Warren and Halpern-Manners (2007).

References

Balfanz, R., & Legters, N. (2004). *Locating the dropout crisis: Which high schools produce the nation's dropouts? Where are they located? Who attends them? Center for research on the education of students placed at risk.* Baltimore, MD: CRESPAR: Johns Hopkins University. Retrieved November 5, 2007 from www.csos.jhu.edu/crespar/techReports/Report70.pdf.

Banks, J. (2003). Multicultural education: Characteristics and goals. In J. Banks & C. M. Banks (Eds.), *Multicultural education: Issues & perspectives* (4th ed., pp. 3–30). New York: John Wiley & Sons.

Bonilla-Silva, E. (2003). *Racism without racists: Color-blind racism and the persistence of racial inequality in the United States.* Lanham, MD: Rowman & Littlefield.

Brown, C. (2005, March 6). Looking at 50/50: Cache, Logan districts tackle low Hispanic graduation rate. *The Herald Journal,* A1, A10.

California Department of Education. (2004). *Language census data.* Sacramento, CA: CDE.

Chamot, A. U., & O'Malley, M. (1994). *The CALLA Handbook: Implementing that cognitive academic language learning approach.* Reading, MA: Addison-Wesley.

Collier, V. (1992). A synthesis of studies examining long-term language minority student data on academic achievement. *Bilingual Research Journal, 16,* 187–212.

Crawford, J. (2000). *At war with diversity: US language policy in an age of anxiety.* Clevedon, UK: Multilingual Matters.

Darling-Hammond, L., & Sclan, E. M. (1996). Who teaches and why: Dilemmas of building a profession for twenty-first century schools. In J. Sikula (Ed.), *Handbook of research on teacher education* (2nd ed., pp. 67–101). New York: Macmillan.

DeCuir, J., & Dixson, A. (2004). "So when it comes out, they aren't that surprised that it is there": Using critical race theory as a tool of analysis of race and racism in education. *Educational Researcher, 33*(5), 26–31.

Delgado, R. (Ed.). (1995). *Critical race theory: The cutting edge.* Philadelphia, PA: Temple University Press.

Delgado, R., & Stefancic, J. (1997). *Critical white studies: Looking behind the mirror.* Philadelphia, PA: Temple University Press.

Delgado-Gaitan, C. (2004). *Involving Latino families in school: Raising student achievement through home-school partnerships.* Thousand Oaks, CA: Corwin Press.

Donato, R., Menchaca, M., & Valencia, R. (1991). Segregation, desegregation, and integration of Chicano students: Problems and prospects. In R. Valencia (Ed.), *Chicano school failure and success: Research and policy issues for the 1990s* (pp. 27–63). London: Falmer Press.

Frankenberg, R. (1993). *White women, race matters: The social construction of whiteness.* Minneapolis, MN: University of Minnesota Press.

Gándara, P., Maxwell-Jolly, J., & Driscoll, A. (2005). *Listening to teachers of English language learners: A survey of California teachers' challenges, experiences, and professional development needs.* Santa Cruz, CA: The Center for the Future of Teaching and Learning.

Genesee, F., Lindholm-Leary, K., Saunders, W. M., & Christian, D. (Eds.). (2006). *Educating English language learners: A synthesis of research evidence.* New York: Cambridge University Press.

Gillborn, D. (2005). Education policy as an act of White supremacy: Whiteness, critical race theory and education reform. *Journal of Education Policy, 20,* 485–505.

Goto-Butler, Y., Orr, J. E., Bousquet Gutierrez, M., & Hakuta, K. (2000). Inadequate conclusions from an inadequate assessment: What can SAT-9 scores tell us about the impact of Proposition 227 in California? *Bilingual Research Journal, 24,* 141–154.

Greene, J. P. (2002). *Public school graduation rates in the United States* (Civic Report No. 31). New York: The Manhattan Institute for Policy Research.

Hakuta, K., Goto-Butler, Y., & Witt, D. (2000). How long does it take English learners to attain proficiency? *University of California Linguistic Minority Research Institute Policy Report 2000–1.*

Johnson, C., & Marx, S. (2009). Transformative professional development: A model for urban science education reform. *Journal of Science Teacher Education, 20*(2), in press.

KewalRamani, A., Gilbertson, L., Fox, M., & Provasnik, S. (2007). *Status and Trends in the Education of Racial and Ethnic Minorities* (NCES 2007–039). National Center for Education Statistics, Institute of Education Sciences, U.S. Department of Education. Washington, DC. Retrieved September 24, 2007 from http://nces.ed.gov/pubs2007/2007039.pdf.

Kincheloe, J., Steinberg, S., Rodriguez, N., & Chennault, R. (Eds.). (1998). *White reign.* New York: St. Martin's press.

Kolchin, P. (2002). Whiteness studies: The new history of race in America. *The Journal of American History, 89,* 154–173.

Krashen, S. D. (1999). *Condemned without a trial: Bogus arguments against bilingual education.* Portsmouth, NH: Heinemann.

Krashen, S., & McField, G. (2005). What works? Reviewing the latest evidence on bilingual education. *Language Learner, 1*(2), 7–10, 34.

Kubota, R. (2004). Critical multiculturalism and second language education. In B. Norton & K. Toohey (Eds.), *Critical pedagogies and language learning* (pp. 30–52). Cambridge: Cambridge University Press.

Ladson-Billings, G. (1999). Just what is critical race theory and what's it doing in a *nice* field like education? In L. Parker, D. Deyhle, & S. Villenas (Eds.), *Race is … race isn't: Critical race theory and qualitative studies in education* (pp. 7–30). Boulder, CO: Westview Press.

Ladson-Billings, G., & Tate, W. (1995). Toward a critical race theory of education. *Teacher's College Record, 97,* 47–68.

Marx, S. (2003). Entanglements of altruism, whiteness, and deficit thinking: White preservice teachers working with urban Latinos. *Educators for Urban Minorities, 2*(2), 41–56.

Marx, S. (2004). Regarding Whiteness: Exploring and intervening in the effects of racism in teacher education. *Equity & Excellence in Education, 37*(1), 31–43.

Marx, S. (2006). *Revealing the invisible: Confronting passive racism in teacher education.* New York: Routledge.

Marx, S. (2008). Popular White teachers of Latina/o kids: The strengths of personal experiences and the limitations of Whiteness. *Urban Education, 42,* 29–67.

McCandless, E., Rossi, R., & Daugherty, S. (1996). *Are Limited English Proficient (LEP) students being taught by teachers with LEP training?* (NCES 1996–IB–7–96). Washington, DC: National Center for Education Statistics. Department of Education. Retrieved October 3, 2007 from http://nces.ed.gov/pubs/97907.pdf.

McIntosh, P. (1989). White privilege: Unpacking the invisible knapsack. *Peace and Freedom,* 10–12.

McIntyre, A. (1997). *Making meaning of Whiteness: Exploring racial identity with White teachers.* Albany, NY: State University of New York Press.

National Center for Education Statistics. (2001). *Teacher Preparation and Professional Development: 2000, NCES 2001–088.* Washington, DC: U.S. Government Printing Office. Retrieved October 19, 2007 from http://nces.ed.gov/pubs2001/2001088.pdf.

National Center for Education Statistics. (2003). *Overview of public elementary and secondary schools and districts: School year 2001–02: Statistical analysis report.* Washington, DC: Lee McGraw Hoffman. Retrieved June 26, 2006 from http://nces.ed.gov/pubs2003/2003411.pdf.

National Center for Education Statistics. (2006). *The condition of education 2006 in brief.* U.S. Department of Education: Institute of Education Sciences. Retrieved September 23, 2007 from http://nces.ed.gov/pubs2006/2006072.pdf.

National Center for Education Statistics. (2007). *The condition of education 2007. Indicator six. Language minority school age children* (NCES 2007–064). Washington, DC: U.S. Government

Printing Office. Retrieved September 21, 2007 from http://nces.ed.gov/programs/coe/2007/pdf/06_2007.pdf.

National Center for English Language Acquisition. (2006). *The growing number of limited English proficient students 1994–1995 to 2004–2005.* Retrieved September 23, 2007 from www.ncela.gwu.edu/policy/states/reports/statedata/2004LEP/GrowingLEP_0405_Nov06.pdf.

National Education Association. (2003, August). *Status of the American public school teacher 2000–2001.* Washington, DC: NEA Research. Retrieved June 26, 2006 from www.nea.org/edstats/images/status.pdf.

Omi, M., & Winant, H. (1994). *Racial formation in the United States: From the 1960s to the 1990s.* New York: Routledge and Kegan Paul.

Orfield, G., & Lee, C. (2004). *"Brown" at 50: King's dream or "Plessy's" nightmare?* Cambridge, MA: The Civil Rights Project at Harvard University.

Ovando, C. J., Combs, M. C., & Collier, V. P. (2006). *Bilingual & ESL classrooms: Teaching in multicultural contexts* (4th ed.). New York: McGraw-Hill.

Ramirez, J., Yuen, S. D., Ramey, D. R., Pasta, D. J., & Billings, D. K. (1991). *Longitudinal study of structured English immersion strategy, early-exit and late-exit transitional bilingual education programs for language minority children.* Washington, DC: US Office of Policy and Planning.

Rodriguez, N. (1998). Emptying the content of Whiteness: Toward an understanding of the relation between Whiteness and pedagogy. In J. Kincheloe & S. Steinberg (Eds.), *White reign* (pp. 31–62). New York: St. Martin's Press.

Rose, M. (1989). *Lives on the boundary: The struggles and achievements of America's underprepared.* New York: Free Press.

Samway, K. D., & McKeon, D. (2007). *Myths and realities: Best practices for English language learners* (2nd ed.). Portsmouth, NH: Heinemann.

San Miguel, G., & Valencia, R. R. (1998). The Treaty of Guadalupe Hidalgo to *Hopwood*: The educational plight and struggle of Mexican Americans in the Southwest. *Harvard Educational Review, 66,* 353–412.

Scheurich, J. (1993). Toward a White discourse on White racism. *Educational Researcher, 22*(8), 5–10.

Shome, R. (1999). Whiteness and the politics of location: Postcolonial reflections. In T. Nakayama & J. Martin (Eds.), *Whiteness: The communication of social identity* (pp. 107–128). Thousand Oaks, CA: Sage Publications, Inc.

Singley, B. (Ed.). (2002). *When race becomes real.* Chicago, IL: Lawrence Hill Books.

Swanson, C. (2004). *Who graduates? Who doesn't? A statistical portrait of public high school graduation, Class of 2001.* Washington, DC: Education Policy Center: Urban Institute.

Tatum, B. D. (1999). *"Why are all the black kids sitting together in the cafeteria?" And other conversations about race.* New York: Basic Books.

Thomas, W., & Collier, V. (1997). School effectiveness for language minority students. NCBE Resource Collection Series, No. 9. *National Clearing House for Bilingual Education.*

Trueba, H. T. (1998). Mexican immigrants from El Rincón: A case study of resilience and empowerment. *TESOL Quarterly, 7,* 12–17.

Valencia, R. R. (Ed.). (1997). *The evolution of deficit thinking: Educational thought and practice.* London: Falmer Press.

Valencia, R. R., & Black, M. (2002). "Mexican Americans don't value education!" – on the basis of the myth, myth making, and debunking. *Journal of Latinos and Education, 1,* 81–103.

Valenzuela, A. (1999). *Subtractive schooling: US-Mexican youth in the politics of caring.* Albany, NY: State University of New York Press.

Warren, J. R., & Halpern-Manners, A. (2007). Is the glass emptying or filling up? Reconciling divergent trends in high school completion and dropout. *Educational Researcher, 36,* 335–343.

Wellman, D. (1977). *Portraits of White racism.* Cambridge: Cambridge University Press.

Part II

Racializing Discourses and Identity Construction in Educational Settings

Racial and ethnic identities are constructed in the web of everyday discourses and educational practices. Students are often constructed as the *Other* by their teachers and peers, whereas culturally responsive pedagogy affirms students' racial backgrounds as positive assets. It is important to understand that the contemporary discourse of racialization tends to discuss racial categorization in cultural terms. This indicates the need to deconstruct discourses of cultural difference from a racialized point of view. Part II features work that addresses issues of identity construction in relation to racialized discourses.

Chapter 6, "Uninhabitable Identifications: Unpacking the Production of Racial Difference in a TESOL Classroom" takes us to a university ESL class in Australia. Constance Ellwood discusses racialization processes in a classroom of students learning English in a second language program. Drawing on the interview and observation data collected as part of an ethnographic study of teacher and student subjectivities, Ellwood analyzes small moments of classroom interaction and demonstrates the ways in which discourses of cultural difference served to fix the identities of the Japanese students in the class. The chapter proposes that one way to disrupt and transform such a racialization process is to employ Judith Butler's notion of the unintelligibility of subjectivity. The author argues that allowing the other to remain unintelligible avoids the tendency of thought to limit itself to what is already known.

Chapter 7, "Understanding the Racialized Identities of Asian Students in Predominantly White Schools," sets a stage in the U.S. South, where the demographics have traditionally been divided into Whites and African Americans. Using Asian Critical Theory as a frame of analysis, Lan Hue Quach, Ji-Yeon O. Jo, and Luis Urrieta, Jr. explore racial relations and racism experienced by nine Asian students who attended predominantly White schools. Interviews with them revealed that schools are a powerful contributing force in the racialization of Asian students. These students were exposed to messages reflecting anti-bilingual sentiments, explicit forms of racism, linguistic imperialism, and the devaluation of heritage languages. The authors discuss the intersection between race, language, and identity along with implications for educators.

In Chapter 8, "Classroom Positionings and Children's Construction of Linguistic and Racial Identities in English-Dominant Classrooms," Laurie Katz and Ana Christina DaSilva Iddings present two case studies of minority children that are juxtaposed to explore the role of power dynamics in linguistically integrated classrooms in the United States. The first study explores the ways in which identity is constructed for two recently arrived second-grade Mexican students and their families with beginning levels of English proficiency. The second study examines the identity construction of African American children in preschool and kindergarten through their oral and written narratives. Utilizing a microethnographic research approach, Katz and Iddings explore how the children positioned themselves and were positioned in relationship to others, how their use of language influenced these positionings, and how the teachers functioned as mediators of their students' constructions of identity in the two distinct case studies. The contrast between the two studies underscores the integration of students' racial, linguistic, and cultural experiences.

In Chapter 9, "Race and Technology in Teacher Education: Where Is the Access?" Francis Bangou and Shelley Wong explore intersections of race and technology through a qualitative study of two Master of Education (M.Ed.) foreign- and second language pre-service teachers, a Latina woman and an African American woman, who learned how to use computer technology to teach Spanish at a large Midwestern university in the United States. The authors discuss how teacher-education programs can support increased access to technology for racial-minority students and argue that the learning experiences of these two pre-service teachers were successful in part because they had the opportunity to reconstruct and reconfigure the technology that was available to them to assert their racialized pedagogical and professional identities and challenge racial stereotypes.

Turning to the Canadian context, in Chapter 10, "Operating Under Erasure: ~~Race~~/ Language/Identity," Awad Ibrahim discusses racialization and how it is connected to identity and second language acquisition. Reviewing the literature and exploring an ethnographic research project that the author conducted in an urban Franco-Ontarian high school in southwestern Ontario, Canada, the author demonstrates that race is salient, if not absolutely pivotal, in the process of second language learning. In this study, a group of French-speaking immigrant and continental African refugee youths enters a social imaginary where they are already constructed as Blacks. This imaginary impacts how their social identities are formed, whom they identify with, and what they learn. They learn Black English as a second language (BESL), which they access in and through hip-hop culture and the language of rap.

6   Uninhabitable Identifications

Unpacking the Production of Racial Difference in a TESOL Classroom

Constance Ellwood

Pre-reading Questions

In contemporary public discourse, the concept of cultural difference is often used as a safer arena to discuss racial difference. Constance Ellwood examines how cultural differences, as perceived by a White teacher of college-level ESL in Australia, affect the ways she teaches.

- What cultural stereotypes exist about "European" students and "Japanese" students in terms of their patterns of classroom participation?
- How could such stereotypes affect the ways teachers teach?

Introduction

This chapter discusses processes of racialization that occurred in a classroom of students learning English in a post-secondary programme in Australia. I demonstrate, within the complexity of classroom life and the contingency of classroom events, the discursive production of students' cultural identities in the classroom practices of white Anglo-Australian teachers, the cultural identifications of students, and the ways in which discourses of cultural difference worked to fix identities and impacted on pedagogy. I draw on interview and observational data collected as part of an ethnographic research project on teacher and student subjectivities in an English-language program at an Australian university. By contextualizing a small moment of classroom interaction, the chapter explicates the complex intersection of discourses which produce the silences of Japanese students in language classrooms. It also employs an elaborated notion of subjectivity as social identity (Butler, 1997, 2004a; Peirce, 1995), as fluid and constructed in interaction, to look in detail at the specific practices of the teachers and students in the research site and to suggest that Butler's notion of "intelligibility" can be usefully employed to think through strategies of disruption and transformation of these racialization processes.

Race and Cultural Difference

Racism has been variously described as "a social reality with devastating effects" (McLaren & Torres, 1999, p. 49); "an ideology of inclusion and exclusion"; and "an assembly of stereotypes, images, attributions and explanations" (Miles & Brown, 2003, p. 104). In the Australian context, the concept of racism is used as a catch-all notion in the language of ordinary citizens to describe "an array of actions which share the common feature that cultural difference broadly understood is often at the heart of socially inappropriate behaviours which help to reproduce forms of social marginalisation" (Poynting & Noble, 2004, p. 18). In other words, practices of differentiation by cultural background, in reconfiguring social experiences as ethnic or racial ones, produce the racialized other as inferior (Miles & Brown, 2003). The term "cultural difference," by appearing to validate difference, disguises the realities of the combined action of power and prejudice, and has been accused of allowing the "violent essentializing of racism" (May, 1999a, p. 24) to be ignored. As Hage has shown, attitudes of tolerance towards cultural difference can be "a form of symbolic violence in which a mode of domination is presented as a form of egalitarianism" (1998, p. 87). It is such attitudes that I discuss here.

Some Aspects of Race in Australia

Debates over the meaning of race and racism have tended to be "sealed within national boundaries" (McLaren & Torres, 1999, p. 5). Whereas, in the United States, the historical significance of slavery has had a crucial impact on conceptions of black–white relations and notions of race (May, 1999b; McLaren & Torres, 1999), in Australia the focus has been rather on the dispossession of the aboriginal inhabitants (Moreton-Robinson, 2004, p. viii) and on what has been referred to as the "spatial dimensions" of the settler colonial project (Ang, 1999, p. 191).

The complexity of Australia's location, on the southeastern fringe of Asia and far from its mother country Britain, along with the way it was appropriated by the British as a homogeneous "white" nation, has produced what a number of writers refer to as "the fear of invasion" (see, for example, Ang, 1999; Stratton, 2004). Encapsulated in the now-defunct Immigration Restriction Act 1901, this fear has, over time, been attached to a shifting variety of Asian countries. The Act, known as the White Australia Policy, required prospective immigrants to pass a 50-word dictation test, and clearly targeted Asians, among others (Yarwood, 1964), although political and trade niceties precluded overt naming of who was required to sit the test (Stratton, 2004). Events such as Japan's victory over Russia in 1904–1905 helped constitute the Japanese as being among the distrusted Others who were capable of carrying out this threat of invasion (Fitzpatrick, 1997). Post-Second World War views of Japanese held by Australians consolidated these attitudes of the Japanese as Other in the public imaginary.

Concurrent with the constitution of many of Australia's northern neighbours as potential invaders is the impact of orientalism (Said, 1991), which collapses people from a variety of Asian countries into one homogeneous group. In Australia, racism against Asians generally is high. Research carried out in 1991 showed that Asians were one of the four groups that suffer the greatest levels of racial aggression (Human Rights and Equal Opportunity Commission, 1991). As recently as 1996, this fear of invasion by Asians was expressed publicly in the parliamentary maiden speech of Pauline Hanson, a far-right member, who stated "I believe we are in danger of being swamped by Asians.... They have their own culture and religion, form ghettos and do not assimilate" (Hanson, 1996). The collapse of a variety of ethnic backgrounds is evident here, as is the ongoing role played by Australia's location in the construction of cultural differences.

While the current official rhetoric proclaims Australia as part of the Asia-Pacific region, and the country has opened up, particularly since 1973, to Asian immigration and, more recently, to the Asian international student market, the changes required of the national psyche, to include what was once emphatically excluded, demand "an enormous adjustment in the national sense of self" (Ang, 1999). Resistance to this change is evident today in various forms of institutional racism (Miles & Brown, 2003; Yarwood, 1964) and a fantasy of white supremacy—a "White Nation fantasy"—which, Hage (1998) argues, operates in multicultural Australian society to maintain the status quo and reinforce the notion of the White Australian as master of—and the ethnic/raced body as Other to—this space.

These historical and contemporary social factors provide the background to my discussion. In this chapter I seek to recast some practices of cultural differentiation which were evident in the Australian language classrooms of my research. I see these practices as acts of symbolic violence—a mode of domination presented as a form of egalitarianism—played out within the wider nexus of the race relations of Australian society.

The Study: The Program, Students, and Teacher

The English-language program consisted of a range of courses, one of which, Critical Reading/Writing, is the focus of this chapter. The overall aim of the language program was to develop students' English-language skills to university entry level. The students participating in the study comprised six Japanese—four female, two male; five French—three female, two male; two German females; a Chinese and an Italian male. Apart from one German student, all were aged in their early 20s. And apart from the Italian student, who had had only 3 years of prior English study, all students averaged 7–10 years of previous English study. The focal teacher—one of four responsible for the program—was a White Australian in her 50s. She had 16 years of teaching experience but had only taught on the language program for 3 years.

The data was collected from classroom observations, interviews with students and teachers, and classroom audio-recordings of both whole-class and small-group activities. In all, 40 classroom hours were recorded at intervals over a 13-week semester, with up to three tape-recorders in simultaneous operation. Additionally, three interviews, each of approximately 40 minutes, were carried out with each participant. My discussion of a moment observed in the classroom draws substantially on this interview data, contextualized within the social factors presented above.

Researcher Race and Reflexivity

Like the teachers in my research, I am categorized as "Anglo-Australian." This term is used to refer to a white-looking person whose ancestors came to Australia from the United Kingdom some time since the 18th century. As an Anglo-Australian, I have the potential to perform the kinds of acts of white supremacy discussed above, and indeed it was through an awareness of the "ethnocentric delusions" (Murphy, 1988) held by me and other teachers (prefigured in Ellwood, 2001), that I was led to carry out the research discussed in this chapter. As such, I engage here with a reflection on what could have been my own practices. At the same time, the events discussed here were experienced as a non-participant observer in an ethnographic research study. From my position at the back of the room, I viewed the classroom from both etic and emic perspectives; there, I found myself identifying with the students and "morally obliged to speak for those the … system seems to leave behind" (Ramanathan, 2005, p. 295). At the same time, I sought to make sense of the racist practices carried out by teachers who I knew to be, like me, well-meaning and well-intentioned. It is in these ways that my white Anglo-Australianness "colours" my understandings.

One Morning in Class…

Thursday morning, second week of a 13-week semester, second meeting of a 2-hour weekly unit on critical reading and thinking. Of the 15 students enrolled, there are 13 present today, seated at desks placed in a u-shape facing the whiteboard. The students look variously expectant or bored. Some are in conversation with a neighbour; others are occupied with papers on their desks. There has been a bus strike, and the teacher jokes with the students who arrive late, "You've got a good excuse today!"

The teacher has met the students on only three occasions previously. Apart from the cultural/raced backgrounds of the students, she has no information on them. Neither ratings of students' language levels nor needs analyses have been provided to her. She herself is relying on time to clarify her knowledge of the students' needs. In an interview in Week 2 of semester, she says, "Maybe as I'm more familiar, and they've settled in and I've got used to them, and I have worked out what their levels and capabilities are, I'll be able to stand back a bit more." She has been given a class list, a subject outline of only a few pages, and a free rein to develop the syllabus. She knows she must teach Critical Reading and Writing Skills but how she does so is up to her.

This unit on critical reading is one segment of a larger programme of full-time study of, and in, English. The teacher has newly developed a unit based around a theme of wildlife harvesting. Although this was a time-consuming process, she is excited by the materials she has found, from a variety of Web and text-based sources, commenting: "I've got terrific readings, I'm really pleased with these readings." She feels the readings, which address both global and local issues, are relevant to the varied cultural backgrounds of the students and their possible interest in Australia; and materials on kangaroo culling appease the implicit pressure to make the course relevant to Australian issues. She plans to work steadily, over the next several weeks, through this material, gradually building up the students' conceptual understandings of terms such as *critique*, *assumptions*, and *values*.

The teacher begins the class by discussing the answers to the homework from the previous week. In responding to the first question, she seeks to facilitate a discussion about terms that derive from the word "critical." One of the two German females is consistently eager to answer. She raises her hand enthusiastically or calls out in response to every question, leaving no pause time between the question and her answer. She interacts with the teacher in an informal and egalitarian manner, "Couldn't it be …?" or "Oh, I didn't know you wanted …". The teacher allows her responses but also calls on other students to participate. "Anyone else got ideas about this?"; "Anybody who wants to offer another suggestion?" She sometimes addresses the group as a whole; sometimes she asks individuals, directly and by name, but as she does not yet know all the names, some students are not called upon. Is it a coincidence that it is the four Japanese females who are not called upon? In the preceding week, the teacher had commented,

> It's so much easier for me to respond to the Europeans as individuals already, um I learn their names much quicker of course because they're familiar and you have a sort of sense of them as personalities, I can see I'm tending to still see the Japanese- I don't have a sense- I haven't been able to learn their names as yet and I don't have a sense of each one.

The teacher, however, has learnt the names of the Japanese males, an aspect of a differential treatment of students by gender (Sunderland, 2004). Importantly, the teacher's reference to "the Europeans" and "the Japanese" indexes the beginnings of a differential treatment of students by cultural background.

As the class continues, the responses can be seen to come from three or four main players. The German female continues to call out, in a strong, almost strident voice, in response to most of the questions. Two French students—male and female—volunteer some answers. Their voices are noticeably quieter and they tend to use predominantly single-word phrases. One Japanese male answers promptly and confidently in a strong voice when addressed directly by name. The Italian male and a Japanese female respond at length, on different occasions, to the teacher's query whether there are further questions. The contributions to the discussion by remaining students—all female, one German, one French, three Japanese—are minimal or non-existent, consisting of rare one-word or one-phrase answers when called upon by the teacher.

The teacher then divides the students, according to where they are sitting, into small discussion groups and hands out a sheet of questions. She circulates among them, working to keep each group on task and prompting with questions, "Maybe there are some other animals that you know about?" She includes me in her wanderings around the room, coming from time to time to interact with me where I am sitting in the back corner of the room. Initially she had not wanted me as observer in the classroom, although she had agreed to interviews. The problem, she had said, was because she saw teaching as

> developing a relationship with students, and having an outside observer would impact on that because I become self-conscious, and also the whole thing of being the teacher, being prepared to make a fool of oneself ... one is inhibited when there's an observer.

After the first week of class, she had changed her mind, expressing an interest in the content of the research, and in seeing "the difference between the teachers' perceptions of what's going on and the students' perceptions of what's going on." She had said, "I'd really like to know what students think, because who knows what they think!"

The teacher continues through the sheet of questions, asking the students for answers. At one point she asks, "So where do our assumptions come from?" The

Japanese female who had spoken up earlier answers, "Culture, from our culture." From the back of the room I hear her comment clearly. However, the teacher, who is standing barely a metre away from her, does not appear to hear. Instead she turns to the eager German female for a response.

The Complexity of Classrooms

I referred, at the beginning of this chapter, to the complexity of classroom processes. Any attempt to give an account of such complexity inevitably falls short since the multiple ambiguities cannot be fully traced. However, while I will focus here on the conditions that made possible this small moment of "not hearing," my aim in narrativizing this description of the classroom is to foreground this complexity and to show that what occurs in the classroom is always contingent on a multiplicity of contextual factors.

Teaching is an intensely complex business. In order to make the act of teaching possible and containable, we can tend, as teachers, to foreclose on some of the multiplicity of the classroom. Nevertheless, if we are to seek to improve our practice and counteract the flaws that become evident in our teaching, in this case, the procedures of racialization, the question becomes not "why are there foreclosures?" but "what foreclosures are taking place and how can language pedagogy be broadened in the light of such foreclosures?"

I referred in the narrative above to the teacher's restricted knowledge of the students, to students' language levels, to the teacher's questioning strategies to which the Japanese students responded when called upon, and to the eager German student. These are some of the complexities I will take up in attempting to tease out the processes of racialization occurring in this classroom. At the same time, in referring in passing to some of the other aspects which were operative in this classroom, such as my own presence as researcher, I hope to implicitly demonstrate the fragility and contingency of these processes. For reasons of space, my focus is on one classroom and one teacher. However, variations of my claims here played out across all the classroom sites in my study.

I begin with one of the conditions that contributed to this moment of "not hearing": the teacher's understandings and knowledge of the students. I use the word "knowledge" advisedly here, foregrounding the power/knowledge nexus (Foucault, 1978) and discursive nature of what is considered to be knowledge. The "discursive" refers to "ways of constituting knowledge, together with the social practices, forms of subjectivity and power relations which inhere in such knowledges and the relations between them" (Weedon, 1997, p. 108). As I discuss here, the teacher's "knowledge" can be seen to be constituted through discourses of cultural identity, and the forms of subjectivity and power relations that inhere in those discourses.

Discourses of Cultural Identity

In an interview at the end of the first week of the semester, the teacher discussed her approach to the unit on critical reading. She had opted for a challenging topic to begin the course because she was anxious that she might otherwise lose the interest of the European students: "I just felt like with the Europeans I had to start this at a level, that they felt they were getting something from it, that they were being challenged to some extent." At the same time, she believed that the work might be too difficult for the Japanese students: "I'm jumping in the deep end with this particular component, starting off with critical thinking, I mean, if I only had Japanese in this class I wouldn't dream of talking about assumptions from the beginning."

The teacher's understanding of the students appears to align the Europeans, as a homogeneous group, with the greater capability to do this work of critical thinking, and the Japanese students, also as a homogeneous group, with the lesser capability. Of interest here are the conditions that have made this view possible, given that, as mentioned above, the teacher's explicit knowledge of these particular students was limited to information about their cultural background. From what source of knowledge then, does the teacher draw understandings of the Japanese students as less capable of critical thinking?

Discussions of categorization of language learners according to stereotypes of cultural identity are familiar in the literature (Harklau, 2000; Holliday, 1999; Kramsch, 1999; Kubota, 1999; Spack, 1997; Thesen, 1997). The motivation for such categorization is normally well-founded and well-intentioned; it issues from an attempt to clarify the struggles that students may have with their language-learning tasks. And this desire to clarify itself issues from the teacher's need to shape the chaos of the diversity that constitutes a classroom. But to what extent are we at risk of such rhetorical construction of students' identities leading to stigmatization, generalization, and inaccurate predictions about students' capabilities (Spack, 1997) and to "a deterministic stance and deficit orientation as to what students can accomplish" (Zamel, 1997)? Writing about Japanese culture specifically, Kubota (1999, p. 9) has critiqued work in applied linguistics that uncritically applies "essentialized cultural representations" of Japanese culture, presenting Japanese students as, for example, lacking capability in critical thinking and self-expression.

Discourses that essentialize Asian students generally are evident across a range of institutionalized educational practices (Kumaravadivelu, 2004). The term "passive," for example, has been seen to operate from within "colonialist/racialized discourses" (McKay & Wong, 1996), essentialized discourses of Japanese culture (Kubota, 1999), and "ideological assumptions" behind teachers' constructions of Asian ESL students (Vollmer, 2000). It is one of the major descriptors applied to Asian learners generally in a number of documents relating to language education (Chalmers & Volet, 1997; Ciccarelli, 1991; Liu, 1996; Nguyen, 1988). Evidence for discourses of Asian cultural identity can also be seen in studies that either reproduce or attempt to counter notions of Asian learners as passive and lacking critical-thinking skills (Ballard, 1996; Ballard & Clanchy, 1984; Burns, 1991; Chalmers & Volet, 1997; Choi, 1997; Susser, 1998; Vollmer, 2000). Ballard (1996) suggests, for example, that, on a continuum of approaches to knowledge, Asian cultures tend to be more "conserving" while Western cultures are more "extending." However, more recent research questions the validity of this notion (Doherty & Singh, 2002), suggesting that conceptions of Western academic skills are an imagined pedagogy, a reification of heterogeneous practices.

That the teacher operates from within a discursive frame which positions the Japanese students as lacking in critical-thinking skills and, as we will also see, unlikely to speak up, and situates the European students in opposition to this, is not surprising in the light of this discourse. The discourse appears to operate hegemonically here, in spite of the fact that, as we saw in the narrative above, the Japanese were not absent from the discussion, and one of the Japanese females showed herself to be a contributor not only when called upon directly, and not only when the class was addressed more generally, but also relevantly and appropriately to the topic. Indeed, as subsequent events proved, the operations of the discourse affected much of what could be seen or thought. Whoever the students were capable of being was thus foreclosed by discourses of cultural identity that predetermined the characteristics of all students in the class. For example, when the European students failed in the first week to complete a class activity according to the teacher's expectations of their abilities, she merely commented: "Even the Europeans didn't come up with those questions … so that was interesting, I would have thought that some of them would."

It was not until the end of the semester that the mismatch between the assumptions produced in the discourse and the actual skills of the students became clear. In the final week of the semester, the teacher commented: "I'm actually finding that the good Japanese students are doing very much better on paper than the Europeans."

And it was not until the final assessment task that assumptions traceable to discourses of cultural identity were understood by the teacher to be assumptions:

> I definitely made assumptions in terms of general competency just because of the oral which were not founded at all … you know, the issues—all the language had been—the ground had been laid for the kinds of analysis that could be done and they weren't well done at all … uh, surprisingly by the Europeans, the stronger Japanese had a good go at them, did better than I expected, so that shifted my perspective.

This teacher's understandings of the students can be clearly seen to derive from discourses that are known to be circulating in society. Discourses of cultural identity intersect here, for example, with discourses about silence in which "oracy, verbal competence, articulateness and participation in discussions will be prized more highly than silent participation, listenership, and observation" (Jaworski & Sachdev, 2004, p. 238). In the case of the small moment of not hearing the Japanese female, the teacher's assumption that the Japanese students were not capable of critical thinking appeared to have foreclosed the possibility of what she could hear.

These foreclosures have a productive function, producing the Japanese students as passive non-speakers. Not only was the student assumed to be capable of neither critical thinking nor speaking up, but also, in the actual moment of not being heard, she was produced in this identity of non-speaker/non-critical thinker. At the simplest level, we can see that when one is consistently not heard, one ceases to speak, and one fails to give one's opinion. And indeed, my data shows that, in relation to speaking up in class, the Japanese students, in the first week of classes, were more participatory than in later weeks.

In terms of the symbolic violence discussed earlier, we have seen that when the teacher applies pre-preconceived views about the capabilities of the Europeans versus the Japanese and positions the Japanese students as lacking in critical-thinking skills, she is the animator of the discourses of Japanese cultural identity. These discourses contain, as we have seen, "an assembly of stereotypes, images, attributions and explanations" (Miles & Brown, 2003, p. 104) including passivity, a lack of critical-thinking skills, and a reduced capacity to contribute orally in class. Insofar as the Japanese students are excluded from the possibility of being critical thinkers and speakers, these discourses foreclose on the students' identities, and "an ideology of inclusion and exclusion" (Miles & Brown, 2003, p. 104) is in operation. In terms of pedagogy, and the communicative goals of language teaching, this exclusion can be seen as "a social reality with devastating effects" (McLaren & Torres, 1999, p. 49). Thus, just as racist stereotypes reduce and fix constructions of the other, leading to exclusions and negative effects, so too do categories of culture. Subtle prejudices, in conjunction with power, have the capacity to play out in similar ways, whether we name the action racist or not.

The Discourse in Institutional Practices

In the preceding section, I referred to the teacher as animator of discourse. In order to emphasize that the teacher's practices were not those of an autonomous subject, I turn now to another way in which the discourse operated.

If it is to be effective and powerful, a discourse needs a material base in established social institutions and practices (Weedon, 1997). As is clear from the many studies about the role of school discourses in producing particular kinds of social relations and social identities, educational institutions in general are prime sites for the construction and perpetuation of particular discursively produced practices. One of the institutional practices at the university under discussion was a systematic reproduction of discourses of cultural identity through the enrolment requirements of the course. Only the Japanese students were required to provide an English-language score, and students whose scores were high enough went into mainstream university courses. This meant that some European students had been admitted whose English level was, effectively, too high. In fact, the English courses provided some of them with an easy pass, enabling them to meet requirements for an English component to complete their degree. As one student commented:

> It was good because—so that I can make the equivalence in France, but it's still frustrating when you—you spent like half—like uh—a term of learning nothing, you know, it's frustrating so, um, but still you know I'll have my degree.

On the other hand, the possibility that a European student may be too low in English level was not considered, although it did in fact occur, as in the case of the Italian student who managed the course by emailing his assignments home to friends in Italy to be corrected.

In this particular class then, differences in language ability were formed along east–west lines with the highest-level speakers tending to be Europeans, although, as we have seen, many were relatively weak in writing. This diversity of enrolments may be excused by some as a product of troubled economic times with underfunded universities caught in an unreflective push towards internationalization. Effectively, however, the university's enrolment requirements both reinforced the discourse and produced it, such that the institution itself contributed to the reinforcement of an asymmetrical distribution of power in the class. This in turn contributed to a sense of inadequacy among most of the Japanese students, producing them again as less likely to speak up in the face of highly competent speakers.

The production, expression, and perpetuation of discourses of cultural identity by the institution through its enrolment practices form just one aspect of the institutional constraints on teachers which contributed to their reproduction of these discourses. Other factors, which for reasons of space I mention only briefly here, include casualized and uncertain conditions of employment which impact on teachers' levels of anxiety and hence on their classroom practices (Johnston, 1997; Vandrick, 1997), as well as the impact of communicative teaching methodology that relies on active participation in order to function (Cortazzi & Jin, 1996).

Student Identifications with the Discourse

Thus far I have discussed the role of the teacher in the perpetuation of discourses of Japanese cultural identity. However, students themselves are not blank slates waiting to be constructed by others; they bring their own previous discursive constructions to any context. An additional complexity can be found in the identifications of the Japanese students themselves.

Work by scholars that discusses educational practices in Japan and the way these impact on identity (see for example LoCastro, 1996; McVeigh, 2002; Nakane, 2007; Turner & Hiraga, 2003; Yoshimoto, 1998) tends to support the attribution of particular characteristics to Japanese students. Nakane (2007), for instance, clearly shows how the literate nature of teaching/learning practices in the Japanese high schools in her study deprivileges oral skills. She gives as an example the teacher's dialogue during a lesson in which the teacher is the only speaker and answers her own rhetorical question by writing the answer on the blackboard, prior to speaking it. As a result, Nakane claims, Japanese students studying in Western-background English-speaking contexts, which privilege oral skills, find themselves at a disadvantage. Similarly, LoCastro (1996), discussing attitudes to English-language education in Japan, refers to the fact that spoken language is considered ungrammatical and therefore deprivileged. Other scholars, writing of Japanese students, refer to the importance of concepts of shame, harmony, and modesty; to preferences for silence; and to a fear of making mistakes and standing out (McVeigh, 2002; Turner & Hiraga, 2003; Yoshimoto, 1998). It is possible to claim, then, that such beliefs and practices have tended to reduce the status of speaking in many Japanese high school classrooms and have, over time, sedimented habits of both behaviour and perceptions of self which are difficult to alter quickly given the drive for a coherent and intelligible subjectivity.

The impacts of such habits of behaviour cannot be discounted, yet these attributions fail to take account of students' own goals. While all the Japanese in my study referred to difficulties in expressing themselves verbally in the class, they also all expressed intense desires to participate. The problem, as they saw it, arose from their own inability to express their opinion: "I can't tell my opinion well"; "I'm not used to say my opinion in Japan"; "I want to answer the question freely"; "I want, I want, I want to be, the person who has the opinion, I want to be the person who can say"; "I wish I could be like them [referring to other students in class] but I'm shy. Really, really, really shy." These comments reveal the students' strong desires to develop their speaking capacities in the classroom context as well as their self-identifications with an incapacity to participate as they would have liked. Importantly, this incapacity was seen as their own fault and thus their own responsibility to change: "It's my problem to solve it, it is a my problem"; "My bad, bad character, I shy or I hesitate, I wanna change this point"; "I'd like to know the way to be motivated."

Since most of these students positioned themselves as shy and as unable to speak up, one may wish to claim that the Japanese are indeed generally passive and not able to express themselves. However, while we can see, insofar as they identified with the characteristic "shy," that the students recognized themselves in the discourse, we can also see from their interview comments that they sought to resist or escape it. However, these attempts at resistance were sometimes blocked by the operations of the discourse. As I have tried to show, the discursive constructions of the Japanese students in this classroom functioned from the beginning of semester to position them strongly as non-speakers. Therefore, while we can expect to see traces of earlier educational practices in the later classroom behaviour of students, teachers must also be open to the possibility that some students may be seeking actively to develop new skills and new identities.

Peer Power Relations

As Peirce (1995) has shown, the social context of the speaking situation and the power relations of the interactants impact strongly on what speaking is possible and on whether "those who speak regard those who listen as worthy to listen, and [whether] those who listen regard those who speak as worthy to speak" (p. 28). One of the main impacts on some of the Japanese students' self-perceptions in my study came in the form of the German student mentioned earlier. This student was, at 33, considerably older than the other students and had a very high level of spoken English; she was described by her compatriot as "obviously um overqualified for this course."

While the teachers appreciated her committed attitude, many of the students found her behaviour irritating or difficult: "I think [she] scares me a bit [...] so yep I won't like to work with her" (female French student); "she's really uh, I don't know, I can't find proper word, aggressive. So I feel more uncomfortable than other classes because of [her]" (male Japanese student). Two of the Japanese females found her attitude particularly inhibiting on their ability to speak up: "Her face is so irritated [...] when I see those face expression I feel more nervous or more frustrated, I can't make opinion more"; "I angry to myself—oh why I couldn't understand this question and why [she] is so clever."

The students' comments illustrate the way relations of power impact on speaking and show how "feelings of inadequacy are frequently socially constructed" (Peirce, 1995, p. 28). The German female's higher-level speaking skills combined with her intense desire to improve her English produced an impatience in her which was experienced negatively by the other students. As Pennycook (2004) discusses, the presence of such students can usefully provoke reflection on key issues, such as gender and class. In this case, the differential treatment this student received and the teachers' positive responses to her attitude can be critiqued in terms of the way in which this appreciation obscured issues of power and privilege attached to "whiteness" (Kubota, 2004a).

Problematizing Intelligibility

In the contemporary context of increasing global flows, language teachers may be called upon to manage an increasingly diverse cohort of students. They accomplish this role, in part, by categorizing students according to currently circulating discourses. As we have seen, both teachers and students reproduced discourses of cultural identity: teachers "recognized" students and students "recognized" themselves through familiar "common-sense" representations.

A number of writers have suggested that we cannot avoid representation of students and that therefore such essentializing moves are inevitable. Nelson, for example, claims that we "cannot not classify" since it "is what our brain does" (Nelson, 1998, p. 798). While categorization has indeed been shown to characterize mental activity, if we are to work to counteract the negative effects of stereotyping, we must also accept our potential to resist automatic, unreflective representations of ourselves and others.

Nelson's view also fails to recognize that language operates along binaries (Butler & Scott, 1992), clustering positive in opposition to negative terms and aligning individuals or groups almost exclusively with one side or the other. The discourse operating here worked in a binarized way to align Japanese students with a number of negative characteristics. As well as being attributed passivity and an inability to think critically, the Japanese were associated with unknowability, unfamiliarity, an undemonstrative quality, and an unwillingness to participate. This was evident in statements by all four teachers in the study: "the Japanese are just very quiet [...] so more passive"; "they had a sort of sullen-looking expression but of course it wasn't sullen it was just their 'devoid of expression' face"; "I mean you just sort of resort to clichés: the inscrutability of the Japanese students"; "there's a sort of alien quality there." At the same time the binary operation of the discourse aligned the European students with activity, engagement, critical thinking, and an ability to be forthcoming. They were not only attributed with energy: "we'd romp along sometimes," and "I could really run with that kind of energy and that fluency," but they also tended to be differentiated as individuals, rather than collapsed into a homogeneous whole, although gender, as we have seen, plays a part here. Thus, two of the female French students were described as "great sparky females," and the outspoken German student as "right on the ball. She knows what's going on!" Further evidence for such differential positioning of Asian and European students (see also Vollmer 2000) can be seen in the reduced number of statements made by teachers about the European students generally, in response to the interview question: 'How is the class going?' compared to the many negative responses about the Japanese students. Thus, while the Japanese students tended to be seen as problematic, the European students were more often seen as representative of a norm which needed no comment, by virtue of the fact that it was the norm.

Such binaries tend to fix subjects in rigid categories and fail to recognize the unstable production of identities in social and temporal relations of power. That both the Japanese and the European students were grouped by teachers into one concept, "Japanese" or "European," respectively, already demonstrates a tendency to ignore the complexity of identities provided by gender, class, sexuality, age, place of origin, and so on. As several researchers have argued (Harklau, 2000; Kubota, 1999; Spack, 1997), there are always students who do not fit the cultural categories which are imposed.

Calls have been made to challenge such fixed and essentialized representations of students. These calls have suggested that teachers need to acknowledge the intracultural diversity resulting from the contingent impacts of social context and to recognize the role of the discursive construction of identities in relations of power (Kubota, 2003; Peirce, 1995). Thus, Kubota recommends that teachers learn to recognize "that their actions either challenge, ignore, or comply with the existing power relations" (Kubota, 2004b, p. 27). Teachers need also to resist being caught in binaries—not only the binary of "us" versus "them," but also a binary that either rejects or champions the notion of cultural difference (Kubota, 2004b) and thereby fails to recognize the complex interplay of the diverse influences that form identities.

Acknowledging diversity and recognizing power relations are clearly vital to undermining the hegemony of these discourses of cultural identity. I propose an additional strategy which derives from the notion of identity employed in my discussion here.

Unintelligibility as a Goal

We are both "subject to" and "subject of" discourses. Not only are our beliefs and practices produced by discourses, but perhaps more importantly, who we are is the result of discourses. This means that not only are our beliefs about ourselves and others discursively produced, but also, in order to be at all, we must constantly be aligned with discourses. We may be experienced as unintelligible if we do not operate within known discourses, since any disjunctures or aberrations from normative behaviours can be seen as failures to be properly human (Butler, 2004b). Because of this, any individual seeks his or her own intelligibility through processes of self-regulation, referred to as techniques of the self (Rose, 1999). In order to be intelligible, we draw on commonly recognized discourses. Additionally, these techniques of the self constitute a drive towards a unified subjectivity, since our intelligibility depends in part on our predictability. There therefore exist strong pressures on students to conform to stereotypes consistent with their understandings of their own cultural identities, just as there exist strong pressures on teachers to conform to stereotypes of teacher behaviour. Conforming to discourses allows each one of us to avoid taking up "an uninhabitable identification" (Butler, 2004a, p. xix). There is thus a certain security and a certain safety in being positioned or constructed by others, even if one is positioned negatively. This security and certainty is sought in the name of intelligibility; we seek above all to be recognizable, knowable, and intelligible.

One way around these impasses of cultural identity then might be to propose unintelligibility as a goal. Foregrounding the idea of unintelligibility means looking at habituated and sedimented behaviours for possibilities for change and relies on a notion of identity as fluid, and constructed "in relation," rather than as stable and autonomous. Rather than try to make sense by categorizing, and thereby fixing identities in ways that can be shown to impact negatively on pedagogy, we can strive to remain open, in a state of unknowingness. For teachers, this means avoiding the comfort of "a settled practice" (Louden, 1991, p. xi) which is not able to accommodate the complexity and fluidity of identity. It means allowing ourselves to have our "plans ruined" (Butler, 2004a, p. 130), which means in turn letting go of some of the power to speak others into being. This will also involve allowing ourselves to be addressed by students in some fundamentally new ways (Ellsworth, 1997). It means recognizing the relative powerlessness of students in the rigidly structured domain of the classroom. It means not merely asking students to "name" themselves (Spack, 1997), but will involve "ruining" students' notions of themselves since it must ask them to question, with teachers, the discourses and power relations implicit in their own statements about themselves. Part of this strategy would be to be alert to the actual and possible gaps between "saying" and "doing." In other words, on the one hand, what are the gaps between students' statements about themselves, which we first must be open to hearing, and teachers'—or other students'—perceptions of their behaviours? On the other hand, how can we bridge the gap between students' strong desires to speak up and statements such as "I can't tell my opinion well"? At the level of classroom activities, this could mean a focus on identity in the curriculum, part of which would be to make the copula of the verb "to be" suspect. Any statement which claims that "someone" is "something" can be material for analysis and deconstruction. Such statements, such as "Japanese students are passive," must be shown to be situated within a discursive legacy, to be of themselves semantically empty.

Conclusion

This contextualized discussion of one moment in an English-language classroom has revealed the operation of processes of racialization through cultural differentiation. These practices of differentiation by cultural background lead to exclusions and stereotypical attributions which produce the racialized other as inferior. It is clear that an essentialized, and thus racialized, cultural representation of Japanese students as passive and noncommittal operated in the classrooms in my research despite a critical body of scholarship which has sought to counteract such representations. As my data have shown, even well-intentioned teachers can fall into understanding their students through cultural differentiation processes which are racist in their effects. The discourse of Japanese cultural identity can be seen to have determined the teacher's choice of teaching approach as well as her expectations about students' capacities to participate orally in class. At the same time, students may also identify with racialized understandings of themselves. The Japanese students here assumed themselves inadequate, on the basis of their apparent inability to participate.

I have suggested the importance of allowing the "unintelligible" as a means of counteracting the limitations of teachers' understandings and students' self-stereotyping, and I have offered some suggestions as to what this might look like in practice. In elucidating the idea of the "unintelligible," I have drawn on a view of subjectivity as multiple, fragmented, changeable, and discursively produced in social relations of power. I have suggested that an alternative understanding of students that allows the unintelligible may contribute to strategies of disruption and transformation of the racialization processes discussed here.

Discussion Questions

1. The author describes a teacher's *not hearing* her students in the classroom. Have you observed such instances in classroom situations? If you have, who were not heard and who were heard? What kind of power relations existed among the participants

in the classroom (between teacher and students, or between students) in terms of their gender, race, ethnicity, and other social categories? What was the topic of discussion? How did *not hearing* affect students' participation in class?

2. The author mentions the relationship between culture and race. More specifically, racialized images of groups of people have been replaced by a discourse of cultural difference. Think about some concrete examples. What parallel do you see between the ways we talk about cultural differences (e.g., characteristics of students from East Asia, the Middle East, Latin America, African American heritage) and hidden perceptions of racial differences?

3. The author proposes *unintelligibility* as a goal for understanding students. What does this mean? What kind of problems can *intelligibility* cause?

4. How can we avoid cultural/racial stereotyping and yet recognize and affirm differences that exist among groups of people?

References

Ang, I. (1999). Racial/spatial anxiety: "Asia" in the psycho-geography of Australian whiteness. In G. Hage & R. Couch (Eds.), *The future of Australian multiculturalism: Reflections on the twentieth anniversary of Jean Martin's The Migrant Presence* (pp. 189–204). Sydney: Research Institute for Humanities and Social Sciences, University of Sydney.

Ballard, B. (1996). Through language to learning: Preparing overseas students for study in Western universities. In H. Coleman (Ed.), *Society and the language classroom* (pp. 148–168). Cambridge: Cambridge University Press.

Ballard, B., & Clanchy, J. (1984). *Study abroad: A manual for Asian students.* Kuala Lumpur: Longman.

Burns, R. B. (1991). Study and stress among first year overseas students in an Australian university. *Higher Education Research and Development, 10,* 61–77.

Butler, J. (1997). *The psychic life of power: Theories in subjection.* Stanford, CA: Stanford University Press.

Butler, J. (2004a). *Precarious life: The powers of mourning and violence.* London; New York: Verso.

Butler, J. (2004b). *Undoing gender.* New York: Routledge.

Butler, J., & Scott, J. W. (1992). Introduction. In J. Butler & J. W. Scott (Eds.), *Feminists theorize the political* (pp. xiii–xvii). New York: Routledge.

Chalmers, D., & Volet, S. (1997). Common misconceptions about students from South-East Asia studying in Australia. *Higher Education Research and Development, 16,* 87–98.

Choi, M. (1997). Korean students in Australian universities: Intercultural issues. *Higher Education Research and Development, 16,* 263–282.

Ciccarelli, A. (1991). Adolescent learners in ELICOS contexts. *EA Journal, 9*(2), 7–20.

Cortazzi, M., & Jin, L. (1996). Cultures of learning: Language classrooms in China. In H. Coleman (Ed.), *Society and the Language Classroom* (pp. 169–206). Cambridge: Cambridge University Press.

Doherty, C., & Singh, P. (2002). *Simulating Western pedagogy: A case study of educational programs for international students.* Paper presented at the ANZCIES Conference, University of New England, Armidale, December 6–8.

Ellsworth, E. (1997). *Teaching positions: Difference, pedagogy, and the power of address.* New York: Teachers College Press.

Ellwood, C. (2001). *Dissolving and resolving cultural expectations: Sociocultural approaches to program development for international students.* Paper presented at the Language and Academic Skills Conference, LaTrobe University, Melbourne Australia, November 27–28.

Fitzpatrick, J. (1997). European settler colonialism and national security ideologies in Australian history. In R. Leaver & D. Cox (Eds.), *Middling, meddling, muddling: Issues in Australian foreign policy* (pp. 98–119). St Leonards, NSW: Allen & Unwin.

Foucault, M. (1978). *The history of sexuality: The will to power* (vol. 1). London: Penguin.

Hage, G. (1998). *White nation: Fantasies of white supremacy in a multicultural society* (2nd ed.). Sydney: Pluto Press.

Hanson, P. (1996). Maiden speech to the Federal House of Representatives, Official Hansard 7. Retrieved May 29, 2006 from www.onenationparty.org/MaidenSpeech.htm.

Harklau, L. (2000). From the "good kids" to the "worst": Representations of English language learners across educational settings. *TESOL Quarterly, 34,* 35–67.

Holliday, A. (1999). Small cultures. *Applied Linguistics, 20,* 237–264.

Human Rights and Equal Opportunity Commission. (1991). *Racist Violence: Report of the National Inquiry into Racist Violence in Australia.* Canberra: AGPS.

Jaworski, A., & Sachdev, I. (2004). Teachers' beliefs about students' talk and silence: Constructing academic success and failure through metapragmatic comments. In A. Jaworski, N. Coupland, & D. Galasinski (Eds.), *Metalanguage: Social and ideological perspectives* (pp. 227–244). Berlin: Mouton de Gruyter.

Johnston, B. (1997). Do EFL teachers have careers? *TESOL Quarterly, 31,* 681–712.

Kramsch, C. (1999). Global and local identities in the contact zone. In C. Gnutzmann (Ed.), *Teaching and learning English as a global language: Native and non-native perspectives* (pp. 131–143). Tubingen: Stauffenberg Verlag.

Kubota, R. (1999). Japanese culture constructed by discourses: Implications for applied linguistics research and ELT. *TESOL Quarterly, 33,* 9–35.

Kubota, R. (2003). Critical teaching of Japanese culture. *Japanese Language and Literature, 37*(1), 67–87.

Kubota, R. (2004a). Critical multiculturalism and second language education. In B. Norton & K. Toohey (Eds.), *Critical pedagogies and language learning* (pp. 30–52). New York: Cambridge University Press.

Kubota, R. (2004b). The politics of cultural difference in second language education. *Critical Inquiry in Language Studies, 1,* 21–39.

Kumaravadivelu, B. (2004). Problematizing cultural stereotypes in TESOL. *TESOL Quarterly, 37,* 709–719.

Liu, Y. (1996). Exploring the links between cultural/educational backgrounds and motivation: A case study of two Chinese EFL learners in an ESL setting. *Carleton Papers in Applied Language Studies, 13,* 53–66.

LoCastro, V. (1996). English language education in Japan. In H. Coleman (Ed.), *Society and the language classroom* (pp. 40–58). Cambridge: Cambridge University Press.

Louden, W. (1991). *Understanding teaching: Continuity and change in teachers' knowledge.* London: Cassell.

May, S. (1999a). Critical multiculturalism and cultural difference: Avoiding essentialism. In S. May (Ed.), *Critical multiculturalism: Rethinking multicultural and antiracist education* (pp. 11–41). London: Falmer Press.

May, S. (1999b). Introduction: Towards critical multiculturalism. In S. May (Ed.), *Critical multiculturalism: Rethinking multicultural and antiracist education* (pp. 1–10). London: Falmer Press.

McKay, S., & Wong, S. (1996). Multiple discourse, multiple identities: Investment and agency in second language learning among Chinese adolescent immigrant students. *Harvard Educational Review, 3,* 577–608.

McLaren, P., & Torres, R. (1999). Racism and multicultural education: Rethinking "race" and "whiteness" in late capitalism. In S. May (Ed.), *Critical multiculturalism: Rethinking multicultural and antiracist education* (pp. 42–78). London: Falmer Press.

McVeigh, B. (2002). *Japanese higher education as myth.* New York; London: M.E. Sharpe.

Miles, R., & Brown, M. (2003). *Racism* (2nd ed.). London: Routledge.

Moreton-Robinson, A. (Ed.). (2004). *Whitening race.* Canberra: Aboriginal Studies Press.

Murphy, E. (1988). The cultural dimension in foreign language teaching: Four models. *Language, Culture and Curriculum, 1*(2), 147–163.

Nakane, I. (2007). *Silence in intercultural communication: Perceptions and performance.* Amsterdam: John Benjamins.

Nelson, G. (1998). Comments on Ruth Spack's "The rhetorical construction of multilingual students": Categorizing, classifying, labeling: A fundamental cognitive process. *TESOL Quarterly, 32,* 727–732.

Nguyen, X. T. (1988). Understanding Vietnamese students: A focus on their passive attitude. *Journal of Vietnamese Studies, 1*(1), 19–25.

Peirce, B. N. (1995). Social identity, investment and language learning. *TESOL Quarterly, 29,* 9–31.

Pennycook, A. (2004). Critical moments in a TESOL praxicum. In B. Norton & K. Toohey (Eds.), *Critical pedagogies and language learning* (pp. 327–345). New York: Cambridge University Press.

Poynting, S., & Noble, G. (2004). *Living with racism: The experience and reporting by Arab and Muslim Australians of discrimination, abuse and violence since 11 September 2001. Report to the Human Rights and Equal Opportunity Commission.* Sydney: Centre for Cultural Research, University of Western Sydney.

Ramanathan, V. (2005). Some impossibilities around researcher location: Tensions around divergent audiences, languages, social stratifications. *Journal of Language Identity and Education, 4,* 293–297.

Rose, N. (1999). *Governing the soul: The shaping of the private self* (2nd ed.). London: Free Association Books.

Said, E. (1991). *Orientalism: Western conceptions of the Orient.* Harmondsworth: Penguin.

Spack, R. (1997). The rhetorical construction of multilingual students. *TESOL Quarterly, 31,* 765–774.

Stratton, J. (2004). Borderline anxieties: What whitening the Irish has to do with keeping out asylum seekers. In A. Moreton-Robinson (Ed.), *Whitening race* (pp. 222–238). Canberra: Aboriginal Studies Press.

Sunderland, J. (2004). Classroom interaction, gender, and foreign language learning. In B. Norton & K. Toohey (Eds.), *Critical pedagogies and language learning* (pp. 222–241). New York: Cambridge University Press.

Susser, B. (1998). EFL's othering of Japan: Orientalism in English language teaching. *JALT Journal, 20*(1), 49–82.

Thesen, L. (1997). Voices, discourse, and transition: In search of new categories in EAP. *TESOL Quarterly, 31,* 487–511.

Turner, J., & Hiraga, M. (2003). Misunderstanding teaching and learning. In J. House, G. Kasper, & S. Ross (Eds.), *Misunderstanding in social life: Discourse approaches to problematic talk* (pp. 154–172). London: Pearson Education.

Vandrick, S. (1997). The role of hidden identities in the postsecondary ESL classroom. *TESOL Quarterly, 31,* 153–157.

Vollmer, G. (2000). Praise and stigma: Teachers' constructions of the "typical ESL student." *Journal of Intercultural Studies, 21,* 53–66.

Weedon, C. (1997). *Feminist practice and poststructuralist theory* (2nd ed.). Oxford: Blackwell.

Yarwood, A. T. (1964). *Asian migration to Australia: The background to exclusion 1896–1939.* Melbourne: Melbourne University Press.

Yoshimoto, M. (1998). The dilemma of perceptual changes: A case study of three Japanese ESL students. *Carleton Papers in Applied Language Studies, 15,* 41–64.

Zamel, V. (1997). Toward a model of transculturation. *TESOL Quarterly, 31,* 341–352.

7 Understanding the Racialized Identities of Asian Students in Predominantly White Schools

Lan Hue Quach, Ji-Yeon O. Jo, and Luis Urrieta, Jr.

Pre-reading Questions

In this chapter, Lan Hue Quach, Ji-Yeon O. Jo, and Luis Urrieta, Jr. focus on the experiences of Asian students who attended predominantly White schools in the southeast region of the United States, which has traditionally been structured socially, politically, and economically by the Black and White racial division. Before reading this chapter, think about the following questions:

- What would your experiences be like if you grew up as an Asian student in the southeastern United States?
- If you were a teacher in this region, what would you do to support new Asian immigrant students?

Imtroduction

When I went to college, I had an Asian roommate. I never really knew an Asian person who was like me before. She got me to join an Asian student organization … All of the people I met told me that I was definitely a "twinkie." Other people called me a "banana." When I asked them what they meant, they all laughed and said that I may be "yellow on the outside", but I was "definitely white on the inside." I told them that growing up, I never had an Asian friend before … They told me that it was pretty obvious and started laughing. I still think a lot about that.

(Anna, self-identified Asian-American female student)

For immigrant children in the United States, school remains the primary site for learning English as a second language and identity development (Suarez-Orozco & Suarez-Orozco, 2001; Valdés, 2001). The increase of Latinos and Asians in the southeastern regions of the United States has changed the racial composition of many classroom spaces that have been historically White and Black. Understanding the schooling experiences of these new immigrant groups has great implications for educators and administrators. While research on Latinos in this area has emerged, few studies have examined race, identity, and language issues as they relate to Asian students.

Wu (2002) states: "More than anything else that unites us, everyone with an Asian face living in America is afflicted by the perpetual foreigner syndrome" (p. 79). Even

U.S.-born Asian Americans are often asked where they are *really* from. Assimilated Asian students with flawless American accents also negotiate this perpetual-foreigner syndrome while finding acceptable racialized identities within their own Asian communities. Anna's case above reflects this complex racial-identity struggle. Although Anna acknowledged herself as both Asian and American, she was often judged as not Asian enough or was critiqued for, in her own words, "knowing nothing Asian." Anna's experience provides insight into the complexities of racial and language-identity constructions for Asian students in North Carolina.

Using semi-structured life interviews, this chapter explores nine Asian students' educational experiences in North Carolina who entered the school system before a sizeable presence of non-Black minorities emerged. In this analysis are embedded discussions of how racialized experiences contribute to and shape Asian students' linguistic, cultural, and racial identities. We argue that our informants' experiences greatly differ from students in areas of the United States that have historically received generations of immigrants such as California, Texas, and New York (Zhou, 2003). For the Asian students in our study, their language and identity development was influenced by the implicit and explicit assimilationist messages received in predominantly White schools.

Asians in North Carolina

While Asian and Latina/o immigrant populations in the United States show an overall increase, these groups have grown dramatically in states like North Carolina[1] (Wortham, Murillo, & Hamann, 2002; Wainer, 2004). Unlike historically identified primary immigrant destination states, these new growth areas[2] are populated by mostly newcomer immigrants (Fix & Passel, 2003). While Latino students have become a research focus in these areas (Wainer, 2004; Wortham et al., 2002), far less emphasis has been placed on studying Asian students in the southeastern United States. Asians represent the second-largest immigrant group and understanding their experiences is important and timely.

Some 12.5 million Asians and Pacific Islanders live in the United States and constitute 4.4% of the total population (Reeves & Bennett, 2003). While 51% of Asians live in the west, 19% live in the southern[3] United States. The U.S. Census Bureau (2005) reported that approximately 156,000 Asians lived in North Carolina in 2005. Compared to other minority groups, Asian students are in schools with the smallest concentration of their own racial group and are considered "the most integrated and by far the most likely to attend multiracial schools" (Orfield & Lee, 2005, p. 3).

Asians' socioeconomic status and educational attainment data in North Carolina contribute to perceptions of their overall success. Economic data indicate that a large portion of the Asian workforce is concentrated in managerial, professional, and successful self-employed occupations (Reeves & Bennett, 2003). For example, Asians own 13.1% of all minority businesses in North Carolina, with the majority of these respectively owned by East Indians, Koreans, and Chinese (Reeves & Bennett, 2003).

Asian students' educational achievement is also high compared to other minority students. Nationally, 88% of the Asian school-aged population graduate from high school and have the highest proportion of college graduates (Stoops, 2004). Of the overall 25 or older U.S. population, 50% of Asians had Bachelor degrees compared to 30% of non-Hispanic Whites and 17% of Blacks. Consistent with national trends, 79% of Asians complete high school in North Carolina; the highest minority group completion rate. While economic status and high educational achievement reports provide a general snapshot of this population, these data often fail to account for the great diversity and struggles within the larger pan-ethnic Asian label.

The Asian label represents the most diverse racial, ethnic, linguistic, and class grouping in the United States. For example, while some studies show that Southeast Asian refugees have adapted well to U.S. life, other evidence suggests the contrary. Cambodians, Hmong, and Laotians experience educational underachievement, language barriers, gang involvement, and teen pregnancy (Smith-Hefner, 1999; Zhou & Bankston, 1998). Southeast Asian refugees account for nearly 30% of the Asian population in North Carolina.

When the participants in this study attended school, Asian (and Latino) students in North Carolina classrooms marked the beginning of an increased racial diversity in a traditionally racially dichotomous region. Unlike in the west with sizeable ethnic communities (i.e. Chinatowns, Korea towns, Little Saigon, etc.) and greater opportunities for cross-cultural interactions, the Asian students in our study were limited in this regard. Even with an increasing diversity in the media, the cultural norms that most influenced these Asian students came from the White mainstream.

Adding to the complexity, the students in this study entered North Carolina classrooms when teachers had little exposure to training and preparation for teaching culturally and linguistically diverse populations. As a result, the Asian students in this study were often invisible in their schools, to teachers and to administrators.

Theoretical Framework

To understand the complexity of race, racial relations, and racism in our participants' fluid and dynamic language-learning experiences and racialized identities, we drew from the existing literature on race, language acquisition, and identity development in immigrant children, while focusing on Critical Race Theory (CRT) and Asian Critical Theory (AsianCrit) as the primary lens for data interpretation. Rather than trying to fit our participants' narratives into a rigid frame or within a particular theoretical model, we acknowledge the influence of these multiple lenses. We also tried to understand our participants' lives in their own terms (Phillion, 1999). Using "predetermined structures and theories to categorize" does little to understand the lives of those who share them with us (Phillion, He, & Connelly, 2005, p. 10).

Intersections of Race, Language, and Identity

Omi and Winant (1993) provide a working definition of race: "[Race is] a concept which signifies and symbolizes social conflicts and interests by referring to different types of human bodies." These "different types" are not based on biological differences; rather, they are socially and historically constructed (p. 55). The concept of race has also been re/articulated not only legally, but also through social and political struggles (Jo, 2004).

Racial identities are inextricably related to linguistic identities for many Asian students in the United States. Skutnabb-Kangas (1988) used "linguicism" or "linguistic racism" to refer to the ideologies and structures which are used to legitimate, effectuate, and reproduce an unequal division of power and resources (both material and non-material) between groups which are defined on the basis of language (on the basis of their mother tongues).

(p. 13)

U.S. linguicism creates inferior identities for nonnative English speakers and ethnolinguistic minority groups; maintaining social hierarchies based on linguistic membership (Skutnabb-Kangas, 1988). Policing Standard English as the only valid linguistic form subordinates and devalues the identities and experiences of ethnolinguistic-minority students, including African Americans (Alim, 2004). Exclusionary/assimilationist school programs (Cummins, 2001) overtly devalue nonstandard dialects and languages, as do uncritical multicultural curricula that essentialize the nonwhite "Other" (Kubota, 1999, 2001).

The imposition of mainstream cultural capital through linguistic forms of power is often at the cost of non-English-speaking students' heritage languages (Skutnabb-Kangas, 2000). U.S. educational schools and institutions do not actively promote bilingual and bicultural identity development. As a consequence, there has been a steady loss of primary-heritage languages (Darder, 1991; Wong Fillmore, 1991). Meanwhile implicit linguistic codes in the culture of power are never clearly revealed to non-Standard English speakers (Delpit, 1995), while the expectation is for these students to somehow learn these codes. To achieve a fully perceived American identity, immigrants and other minorities are encouraged to speak English (Tollefson, 2000) while trying to fit into the whitestream,[4] often at the cost of home languages and cultures.

Language is inseparable from cultural identity (Anzaldúa, 1999; Schmidt, 2000), and race, language, and cultural identity development is directly influenced by social contexts. For the English-language learner (ELL), schools become the place where interactions with native English speakers significantly shape their own self-perceptions (Ibrahim, 1999; McKay & Wong, 1996). Ethnographic studies of ELLs' racialized identity constructions find that this is a complex, multiple, and fluid process (Harklau, 2000; McKay & Wong, 1996). The politics of these cultural and linguistic identities are directly connected to power distributions (privileges accorded or denied) to cultural groups in the United States (Crawford, 2000). Language thus contains more than just linguistic elements and is considered a powerful social medium (Kouritzin, 1999). Racial, cultural, and linguistic identities for minority students are formed within this whitestream U.S. context.

Our participants' language experiences were particularly informed by the dichotomized racial school contexts they attended. We discuss participants' language experiences as personal language history-in-process, composed of each individual's overall experiences with language. Personal language experiences consisted of daily interpersonal language interactions shaping and reshaping personal language histories throughout one's life.

Asian Critical Theory

Although CRT has made contributions in understanding the intersectionality and race in the experiences of students of color (Ladson-Billings, 1995, 2000; Wortham et al.,

2002), scholars have critiqued CRT for failing to recognize the experiences of non-Black minorities. As a result various subgroups within CRT have emerged: Latina/o Critical Theory (LatCrit), Asian Critical Theory (AsianCrit), Feminist Critical Theory, Queer Critical Theory (QueerCrit), and Tribal Critical Theory (Wing, 2001). Each group emphasizes their unique experiences and subject positions while recognizing the multiple lenses and identities existent within their cultural communities. To understand the complex racial-identity experiences of the nine Asian students in this study, we used AsianCrit to frame our theoretical and analytical lenses. We also acknowledge other CRT subgroups' contributions, since Asian Americans also occupy various subject positions such as gender, sexuality, and multiraciality.

Both LatCrit and AsianCrit scholars share similar experiences on issues related to immigration, language rights, accent, citizenship, and discrimination based on national origin (Delgado & Stefancic, 2001); however, they acknowledge the differences that exist within groups in U.S. history. LatCrit and AsianCrit scholars also acknowledge the diverse experiences each community has in racialization processes, discrimination, representation, history, and politics.

AsianCrit scholars assert that Asians are often portrayed as the "reticent minority," the group that fails to speak up for their rights and is complacent about racial discrimination. Asians are also portrayed by neo-conservatives as the model minority (Lee, 2001). Scholars also argue that these seemingly unharmful and often celebratory images are actually used to manipulate Asians and to uphold White privilege by dividing minority groups in the United States.

Asian students generally experience school negotiating both negative and positive stereotypes created and maintained by the popular press and media (Spring, 2004). Historically, these images include the coolie, the deviant, the yellow peril, the model minority, and the gook (R. Lee, 1999). Whether portrayed as a servile Asian worker, an opium abuser, or an immigrant ready to overrun the U.S. labor market, Asians have been constructed as a "threat to the American national family" (Spring, 2004, p. 67). Although the model minority and model student stereotypes present positive Asian-American representations, they also create racial tensions with African Americans and Latina/os when used to criticize low-achieving minority students (Spring, 2004). The model minority stereotype is highly condescending toward all racial minorities. Wu (2002) states that this "impl[ies] that Asian Americans are remarkable, given that we are a racial minority group. We are 'model' at least for people of color" (p. 59).

How the Asian students in our study experienced race, racism, and racial relations in North Carolina significantly impacted their identity constructions and language-learning experiences. This chapter focuses on the Asian students' struggles with the stereotypes they faced as part of the *model minority* (S. Lee, 2001) and the pressures to be *whitened* (Ong, 1999). We use AsianCrit not only to hear the silenced voices of Asian college students in North Carolina, but also use their narratives to uncover the deeply engrained social and educational racism and inequity they experienced. We hope to highlight Asian students' struggles as they learned to negotiate racism and assimilationist policies.

Method

Qualitative researchers have long recognized the power of voice and the use of narrative in examining lived experiences (Denzin & Lincoln, 2001; Kramp, 2004). According to Delgado and Stefancic (2001), "critical race theorists have built on everyday experiences with perspective, viewpoint, and the power of stories and persuasion to come to a better understanding of how Americans see race" (p. 38). Through the use of CRT and AsianCrit, we use both narratives and counter-narratives to further understand the racialization of Asian students living in an area of the United States where race has been primarily understood through a Black–White binary.

Specifically, we use a retrospective interview methodology (Gándara, 1995) or a modified version of life-history interviews (Davies, 2001) to explore the lived experiences of our participants. These data are presented in context using an interpretive (Geertz, 1973) and non-prescriptive approach. We situate this study in the South and, rather than a limitation, we believe that one of the strengths of this study is the context—one that represents a rapidly changing racial demographic. We used the following primary question to guide our inquiry: How is identity and language development in Asian students shaped by race, racial relations, and experiences with racism in school?

Our Informants

The participants for the study were recruited using a purposeful or convenience sampling method (Gall, Borg, & Gall, 2003). Included in this study are the voices of nine 1.5⁵ and second-generation Asian students who grew up in North Carolina and graduated from high school between 1996 and 2000. At the time of the interviews, all of the participants were attending a prestigious state university in North Carolina. The participants included 1.5 and second-generation immigrant students from Korea, China, Taiwan, the Philippines, and Vietnam. For the 1.5-generation student, knowledge of their native language is usually limited to informal registers rather than functional literacy or is lost completely (McKay & Wong, 2000; Thonus, 2003). Second-generation students are defined as children of immigrants who were born in the United States but whose parents immigrated from another country. All of the participants in this study described having knowledge of their native languages at the beginning of their schooling experiences. The participants also shared similar levels of socioeconomic status.

Table 7.1 provides a general profile of each participant. All of the names are pseudonyms that are consistent with the names the participants used to identify themselves. For example, with the exception of one participant, all of the others preferred to go by their American names rather than their given ones.

Data Collection and Analysis

Data were collected using an in-depth, retrospective, semi-structured life-interview model (Gándara, 1995; Davies, 2001). All of the interviews were conducted over the course of one academic year (2001–2002). During each interview, we used open-ended (Gubrium & Holstein, 1995) rather than standardized forms of questioning. Although

Table 7.1 List of Participants

Name	Gender	Age on arrival	Heritage language	Heritage country
Chris	Male	Born in United States	Mandarin Chinese	Hong Kong
Joan	Female	Born in United States	Mandarin Chinese	Taiwan
Anna	Female	Born in United States	Cantonese	Vietnam
Rick	Male	Born in United States	Tagalog	Philippines
Helen	Female	9 months	Korean	Korea
Michelle	Female	1 year old	Cantonese	Hong Kong
Jun	Male	8 years old	Korean	Korea
Liz	Female	10 years old	Mandarin Chinese	Mainland China
Stacy	Female	11 years old	Korean	Korea

there were general questions used to guide the interviews, much of the time we spent with the participants became more like informal dyadic conversations, enabling both the researcher and the participants to engage in the process of dialogical authoring (Bakhtin, 1981). All interviews were transcribed, and over 600 pages of raw interview data were collected. Additional data included email exchanges about queries that arose after transcription, telephone conversations, and follow-up interviews. The bulk of the data used in this article was based on each participant's autobiographical memory as the archival epistemological foundation (Hoffman & Hoffman, 1990; Pavlenko, 2001).

The investigators sorted and coded interview data individually and collectively to identify themes. Interview transcripts were actively used to triangulate data and to substantiate and/or refute claims (Davies, 2001). After themes were identified and data sorted into domains (LeCompte & Schensul, 1999), specific examples from the interviews were cited to support each of the emergent themes.

Findings

Memories of language exchanges or interpersonal interactions that highlight language issues varied with each participant. Differences in experiences varied with race and within race and often related to whether participants were of the 1.5 or second-immigrant generation. Family culture, gender, perceived cultural identity, heritage-language use, experiences with discrimination and racism, experiences in higher education, including heritage-language and cultural-identity revival, were part of the general experiences of most participants. The following sections highlight the contradictions the Asian students in this study experienced in predominantly White schools where they were part of neither the White majority nor Black minority.

Negotiating School in Isolation

Chris, Joan, Anna, and Rick were born in the United States in areas of the south or southeast. What they shared was the experience of being "the only or one of very few Asian families" in the areas in which they lived. Helen and Michelle were two Asian females who immigrated to the United States before the age of one. Stacy, Liz, and Jun came to the United States in elementary or middle school. Early inquiry into their experiences revealed that despite generational status, all of these informants felt "isolated," "too different," or "very alone" as the "true minority" during their early schooling experiences. The lack of exposure to other students who "looked like them," impacted how they saw themselves. For example, Michelle stated,

> As a child, getting on the school bus was a terrifying experience. I remember throwing up because I was not used to the food teachers forced me to eat. I felt very alienated and alone growing up. I really didn't have any other person who had the same experiences to talk to.

Stacy came to the United States in middle school but experienced similar challenges to Michelle. She stated,

> I think, before I came to the U.S., I had the mindset that my immigration was going to enrich my educational experience and broaden my opportunity. I guess my curiosity of just experiencing American school was a big thing for me. I was in a state of happiness, but within the first week, I realized I didn't have any friends.

With very few other students around who "looked like them," this isolation impacted how these Asian students negotiated their identities. This is best illustrated in the words of Helen, who said that "Having no other Asian students in my school definitely affected how I saw myself. It was hard to hold on to our Asian-ness."

Embedded in the isolation were examples of the racism students felt on a daily basis. Being the only one or one of few Asians in school, the participants discussed how others treated them and how these experiences affected them, even many years later. Jun, for example, showed great emotion when he talked about this time in his life. He described his experiences as "difficult" and stated,

> When I was in elementary school, kids were making slanted eye gestures or making karate sounds, but I thought maybe there weren't a lot of people like me. When I heard it more and more, I realized that I wasn't really welcome.

Others described similar negative experiences. Helen said,

> Teachers and kids at school thought I was mute because I didn't speak. I was picked on and I cried a lot. My parents felt helpless because they could not help me adjust. I remember when another child actually scratched my face because I was different.

Joan shared that,

> When I was in kindergarten or first grade ... don't remember exactly..., I didn't know I was different. Everybody made fun of me when the teacher couldn't see us. I realized then, I was different. I always wondered why couldn't I talk and look like them? Children are cruel and you know they have to learn this kind of hate from somewhere.

These examples of racism in the form of gestures and jokes reflect how these students are racialized and became targets of racial discrimination. In response to this racializing process, students internalized the need to be more than just an American. Many of these informants expressed the strong desire to become a part of the White American culture and took extreme measures to achieve this goal. Participants could vividly recall other students using pejorative descriptors such as "chink" and "gook" to get their attention in the halls. Other students and peers imposed identities on these participants by using common negative racial stereotypes to describe them to others.

Choosing Whiteness

The participants in this study explicitly chose to forge friendships with White students rather than Black or Latino students as a way to gain access to the dominant culture. The participants made purposeful moves of power by choosing White friends, learning Standard English, and changing their physical appearances as a way to connect to the dominant culture while distancing themselves from minority groups who were perceived as less successful.

Anna specifically described herself as "kind of racist" when she reflected on the kinds of friends she had in school. She stated,

> I could tell early on that the Black students were not as respected by teachers in school as the White students. They weren't interested in school and always got in trouble. Why would I want to hang out with them?

Stacy described her conflict with Black students in the following vignette.

> Another incident that happened to me was on a school bus in high school. The bus was very crowded. I asked a Black girl to scoot over and I sat next to her, but she kicked me and I fell. That was pretty traumatizing. I did not say anything and I knew that was just absolutely an immature act on her part. Stuff like that happened a lot with that group so I didn't really want to be around them.

Helen added,

> I learned pretty quickly that the Black kids didn't get as much respect from teachers or other people. They didn't do as well on tests and things, so I didn't try very hard to be like them. I think I was accepted by the White students because I was smart.

Michelle stated,

> I remember picking up on English pretty fast. Once I was like everyone else, I hung around White kids, not Black. I don't really know why. I think because I had more in common with them [White students] ... like making better grades. Actually when I think about it, even when I didn't speak English that well, the few friends I did have were White. I guess I had very little in common with the other students.

In addition, Michelle stated,

> I remember hearing the word "chink" for the first time in high school. I guess I believed that there was no way that could have been addressed toward me since I had a White boyfriend and I wasn't like the other (Asian) students.

Some students had experiences of trying to change their physical appearances to fit into the whitestream culture. Some wore green contacts, changed their hair color, and Anna even talked about how she tried to stay out of the sun so she "wouldn't be so dark." Other students forged and maintained relationships with only White friends. As Asian students who attended school where the majority of the student population was White, many of them experienced moments in their lives where they wanted to look White. Anna described wanting to change herself physically by stating,

> When I was young, I really wanted to be White like my friends, my classmates and the people on TV. There were not a lot of Asians where I grew up. When I think about school, I remember that other kids used to tease me when I was little and call me offensive things. I used to feel ashamed of being Chinese because everybody else was White. I always wanted to have blonde hair and White skin.

For Chris, negotiating the challenges of school required that he forge relationships with White students. In his interview, he stated, "Since there was no exposure to other kids like me, I grew up with White friends, doing things that White people did. I wanted to be like them." Jun described his experience as a positive force in helping him to assimilate. He said,

> When I grew up, there weren't any Asians. I was probably the only one in school. Back then, I affiliated more with American people and there wasn't much conflict. I liked having White friends. That helped me a lot to learn English and how to act more American.

There were also examples of counter-narratives that in fact resisted assimilation into Whiteness. Jun remembered being frustrated with Asian students he knew who changed their names and "acted White." However, although he reported this frustration, he also acknowledged the need for him to develop friendships with students of the dominant culture. Like Jun, all of the informants discussed the importance of assimilating to American culture by learning English well. For many of the participants, learning English ultimately meant that they lost their native languages as a result.

The Cost of Learning English

The students who were born in the United States or who came during their elementary school years all spoke their heritage languages as their first language at home prior to attending school and some of the students were in English as a second language classes for at least the initial few years. All of these students spoke their native languages fluently at the time they entered school. In describing their ability to maintain fluency in their native languages, the informants attributed this to family members.

Michelle attributed her language proficiency to extended family when she stated, "I have lived in North Carolina since I was three years old and my grandmother was the only one I spoke Chinese to. She is the reason I can speak it now." Although despite some parents' attempts to use their native languages with their children, teachers discouraged its use and instructed parents to speak only English. Joan described the effort her parents made to encourage her to be bilingual. She stated,

> My parents tried really hard for me to learn Chinese and wanted me to learn about my heritage, but I resisted. I wanted to fit and be American so I never wanted to learn about my language and my culture. I went to a weekend Chinese language school for two years when I was young, but I just quit. When I tried to learn Chinese by myself in high school, I quit then too because it was so hard.

In contrast, Joan talked about school as a primary influence on her earlier language experiences. She stated,

> In preschool and kindergarten, I had difficulty in learning English. I entered preschool speaking mainly Mandarin Chinese, but in first and second grade, my primary language was changed to English. My parents mainly speak Mandarin, but teachers told them not to talk to us in Chinese. I am fully fluent in listening, but can't speak it at all. It's sad to me now.

For most of the participants, teachers thought that the maintenance of heritage languages hindered their success in learning English. As a result, the participants recalled that most of their teachers either explicitly or implicitly discouraged the use of native languages in classrooms and schools. For the informants who were born in the United States or came as young children, many described teachers and friends as the most powerful influence in contributing to their first language loss. Chris stated, "I learned somewhere that knowing Chinese hindered my brain capacity to use English. It was also difficult to stay fluent because all of my friends were White and English speaking." Despite the efforts of their families to retain their native languages, all of the informants experienced a great sense of loss and remorse for "not being more fluent." As a second-generation immigrant born in the United States, Rick described his experience in the following way:

> Learning English was never a problem for me since I was born here. However, I have always regretted not being able to speak Tagalog. When I think about my language, I feel that I missed out. There is a definite language barrier when I go back to the Philippines. They speak some English but I cannot ever have an in-depth conversation with them or any of my relatives.

For all of the participants, discussing their language experiences was emotional. Despite their current level of fluency or loss in their native languages, all nine informants described learning English as necessary to become fully integrated into American society. Throughout the interviews, all of the participants described how teachers and schools emphasized the learning of English, no matter what the cost. One informant recalled a teacher telling him explicitly that the only language he needed to know was English because, "anyone who was important could speak English and that it was the world language."

Shifting and Contesting Identities

Informants were asked how they identify themselves today and how those identities evolved over time. All of the students described the importance of "being Asian" and tried to claim it as a part of their racialized identity. As college-age students at the time of the data collection, the informants constructed themselves as having a duality of identities or hybridized identity. They used descriptors such as "Asian-American," "Korean-American," "American-born Chinese (ABC)." Jun was quite adamant in describing himself as an "Asian in America." He stated that,

> I identify myself now more as an Asian in America, not an Asian-American because the beliefs that I am holding on to are more on the Asian-side. So, I may speak the American language [English], but I don't really consider myself as a true American.

Another student said, "I see myself as both Chinese and American and never try to generalize myself as Asian American." Some associated language proficiency with levels of "Asian-ness." Rick said,

> I think that Asian Americans have a difficult time establishing an identity. I personally don't think there is one way to be an Asian-American. Some people say that I can't really call myself a real Filipino if I can't speak my own language. You have to realize where you come from and who you are. I am definitely both, even though I don't know my native language.

Michelle described her level of frustration with how others construct her in terms of how much she knows about her heritage language and culture,

> I get really embarrassed when White people ask me questions about my country, heritage or traditions and I have to respond, "I don't know." Sometimes I wonder why I am expected to know this. Just because I look Asian doesn't mean I know everything about Asia.

When they were asked to describe how these identities have changed or shifted over time, all described experiencing states of transition. Stacy said,

> I came to the United States when I was about eleven years old. I identify myself more with Korean, even though I became a naturalized citizen of the United States. I think I find myself kind of in the middle: not completely an Americanized Korean and at the same time not an immigrant.

Anna added,

> Now, I consider myself Chinese-American because of this experience. I am neither here nor there; I am a mix of both. I think it is interesting that I actually have two separate groups of friends—White and Asian. There is never any mixing. I think I identify this way because I was able to spend some time in China. If not for this, I would be like my sister who we call an "Asian blonde" because all she cares about is being White. She even dyes her hair and has fake contacts. I think it's sad. She doesn't even eat ethnic food.

For others, identities were constructed based on length of time spent in the United States and shifted depending on the spaces they negotiated. Michelle told us that,

> Chinese people who come when they are younger are more Americanized than those who come when they're older. I feel lucky because I identify more with the Chinese part of me more now than when I was younger. My parents tried very hard to help me retain some cultural appreciation by sending me to China as much as possible. In America, I feel Chinese. In China, I feel American.

The length of residence was also used as a divider and ruler that decided who was a "real" Asian and who was not. According to Liz,

> There is really no difference between a White person and an Americanized Asian. I think the cut-off age is 10 years old. After that they speak with a little accent and are still really into the food and culture, more so than those who were born here.

Throughout the interviews, the informants described in detail their understanding of race and their experiences with racism. All of them discussed how this contributed to their understanding of themselves. For Joan, race was blurred with national identity. She stated,

> I identify myself mostly as an American. All my friends are American, and I don't really have Asian friends. I do not really see myself as a certain race. I feel that way because I grew up in this area and there were very few Asians who lived here. In elementary school, there were no Asians in my grade.

By conflating national and racial identity, Joan claimed not to see race, reflecting a colorblind view of race. Other students saw race and racial inequity more clearly. Anna stated,

> I had all White friends, and I think I even grew up kind of racist. I never associated myself with them [Black students] or even other Asians because they were not people I could really connect with. I knew it was bad when my mother decided I was "too American," and she sent me away to Taiwan for a year to make me relearn how to respect my culture.

The dominant racial stratification and prejudices did not stop at one-on-one interaction between students and their peers. For many students, their teachers were not the
people who educated them to overcome or critique this racist structure. Surprisingly,
the teachers themselves were often the bearers and transmitters of this persistent racist
practice. Rick stated,

> When I was in school I do remember that one of my teachers once told me that
> you should marry within your race and not to mix. She told me if I did, that I
> would have a lot of problems in life otherwise. When I think back on some of these
> negative experiences, I am amazed that I even identify myself as Asian at all.

Negotiating Gender, Class, and Institutional Realities

While the focus of the study and overwhelming themes that emerged from the narratives were on racialized identity construction and language experiences, it is also apparent that the participants' own gender and class status were intertwined with their racial
and language experiences. As evidenced throughout the periphery of the interviews,
students in this study worked to maintain what was described by Anna as "girl things."
Female students not only made efforts to transform themselves to emulate their White
peers, but also conformed specifically to traditional gender roles and the societal construction of what is an "American girl." The male participants engaged in "boy" activities (i.e., contact sports and video games), while the female students talked about the
importance of image. One young woman talked at length about how important it was
to "find the perfect dress for prom and to get make-overs." Another described the
importance of participating in activities that were "safe … like tennis. Soccer is too
rough."

Expectations from the parents differed from the expectations of teachers, particularly for the female participants in the study. While most of the participants came from
working- or middle-class families, all of their parents had high expectations for them
to pursue professional careers. All female students described the importance their
parents placed on them getting "high-powered" or prestigious jobs that included law,
medicine, or engineering. Some of the participants even talked about how their parents
discouraged them from jobs that "society does not value as much." One of the student's
grandmother, who was a teacher in her native country but worked as a custodian in a
school in this country, told her "teachers do not get the respect they deserve in the U.S.
It's not worth it. They work so hard, but no one notices."

In contrast, some female students described how teachers had lower expectations for
them because they were girls. For a few female students interviewed, they recalled that
many of their teachers expected high academic achievement from them in the areas of
science and math, but were not pushed as hard as their White male counterparts. Some
female students talked about never being chosen to be group leader or the one to
"present to the class." While not the main focus of the study, all of the participants
made references to the role of gender and class status in informing the construction of
these students' racialized identities. These implicit and often overlooked examples, as
described by the participants in this study, reflect the ways in which the institution of
schooling constructs and reinforces gender roles, social class, and racial stereotypes.

With all of these points of intersections, these data show the complexity that exists in the experiences of Asian students in North Carolina.

Emergent Themes

All of these students experienced schools at the K–12 levels in predominantly White schools. As one of very few Asian students in a school where the largest minority population was Black, the participants in this study experienced great conflicts when learning English and in the development of racialized identities. Students felt isolated and experienced much racism in response to the lack of understanding from the community and teachers. This experience contributed to their understanding of what they needed to achieve in order to be successful in these schools. As a result, many of our participants assimilated quickly by learning English (often with little support from teachers), developing relationships with White students, and by trying to act and look like them. Despite their longing to be like their White peers, many were reminded that they were, in fact, different. These experiences, coupled with both the implicit and explicit messages they received to learn English quickly, resulted in their failure to retain their heritage languages.

As deeply embedded in language, identity development for these participants was confusing and conflicting at times. Their memories about race, racial relations, and racism were connected to their language-learning experiences, ultimately shaping their racialized identities. As they grew older, their identities evolved. For most of the participants, it became more important to claim their *Asian-ness*. Their understanding became more reflective and the language that they used was more purposeful. Despite the attempts of these Asian students to acknowledge their multiplicity of identities, society continued to create one racialized pan-ethnic Asian identity for them. The data show that race, racial relations, and experiences with prejudice and racism shaped how others viewed them and how they constructed an understanding of themselves. Although gender and social class were not identified as dominant themes, the role they played in how these students saw themselves and how they reconciled this with the way society constructed them was noteworthy. Ultimately, the experiences of these Asian students reflect the complexity, fluidity, and intersections between, within, and among race, language, and identity.

Discussion

We assert that race is a social construction that intersects with social, political, and educational forces—ones that played out in the daily experiences of our participants in powerful ways. These students had unique experiences as the only or one of very few Asian students in schools dominated by White students. As clearly different from their African American peers, administrators, teachers, and other students could not easily place these Asian students in their existing construction of *minority*. Instead, Asian students experienced school in a space of isolation until forces of assimilation elevated them to an Americanized status. Their language development and racialized identities were shaped through ongoing interactions with the dominant and minority cultures that were contradictory at times and dismissive at others.

Race, situated in schools where these participants were the only Asians, was a prevalent force (during their K–12 and college experiences) in shaping their identities and language-learning experiences. For these students, racial-identity development was a complex process that was complicated by racial stereotypes and societal expectations to assimilate to White mainstream culture. Decisions to identify and relate to specific racial groups while rejecting others were made based on both explicit and implicit messages these students received from their teachers and peers.

Asian Racialization and Identity Renegotiation

We argue that the experiences the Asian students in this study had in their K–12 schools contributed to their constructions of a racialized Asian identity. Despite their diverse national and cultural identities, all of the informants were perceived by their teachers to be all the same. Students experienced racism on a daily basis in the form of jokes and/or derogatory gestures and comments that were based on their physical appearances. Throughout the interviews, we also found that teachers contributed to the racialization of Asian students through anti-bilingual sentiments, linguistic imperialism, and explicit messages for students to learn English quickly, often at the cost of their own heritage languages. Inter- and intra-racial conflicts were also evident in the experiences of our participants. These conflicts often created an internalized racial hierarchy and contributed to the overall racialization of Asian students.

Identities were constructed, co-constructed, and then renegotiated as the participants in this study matured over time. Comments such as "I can't speak my language, but I still consider myself as Asian American" illustrate the dynamic relationship between language development and the identities that participants constructed. Identity, as it relates to language, is both multidimensional and interconnected. While knowledge of their heritage language did not define the participants' identities, their individual levels of proficiency and fluency (or lack thereof) contributed to how these Asian students saw themselves and how others perceived them. All of the participants struggled to find a connection between their own heritage and their American identities. Many also developed separate groups of friends (both White and Asian), and were very careful not to mix these groups.

Implications for Educators

Given the isolating racial context that our participants experienced as immigrant students in North Carolina, this study revealed tremendous gaps in educating students of color, particularly for those learning English as a second language. Unfortunately, the schooling experiences of Asian students in the areas experiencing this new growth were more negative than positive. Consistent with existing literature, these students faced particular challenges in learning English as a second language in limited time and were expected to assimilate to American dominant culture, usually at the cost of their native languages and identity development.

Their experiences in these predominantly White schools show that what has been identified as important for the developing second language learner is still not well-institutionalized. Educators who are uninformed and underprepared to meet the needs of the ELL population will continue to send messages that devalue students' native languages and cultures, ultimately negatively impacting the development of their racialized, cultural, and linguistic identities. For our informants, through both the implicit and explicit messages they received in schools, they learned that they needed to become fluent English speakers and fully assimilated into American society in order to be successful. This success was achieved at great cost, usually resulting in the loss of their first languages and often a denial of their racial and ethnic identities. They learned to negotiate this system of power through access to higher education.

In this culturally rich and diverse society, schools should actively participate in helping Asian students (and other immigrant students of color) to claim bilingual and bicultural identities rather than undermine this development. We charge educators, researchers, and teachers to continue to work as advocates for students who society has constructed as *at risk* or *deficient* by debunking harmful stereotypes, affirming native languages and cultural identity, and forcing schools to re-examine essentializing, uncritical (or in some areas non-existent) multicultural curriculum. It is our hope that the experiences of the participants that we present in this chapter provide some insight into how Asian students are forced to negotiate and renegotiate race, racial relations, and experiences with racism on a daily basis and how these societal forces intersect their experiences with language and identity development.

Discussion Questions

1. The authors mention that Asians in the United States are perpetual foreigners. Why does this image exist? What are the situations in other parts of the world? Think about demographics and immigration patterns.
2. Asians in the United States are often considered to be "model minorities" in terms of academic and economic achievements. However, there are many challenges that they face, as the authors point out. What are some of the challenges? How can they be overcome?
3. How does racism influence the desire to become White?
4. Interview Asian (or other immigrant) students who are ethnic minorities. Ask about their experiences of schooling in the dominant society. What were their challenges? How did they overcome them? Share what you have found out with your peers and compare/contrast various experiences of minority students.
5. Many informants in the study had painful experiences of feeling pressured to assimilate through learning English and abandoning their racial/cultural background. If you were a teacher or a teacher educator, how would you reverse this assimilationist trend in the classroom and school community? Think about some concrete strategies.

Notes

1. North Carolina is the focus of this study. Between 1990 and 2000, North Carolina experienced the fastest immigrant population growth of any other state in the nation (Wainer, 2004).
2. New growth states are areas where the population of immigrants grew at a rate that was faster than Texas, where the numbers grew to 91% in the 1990s (Capps, Passel, & Fix, 2003).

3. The South includes Alabama, Arkansas, Delaware, District of Columbia, Florida, Georgia, Kentucky, Louisiana, Maryland, Mississippi, North Carolina, Oklahoma, South Carolina, Tennessee, Virginia, and West Virginia.
4. Sandy Grande (2000) refers to "whitestream" as the cultural capital of Whites in almost every facet of U.S. society. Whitestream in this chapter refers to the official and unofficial texts used in U.S. society that are founded on the practices, principles, morals, values, and history of White Anglo-American culture, i.e. White cultural capital. We must clarify that whitestream indoctrination is not exclusively the domain of Whites in U.S. society, but of any person actively promoting White models as "standard."
5. We define 1.5 generation using Harklau's (2000) definition of immigrant students who were born in another country but came to the United States as a child and were educated in the United States.

References

Alim, H. S. (2004). *You know my steez: An ethnographic and sociolinguistic study of styleshifting in a Black American speech community.* Durham, NC: Duke University Press.

Anzaldúa, G. (1999). *Borderlands/La Frontera: the new mestiza* (2nd ed.). San Francisco, CA: Aunt Lute Books.

Bakhtin, M. (1981). Discourse in the novel. In M. Holquist (Ed.), *The dialogic imagination* (pp. 259–422). Austin, TX: University of Texas Press.

Capps, R., Passel, J., & Fix, M. (2003). *The new neighbors: A users' guide to data on immigrants in U.S. communities.* Washington, DC: Urban Institute.

Crawford, J. (2000). *At war with diversity: U.S. language policy in an age of anxiety.* Clevedon, UK: Multilingual Matters.

Cummins, J. (2001). *Language, power, and pedagogy.* Clevedon, UK: Multilingual Matters.

Darder, A. (1991). *Culture and power in the classroom: A critical foundation for bicultural education.* New York: Bergin & Garvey.

Davies, C. (2001). *Reflexive ethnography, A guide to researching selves and others.* London: Routledge.

Delgado, R., & Stefancic, J. (2001). *Critical race theory: An introduction.* New York: New York University Press.

Delpit, L. (1995). *Other people's children: Cultural conflict in the classroom.* New York: The New Press.

Denzin, N. K., & Lincoln, Y. S. (Eds.). (2001). *Handbook of qualitative research* (2nd ed.). Thousand Oaks, CA: Sage.

Fix, M., & Passel, J. S. (2003). *U.S. Immigration: Trends and implications for schools* (Report No. UD-035–556). Washington, DC: Urban Institute.

Gall, M. D., Borg, W. R., & Gall, J. P. (2003). *Educational research: An introduction* (7th ed.). White Plains, NY: Longman.

Gándara, P. (1995). *Over the ivy walls: The educational mobility of low-income Chicanos.* Albany, NY: State University of New York Press.

Geertz, C. (1973). *The interpretation of cultures: Selected essays.* New York: Basic Books.

Grande, S. (2000). American Indian geographies of identity and power: At the crossroads of indígena and mestizaje. *Harvard Educational Review, 70,* 467–498.

Gubrium, J., & Holstein, J. (1995). *The active interview.* Thousand Oaks, CA: Sage Publications, Inc.

Harklau, L. (2000). From the "good kids" to the "worst": Representations of English language learners across educational settings. *TESOL Quarterly, 34,* 35–68.

Hoffman, M., & Hoffman, H. S. (1990). *Archives of memory.* Lexington, KY: University of Kentucky Press.

Ibrahim, A. (1999). Becoming black: Rap and hip-hop, race, gender, identity, and the politics of ESL learning. *TESOL Quarterly, 33,* 349–369.

Jo, J. O. (2004). Educating "good" citizens: Imagining citizens of the new millennium. *The High School Journal, 87*(2), 34–43.

Kouritzin, S. G. (1999). *Face[t]s of first language loss.* Mahwah, NJ: Lawrence Erlbaum Associate.

Kramp, M. K. (2004). Exploring life and experience through narrative inquiry. In K. deMarrais & S. D. Lapan (Eds.), *Foundations for research: Methods of inquiry in education and the social sciences* (pp. 103–122). Mahwah, NJ: Lawrence Erlbaum Associates.

Kubota, R. (1999). Japanese culture constructed by discourses: Implications for applied linguistic research and ELT. *TESOL Quarterly, 33,* 8–35.

Kubota, R. (2001). Discursive construction of the images of U.S. classrooms. *TESOL Quarterly, 35,* 9–38.

Ladson-Billings, G. (1995). Toward a critical race theory of education. *Teachers College Record, 97,* 47–68.

Ladson-Billings, G. (2000). Racialized discourses and ethnic epistemologies. In N. K. Denzin & Y. S. Lincoln (Eds.), *Handbook of qualitative research Vol. 2* (pp. 257–278). Thousand Oaks, CA: Sage.

LeCompte, M., & Schensul, J. (1999). *Analyzing and interpreting ethnographic data.* Walnut Creek, CA: Altamira Press.

Lee, R. (1999). *Orientals: Asian Americans in popular culture.* Philadelphia, PA: Temple University Press.

Lee, S. (2001). More than "model minorities" or "delinquents": A look at Hmong American high school students. *Harvard Educational Review, 71,* 505–528.

McKay, S. L., & Wong, S. C. (1996). Multiple discourses, multiple identities: Investment and agency in second-language learning among Chinese adolescent immigrants. *Harvard Educational Review, 66,* 577–608.

McKay, S. L., & Wong, S. C. (2000). *New immigrants in the United States: Readings for second language educators.* Cambridge: Cambridge University Press.

Omi, M., & Winant, H. (1993). On the theoretical status of the concept of race. In W. Crichlow & C. McCarthy (Eds.), *Race, identity, and representation in education* (pp. 3–10). New York: Routledge.

Ong, A. (1999). Cultural citizenship as subject making: Immigrants negotiate racial and cultural boundaries in the United States. In R. Torres, L. Miron, & J. Inda (Eds.), *Race, identity, and citizenship: A reader* (pp. 262–293). Malden, MA: Blackwell Publishing.

Orfield, G., & Lee, C. (2005). *Why segregation matters: Poverty and educational inequality.* Cambridge, MA: The Civil Rights Project at Harvard University.

Pavlenko, A. (2001). Language learning memoirs as a gendered genre. *Applied Linguistics, 22,* 213–240.

Phillion, J. (1999). Narrative and formalistic approaches to the study of multiculturalism. *Curriculum Inquiry, 29,* 129–141.

Phillion, J., He, M. F., & Connelly, F. M. (Eds). (2005). *Narrative and experience in multicultural education.* Thousand Oaks, CA: Sage Publications.

Reeves, T., & Bennett, C. (2003). *The Asian and Pacific Islander population in the United States: March 2002* (Current Population Reports, P20–540). Washington, DC: U.S. Census Bureau.

Schmidt, R. (2000). *Language policy and identity politics in the United States.* Philadelphia, PA: Temple University Press.

Skutnabb-Kangas, T. (1988). Multilingualism and the education of minority children. In. T. Skutnabb-Kangas & J. Cummins (Eds.), *Minority education: From shame to struggle* (pp. 9–44). Philadelphia, Multilingual Matters.

Skutnabb-Kangas, T. (2000). *Linguistic genocide in education—or worldwide diversity and human rights?* Mahwah, NJ: Lawrence Erlbaum Associates.

Smith-Hefner, N. J. (1999). *Khmer American: Identity and moral education in a diasporic community.* Berkeley, CA: University of California Press.

Spring, J. (2004). *Deculturalization and the struggle for equality: A brief history of the education of dominated cultures in the United States* (5th ed.). New York: McGraw Hill.

Stoops, N. (2004). *Educational attainment in the United States: 2003* (Current Population Reports P20–550). Washington, DC: U.S. Census Bureau.

Suarez-Orozco, C., & Suarez-Orozco, M. (2001). *Children of immigration.* Boston, MA: Harvard University Press.

Thonus, T. (2003). Serving generation 1.5 learners in the university writing center. *TESOL Journal, 12*(1), 17–24.

Tollefson, J. W. (2000). Policy and ideology in the spread of English. In K. Hall & W. G. Egginton (Eds.), *The sociopolitics of English language teaching* (pp. 7–21). Clevedon, UK: Multilingual Matters.

U.S. Census Bureau. (2005). *State and county quickfacts, 2005* [Data file]. Retrieved November 3, 2008 from http://quickfacts.census.gov/qfd/states/37000.html.

Valdés, G. (2001). *Learning and not learning English.* New York: Teachers College Press.

Wainer, A. (2004). *The new Latino South and the challenge to public education: Strategies for educators and policymakers in emerging immigrant communities.* Los Angeles, CA: Tomás Rivera Policy Institute.

Wing, A. K. (2001). USA2050: Identity, critical race theory, and the Asian century. *Michigan Law Review, 99,* 390–1408.

Wong Fillmore, L. (1991). When learning a second language means losing the first. *Early Childhood Research Quarterly, 6,* 323–346.

Wortham, S., Murillo, E., & Hamann, E. (Eds.). (2002). *Education in the new Latino diaspora: Policy and the politics of identity.* Westport, CT: Ablex.

Wu, F. (2002). *Yellow: Race in America beyond black and white.* New York: Basic Books.

Zhou, M. (2003). Urban education: Challenges in educating culturally diverse children. *Teachers College Record, 105,* 208–225.

Zhou, M., & Bankston, C. (1998). *Growing up American: How Vietnamese children adapt to life in the United States.* New York: Russell Sage Foundation.

8 Classroom Positionings and Children's Construction of Linguistic and Racial Identities in English-Dominant Classrooms

Laurie Katz and Ana Christina DaSilva Iddings

Pre-reading Questions

Linguistically diverse students are often deprived of the opportunity to express their voices and participate fully in educational activities. However, teachers can transform the oppressive structure as agents for change through their critical consciousness. Laurie Katz and Ana Christina DaSilva Iddings present two studies on young, linguistically diverse students, one on Mexican students and the other on African American students.

- What would effective teachers do to encourage diverse students to express their own voices?
- How would such teachers work with families of students from diverse backgrounds as equal partners?

Introduction

Recent standard-based reforms in U.S. schools have endorsed specific knowledge bases, promoted standard ways of using language, and established a general framework for defining success. Although some of these reforms may hold compelling purposes, they fail to take into account the racial, ethnic, social, cultural, and linguistic composition that makes up the student population. School achievement and graduation rates continue to favor White middle/upper-class students and to maintain power structures that sustain and preserve dominant societal groups. The National Center for Educational Statistics (2000) has reported that in the United States, 28.6% of Hispanics and 12.6% of Blacks between the ages of 16 and 24 years old drop out of school as compared to 7.3% of Whites. In addition, achievement rates in reading and math were still lower for Blacks and Hispanics than for Whites at ages 9, 13, and 17 (National Assessment of Education Progress, 2004). In view of these figures, the circumstances of Blacks and Hispanics in U.S. schools have been a concern to politicians and educators.

Our research focuses on how the social dynamics of classrooms serve to position children in certain roles and identities that function to promote or constrain the learning of students from non-white, non-middle-class communities. This study specifically addresses students from non-middle-class Latino and African American communities. First, a literature review is presented to clarify what we mean by race and how we approach the concept of *positioning* in the study of children's identities in educational settings. Then we compare and contrast two cases: the first data set explores the identity construction of two recent-immigrant Mexican students (and their families) with beginning levels of English proficiency that were included in an English-dominant second-grade classroom and whose family members participated in a family literacy after-school program. The second data set examines the identity construction of African American children in preschool and kindergarten through their written and spoken narratives. The comparison of case studies is used as a tool for revealing and framing otherwise invisible social and cultural processes and derives from applications of cultural anthropology and the ethnography of communication to education (cf. Hymes, 1980, 1996). In brief, as we apply those logics-of-inquiry, by working back and forth across the two cases, variations and similarities in how particular social processes and learning opportunities are realized and contextualized become visible. The findings we report are accompanied by suggestions for mainstream and second language teachers in bridging children's home and school identities.

The Development of Ethno-Racial Identities in Relation to Language

There have been relatively few studies that address how racially and linguistically diverse students construct ethno-racial identities *and* come to validate their linguistic and cultural norms within institutional contexts where (standard) English is dominant (Gee, 1996). The scarcity of studies relating language, race, and identity may point to the inherent difficulties in trying to define *race*.

In his 1994 studies about race, the anthropologist Mark Cohen, for example, concluded that "races as imagined by the public do not actually exist. Any definition of race that we attempt produces more exceptions than sound classifications. No matter what system we use, most people don't fit" (p. 4). It follows, then, that race may not be clearly definable. However, classifications based on race have created human taxonomies, which often favor White, middle/upper-class, monolingual, and monodialectal populations and have frequently resulted in gross exaggerations or stereotypes (Nieto, 2000).

In this chapter, race is viewed as socially constructed and not a biological fact. Thus, it is important to understand how race becomes operationalized as a socially and culturally constructed ideology related to modes of being, speaking, and behaving in a society. In particular, our emphasis is placed on school practices, and on how these practices often exclude the cultural norms of Latinos and African Americans as members of nondominant racial and linguistic communities. For example, students from nondominant groups may be stigmatized and labeled because of their particular discourse patterns, which may differ from Standard English. Therefore, the way these students are positioned in classrooms in relation to their counterpart peers (e.g., inferiorly labeled, grouped, and tracked sometimes for the length of their schooling) can place them in jeopardy for school success (Nieto, 2000). Thus, for our analysis of Latino and African American students' classroom performances in the two different settings we observed, we rely on the concept of positioning, as explained below.

Positioning

The concept of *positioning* refers to the manner in which different categories of people (e.g., men and women, adults and children, professors and students) enter into interactions (Davies & Harré, 2000). The positionings that each individual occupies within certain communities are influenced by the participants' perceptions of their rights and obligations, and of the *place* they occupy in relation to the sociocultural context in which they interact. The distribution of power in the group is closely tied to the assignments and appropriations of rights and duties. For example, a more skilled member of a given community may provide assistance to a more novice member as they, together, work on a task. In this case, the more skilled person may assume the position of a mentor with a given set of skills, while the novice is positioned as the pupil who has yet to learn these pertinent skills.

The concept of positioning moves beyond role theory used to describe a more static social typification, one that is long-term, often formally assigned, not easily relinquished, and with a profound influence on the lives of those who occupy them. Conversely, positioning theory concerns conventions of speech and action that are shifting, contestable, and ephemeral (Harré & van Langenhove, 1999). It is important to note that within positioning theory, human beings are not seen as objects that are caused to behave by forces acting on them. Instead, they are regarded as agents, moved by intentionality, continually seeking to understand and trying out ways of giving meaning to things around them. Thus, individuals act as agents through the mediation of signs including language (Holland, Lachicotte Jr., Skinner, & Cain, 2001). This theoretical stance presupposes that the sense of *self* is an experience, and to experience oneself as having a location in a manifold of places and in relation to others is a necessary condition to understand the self. Viewed in this way, human subjectivities are given significance by the discourses in which they appear. However, it is important to note that certain boundaries apply as an individual negotiates his or her life events. The need to cohere, or to make sense, the need to adapt to situations, and the fact that we inhabit many different discourses, each of which with its own cluster of significations, constrain the meaning that an individual may apply to a given situation. Therefore, this theoretical stance identifies a person as having a coherent identity that is fluid, as individuals who adopt various positions within different discourse locations, while fashioning for themselves, however intentionally or unintentionally, a unique complex of subjectivities with some consistency within their life stories. We next provide an overview of how this concept may unfold in classrooms.

Classroom Positionings

The role of power dynamics in linguistically integrated classrooms has increasingly gained attention in recent educational investigations (for a review of these studies see DaSilva Iddings, 2005). As a disproportionate number of students in the *lower-track* classes are from a linguistically diverse background (Johannessen, 2004), researchers have begun to question how these students are differentially powered and positioned in the language-integrated classroom (i.e., who has power to speak, who is recognized as the *most able*, and who should automatically be uninterested or not be able to contribute significantly to the discussion at hand). Whether or not students feel that they are academically capable, or accepted by their peers for what they have to say, are important considerations for language-integrated classrooms. Lewis (2001), for example, has observed that in peer-led group discussions, language was often used as a way of achieving social and interpretive power (p. 97). In addition to literally having a voice, Moje and Shepardson (1998) discuss power differentials as impacting social and academic positionings, as well as roles and relationships within the classroom. These issues are prevalent in classroom communities where there are inevitable differences in linguistic abilities in English (as the dominant language of the classroom). Moje and Shepardson (1998) further explore how peer interactions influence learning: "peer interaction has been promoted as a pedagogical approach, and yet, we must ask how others' different intellectual, experiential, or social and cultural status shapes the interaction that transpires and the learning that results" (p. 227).

Using examples from a kindergarten class including English-language learners (ELL) and monolingual English speakers, Toohey (2000) examined the social positionings of ELLs in relation to the practices and resources available for newcomers to that community. In addition, she inquired how the social structure of the classroom, its power relations and its conditions for legitimacy defined the possibilities for learning. Toohey's findings suggest that all kindergarteners in her study were actively engaged in negotiating their identities and access to participation and resources in the variety of practices of the classroom community (see Lave & Wenger, 1991). She emphasizes, however, that identity and access to participation in these various communities were historical, dynamic, and problematic for the children.

In sum, this discussion suggests that the social and discursive context in which human beings operate has powerful implications for how students experience a sense of *self*. Our work further addresses the relationship between students' sociocultural experiences and their language acquisition by focusing on children's identities in an educational context. It invites teachers to examine learning situations and students' positionalities in relation to educational purposes and procedures in order to meaningfully integrate linguistically diverse students in their classroom settings. This research places concepts such as situatedness of learning, distribution of the rights and duties of talk, and positioning at the core of the investigation.

The Studies

We juxtapose two case studies; one focusing on Latino students and the other on African American students to examine classroom practices that may influence the learning circumstances of linguistically diverse students. It is important to note that our use of these studies is not to represent the educational situation of any one linguistically diverse group, but to use a comparative/contrastive perspective for identifying and describing practices occurring in these classrooms. There are limitations to comparing/contrasting these studies. First, the composition of the student population is different in both classrooms; one classroom has a few Latino students within a predominantly Caucasian student population, while the other has almost all African American students. Second, teacher preparation and their experiences are different in both classrooms. These limitations, in addition to context variables, probably affected teaching practices within both classroom settings. The authors, in noting the limitations, selected these studies based on better understanding of how language is used and validated in classrooms of students who represent different linguistically diverse groups.

Methodology and Analytical Frameworks

A microethnographic discourse analysis (cf. Bloome, Carter, Christian, Otto, & Shuart-Faris, 2005) was used in our research to examine narratives involving participants' home and school identities within both studies. This particular approach refers to the ethnography of communication (cf. Gumperz, 1986; Hymes, 1974) and was selected to analyze the language in classrooms that referred to the children's positionalities and identities. The analysis involved events from both studies. Events from the Storytelling Study consisted of the children's oral and written narratives from their activities of writing in their journals and telling stories to their classmates and teachers/researchers. The events from the Family Literacy Study were classroom interactions between peers and oral narratives of students' family members and the classroom teacher during parent–teacher conferences. Bloome et al. (2005) describe events as empirical circumstances where researchers can inquire into how people create meaning through their actions and reactions to each other. Within these events individuals' actions and reactions are characterized as linguistic processes in that their actions and reactions are derived from language systems for making meaning.

Transcripts from these events were further analyzed and broken into message units. Bloome et al. (2005) build on the work of Green and Wallat (1981) to interpret the message unit as the smallest unit of conversational meaning. Each numbered line represents one message unit. Although prosodic markers are part of these types of analyses, only some prosodic cues are included in our transcripts when it is important to discuss an issue in the data analysis.

The children's socio-constructions of identity in relation to race and language were analyzed according to (a) how they positioned themselves and were positioned in relationship to others; (b) how their use of language influenced these positionings; and (c) how the teachers functioned as mediators of their students' socio-constructions of identity. Following are the two studies presented, beginning with the Family Literacy Case Study. Each study describes the participants, setting, and methodology.

The Family Literacy Case Study

Participants and Setting

The Family Literacy Study was a part of a larger project designed to investigate the social and academic interactions between native speakers of Spanish and native speakers of English over 1 school year. This project was conducted in an elementary school in the southwest United States. The school, previously characterized by a predominantly White, English-monolingual population, was receiving a sudden large influx of immigrant Latino students. The principal was interested in establishing solid relationships with the immigrant families that were moving into the neighborhood and in creating a family literacy program to support the academic achievement of English-language learners. A second-grade classroom was selected based on the principal's recommendation of a teacher who had designed and implemented a family literacy after-school program, aiming to attain a greater understanding of the family lives of students in her classroom and to support students' academic performances in the classroom. Both adults and children participated in the classes together. The main data for this study pertain to the activities recorded during family literacy meetings, which happened one evening a week, and to classroom observations and recordings, which happened twice a week during regular curricular activities.

The classroom teacher, Ms. W, was a White middle-class woman and a native speaker of English with no background in the Spanish language. She was a veteran teacher with about 22 years in the profession. She had spent most of her teaching career in Special Education resource classrooms and had about 2 years of experience working with English-language learners. There were 22 students in the class. Of the classroom students, 14 were Anglo native speakers of English, two were Black native speakers of English, six others were Hispanic native speakers of Spanish. We paid particular attention to two of the six Hispanic students because they had recently emigrated from Mexico (resided in the United States for less than 5 years) and were thus considered newcomers to the classroom community.

Procedures

The researcher (author, DaSilva Iddings), is a Latina who immigrated to the United States as an adult and speaks English and Spanish fluently. She served as a translator during parent–teacher conferences and on other many occasions upon teacher's request. She was a participant observer in the classroom as well as in the Family Literacy program held after school. The Family Literacy Program consisted mostly of parent–teacher conferences with the purpose of helping parents support their children's academic progress at home. These conferences were held with the aid of a translator (who was also the researcher) and served to inform the teacher about children's experiences at home. Social and academic interactions between teachers and students as well as among peers were recorded. In addition, the researcher interviewed the teacher throughout the investigation to obtain a general understanding of her pedagogical beliefs regarding second language learners and to determine if she had any changes in these beliefs over time.

Ongoing interviews were also conducted with the participating students (in English and in Spanish) as well as their parents (in Spanish). These interviews provided information regarding the families' cultural backgrounds as well as further insight into the students' classroom interactions. There were approximately 30 hours of video- and audio-tapes of interviews and of regular classroom interactions. Trustworthiness of findings was ensured through the use of prolonged engagement (i.e., long-term observation in the field), purposive sampling, triangulation of sources (i.e., teacher, students, parents, artifacts), and triangulation of methods (i.e., observations, interviews, field notes, video and audio taping).

The Storytelling Case Study

Participants and Settings

The Storytelling Study was also a part of a larger project that examined young children's written and spoken narrative development in preschool and kindergarten classrooms over a 4-year period. The project was located in a low socioeconomic urban community in the southeast region of the United States. The first 2 years was conducted in a 4-year-old classroom housed in a community center in a predominantly Black neighborhood. The main data of this study come from the following 2 years of the project, which took place in an early childhood center of the public school system. The first year in this setting was in two pre-K (4-year-old) classrooms. For the next year, the study followed many of these children into two kindergarten classrooms, as well as conducting the project in two additional pre-K classrooms (four classrooms in total). All the classrooms were composed of African American children except for one White child. All the classrooms had teachers with pre-K to fourth-grade or K to eighth-grade certification. There were two African American teachers and two White teachers. In both preschool classrooms were African American paraprofessionals who also assisted with the project.

Procedures

Twice a week for the duration of the study, the following format was implemented to collect children's oral and written stories. First, one of the members of the research team (including the classroom teachers and university faculty and students) told or read a story of varying genres (e.g. folktales, modern children's stories, personal stories) while the children were gathered in a rug area. All the stories were either traditional African American or African stories about African or African American life or personal stories by the African American members of the research team. Second, the students volunteered to tell a story. Third, the students went to a table area where they wrote and drew stories in their *author books*. During this time, the research team circulated among the students, dating the children's pages and writing each child's dictated story in standard orthography. The final part involved the students returning to the rug area where they volunteered to *read* or *tell* a story from their author books. Data collection consisted of the children's books as well as audio/video-tapes and fieldnotes of the children's oral and written narratives. In addition, interviews were conducted with the teachers. As one of the researchers (author, Katz), I identify myself as an American Jew of the Caucasian race. My role as a participant observer along with the procedures of the project allowed me opportunities to gain access and to become familiar with the children whose identities were very different from mine. My focus on the content of their oral and written stories helped to demonstrate my validation of their own experiences.

Findings and Discussions

Our analysis of classroom events are organized according to our observations of (a) how the children positioned themselves and were positioned in relationship to others;

(b) how their use of language influenced these positionings; and (c) how the teachers functioned as mediators of their students' socio-construction of identity. Analyses from six transcripts (two from the Storytelling Project and four from the Family Literacy Project) representative of typical events from the data are discussed in relationship to the three research questions. We begin by presenting the data from the Family Literacy Study, then the data from Storytelling Study. Following, we will discuss the studies comparatively in relation to the facilitating and mediating factors that afforded or constrained the construction of ethnic/linguistic identities in the classroom as well as the role of the teachers as mediators of classroom practices.

The Family Literacy Case Study

Findings from the Family Literacy case study involve transcripts of two students, Oswaldo and Lucas, and their respective parents who had recently immigrated from Mexico. These two students and their parents are representative of other Hispanic families in their school. Oswaldo is an 8-year-old Mexican student who had come to the United States when he was aged 6. His father, Jacinto, was a woodworker, and his mother, Elena, worked at a Burger King. Both parents were participants in the Family Literacy Program. Oswaldo was at the beginning stages of proficiency in English. Although he spoke Spanish at home, he resented being talked to in Spanish at school, and preferred to be called *Oswald* rather than Oswaldo.

Lucas is also an 8-year-old Mexican student. He had immigrated from Mexico just before he entered second grade. He spoke virtually no English. Lucas's mother, Dora, worked as a hotel maid, and his father, Dito, was a construction worker. Only the mother was a participant in the Family Literacy Program.

The transcripts below are examples of interactions between students as they participated in classroom practice. In addition, excerpts taken from parent–teacher, parent–researcher, and teacher–researcher interviews conducted during the Family Literacy Program are presented to illustrate instances relating to the construction of ethnic and linguistic identities for the two English-language learners.

Oswaldo

The example below is an excerpt from an interview with the teacher regarding Oswaldo's performance in school. During our conversation the teacher stated her concerns about Oswaldo's absences. She seemed to have made assumptions that his absences could be a cause for his slow progress in school (lines 01, 02). Moreover, she attributed these absences (lines 01, 04, 05, 06) to his being doted on by the mother and, therefore, allowed to stay home—especially on rainy days (lines 02, 03). In addition, Ms. W attributes the trait of being protective of children as characteristic of Hispanic cultures (line 01).

Transcript #1

W: Ms. W (teacher).

01.   W: He is a baby! Hispanic mothers are doting of their boys. Oswaldo could be doing
02.   much better if he just came to school everyday, but he is out a lot. He is always out
       when
03.   it rains ... There are some cultural things that become a factor on how
04.   Hispanics perform at school. For example, when it rained yesterday, all my
05.   Hispanic kids didn't come to school.

Although the teacher's assumptions about Oswaldo, his mother, and his home life did not seem to be intentionally diminishing, they signaled helplessness and deficiencies ("he *is* a baby," he *is* doted on, he *could be* doing better). Early into the school year Oswaldo began to enact dependency in the class and by the end of the study he hardly engaged in school assignments by himself. In the classroom he was often quiet and reserved. He did not seem to want to venture to answer questions and, if asked a question directly, he usually mumbled: "Inono [I don't know]." He concealed his schoolwork so that others would not see it, and only uncovered it (sheepishly) if the teacher came to check it. Although his English was limited, he seemed to be able to hold a casual conversation. He was self-conscious about speaking Spanish and preferred to speak in English even to his Spanish-speaking peers. Perhaps the emphasis on the English language as the primary vehicle for success was a factor in constraining Oswaldo's autonomy in the classroom as well as his overall sense of ethnic identity.

During an interview, Oswaldo's mother, Elena, responded to the teacher's concerns about Oswaldo's frequent absences by explaining that sometimes she needed him to stay home to help the family on household-management tasks such as going to the store or to the bank (lines 01, 02). Although Oswaldo's proficiency was limited, he often performed the role of language broker for the family (lines 02, 03). Elena expressed a wish to speak English more fluently and often referred to herself as stupid (line 04) for not being able to do so.

Transcript #2

E: Elena (Oswaldo's mom).

01.   E: *Si, a las veces yo necesito que el vaya comigo a la tienda o a pagar las cuentas. Yo no se lo que haria sin ese nino!* (Yes, sometimes I need him to go with me to the store or to pay the bills. I don't know what I would do without this child!)
02.   *El me ayuda a hablar con todos y en toda parte que voy.* (He helps me to talk to everyone, everywhere I go.)
03.   *I mi me gustaria hablar major el ingles para no tener que contar con el a todo momento.* (I wish I spoke better English so that I wouldn't have to count on him all the time.)
04.   *Pero, yo soy muy burra y no sey nada de ingles.* (I am very stupid. I don't know any English.)

05. *Cuando me toca a ir a la tienda sola, nadien me entiende.* (When I go to the store alone, no one understands me.)

In this transcript, contrary to his circumstances at school, Oswaldo is positioned as reliable, helpful to his mother (lines 01, 02), and a competent language user (line 04). It is also notable in the excerpt that the ability to speak English was held in high regard for the mother (lines 02, 03). This is congruent with Delgado-Gaitan's (1994) discussions about the contextual discrepancies in identity development within the home and school for Mexican immigrant children. In her ethnographic studies of three Mexican immigrant families living in California, Delgado-Gaitan found that for these children, developing identities of competence within the home involved following family values, including morals to live by (e.g., respect for adult authority), collaboration and responsibility toward family tasks and goals, and developing one's sense of autonomy. Identity within school was directly intertwined with English proficiency, standardized tests, and modes of thinking and acting (e.g., ways of conceptualizing stories) according to the expected cultural norms of the institution.

Lucas

Contrary to Oswaldo, Lucas purposefully sought to be noticed throughout the classroom day. He directed attention to himself by poking other students with a pencil, constantly calling out to the teacher, and tattling on other students. The teacher reported that Lucas had difficulty relating with others and that he had a poor attitude toward school. Although he spoke very little English at the time of the study, the teacher and researcher observed that he did not seem to want to speak Spanish (i.e., his home language) to his friends who were also native speakers of Spanish. Even if he did not know certain words in English, he actively tried to interact with his classmates. Unfortunately, these interactions were often confrontational, but they were also instrumental in helping position himself in relation to others in his class. In the following transcript Lucas is being strategic in claiming ownership of a school object (scissors) with his limited proficiency of English that involves not knowing the English word for scissors. For example, in line 01 he gestures using opening and shutting motions with his two fingers as though he was cutting something. His friends promptly recognized the gesture and engaged him in a game of sorts by taking his scissors away and passing them back and forth to each other, bypassing Lucas (line 02). Recognizing that Lucas did not have the word in English to claim his object, while playing the game, the students uttered the word scissors slowly, emphatically, and repeatedly (lines 02, 04), as if they wanted him to learn it.

Transcript #3

L: Lucas; A: Alicia; D: Damian.

01. L: [gesturing to A with his two fingers as if he was cutting something, referring to a pair of scissors A had taken from him] Hey, mine.

02.   A: [passing the scissors to D] No, those are not your *scissors* [emphasizing the word in a didatic manner]; they are D's.
03.   L: [to D]: Gimme! [gesturing as if cutting] Mine! Teacher!
04.   D: [being deceiving] I don't have your *scissors* [emphasizing the word].
05.   L: [aggressively walking to D's desk and looking inside it] You taked my *scissors*! Gimme! Teacher!

It is interesting to note that Lucas chose not to speak in Spanish to Alicia and Damian (who were both native speakers of Spanish). Instead, his gesturing of the word he did not know in English (*scissors*, line 01) proved strategic in enticing Damian and Alicia to help him learn the word. By the end of the first semester of the academic year, the teacher reported that he was eagerly trying to speak only in English, even though she and his classmates did not always understand him. It appeared that Lucas had realized that using English was important in the classroom and gained him status among his classmates and teacher. In some respects, Lucas was letting go of linguistic resources which in the past had allowed him to establish friendships and cultural solidarity with other native speakers of Spanish in the class. Lucas's willingness to give up those resources was perhaps reflective of the struggles his family was having in becoming established in the community (see transcript #4 below).

Lucas's mother, Dora, during a parent–teacher conference reported that Lucas was not confrontational at home nor when interacting with his Spanish-speaking peers. She thought that his poor attitude in school (as described by the teacher) stemmed from his frustration at not being able to express himself. In the excerpt below, Dora revealed in line 01 that Lucas has recently been complaining about the other children making fun of him because he was not fluent in English. She took the initiative to help him learn English (lines 02–03)—buying computer games and having him practice on the computer. In line 05 she explained that she did not want Lucas to suffer for not speaking English like she had as an adult. In lines 06–07 Dora indicated that she did not realize how difficult it would be for her in the United States without knowledge of English. In line 08 she explains that her suffering is due to her lack of English. In line 09, she reiterates her desire and reasons for Lucas to learn English quickly.

Transcript #4

D: Dora

01.   Dora: *[Lucas] reclama mucho de los amiguitos. Los niños siempre lo molestan por su ingles.* (He complains about the kids. They are always making fun of him because of his English.)
02.   *Yo compré un monton de juguetes para la computadora para el aprender ingles. El trabaja en*
03.   *la computadora por lo menos dos horas por dia.* (I bought a lot of computer games for him to learn English. He works on the computer at least 2 hours every day.)
04.   *Yo no quiero que el sufra como yo. Ahora [como una adulta] ya esta mais dificil para mi*

05. *aprender [ingles].* (I don't want him to suffer like me. Now [as an adult] is much harder to learn [English].)

06. *Todo es muy difícil aqui. Nosotros venimos con la idea que todo iva ser muy mas facil,*

07. *pero me parece que todo es muy difícil...* (Everything is so difficult here. We came with the idea that everything would be easier, but everything is so difficult...)

08. *...Todo es muy difícil sin ningun apoyo y sin hablar English.* (Everything is hard without any support and without being able to speak English.)

09. *Por esso yo quiero que Lucas aprenda ingles lo mas rapido possible.* (That's also why I want Lucas to learn English as soon as possible.)

The urgency in learning English, present both at home and at school for Lucas, imposed serious constraints in the construction of a linguistic/ethnic identity as a bilingual or even as a native speaker of Spanish. As language is linked to development, bonding with family, learning to think critically, and learning to negotiate and communicate with others, Lucas was rapidly losing valuable tools to mediate the world around him.

Summary

These narratives document activities that children perform at home and school. Their home and school roles appear to be separate as well as conflicting in strengthening their ethnic/linguistic identities. Oswaldo is positioned as very helpful and competent, being able to carry out responsibilities that are essential for his mother, and as having enough English-language proficiency to be perceived as competent in his home. However, this degree of competence is not perceived as sufficient to be a successful student. As the use of English held high status in that classroom, the ELLs were primarily silent or hesitant to speak, perhaps thinking the other children might be judging them according to their English proficiency. Parents understood the importance of learning English; however, their efforts to help their children learn English did not seem to be validated in the school setting.

The Storytelling Case Study

Children in the Storytelling Study talked about their performed roles both at home and at school through their oral and written narratives. As they discussed these roles, they identified themselves within specific discursive groups (e.g., their families and people in the classroom—teachers and classmates). The children established themselves within these groups in several ways: (a) by explicit naming; (b) by using relational terms such as momma, daddy, grandma; (c) by using icons and pictorial representations; and (d) by describing the story's location. Furthermore, the children claimed their status within their discursive groups by how they positioned themselves in relation to the people of importance in their lives as well as their relationship to locations that were also considered of high value to them. Transcript #5 is a transcript of Nicki's written narrative accompanied by her story from one of her author books. Nicki is a 4-year-old African American girl in a preschool classroom.

Figure 8.1 "Me and my momma."

Transcript #5

"Me and My Momma" (Nicki's written narrative).

01.   Jamal drunk all the hot sauce.
02.   My momma said "I gotta go buy some more hot sauce."
03.   He ate the pepper and some salt.
04.   He took a bath.
05.   I runned his water and it was all hot.
06.   My momma wanted to play outside and we did.
07.   I pour some water on him.
08.   We went to Chuck E. Cheese I put a box on him.
09.   He couldn't go cause the door was locked. The end.

One of the ways Nicki claims her identity within the domain of her family is when she titles her story "Me and My Momma" and refers to her mother again in lines 02 and 06. (In other narratives in the Storytelling Project, not shown in this chapter, "Mother" was referenced the most when children claimed their identity with their family.) Nicki's mother seems very important to her. Not only does she title her story by associating herself with her mother but she indicates that she (Nicki) must go buy more hot sauce because her mother has said to do this (line 02). In line 06 she also follows her mother's wishes by playing outside. Another person is mentioned in Nicki's narrative—Jamal. It is unclear as to Jamal's relationship with Nicki but she positions herself as older than him and as doing something that a "big girl" or her mother would do by indicating in lines 04–05 that Jamal took a bath and she ran the water—all hot. Nicki appears to continue this topic in line 07 by pouring water on Jamal. Nicki refers to several icons in this narrative: hot sauce, pepper, and salt. They appear to be important spices or used often in Nicki's food because she associates these spices with people who are important to her. Children refer to food that is important in their lives, such as cakes (birthdays or special treats), candy, marshmallows, sweet potatoes, and chicken. Nicki also locates herself at Chuck E. Cheese (line 08); a valued location mentioned by many of her classmates in their oral and written narratives.

Nicki demonstrates her role as a student through the use of school practices that involve counting and learning how to develop a story structure. Also, Nicki's written narrative allows her the opportunity to implement aspects of writing. Nicki adopts a story structure posed by her teacher. First, she writes numbers in the top left-hand corner of her written story in correct order from one to nine. Her writing of numbers is an indication that she is school "smart." Second, she titles her story and ends her story (line 09). Her narrative story appears to be topic-centered, consisting of several topics (e.g., Jamal's bath, playing outside, and going to the Chuck E. Cheese restaurant). Although it is difficult to follow some of the topics, there is some understanding of sequencing. In the Storytelling Study, many of the children's narratives were filled with actions similar to Nicki's that presented themselves in the roles of grown-ups and heroes (e.g. fighting monsters and saving daddy).

Children in the Storytelling Study were able to use their repertoire of narrative styles, structures, and content available to them from formal instruction, informal instructional context, and family contexts. They adopted and adapted the narratives available to them as they socially constructed their stories (cf. Bloome, Champion, Katz, Morton, & Muldrow, 2001). Children's adoption of narratives includes their imitation and reproduction of narratives in the ways they experienced them (e.g., they may attempt to tell *Goldilocks and the Three Bears* in the same manner in which they were told the story). Children's adaptation of narratives involves various hybridizations and transformations of extant narratives. Transcript #6 is an excerpt from a larger narrative showing how Sheila, a 5-year-old kindergartener, adopts and adapts her story according to her repertoire of narrative structures. Sheila stands in front of the other children who are sitting on the floor. One teacher sits next to Sheila while the other researchers are sitting with the other children.

Transcript #6

Sh: Sheila; Ss: Students; Sx: unidentified student; T: Teacher (Ms. Mansfield); DB: Researcher.

01:	Sh: Tiana came over my house
02:	Kimberly came over my house
03:	Mr. Block came over my house
04:	My mama looked downstairs and saw all of us
05:	She saw us making a [undecipherable]
06:	he was playing downstairs
07:	[giggling from students]
08:	Sh: Ms. Mansfield was sleeping with Jamisha
09:	Ss: oooooooo ooooooooo ooooooooo
10:	T: [undecipherable] a soap opera
11:	Sh: Nina was sleeping down the [undecipherable]
12:	Ss: oooooooo ooooooooo oooooooo
13:	Sx: I sleep with a girl
14:	Sh: Jamisha was sleeping up top
15:	Sx: oooooo ooooo
16:	Sh: I was … I was sleeping by my own self
17:	[giggling from students]
18:	Sx: [undecipherable] sleep with a boy
19:	[giggling from students]
20:	T: [undecipherable]
21:	Sh: Sheila was sleeping on the top bed
22:	[giggling from students]
23:	Sh: Mr. Bloch [DB] was sleeping downstairs on the couch
24:	[giggling from students]
25:	Sh: Ms. Mansfield was sleeping on the other couch
26:	Sx: so she can sleep [undecipherable]
27:	Sx: [undecipherable]
28:	Sh: Tommy and Jamal was making them a [undecipherable]
29:	[giggling from students and various undecipherable comments]
30:	Sh: and I was sleeping on the … the bottom bed
31:	[various undecipherable comments]
32:	Sh: and I was sleeping
33:	Sh: and momma woke up and saw all of us sleep
34:	Sh: my momma woke up and took us to school
35:	Sh: quit coughing and get off of me Demonte
36:	T: [undecipherable comment]
37:	[extended silence and background whispering]
38:	Sh: and Demonte was playing to the park
39:	Sh: my momma gave us a dollar
40:	Ss: ooooooo ooooooooo
41:	Sh: my momma gave us two dollars

42:    Ss: oooooo
43:    [extended silence]
44:    Sh: then my momma gave us three dollars
45:    Ss: oooooo
46:    Sh: and then my momma gave us four dollars
47:    Ss: oooooo
48:    Sh: all of my kids came over my house and got em four four dollars
49:    Ss: oooooo ooooooooo
50:    Sx: [undecipherable comment]
51:    Sh: and and
52:    Sh: [undecipherable] five dollars
53:    Ss: oooooo
[...]
54:    DB: very good story
55:    Sx: yes yes

Sheila's story contains people from her family (i.e., her momma) as well as her class-mates and teachers. Her narrative is performance-based (Bauman, 1986) as she holds the floor or captures her audience by reacting to the responses of her classmates. In line 08 she reports two children sleeping with each other. The children respond to this taboo subject in line 09. Sheila continues to construct her story by reporting other children who are also sleeping at her house. Each time she reports a child is sleeping, the children respond (by giggling or saying ooooo). In line 39 she changes her topic to her momma giving them a dollar. Both having money and being given the money by her mother are signs of status. Sheila reacts to the students from lines 41–53 by continuing this topic. Each time she increases the value of the money, the children react (ooooo). Each additional dollar is also part of her school identity as she demonstrates her counting skills. Sheila ends her story by changing locations from her home to her school; two important places that are valued in her life.

Summary

The activities the children in the storytelling study engaged in were (1) telling stories in front of their classmates and teachers, and (2) writing stories in their author books. During these activities they told or wrote stories that positioned themselves with people who were important in their lives. Their stories contained activities performed with people who were considered "grown up" and were performing important roles. For example, Nicki helps her mother by giving Jamal a bath. Nicki also acts as a student by writing numbers in her author book and telling a story that represents beginnings of a story-structure format. Sheila also positions herself as both a daughter and a student but through different representations than Nicki. Her story contains both her mother and her classmates, and her mother giving her and her classmates money that she counts out correctly.

Implications and Conclusion

The comparison of the two case studies was instrumental in identifying how children from linguistically diverse backgrounds are positioned in classrooms to promote or constrain their home and school identities. Findings from these cases are not population-specific but associated with classroom practices that mainstream and second language teachers can implement to promote the integration of home/school identities of all children's ethnic, racial, and socioeconomic backgrounds. Our findings suggest three major factors that can be instrumental in facilitating this integration.

The first factor refers to classroom activities that are both text- and oral-based. These activities provide opportunities to bring aspects of the social and cultural practices of the home that are either rich in print or oral traditions into the classroom. Being able to express oneself in a familiar modality allows children to position themselves in events and use familiar words that associate themselves with their families, community, and school. For example, in the Storytelling Study, children were able to make (draw/write) or tell their stories. They used narrative styles, structures, and content available to them from their home and community, and adopted and adapted these styles into the classroom setting. Furthermore, they were proud of their stories because of how their stories represented their social relationships and other features that were important to their lives.

The second factor refers to teachers as mediators of classroom activities who position children as both competent in their homes and classroom communities. For example, teachers in both studies provided students with feedback, instilled cooperative behaviors in the classroom, and created a disciplined environment in the classroom where students were learning the academic content. However, teachers in the Storytelling Project provided opportunities for children to choose the topic(s) for their stories and have their own author books, positioning the children as having some ownership of their learning and being perceived as part of the classroom. This type of choice and ownership is based on ideas of best practices for teaching young children according to the National Association for the Education of Young Children (Bredekamp & Copple, 1997). Some of the best practices the teachers followed included making the curriculum meaningful and of interest to their children. Furthermore, they strived to promote their children's creativity and develop their emerging literacy by validating the children's discourses; for example, praising their stories and encouraging them to continue writing or telling their stories even if they were not understood or told in a specific format.

The teachers' mediation of the storytelling activities within a group also helped to validate the students' home and school identities. Children listened to each child tell their story and reacted to parts of their stories by interjecting, giggling, and applauding. Their stories were considered a reflection of their lived experiences. Similarly to Toohey's (2000) kindergarten study, these teachers mediated activities to promote children's access to the classroom community. In the Family Literacy Study, the children's perception of their lack of English proficiency for classroom purposes inhibited them from telling their own stories to the class, thus inhibiting their relationships with other children as well as their engagement in classroom assignments. That is, the children's identities in the classroom were largely constructed by how their English proficiency was perceived by others and by what others said about them.

The third factor refers to the meaningful inclusion of all children within classroom practices. In general, classroom practices that integrate both home and school identities position all children, regardless of race, culture, language, and socioeconomic class as being actively engaged in all activities and perceived as contributing members of the classroom. This means that there are deliberate efforts by teachers to: (a) create opportunities for family and community lives to intersect with school practices; (b) organize their classrooms to ensure students have equitable access to instructional content; and (c) willingly accept any type of writing/oral narratives as authentic and to validate the students' responses. Some of these practices were present in both studies. For example, in the Family Literacy Study the teacher made a concerted effort to hold frequent parent–teacher conferences so that she would be able to learn about each family's histories and home practices that may have been of relevance to the children's learning. However, the concern with academic gains and the privileging of English precluded the creation of conditions for these histories and/or practices to be an integral part of classroom activities. In the Storytelling Study, all children regardless of race, culture, language, socioeconomic class, or disability were actively engaged and perceived as contributing members of the classroom. For example, teachers structured the classroom in such a manner that all the children had opportunities to share their stories. None of their stories were perceived as being more or less valuable than others. In our observations, the students in both studies were actively attempting to exert agency in authoring and in hybridizing their multiple *selves* through their participation in the available practices of the classroom. However, in the absence of those previously mentioned facilitating factors, individuals' agency was curtailed and identities remained compartmentalized and fragmented. Our findings suggest that although individuals were able to actively negotiate their identities, this process was severely complicated by the devaluation of home language for the new immigrant students.

In view of the rising numbers of linguistically and racially diverse students in mainstream classrooms, the need to adequately prepare teachers to support these students' learning in U.S. schools has become ever more pressing. The two studies demonstrate the importance of promoting teachers' awareness of students' language, race, and identity. These are inherent aspects of being a student and thus need to be taken into account when academic performance is at issue. Classroom practices that account for these variables help children negotiate their home identities and become full participants in classroom environments.

Discussion Questions

1. In the Storytelling Study, students' lived experiences were heard, valued, and shared. What are positive consequences of this type of classroom experience for the students? Can this activity be adapted to a classroom with older students?
2. How could the teacher in the Family Literacy Study make the curriculum and instruction meaningful and interesting for all students? Think of some concrete activities and strategies.
3. Observe classrooms that enroll linguistically diverse students and identify how the students are encouraged (or discouraged) to express their own ideas and experiences and to take pride in their own cultural, ethnic, and linguistic identity.

4. The authors conducted interviews with Latino parents as part of the data collection in the Family Literacy Study. What kind of perspectives and insights would such interviews provide to researchers or classroom teachers? Share your own experiences of interviewing linguistically diverse parents, if any, or predict what kind of issues could be discovered (e.g., communication at home, information about siblings).

References

Bauman, R. (1986). *Story, performance and event.* Cambridge: Cambridge University Press.

Bloome, D., Carter, S. P., Christian, B. M., Otto, S., & Shuart-Faris, N. (2005). *Discourse analysis and the study of classroom language and literacy events.* Mahwah, NJ: Lawrence Erlbaum Associates.

Bloome, D., Champion, T., Katz, L., Morton, M. B., & Muldrow, R. (2001). Spoken and written narrative development: African American preschoolers as storytellers and storymakers. In J. L. Harris, A. G. Kamhi, & K. E. Pollack (Eds.), *Literacy in African American communities* (pp. 45–76). Mahwah, NJ: Lawrence Erlbaum Associates.

Bredekamp, S., & Copple, C. (Eds.). (1997). *Developmentally appropriate practice in early childhood programs serving children from birth through age eight.* Washington, DC: National Association for the Education of Young Children.

Cohen, M. (1994) Demographic expansion: causes and consequences. In T. Ingold (Ed.), *Companion encyclopedia of anthropology: Humanity, culture and social life* (pp. 1–23). New York: Routledge.

DaSilva Iddings, A. C. (2005). Linguistic access and participation: Second language learners in an English-dominant community of practice. *Bilingual Research Journal, 37,* 223–236.

Davies, B., & Harré, R. (2000). Positioning: The discursive production of selves. In B. Davies (Ed.), *A body of writing, 1990–1999* (pp. 87–106). Walnut Creek, CA: Alta Mira Press.

Delgado-Gaitan, C. (1994). Sociocultural change through literacy: Toward the empowerment of families. In B. Ferdman, R. Weber, & A. Ramirez (Eds.), *Literacy across languages and cultures* (pp. 143–171). Albany, NY: State University of New York Press.

Gee, J. (1996). *Social linguistics and literacies: Ideology in discourses.* London: Palmer.

Green, J., & Wallat, C. (1981). Mapping instructional conversations. In J. Green & C. Wallet (Eds.), *Ethnography and language in educational settings* (pp. 161–195). Norwood, NJ: Ablex.

Gumperz, J. (1986). *Discourse strategies.* New York: Cambridge University Press.

Harré, R., & van Langenhove, L. (1999) *Positioning Theory.* Oxford: Blackwell.

Holland, D., Lachicotte, Jr., W., Skinner, D., & Cain, C. (2001). *Identity and agency in cultural worlds.* Cambridge, MA: Harvard University Press.

Hymes, D. (1974). *The foundation of sociolinguistics: Sociolinguistic ethnography.* Philadelphia, PA: University of Pennsylvania Press.

Hymes, D. (1980). *Language in education: Ethnolinguistic essays, language and ethnography series.* Washington, DC: Center for Applied Linguistics.

Hymes, D. (1996). *Ethnography, linguistics, narrative inequality: Toward an understanding of voice.* London: Taylor & Francis.

Johannessen, L. R. (2004). Helping struggling students achieve success. *Journal of Adolescent and Adult Literacy, 47,* 638–648.

Lave J., & Wenger, E. (1991). *Situated learning: Legitimate peripheral participation.* New York: Cambridge University Press.

Lewis, C. (2001). *Literacy practices as social acts: Power, status and cultural norms in the classroom.* Mahwah, NJ: Lawrence Erlbaum Associates.

Moje, E. B., & Shepardson, D. P. (1998). Social interactions and children's changing understandings of electric circuits: Exploring unequal power relations in "peer" learning groups. In B. Guzzetti & C. Hynd (Eds.), *Theoretical perspectives on conceptual change* (pp. 225–234). Mahwah, NJ: Lawrence Erlbaum Associates.

National Assessment of Education Progress. (2004). Washington, DC: U.S. Government Printing Office. Retrieved July 26, 2005 from http://nces.ed.gov/nationsreportcard/.

National Center for Educational Statistics. (2000). Washington, DC: U.S. Government Printing Office. Retrieved July 15, 2005 from http://nces.edu.gov.

Nieto, S. (2000). *Affirming diversity: The sociopolitical context of multicultural education* (3rd ed.). Reading, MA: Longman.

Toohey, K. (2000). *Learning English at school: Identity, social relations and classroom practice.* Clevedon UK: Multilingual Matters.

9   Race and Technology in Teacher Education

Where Is the Access?

Francis Bangou and Shelley Wong

Pre-reading Questions

In this chapter, the authors illustrate the complexity of the interrelationships between technology, teacher education, and social inequality. More precisely, they describe how infusing technology into a teacher-education program enabled two pre-service teachers of color to fight racism by providing them with the opportunity to "reconfigure" the technology that was available. Before reading this chapter, please consider the following questions:

*   What are your schools' policies regarding access to computer labs and computer use? What is done to address the "digital divide" between affluent students and students who do not have a computer nor Internet access at home?
*   Is race invisible in cyberspace? How do representations of racial identity and racial stereotypes affect white students and students of color?
*   In your view, how does technology change teaching and learning?

Introduction

Although some claim that technology is racially neutral, others argue that the use of technology in the United States has exacerbated the racial and class divides by allowing those with resources to benefit from technology and those who are poor to be denied access (Cummins & Sayers, 1995). In the context of mandated testing and accountability demands placed by No Child Left Behind, which was signed into federal law in 2002, many school districts have turned to educational technology as a means to address achievement gaps.

In the field of kindergarten–grade 12 (K–12) foreign/second language education, it has become imperative for both pre-service and in-service teachers to be able to use computers as an integral part of their teaching (Tognozzi, 2001). However, many of the studies concerning foreign-language teaching and technology have no explicit discussion of the impact of these technologies on minority students. Foreign-language education in the United States has produced limited success. It is due in part to the monolingual mindset of many Americans, the limited support for foreign-language education and the social expectations of failure (Reagan & Osborne, 2002). In the United States, foreign-language classes are not a requirement for high school graduation and often restricted to students who are on the "college track." The low representation of students of color in foreign-language education parallels the racial divide in high school graduate rates and university admission. Indeed, many studies of technology and foreign-language teaching do not present data on the racial composition of foreign-language classes, and there are few studies on racial-minority recruitment or achievement in the field of foreign-language education in the United States.

In this chapter, we will explore intersections of race and technology through a year-long qualitative study of two pre-service teachers in the Foreign and Second Language Master of Education (M.Ed.)—a Latina woman and an African American woman, who learned how to use computer technology to teach Spanish at a large Midwestern university. The case studies of these two women will be analyzed to gain insights into how teacher-education programs can support increased access to technology for racial-minority students. It will be shown that the learning experiences of these two pre-service teachers were successful in part because they had the opportunity to reconstruct and reconfigure the technology that was available to them to assert their racialized pedagogical and professional identities (Paradies, 2005) and challenge racial stereotypes (Fouché, 2000).

Race and Computer Technology

In the following review of the literature, we argue that racial and social class inequalities contribute to lack of access to technology and lower-level technology skills for students of color from poor and working-class families. Moreover, inequalities and discrimination that exist in the real world are reproduced in the virtual world. Some students have had computers at home since they were young children, while others do not have a computer at home to complete an assignment. It is crucial, then, to address issues of racial and class inequalities. It is also important to understand how to support racial minorities who have traditionally been denied access to technology.

Access

Research has shown that race and ethnicity impact access to computer technologies. Mossberger, Tolbert, and Stansbury (2003) found that African Americans, Latinos, the poor, older individuals, and the less-educated are all statistically less likely to have access to home computers, the Internet, and the e-mail. They also found that race, ethnicity, education, income, and age are all statistically significant predictors of lower levels of self-reported technology skill. Reid (2001) highlighted the fact that although computers at school improved access for some racial and ethnic groups, African American and Hispanic students did not log on to the Internet as often as their white classmates. She found that some possible factors that influenced racial and ethnic disparities in computer use included "discrimination, minority students' relative lack of exposure to computers, and a dearth of racially and ethnically diverse content on the Internet" (p. 2). Hanson (1997) argued that rather than act as an education panacea, the use of computers often exacerbates inequities for students of color and poor students. Mossberger, Tolbert, and Stansbury (2003) concluded that "the optimistic scenario depicting information technology diffusion throughout society may be unrealistic without some policy intervention in low-income and minority communities" (p. 6).

Race in Cyberspace

The concept of cyberspace might suggest that there is an online universe that is different from the real world (Warschauer, 2000). "Cyberspace is a type of fantasyland where we take on cyber-identities and engage in virtual reality. But then, when we leave cyberspace, we come back to the real world" (p. 1). Yet, Warschauer argues, we need to realize that "online communication lies not in its separation from the real world, but rather in how it is impacting nearly every single aspect of the real world" (p. 1).

"There is no race. There is no gender. There is no age. There are no infirmities. There are only minds" (television commercial for MCI, in Nakamura, 2000). This television commercial illustrates a traditional "color-blind" view of race in cyberspace. The Internet has traditionally been perceived as a space where racial and other physical markers are not relevant because they are invisible to the eye—they cannot be seen. Such claims are based on the assumption that race is primarily biological, embodied in physical space. Proponents of such perspectives are then able to avoid any discussion related to race and technology by claiming that it is irrelevant (Kolko, Nakamura, & Rodman, 2000). However, if we conceive of race as rooted in culture and discourse rather than nature and biology, it becomes crucial to address the issue of race when discussing computer technology and virtual reality.

Indeed, as Kolko et al. (2000) point out, "because all of us who spend time on-line are already shaped by the way in which race matters off-line, we can't help but bring our own knowledge, experiences, and values with us when we log on" (p. 5). This is why in a discussion of technology it is necessary to address the issue of race (Warnick, 2002). Race becomes an issue, consciously or unconsciously, when people have to create a virtual presence on the Internet. To do so involves "deliberately constructing an identity for yourself, whether it is choosing an e-mail name, putting together a webpage, designing a graphical avatar, or creating a nickname for a chat room or virtual world" (p. 6).

Within the context of K–12 school in the United States, social identities are extremely racialized. Stereotypes that exist in the real world are reproduced on the Internet (Nakamura, 2000). Silver (2000) stated "communities—geographic and on-line—are defined not only by who and what are included but also by who and what are excluded" (p. 143). "Today the Internet remains a largely (though not entirely) white space" (Sterne, 2000, p. 195). According to Warschauer (2000) "because of this basic contradiction, the Internet can both magnify existing inequalities in society while also facilitating efforts to challenge these inequalities" (p. 13). What then are the implications of including non-white voices and non-white representations in virtual reality? How does one locate the discussion of race in cyberspace? For those who want to address equity by increasing access to technology for under-represented students, the accounts of minority teachers' use of technology may be instructive.

Interacting with Technology

According to Fouché (2000), technologies have historically silenced African American people and have often rendered them invisible. At present African Americans "are still struggling to build independent and critical technological voices" (p. 2). Fouché argued that there is a need to study racially marginalized people's cultural needs, desires, aesthetics, and priorities, which can produce and redefine technological artifacts, practices, and associated knowledge to subvert the architecture of constructed dominant meanings of technologies. To do so, it is important to understand how racially marginalized people "see, view, feel, understand, and interact with technologies from their own perspectives" (p. 5). According to Fouché (2000), "a great deal of energy within African American life is dedicated to negotiating negative representations that have been used to present African Americans as racially inferior" (p. 11). Resistance has been a means of gaining control and producing alternative forms of identification. Within that context

> representation and resistance provide the most basic of frameworks through which to examine how technology is used to suppress African Americans and alternatively to assess the processes by which African Americans reconstruct and reconfigure technologies to reclaim a portion of this stolen agency.
>
> (p. 11)

While African American students and teachers and other people of color may invest a great deal of energy resisting negative images of themselves in teaching materials, white teachers may not be conscious of these racist processes. In fact, the view that cyberspace is a "neutral" rather than a "white" space may itself be conditioned by one's own consciousness of the problem of race. That Whiteness is unmarked and goes unnoticed is a very important issue in the professional identity of teachers. "I don't care if you are white, black or purple, I treat all students alike" is an example of colorblind ideology (Howard, 1993). A number of critical scholars have pointed out that part of becoming aware of racism is to recognize that white is a color and to identify the ways in which the superiority of Whiteness gets constructed in wider discursive practices.

The Study

In this study we illustrate some of the processes of racial representation and resistance to dominant views on racial minorities of two pre-service teachers of color who were able to integrate technology into their teaching practice by fighting against racism and claiming professional pedagogical identities as women of color. In the following section we will introduce the context of the study and our objectives. Then, we will describe our methodology.

Context

This research took place in a Foreign and Second Language Education (FSLED) M.Ed. program at a large Midwestern university. In 2000, the College of Education was the recipient of a 3-year grant entitled "Preparing Tomorrow's Teacher to use Technology" (PT3). The aim of the grant was to infuse technology into the various M.Ed. programs. The main goal of the PT3 project was to create systemic change and improvement in the university's teacher-education programs to ensure that all graduates of the programs were able to make appropriate use of technology to improve teaching practices and student learning. The authors of this chapter were members of the Technology and Foreign and Second Language Community of Inquiry. The first author was the PT3 graduate research assistant and technology specialist. He was hired as a technological assistant to infuse the use of technology into the FSLED M.Ed. program and transform the curriculum. The second author served as the M.Ed. foreign-language faculty coordinator, PT3 principal investigator, and faculty sponsor. Both researchers are foreign- and second-language educators who identify themselves as minority scholars of color—more precisely, a French West Indian and an Asian American.

During the research, 26 students were enrolled in the five-quarter intensive FSLED M.Ed. program with teacher licensure. The racial/ethnic make up of the cohort included: 20 Caucasian/White/European Americans; 2 African Americans; 3 Latinas; and 1 Asian American.

The researchers utilized the Methods of Teaching Foreign Languages courses to provide a sound theoretical and practical framework for students to familiarize themselves with the use of technology. We started working with the M.Ed. program in January 2001.

Both of the researchers' teaching practices have been informed by sociocultural and critical frameworks (Norton & Toohey, 2004). We thought that it was important for language teachers to be aware of issues of power, social justice, and equity (King, Hollins, & Hayman, 1997; Blackburn & Clark, 2007). Traditionally, such topics were not addressed in the M.Ed. program. Talking about race in teacher education is still a challenge. Pre-service and in-service teachers often wonder how they could fit multicultural perspectives into their curriculum without creating or reinforcing racism (Bolgatz, 2005). The first author who took the lead in infusing technology into the methods courses believed that learning to use technology as a pedagogical tool could be an effective way to reflect on these issues. He strongly encouraged the pre-service teachers to design web-based units that dealt with power, social justice, and equity (Merryfield, 2001). He consciously modeled critical multicultural perspectives and practices (Canagarajah, 1999) in his demonstrations and lectures. For example, the first author modeled how to assess a website from a critical perspective (Warnick, 2001) by asking questions such as: Who is represented? Who is not? To whom is this website addressed? Then, the pre-service teachers were asked to do the same with the websites they would include in their web-based unit plans. Posing the question "whom does knowledge serve?" or "knowledge for whom?" is important when our students are marginalized with respect to class, race, gender, or constructions of difference (Wong, 2006).

The first author also used his own experience as a French teacher of color to provide the pre-service teachers with the space to debate issues of race and language education. For instance, he talked about his students' surprise on the first day of class when they saw a Black man entering the room and comments he received such as: "I didn't know there were Black people in France."

Purpose

The two pre-service teachers discussed in this chapter were part of a broader study that investigated how a group of six pre-service teachers constructed a knowledge base related to using technology to improve their professional practice through the tripartite framework of the teacher-learner, school and schooling, and the nature of language teaching and learning (Freeman & Johnson, 1998). Race is part of all three domains in the tripartite framework and has an impact on the development of the teacher-learner, our analysis of school and schooling, and the nature of language teaching and learning.

Selection of the Participants

First, we wanted the research participants to represent a diversity of technological skills. Second, we wanted research participants' motivation to integrate technology into their teaching practice to be different. Third, it was important to have diversity of languages and experiences. Fourth, as racial and ethnic minorities interested in multicultural education, we wanted to have different genders, races, and ethnicities represented. Finally, the research participants needed to be enrolled full-time in the program.

The participants in the larger study were six full-time graduate students who completed the M.Ed. program in either French, German, Spanish, Latin, or Japanese. In this chapter we are going to focus on two of the participants named Michaela and Andrea (pseudonyms) whose honesty and experience caught our attention. We choose to foreground their stories, because for each of these two women, integration of technological tools to enhance their teaching was deeply intertwined with their own identity as women of color.

Michaela

Michaela was a 22-year-old Venezuelan born in the United Kingdom. Her parents were both from Venezuela. She was a single mother of a 2-year-old boy. Her childhood was spent between three countries: Venezuela, the United Kingdom, and the United States. When she was 12, her family had a computer with Microsoft Works software. She learned how to use word processing on her own. When she was a student abroad she worked for an oil company as a secretary. The company provided her with free training for Windows. She admitted that compared to the other learners she was the "slowest" and she did not like it.

Michaela was one of the students who had the most antagonistic reaction when we introduced the web-unit plan to the class. She almost cried. Before entering the M.Ed. program, she taught English as a Foreign Language abroad for 6 months, and then 6 months at the College Literacy Council. Before the M.Ed. program, she used her personal computer primarily to do word processing and email. She had never attended a class where computers were used as an integral part of instruction.

Andrea

Andrea was a 29-year-old African American female who was always quiet in class and rarely participated in class discussions. Like Michaela, she planned to teach Spanish. Before enrolling in the M.Ed. program she worked as a nurse. She was born on the East coast of the United States and moved to the Midwest when she was an adolescent. She remembered that her parents bought a Commodore 64 and "it was mainly used for computer games."

After moving to the Midwest, she went to a suburban school and used computers to type her assignments on a word processor. When she was a student, she "really started using more" computer technology. She did word processing and sent emails daily. As a nurse she had used the computer to do her "charting" but she did not like it because "the computers were never working." At the time of the research she was living with her parents and had access to three computers at home. Before the M.Ed. program, she had never taught or attended a class where computers were used for instructional purposes.

Methodology

From June 2001 to June 2002, the research participants were observed both at the university and in their field placements for teaching practicum. Some of the pedagogical strategies that participants used to teach the language and the ways in which technology was implemented were recorded.

Each participant was also interviewed once during the fall quarter of 2001, and the winter and the spring quarters of 2002. The goal of the interviews was to understand participants' interpretations of their own experiences and feelings. During interviews, care was taken not to control or predict their responses. The interviews were divided into three major themes: the technological tools used in their field placements and at the university; the curriculum both in schools and at the university; and students' relationships with their peers, instructors, mentor teachers, and field educators. However, the interviews remained open to allow the participants to elaborate on their experience and feelings that they had in different classes regarding technology-enhanced teaching and learning.

Moreover, we met with the participants seven times from November 2001 to June 2002 to discuss collectively in a chat room issues related to technology and education (e.g., technology and gender, technology and linguistic diversity). The chat-room discussions were always 1 hour long and usually took place at the end of the day. Participants were encouraged to initiate discussion but they always relied on us to choose the topic.

We also collected participants' capstone projects and examined their electronic portfolios and their web-based unit plans. In the capstone project and the electronic portfolio, "the participants identified issues in foreign language education that were of importance to them" (Raymond, 1999, p. 66). Participants' teaching philosophy and pedagogy as they were expressed in these documents were also highlighted. Furthermore, we watched the videos of the workshops organized during the fall quarter and underlined some of the pre-service teachers' concerns in our field notes.

We compared the data from diverse documents and identified recurring themes and patterns. The data were classified chronologically according to the quarter in which the research took place (summer, fall, winter, spring, summer). Taking a developmental approach, we investigated how the themes and patterns changed over time. In this study we looked for patterns and we also highlighted some of the contested issues that we as racialized scholars of color found significant in supporting academic achievement for racial minority students.

Andrea's and Michaela's Racialized Lived Experiences in the M.Ed. Program

"I am a Minority." "Diversity is a huge problem on here [campus]. Maybe not a problem per se but it's something I'm aware of because most of the classes are not diverse whatsoever. I'm the sole and only person of a different color." "I thought I was the only minority person in this all city."

The above quotes are what Andrea and Michaela said about their experiences in the city and on campus. In this section, we will highlight some of Andrea's and Michaela's lived experiences as women of color in a predominantly white or European American M.Ed. program. Indeed, they were the only participants who described their experiences in the school and in the program through the lenses of their racialized identities. It will be shown that their own experiences with racism in the program and in society had both a negative and positive impact on their motivation to become teachers.

The student population in the M.Ed. program was mainly made of White, middle-class women. Andrea said that she was surprised to find another African American woman in the program: "I was shocked, I truly was." She admitted that being one of two Black students was an improvement compared to her experience as an undergraduate student, laughed softly and quipped ironically in an understated way, "We've come a long way."

Both Michaela and Andrea became quickly aware of the lack of racial diversity in their school placements in elementary, middle, and high schools as foreign-language student interns. Andrea started counting the number of students of color that she would see in her placements: "I find myself throughout the day counting how many kids of a different race there are. To this date, I have seen two black kids in the whole school."

Confronting Stereotypes

Andrea reported that the M.Ed. program did not provide students with a fair representation of the inner-city schools: "There is a big stigma that this program has put on inner city schools ... it's always inner city kids that have all the problems, but in Weatherston and Gaithertown [pseudonymous suburban school districts] they would be great." One of Andrea's goals was to provide students in the M.Ed. program with an awareness of different cultures and realities: "These teachers that I had in the past do not really have any exposure to any other cultures ... So I think my thing is to make these students in the M.Ed. program aware of other cultures." Nowadays, with the dominant ideology of colorblindness (Bonilla-Silva, 2002) the use of overtly racial epithets is usually perceived as inappropriate. In such contexts, Whites often develop a set of strategies to code-talk about people of color (Edsall & Edsall, 1992). Although racial epithets were never used in the M.Ed. program, students and faculty were still able to create a veiled discourse around race and people of color. "Suburban" and "inner city" were ways of coding race and class difference without mentioning "race." "Culturally diverse" rather than "racially diverse" was the preferred label used to refer to nonwhite learners. Within the M.Ed. program, "cultural diversity" was also used to refer to "inner-city schools." Moreover, most of the inner-city schools where the pre-service teachers were placed had little access to technology. In some schools, teachers had difficulty using a VCR for their instruction. In contrast, most of the pre-service teachers placed in suburban schools had an elite access to technology. For instance, in one of the suburban schools, the pre-service teachers could use laptops in their classrooms with a wireless Internet connection. It appears, then, that access to technology reinforced the negative stereotypes of academic underachievement associated with inner-city schools. The majority of students claimed that they could not fulfill their technological requirement in inner-city placements because they did not have easy access to technology. Rather than critically addressing the inequalities of resources, student teachers tended to locate blame on inner-city schools (Bonilla-Silva, 2003). Within the M.Ed., access to technology was part of the discourse that stigmatized inner-city schools and their communities.

Moreover, the technological teaching materials available in the M.Ed. program had little representation of people of color. The teachers and the native speakers of the target languages represented on the websites and in electronic courseware were mostly White. Such representation reinforced the idea that teaching a foreign language was not meant for people of color. As a woman of color, Andrea was aware of that discourse. She believed that as a member of the "other culture," she had an awareness that the other pre-service teachers in the program did not have. Her mission was to "make the other pre-service teachers aware of other cultures" so that they realized that the discourses in place in the M.Ed. program masked institutional racism.

Michaela felt that her peers were unaware and uninterested in the rest of the world. She commented,

> They [students in the M.Ed. program] are just so far away from reality. So even like in France, you do your own stuff, but you're so aware of the rest of the world. Here, you are aware of Dayton [a neighboring town] and that's it.

Moreover, Michaela was a single mother and she sometimes had difficulty fulfilling the program requirements. She often had to justify herself to the program managers and to some of her classmates. For instance, once she was almost dismissed from the program because she was often late to class. As part of the requirements, the pre-service teachers had to design a web-based unit plan in groups. The requirement was quite demanding, but Michaela preferred working on her own, because she knew that she would not have been able to follow the schedule of her group-mates and she did not want to create more conflicts. The full-time intensive M.Ed. program required a great deal of work for the students. As a woman and as a teacher of color, Michaela was confronted everyday with classmates and faculty who were either indifferent or unaware of her responsibility as a single parent.

During an informal conversation, Michaela declared that she was very pleased with a classroom activity that she created, because it allowed her to break stereotypes about Latin America. She declared that she wanted her students to realize that in Latin America "people were not riding donkeys all the time." Both Andrea and Michaela had a "double consciousness" (Dubois, 1961). They were aware that they were constantly being measured by a standard that saw them as different and each of them accepted the responsibility to "represent the race." Both had the desire to "give back" to their communities and to those who are less fortunate with respect to resources.

It seemed that Andrea's and Michaela's motivation to teach was negatively impacted by such lack of diversity in the placements and lack of cultural awareness. Andrea said:

> Maybe it's the assignment that I'm in now, that it's not where I wanted to be. I honestly wanted to be in an urban setting to have a diversity of kids and I don't have that and I just lost interest in it [teaching] and I find it [teaching] old.

Michaela said about the school system: "I think it's how the system is set up, and the kids are products of that system and I don't like it … it frustrates me, it frustrates me a lot."

When talking about their experiences on campus and in the community, none of the other participants mentioned their racial identities to the researchers. For instance, they addressed issues related to the management of their time or the size of the classes. Research has pointed out the differing impact of awareness of racism and racial identity for teachers and students of color (Bush, 2004). In Bush's study at a university in New York, when asked "how much has racial identity affected your life?", 66.7% of Asians, 54% foreign-born Blacks, 53.5% of U.S.-born Blacks, 42.8% of Latinos, 41.9% of U.S.-born Whites and 39% of foreign-born Whites answered "A lot." In contrast to the White students in their cohort, Andrea's and Michaela's racial identities were significant in the ways that they openly discussed their experiences within the M.Ed. program. They clearly identified themselves as women and teachers of color and they were aware of the impact of their racial identities on their everyday life as individuals and as professionals. In the following section, it will be shown that such awareness had an impact on the ways that they interacted with the technology.

Technology as a Means of Resistance

As shown in the previous section, Andrea and Michaela were very much aware of the colorblind racism (Bonilla-Silva, 2002) that existed in the M.Ed. program. Foreign-language education is essential for building cultural and world knowledge. Indeed, through their practice, foreign-language educators have the opportunity to engage learners in challenging their notion of otherness (Reagan & Osborn, 2002). In this section, we will describe how Michaela and Andrea, through the teaching of otherness and the use of technology, broke stereotypes and claimed their identities as women and teachers of color (Motha, 2006).

Opening Students' Eyes to the World

It seemed important to both Michaela and Andrea to "open students' eyes to the world." Andrea said:

> I would like to as teacher to open up the kids eyes to the world … to have them understand that there is more to the world than what they see in the Upper Cliff [pseudonym] situation [wealthy school district where Andrea was doing her teaching practicum].

Andrea added: "There are so many things out there. There are people of *many* colors that speak this language [Spanish]. It's not just Spain. You know what I'm saying?" Michaela reported that what she wanted to do as a teacher was to "just have them [students] think beyond the preterit and think beyond Spanish ... and have a little bit of awareness of the world they live in."

Both Michaela and Andrea wanted to provide their students with life skills. Andrea and Michaela defined life skills as qualities they thought would be beneficial to anybody. One of these qualities was to be tolerant and respectful of other people. Andrea said,

> I'm not just teaching a language, I'm teaching them life skills and that's what I have to do. I have to teach them or at least model for them to respect me as a person, to respect each other as people, to be considerate, to be responsible.

Michaela said,

> I want to teach my students life skills that I thought were useful to me when they were taught to me. It's just personal things that are really like your little box of tools you know like tolerance, patience, self control.

Most of the pre-service teachers wanted to open their students' eyes to the culture of the target language. It was mainly to help their students "function" in the target culture or to "meet" people from the target culture. Michaela and Andrea were the only participants who explicitly referred to concepts such as "tolerance," "life skills," and "respect of people," and included themselves: "respect *me* as a person." Moreover, Michaela and Andrea wanted students to acquire life skills that could be useful when interacting with people from any culture and not only from the culture of the language they were teaching. This emphasis for them on "life skills" was connected holistically to tolerance and respect for other people.

As stated earlier, Michaela and Andrea wanted to use their professional practice to challenge and eradicate the inequities that they experienced as women of color in their daily life and in the M.Ed. program. To do so, they had to appropriate the discourse that was in place in the M.Ed. program. They never specifically referred to race and racism but instead they used the terms of "diversity," "tolerance," and "culture." It is a strategy that is often used by minorities when they want to be heard. They often have to "recycle" the discourse in place in order to be considered by the majority as an equal and non-threatening interlocutor. We cannot take for granted that people in power think that speakers in subordinate positions are worthy to be listened to (Norton, 1998; Albright & Luke, 2008). We previously argued that technology was part of the discourse of stigmatization that was in place in the M.Ed. program. In the following section we are going to describe the ways that Michaela and Andrea reconstructed technology to fulfill their goals.

Reconstructing Technology

Both Michaela and Andrea seemed to believe that technology was a good way to diversify students' world-views. Michaela commented, "I think it's [technology is] a great way to broaden anyone's horizon, you know, just giving you a different prospective in life." Andrea commented that technology was useful in that it allowed students "to get in touch with other parts of the world." Michaela and Andrea reconstructed the technology in two different manners. They integrated racially diverse pictures of teachers, language learners, and speakers of the target language into their electronic portfolio and in their teaching material. They also used the technology to virtually immerse the language learners in the target culture.

To diversify her students' world-views, Andrea infused in her teaching activities images of people of different races:

> I try to find people of a different color, I do try to incorporate that somehow ... Even for lesson plans that I did for school, I try to find clip arts for the different things to show the verbs. So instead of only having White I really have to search to find clip arts of people of a different race.

For instance, during her practicum at an elementary school, Andrea made a book about winter. In that book she included clip arts of children from different races. Later, she commented, "The clip arts, all the clip arts, I had Black kids, Spanish-looking kids ... I mean it's very diverse. I'm very happy about it." As part of her electronic portfolio, she created a web-based unit plan about Mexican culture. In this unit students could visit different websites to familiarize themselves with Mexican culture. Finally, Andrea created a lesson related to the Day of the Dead, a Mexican holiday. In this activity, students had to read a website and respond to historical questions related to cultural practices involved in honoring the dead.

Michaela also used the Internet to diversify her students' world-views and break stereotypes. She said, "I don't know how it [the Internet activity] came about but I really wanted them to think of what real life would be in a Latin country." She created an activity where students had to pretend to be citizens of a South American country of their choice. Then, her students adopted a particular identity (e.g., as a single mother, married, teacher, etc.). According to their chosen identity her students performed different tasks (e.g., find an apartment, go on vacations). Michaela's students also answered different questions such as: What is the constitution of this country? Where do you work? How much is the rent? How much do you earn? Students had to use the Internet to find the information that they needed. After collecting the data and answering the questions, Michaela's students reflected on their experience and gave a class presentation. They were encouraged to use technology for their presentation. Some students created videos and others used PowerPoint. Michaela seemed to be pleased with the activity. She said, "I thought it was really, really successful." As part of her electronic portfolio, Michaela created a web-based unit plan about Latin American tales and legends. One of the goals of this unit was to place these tales and legends within a historical and cultural framework. By visiting different websites and completing different tasks, students came to the understanding that these tales and legends were intrinsically linked to people's history, oral culture, and mysticism.

Other participants also used technology to allow their students to discover the target culture. However, these activities tended to be used to help students communicate and function in a pragmatic manner in the target culture. For instance, a participant, Pam, created an activity about subways in Germany. Students would visit the website of a German subway company and create an itinerary for a trip. They select a point of departure and arrival and talk about what they would visit in the neighborhood that they chose. She also created a web-based unit plan on racism in Germany. It was based on her experience as a teacher in Germany where she witnessed racism toward Turkish immigrants. The goal of the unit was to talk about issues of immigration in Germany and the United States. She was apparently inspired by the workshops that the first author conducted in the M.Ed. program. Although this student wanted to raise awareness about racism she was not able to do it from the perspective of an insider. Contrary to Michaela and Andrea, she did not use her own racial and ethnic identity as a platform. She was a White outsider (witness) who talked about racism experienced by a group of people of color she did not belong to. None of the White participants used their own racial and ethnic identity as a platform to diversify their students' worldviews. As teachers educators, what we learned from this experience was that it is necessary to provide pre-service teachers with the opportunity to address issues of inequity from both a privileged and subordinate perspective.

Identity and Learning Technology

In this section, we will demonstrate that Michaela and Andrea's motivation to incorporate technology into their teaching was enhanced in part because they had the opportunity to use the computer to assert their racial identity within the M.Ed. program.

Both Michaela and Andrea did not understand at first why they had to learn about computer technology in a FSLED M.Ed. program. Andrea believed that technology had the potential to enhance foreign-language education. However, she was also very skeptical. She liked to "teach the old fashion way and maybe enhance it with technology." As a student, she acquired skills that enabled her to not be dependent on computer technology; she also believed that computer technology should be used only to enhance one's teaching and that students should also acquire skills that would allow them not to be too dependent on computer technology. For example, once she expressed her surprise when she realized that students in her schools were incapable of calculating without a machine. According to Andrea, "You need to be able to still do long division. If you don't have a calculator, you need to be able to do that." To her, the trend to integrate technology into teaching could be detrimental to students' learning.

Michaela did not understand why she had to learn more about technology. She stated,

> I hated everything. I wasn't too sure how we should include technology. I wasn't really sure why. I didn't understand why it was in style now. It's like I don't want to be hype, just let me go. I hated it.

Michaela once compared designing a web-based unit plan to a mathematics class: "I just saw it like a Math class and Math has been my biggest challenge in class." To her, learning about computer technology was not relevant and challenging. As stated before, she was going through a difficult time in her personal life and she felt that she could not afford to fail. Moreover, from her experience she believed that she did not have the same technological capital as the other students and that she could once again be marginalized because of her lack of skills. Technology became a serious risk to her success in her M.Ed. program, as observed in her comment, "Yeah, it [technology] could be a threat."

It seems that one factor that enhanced Andrea's and Michaela's motivation to learn computer technology was to be able to use the computer to assert their racial identity. As part of their electronic portfolios, students in the program had to provide information about their background, their teaching philosophy, etc. In fact, they had to construct an identity online. It was important for Andrea to identify herself online as an African American teacher. As Andrea commented:

> I think it kind of gives the person that is looking at my website a little bit of who I am ... There's a part where I have my students' handbook and it's a little black teacher at the board and I love it because that is me. I don't think many people would expect to see that.

When asked if having the possibility of representing who she was racially made the assignment more appealing to her, she answered,

> Sure, sure ... how to personalize that web space more into whom I am. I wish I had a scanner because I would have included some of the pictures that I have at home, but I don't have that so my next best thing is to download clip art. That's what I do.

To our surprise, during the teaching practicum, Michaela was one of the students who used the most computer technology in her class. She transformed herself from being the most technology-phobic in the cohort to being the model student of technology. Michaela started using computer technology more extensively when she realized that it allowed her to broaden students' world-views. She commented,

> The main conclusion that I came to was that I can use it [computer] to do what I wanna do in the classroom, which is to make them [students] feel creative, and let them think outside the box ... have a little bit of awareness of the world we live in.

At the beginning of the M.Ed. program, neither Andrea nor Michaela were as enthusiastic as the majority of the participants about using computer technology. However, when they realized that the technology could be used to assert their racial identity, their enthusiasm rose and they started to infuse the technology extensively into their teaching. Merely having physical access to technology was not enough for them to incorporate it into their teaching.

Providing Access to Technology

The digital divide is often described as a difference between those who have physical access to technology and those who do not. Yet, it is not necessarily true that providing people with computers will decrease the divide and close the gap between minority and

White achievement. Indeed, having physical access to computers in the schools does not necessarily mean that teachers and students will use them, because having access is also influenced by historical and institutional practices (Damarin, 1998).

Access to technology cannot be solely reduced to its material and mechanical dimensions. Through the stories of Michaela and Andrea, we highlighted the fact that one's use of technology is highly complex. Access to technology is also rooted in people's history, beliefs, and identities. We believe that racism is shaped by the discourses that characterize historical and institutional practices (Foucault, 1975). We highlighted the fact that Andrea and Michaela were aware of the discourses concerning race that circulated in the M.Ed. program. When we use technology we bring with us our own knowledge, experience, and values. Michaela and Andrea's interactions with the technology that was accessible to them were in part influenced by their experiences as women of color. These experiences were rooted in historical and institutional practices. To access technology also means to make it our own, so that technology becomes an intrinsic part of the multiple ways we interact with the world(s) around us. The common belief concerning technology is that it is a neutral and passive tool that is subject to its user (Zhao, Alavarez-Torres, Smith, & Tan, 2004). Such a definition is problematic because it overshadows the fact that technology, like any tool, is a cultural artifact that comes with shapes, expectations, and pedagogical as well as philosophical biases. What a user does with the tool is shaped by the user's history and experiences. When using Microsoft Word 2000, Andrea was unable to find racially diverse clip art of teachers and struggled to find such images even on the Internet. Accessing technology also means that one is able to reconstruct the technology and to make it one's own. By building an identity online, through the design of their electronic portfolio, Andrea and Michaela were provided with the space to challenge the existing discourse and reclaim their identity as women and teachers of color. By reconstructing the technology into their own image they truly made it their own.

Considering technology as a cultural artifact rather than a neutral tool has implications for foreign/second language teacher education. When integrating technology into a teacher-education program, it is crucial to provide pre-service teachers with the skills to critically assess the technology, including images and texts available to them. Such assessment should enable them to both highlight the unique features of each technological device and understand that these features have a significant impact on users' social, linguistic, and psychological expression (Zhao et al., 2004).

Pre-service teachers should also be able to critically assess the content of the information provided online. Foreman, Buckmire, and Maeda (1998) have shown that using technology to teach from a critical point of view could help decrease the digital divide by providing students with the "critical expertise to communicate effectively in the post-industrial, post-affirmative action, information, era" (p. 1). Ladson-Billings (1994) argued that successful teachers of students of color were teachers who adopted a culturally relevant approach to their teaching. According to her, the primary goal of culturally relevant teaching is to assist in the development of a relevant personality that allows students of color to be successful academically and still identify with their home culture. Ladson-Billings described culturally relevant teaching as a pedagogy that "empowers students intellectually, socially, emotionally, and politically by using cultural referents to impart knowledge, skills, and attitudes" (p. 8). Foreign-language teaching provides a perfect platform for teachers to be social activists by challenging their notion of otherness (Reagan & Osborne, 2002). Michaela's and Andrea's learning processes of technology-integrated language education were in part enhanced by the fact that these women had the opportunity to relate the subject matter to their personal experience and to empower themselves as women teachers of color by using the technology as a tool of resistance. We believe that a critically relevant pedagogy is crucial for any teacher-education program. What is also critical for teacher education is to explore how racial and ethnic minorities can critically utilize instructional and information technology.

Conclusion

Through describing the experiences of two pre-service teachers of color with technology in an M.Ed. program, we were able to highlight the ways in which race interacted with technology and impacted the participants' learning experiences. Moreover, this study enabled us to problematize the notion of access by situating it within a sociocultural and critical framework. Issues of race, access, and technology have been the topic of many studies. However, few studies address these issues within the context of a pre-service language-teacher education program. Race is just one of the multiple layers that characterize the ways in which one interacts with technology. We believe that gender, class, sexual identity, and religious beliefs also play an important role in the way that one may access the available technology. To keep improving minority access to technology, there is a need for more research on technology-enhanced language teaching, which examines the intersections of various dimensions of social identity (e.g., gender, race, class, sexual identity) and power. More research on the ways in which technology can support those who have been traditionally excluded from education is also needed. Furthermore, it is important to explore how technology can help teachers and students critically address racial identities and racism in foreign-language classrooms.

Discussion Questions

1. Think about one instance where you had created a profile online (dating service, blogs, personal websites, etc.). Have you ever tried to alter your identity online and why?
2. When you send an email or when you are chatting, do you think about the gender, race, or religion of the person you are writing to? Are there any signs that enable you to "read" a person's racial identity? How does such representation affect your interaction with this person?
3. The authors argue for a culturally relevant and responsive approach to teacher education. How can culturally responsive teaching support racial-minority students in developing proficiency in computer technology?
4. The authors argue that for racial-minority learners, physical access to technology is a critical first step but is not sufficient. What else must be present before technology can ensure academic success for minorities such as women, poor, and working-class learners?

Acknowledgments

This research was supported by the United States Department of Education's "Preparing Tomorrow's Teachers to Use Technology" (PT3) grant program. Implementation: P342A000135.

References

Albright, J., & Luke, A. (2008). *Pierre Bourdieu and literacy education*. New York: Routledge.

Blackburn, M. V., & Clark, C. T. (2007). *Literacy research for political action and social change*. New York: Peter Lang.

Bolgatz, J. (2005). *Talking race in the classroom*. New York: Teachers College Press.

Bonilla-Silva, E. (2002). The linguistics of color blind racism: How to talk nasty about blacks without sounding "racist." *Critical Sociology, 28*(1), 42–64.

Bonilla-Silva, E. (2003). *Racism without racists: Color-blind racism and the persistence of racial inequality in the United States*. Lanham, MD: Rowman & Littlefield.

Bush, M. E. L. (2004). *Breaking the code of good intentions: Everyday forms of whiteness*. Lanham, MD: Rowman & Littlefield.

Canagarajah, A. S. (1999). *Resisting linguistic imperialism in English teaching*. Oxford: Oxford University Press.

Cummins, J., & Sayers, D. (1995). *Brave new schools: Challenging cultural literacy through global learning networks*. New York: St. Martin's Press.

Damarin, S. K. (1998). Technology and multicultural education: The question of convergence. *Theory into Practice, 37*(1), 11–19.

DuBois, W. E. B. (1961). *The souls of Black folk*. Greenwich, CT: Fawcett Publications. (originally published in 1903 Chicago: A. C. McClurg & Co.).

Edsall, T., & Edsall, M. D. (1992). *Chain reaction*. New York: W.W. Norton.

Foreman, G., Buckmire, R., & Maeda, D. (1998). *Race, gender, and justice at Occidental College*. Retrieved October 15, 2004 from www.georgetown.edu/crossroads/AmericanStudiesAssn/newsletter/archive/articles/fore.html.

Foucault, M. (1975). *Surveiller et punir*. Paris: Gallimard.

Fouché, R. (2000). *"Say it loud, I'm black, and I'm proud": African American and vernacular technologic creativity*. Retrieved October 15, 2004 from www.rpi.edu/~fouche/fouchesayitloud.htm.

Freeman, D., & Johnson, K. (1998). Reconceptualizing the knowledge-base of language teacher education. *TESOL Quarterly, 32*, 397–416.

Hanson, K. (1997). *Gender, "discourse," and technology*. (ERIC Document Reproduction Service No. ED 418 913.)

Howard, G. R. (1993). Whites in multicultural education: Rethinking our role. *Phi Delta Kappan, 75*, 36–41.

King, J., Hollins, E., & Hayman, W. (1997). *Preparing teachers for cultural diversity*. New York: Teachers College Press.

Kolko, B. E., Nakamura, L., & Rodman, G. B. (2000). *Race in cyberspace*. New York: Routledge.

Ladson-Billings, G. (1994). *The Dreamkeepers: Successful teachers of African American children*. San Francisco, CA: Jossey-Bass Publishers.

Merryfield, M. (2001). Moving the center of global education: From imperial world views that divide the world to double consciousness, contrapuntal pedagogy, hybridity, and cross-cultural competence. In William B. S. (Ed.), *Critical issues in social studies research for the 21st century* (pp. 179–208). Greenwich, CT: Information Age Publishing.

Mossberger, K., Tolbert, C. J., & Stansbury, M. (2003). *Virtual inequality: Beyond the digital divide.* Washington, DC: Georgetown University Press.

Motha, S. (2006). Racializing ESOL teacher identities in U.S. K-12 public schools. *TESOL Quarterly, 40,* 495–518.

Nakamura, L. (2000). Where do you want to go today? Cybernetic tourism, the Internet, and transnationality. In B. Kolko, L. Nakamura, & G. Rodman (Eds.), *Race in cyberspace* (pp. 15–27). New York: Routledge.

Norton, B. (1998). Rethinking acculturation in second language acquisition. *Prospect: A Journal of Australian TESOL, 13*(2), 4–18.

Norton, B., & Toohey, K. (Eds.) (2004). *Critical pedagogies and language learning.* Cambridge: Cambridge University Press.

Paradies, Y. (2005). Anti-racism and Indigenous Australians. *Analyses of Social Issues and Public Policy, 5*(1), 1–28.

Raymond, H. (1999). Learning to teach foreign languages: Case studies of six pre-service teachers in an education program. (Doctoral dissertation, Ohio State University, 2000.) *Dissertation Abstracts International, 61*(5), AAT 9971625.

Reagan, T., & Osborne, T. (2002). *The foreign language educator in society: Toward a critical pedagogy.* Mahwah, NJ: Lawrence Erlbaum Associates.

Reid, C. S. (2001). Technology counts 2001: Racial disparities. *Education Week, 20*(35), 16–17.

Silver, D. (2000). Margins the wires: Looking for race, gender, and sexuality in the Blacksburg electronic village. In B. Kolko, L. Nakamura, & G. Rodman (Eds.), *Race in cyberspace* (pp. 133–151). New York: Routledge.

Sterne, G. (2000). The computer race goes to class: How computers in schools helped shape the racial topography of the Internet. In B. Kolko, L. Nakamura, & G. Rodman (Eds.), *Race in cyberspace* (pp. 191–213). New York: Routledge.

Tognozzi, E. (2001). Italian language instruction: The need for teacher development in technology. *Italica, 78,* 487–498.

Warnick, B. (2001). Rhetorical criticism in new media environments. *Rhetoric Review, 20,* 60–65.

Warnick, B. (2002). *Critical literacy in a digital era: Technology, rhetoric, and the public interest.* Mahwah, NJ: Lawrence Erlbaum Associates.

Warschauer, M. (2000). Language, identity, and the Internet. In B. Kolko, L. Nakamura, & G. Rodman (Eds.), *Race in cyberspace* (pp. 151–171). New York: Routledge.

Wong, S. (2006). *Dialogic approaches to TESOL: Where the ginkgo tree grows.* Mahwah, NJ: Lawrence Erlbaum Associates.

Zhao, Y., Alavarez-Torres, M., Smith, B., & Tan, H. (2004). The non-neutrality of technology: A theoretical analysis and empirical study of computer mediated communication technologies. *Educational Computing Research, 30,* 23–55.

10 Operating Under Erasure

~~Race~~/Language/Identity[1]

Awad Ibrahim

Pre-reading Questions

This chapter is about race—or better racialization—and how it is connected to identity and second language acquisition. It looks at a group of French-speaking immigrant and refugee continental African youth and their language-learning experience in North America. Their *Blackness* is central to this experience and hip-hop and rap are figured prominently. If you were a part of this group,

- would you consider yourself *Black*?
- how would you define race in general and Blackness in particular in this context, and how would Blackness relate to your language learning and identity formation?
- that is, generally speaking, what is the link between race, language, and identity?

Introduction

> Identity is not as transparent or unproblematic as we think. Perhaps instead of thinking of identity as already accomplished fact, we should think, instead, of identity as a production, which is never complete, always in process, and always constituted within, not outside, representation.
>
> (Hall, 1990, p. 222)

Recruited under the umbrella of *crisis*, identities are coming back, Hall continues, they are *returning*. By *return*, Hall is not implying that the question of identity ever went away—after all, invisibility only means misrecognition, not inexistence—but that it is returning with a *particular kind of force*. This forceful return, in my view, is linked to poststructural, postcolonial, postmodern, antiracist, and feminist discourses which place identity formation and performance in that complex intersection of multiple discourses, including discourses of difference, subjectivity, language, history, memory, and power relations (cf. Althusser, 1971; du Gay, Evans, & Redman, 2000; Norton, 1997; Pennycook, 2000; Rajchman, 1995; Woodward, 1997; Yon, 2000).

This *return of identities* into the field of Second Language Acquisition (SLA), and bilingual processes in general, is exceptionally forceful. In fact, a plethora of work in applied linguistics that looks at the intersection of multiple axes of identity is now emerging (cf. Amin, 1997; Cummins, 1996; Goldstein, 1997; Gumperz, 1982; Heller et al., 1999; Ibrahim, 1999, 2000, 2001; Morgan, 1997, 1998; Nelson, 1999; Norton, 1997, 2000; Pennycook, 1999, 2000; Rampton, 1995; Toohey, 2000; Wong, 2000; among many others). This literature calls attention to two significant phenomena: the dialectic or dialogic relation between the macro and micro on the one hand, and the connection between identity and second language theories and technologies of teaching and learning on the other. Within these axes of identity, however, race has received little attention, if any. My intention in this chapter, therefore, is to fill in some of that gap by looking at both phenomena. That is, I intend to ethnographically explore the dialogue between the macro and the micro and to see, in turn, the extent to which this dialogue influences not only the identity-formation processes but language learning as well.

The chapter is guided by the following questions. If identities are ongoing *production*, unstable points of identification or "suture" (Silverman, 2000, p. 76)[2] that are given birth to at the borderland between the Self and the Other (Bakhtin, 1990, p. 365; Woodward, 1997, p. 39), and if this interstitial relation between the Self and the Other is based on unequal historical relations of power, first, what is the impact of this relation on how the Self forms and performs itself and, second, how are these identity-formation processes implicated in how and what one learns? Put otherwise, do societal macro structures play any role in our micro identity-formation processes and are these processes, in turn, connected to SLA? If so, how? In the case of race—the present that is made absent in SLA literature—how does one conceptualize its relation to identity-formation processes and second language learning in general?

Based on a critical ethnographic research project, this chapter will trace the impact of *becoming Black* on ESL learning, that is, the interrelation between the technologies of identity formation and second language learning. It contends that a group of French-speaking immigrant and refugee francophone-African youth that is attending an urban Franco-Ontarian high school in southwestern Ontario, Canada, enters, so to speak, a *social imaginary*—a discursive space in which they are already imagined, constructed, and thus treated as *Blacks* by hegemonic discourses and groups. This imaginary is directly implicated in who they identify with (Black America), which in turn influences what and how they linguistically and culturally learn. They learn Black English as a Second Language (BESL), which they access in hip-hop culture and rap lyrical and linguistic styles. This critical ethnography shows, I conclude, that (ESL) learning is neither neutral nor without its politics and pedagogy of desire and investment.

In what follows, I shall first review the literature that looks at the intersection of race, identity, and second language learning and, second, given its centrality in my research I shall pay special attention to the politics of identity. I then discuss my ethnographic study where I also offer a conclusion on the need to link the macro and the micro, identity and learning, classroom pedagogy and the political and the cultural.

The Alchemy of Race, Identity, and Second Language Learning

The ethnolinguistic terms in which the children of Dominican immigrants in Rhode Island think of themselves, i.e. as "Spanish" or "Hispanic," are frequently at odds with the phenotype-based racial terms "Black" or "African American," *applied to them by others* in the United States. Spanish language is central to *resisting* such

phenotype-racial categorization, which denies Dominican Americans their Hispanic ethnicity.

(Bailey, 2000, p. 555; my emphasis)

After a punctilious and painstaking review of the literature, this statement by Benjamin Bailey (2000) is as close as I got to what I want to explore in this chapter: linking
race, language, and identity. Bailey's main interest, which I shall explore later, is interconnected twofold. First, to investigate how Black immigrants translate and negotiate[3]
the North American Black/White dichotomy, and see, second, how the Spanish language is invoked as an identity location, a way of saying: "Contrary to what you see, this
is where I want to be located; as Hispanic." Significantly, both phenomena are *performed* against the backdrop of the racial politics in North America.

In North America, bodies are marked by history where Blackness is read not so
much in terms of ethnicity but through an essentialized gaze where skin color, hair,
nose, and so on determine who one *is* (hooks, 1992; Ibrahim, 2000, 2008; Omi &
Winant, 1998; West, 2000). However, we know by now that scientifically, i.e., biologically speaking, race does not exist. In fact, it is long declared dead[4] (Back & Solomos,
2000; Gilroy, 2000). And if the meaning does not lie in the object (Hall, 1997), pheno-
types for example, then what exactly are we talking about when addressing *race*?

In the social sciences, especially after the mid 20th century, the biologistic notions of
race have been rejected in favor of an approach which regards race as a social, historical, and political category (Cox, 2000; Essed & Goldberg, 2002; San Juan, 2002). The
biological death of race should thus be equated with its social, historical, and political
birth, since without a racial identity in North America, "one is in danger of having no
identity at all." This is because "We utilize race to provide clues about *who* a person is.
This fact is made painfully clear when we encounter someone whom we cannot conveniently racially categorize ... Such an encounter," Omi and Winant (1998, p. 16)
explain, "becomes a source of discomfort and momentarily a crisis of racial meaning."
Statements such as, "Funny, you don't look black," for Omi and Winant (1998, p. 16)
"betray an underlying image of what black should be." How one *looks like* here is con-
jugated as how one *is like*. Corollary, race becomes a *process* of signification, an ideological *event* where the meaning does not lie in the object (skin color, for example) but in
how the object is signified. The emphasis should therefore be not on *race* but on the
process of its signification: racialization, which is a product of what Lopez and Espiritu
(1990) call *racial lumping* which, in turn, produces a *panethnic* formula. This is a
formula where race and ethnicity (defined in terms of language, culture, and religion)
are fused together, and the internal difference among and within the so-called racial
groups is erased because, from the outsider's point of view, "They all look alike!" The
process of racial lumping or racialization, importantly, is closely connected to racism
and the establishment and maintenance of a "color line" (Omi & Winant, 1998, p. 20).

This racial logic for Omi and Winant (1998) is historical and began with slavery in
North America. By the end of the 17th century, Blackness was consolidated as the
umbrella under which Africans—whose specific identity was Ibo, Yoruba, Fulani, etc.—
were rendered one racial(ized) group; thus moving from ethnicity to race where the
latter obscured or rendered the former secondary. Following Omi and Winant (1998), I
use

the term racialization to signify the extension of racial meaning to a previously racially unclassified relationship, social practice or group. Racialization is an ideological process, an historically specific one. Racial ideology is constructed from pre-existing conceptual (or, if one prefers, discursive) elements and emerges from the struggles of competing political projects and ideas seeking to articulate similar elements differently.

(Omi & Winant, 1998, p. 18)

It is significant therefore, I conclude, to put the emphasis not on the definition of *race* but on the process of racialization and on one of its painful effects: racism. Hence, one might talk about *racism without race.*

This alchemic formula[5] of racialization is directly implicated in the identity-formation processes which in turn mediate what one learns and how. As I already stated, identity is not a static category, it is a dialogic process, a split between the Self and the Other. It is in this dialogue with the Other that the Self knows its virtues; it is in that split that the Other enters the Self. Such dialogue, I will show in my research, especially between Blackness and Whiteness, governs (Foucault, 1984) not only how the former sees itself, but also how it is seen by others. The Self, the Identity, the Subject is no longer found in isolation nor is it a saturated point. On the contrary, it is a meeting point between multiple discourses, including discourses of race and Otherness. Stuart Hall (2000) refers to this process of identity formation as the *New identity* which he distinguishes from the *Old identity*. Old and New identities are interchangeably used with Old and New ethnicities. The discourse and the logic of the Old identity, Hall (2000, p. 145) explains,

contains the notion of the true self, some real self inside there, hiding inside the husks of the false selves that we present to the rest of world. It is a kind of guarantee of authenticity. Not until we get really inside … do we know what we are really saying.

It is, in short, an expression of the Cartesian stable self where the subject is situated within static discourses of history, self, and memory.

The New identity discourse on the other hand is more complexly different. It neglects neither history (and the multiple discourses within which the subject finds itself and the contradictory nature of these discourses) nor power relations, the politics of positioning, nor the dialogic relationship between the Self and the Other. For Bakhtin (1990, p. 365), this dialogic relationship is indeed "a dialogue of social forces perceived not only in their static co-existence, but … as a dialogue of different times, epochs and days." It is "a dialogue that is forever dying, living, being born: co-existence and becoming are here fused into an indissoluble concrete unity that is contradictory, multi-speeched and heterogeneous."

The SLA, according to Hall and Eggington (2000), is still dominated by the discourse of Old identity, cognitive psychology and psycholinguistics. And when it comes to the public discussions on the teaching of English as an additional language, Hall and Eggington (2000, p. 1) find they "typically focus on such aspects of pedagogy as the latest teaching methods and techniques, multimedia materials and resources available for student use, and the 'how to's' of managing student behavior."

Obviously, the discourse of Old identity does not allow for a dialectic relation between the micro—'how to's—and the macro—linking classrooms and the students in terms of social class, age, race, gender, and location to broader social, cultural, and political contexts (Pennycook, 2000).

In spite of this, the influence of the New identity in the field of SLA is steadily increasing. Briefly, I want to review the literature that makes use of the intersection of race, identity, and second language teaching and learning. Its size is still remarkably small. Somehow most of the literature uses *ethnicity* as an operative or theoretical tool, largely at the expense of *race*, while others use the couplet race/ethnicity.

Mapping the Field

Approaching SLA chiefly from a largely theoretical, sociohistorical, and political vantage point, Pennycook (1998, 1999, 2000) is exceptionally insightful in exploring the connection between the political, the cultural, and English-language teaching (ELT) and, to a lesser extent, learning. Pennycook points to the need for a critical applied linguistics that does not take very lightly the idea nor the discourse of teaching English as an international language. The English language and its teaching (and learning), Pennycook contends, has a long and dark history of empire and colonialism. He sees a strong connection between the discourse of Old identity, colonialism and ELT. As he puts it,

> I want to argue that ELT theories and practices that emanate from the former colonial powers still carry the traces of those colonial histories both because of the long history of direct connections between ELT and colonialism and because such theories and practices derive from broader European cultures and ideologies that themselves are products of colonialism.
>
> (Pennycook, 1998, p. 19)

There is a need, he continues, to see the classroom not as a "closed box" where teachers try to help their students learn a language, which "is a set of structures, pronunciation, or acts that students need to learn" (Pennycook, 1998, p. 19). In lieu, he concludes, we need to see the classroom as a site of possibility, struggle, and complex social and cultural space where the macro is interwoven with the micro.

In their ethnographic study of the relations of students' in- and out-of-class cultural learning during a 5-week study-abroad program in Spain, Talburt and Stewart (1999) concurred with Pennycook. In it, the authors found a strong correlation between formal and informal learning experiences and students' gender and race. The only African American student in this program, Misheila, experienced the most restrictive access to and interactions with members of the host culture (Spain); indeed, she encountered insidious racism that hindered not only her second language learning but also her relation to her classmates. As professors, Talburt and Stewart themselves were not prepared for such a situation nor was it anywhere in the literature they reviewed. They hence called for a sustained discussion of students' sociocultural differences as part of the formal curriculum.

Eckert and McConnell-Ginet (1999) explore ethnographically the complex ways in which linguistic practices are used to demarcate territories, invoke identities, and eventually create a "community of practice," which they define as "a group whose joint engagement in some activity or enterprise is sufficiently intensive to give rise over time to a repertoire of shared practices" (Eckert & McConnell-Ginet, 1999, p. 185). Their study is about a crowd of Asian-American kids in an ethnically very heterogeneous junior high school in northern California "who hangs out in a spot that is generally known in the school as 'Asian Wall'" (Eckert & McConnell-Ginet, 1999, p. 185). The authors point to the internal diversity of "Asian Americanness," a category both embraced and resisted by the kids. Those who embrace or enter the Asian Wall, they explain, do so not "so much out of a sense of a pre-existing commonality, as out of a shared need to construct a commonality around which they can join forces" (Eckert & McConnell-Ginet, 1999, p. 186). One conclusion of interest to my study is the strong dependence and co-construction of gender, race/ethnicity, heterosexuality, life stage, and social status. In other words, none of these categories dealt (or could be dealt) with separately. Language here is both a medium of expression and of construction.

In an interesting way, Eckert and McConnell-Ginet's study is similar to Ben Rampton's (1995). In a detailed ethnographic study, Rampton looks at how linguistic practice is used both to abuse and create solidarity. This is done through *ritual expressions* that bank on certain expressions of the second language and do not require a full mastery of the language. Here language is also used as a social demarcation. Heller et al. (1999) find a similar phenomenon in their study of young Franco-Ontarians, where English is used contextually to mark oneself differently. The young use English, more fluently though, to sustain friendship and to mark themselves as bilingual or multilingual. They do so, precisely, because they are asked not to, where speaking French becomes *not cool*.

Using influential theorists like Cummins (1996) and Bourdieu (1991), Norton (1997, 2000) introduces a poststructural theory of subjectivity to the fields of SLA and TESL (Teaching of English as a Second Language). She argues that the question "Who am I?" cannot be understood apart from the question "What can I do?" She defines subjectivity or identity as "how people understand their relationship to the world, how that relationship is constructed across time and space, and how people understand their possibilities for the future" (Norton, 1997, p. 410). Like Pennycook, Norton argues that a successful learner is someone who is able to summon up or construct a social identity that enables him/her to invest in, struggle over, and hence create a symbolic capital, a linguistic repertoire. Learning here is linked to what one does with the language and how much access one has to it. Using Norton's theory, Amin (1997) found a strong correlation between accent, race, and ELT. People of color who may have English as their first language but who perform non-European, non-North American ways of speaking (such as in Caribbean, African, or Asian countries) are not considered natives of English. Hence, she found in the students' minds, native English speakers are Whites.

Benjamin Bailey's (2000) study, however, deserves special attention given its similarity to my own. Bailey looks at how young Dominicans negotiate identity, language, and the politics of racialization in the United States. Taking place in Rhode Island, Bailey's study shows the ongoing tension between how, in the case of Black immigrants, one defines oneself and how one is defined. As he put it,

> Dominican American self-definition of race in terms of ethnolinguistic heritage—as Spanish, Dominican, or Hispanic—runs counter to popular and historical US notions of race in which African-descent phenotype has preceded all other criteria (e.g., national origin, language, or religion) for social classification.

(p. 555)

This is because "African-descent RACE has historically been treated as equivalent to African-descent ETHNICITY in the US..., with the result that immigrants of African descent have largely merged into the African American population by the second generation" (Bailey, 2000, p. 555). Of interest in Bailey's study is the success that Wilson, a 17-year-old first-generation Dominican, has in using language to invoke, express, and negotiate his multiple ethnic/racial identities. He was able, for example, to use skillfully multiple language varieties to situationally highlight Dominican, American, and African American facets of his Dominican-American identity. Bailey thus concludes,

> Language is a medium which affords individual social actors the freedom to highlight various aspects of identity; but it is also a medium through which constraining, hegemonic forms of ascription—e.g. social classification based on phenotype—are invoked and reconstituted.
>
> (Bailey, 2000, p. 557)

An Ethnography of Performance: Methods and Data

The present research constitutes part of the larger critical ethnographic research[6] I conducted at Marie-Victorin (MV)[7] between January and June 1996. MV was a small, urban Franco-Ontarian intermediate and high school (grades 7 to 13) in southwestern Ontario, with approximately 400 students from various ethnic, racial, cultural, religious, and linguistic backgrounds. In the research, I asked the following questions. First, what are the roads taken by African youth in their journey of integration in Canadian society, the journey of *becoming Black*? What is the role of racialization—and racism—in their identity formation, and translation and negotiation of the North American Black/White dichotomy? How are continental African youth imagined, positioned, and constructed in and out of school? What are the implications of this construction in the youth social-identity formation? And what are the cultural, linguistic, and identity outcomes of this journey?

The research made use of the *ethnography of performance*, a methodological approach I developed elsewhere (Ibrahim, 1999, 2001, 2004). This is an ethnographic approach/method that builds on Butler's (1999) notion of *performativity*. For Butler, performativity is a concept that assumes not fixity but repetition, parody and continual act of becoming; it suggests that the subject can never *be* in full and complete, it is always to become, always in progress. Gender and race corollary are not static categories but the repeated stylization of the body, a set of recurrent acts, words, gestures, or what Roland Barthes (1983) calls complex semiological languages. These are signs that are open for signification and different readings since they cannot produce verbal utterances, yet they are ready to be spoken. These complex languages, Butler explains, are produced and performed on the surface of our bodies: in and through our modes of dress, walk, hairstyles, lip gloss, and so on. I am thus contending that we perform our identities, desires, investments, at least in part, in and through the complex semiological languages of dress, walk, and talk.

Methodologically, this theory of subjectivity has direct implications for ethnographic research. Ethnography of performance argues that, if identities are performed in and through the complex semiological languages of our dress, walk, and talk, then they become our best access as researchers to our research subjects' inner identity, what they think and desire, and how they long to represent themselves and to be represented. In other words, the inner selves/identities are best accessed in and through observing what people do and perform on the surface of their bodies. And to have a complete picture of our research subjects' identities, if ever this is possible, we need to follow them extensively in different places, at different times, and over extended periods of time, and ask them to verbalize and reflect upon their own performances/actions. And this is what I did.

First, it is worth noting that, at the time of the research, I was well-acquainted with MV and its population—especially its African population—since I worked on another research project in the same school for almost 2 years. I started the research by *hanging out*[8] with African students at least once a week, and in most cases, two or three times from January to June 1996. I was a participant-observer, keeping regular notes and diaries. I then chose for extensive observation 16 students—10 boys and six girls—between the ages of 14 and 20. The girls were Somali-speakers from Somalia and Djibouti. Of the 10 boys, six were Somali-speakers—from Somalia and Djibouti—two Senegalese, one Ethiopian and one Togolese. With no exception, all of the African students in MV were at least trilingual, speaking English, French, and their mother tongues, with various postcolonial histories of language learning and degrees of fluency in each language. They also varied in their length of stay in Canada and their legal status (some were immigrants, but the majority were refugees). I observed them in and out of the classrooms as well as in and out of school. With the consent of students and their parents, I interviewed them, individually or in groups, either in English or French; the majority, however, were in French. I also videotaped and on two occasions handed over the tape recorders to students to capture their natural interactions among themselves when I was not present. I attended soirées, plays, basketball games, and graduations, and was delighted to be invited to their residences. I transcribed and translated the interviews and some of the videotapes, and analyzed the data by grouping them by theme, category, and subject.

Though MV is a French-language school, the language spoken by students in the school corridors and hallways was predominantly English; Arabic, Somali, and Farsi were also spoken at other times. The research describes the journey of African youth in the school, Canada, and North America in general. Besides their gendered and racialized experience, their youth and refugee status was vital in their *moments of identification*, that is, where and how they saw themselves reflected in the mirror of their society. Put differently, once in North America, I contend, these youths were faced with a *social imaginary* in which they were already (seen and imagined as) Blacks. This social imaginary was directly implicated in how and with whom they identified, which, in turn, influenced what they learned, linguistically and culturally. What they did learn is Black Stylized English (BSE), which they accessed in and through Black popular culture. They learned by taking up and re-performing the rap linguistic and musical genre and, in different ways, acquiring and re-articulating the hip-hop cultural identity.

To explain, BSE is a subcategory of Black English (BE). BE is what Geneva Smitherman (2000) refers to as *Black talk*, which has its own grammar, morphology, and syntax. BSE, on the other hand, refers to ways of speaking that do not depend on a full mastery of the language. It banks more on ritual expressions such as *whassup, whadap, whassup* [what is happening] *my Nigger*, and *yo, yo homeboy* [cool friend], which are performed habitually and recurrently in rap. These rituals, I explain elsewhere, are more an expression of politics, moments of identification, and desire than they are of language or of mastering the language per se (Ibrahim, 1999). It is a way of saying, "I too am Black" or "I too desire and identify with Blackness."

Here, Black popular culture refers to films, newspapers, magazines, and more importantly music, such as rap, reggae, pop, and rhythm and blues (R&B). By *hip-hop*, more skeletally, I am referring to a way of dressing, walking, and talking. The dress refers to the myriad shades and shapes of the latest *fly gear*: high-top sneakers, bicycle shorts, chunky jewelry, baggy pants, and polka-dotted tops (Rose, 1991). The *walk* usually means moving the fingers simultaneously with the head and the rest of the body while walking. The *talk*, however, is BSE. In patterning these behaviors, African youth enter the realm of becoming Black. In sum, becoming Black is a *subject-formation project* (i.e., the process and the space within which subjectivity is formed) that is produced in and simultaneously produced by the process of language learning—BESL (Black English as a second language) learning in this case. More specifically, becoming Black means learning BESL; yet the very process of BESL learning produces the epiphenomenon of becoming Black.

Becoming Black is both a psychic and phenomenological event and takes place when Black immigrants *realize* how they are perceived and hence treated as *Blacks*, where the latter oscillates more toward the negative than the positive (West, 2000). Much like Bailey's study, explored above, African youth find themselves under a hegemonic gaze—a space of psychic formation—where their multiple identities are under erasure. As a continental African, for example, I was not considered Black in Africa; other terms served to patch together my identity, such as *tall, Sudanese,* and *basketball player*. However, as a refugee in North America, my perception of self was altered in direct response to the social processes of racism and the historical representation of Blackness whereby the antecedent signifiers became secondary to my Blackness, and I retranslated my being: I became Black.[9] In the case of African youth, becoming Black is phenomenologically performed in and through their dress, walk, and talk.

BESL Learning and the Politics of Identity/Identification

In Canada, the English language is normally the medium of everyday interaction, except in Quebec. And if African youth wanted to participate in its public life, they would have to learn English rapidly. Popular culture, especially television, as well as friendship and peer pressure, are three mechanisms that hasten the speed of learning the language (Ibrahim, 1999). However, making friends, and even learning English, is influenced by the popular imaginary, projected through the dominant source of representation: television. When I asked students in all the interviews, "*Où est-ce que vous avez appris votre anglais?*" [Where did you learn English?], "*télévision,*" they all responded. Within this *télévision*, significantly, is a particular representation—Black popular culture—that seems to *interpellate*[10] (Althusser, 1971) African youth identity and identification. Because African youth at first have few African Canadian/American friends, they access Black cultural identities and Black linguistic practice through Black popular culture, especially rap music video-clips, television programs, and Black cinema. When I asked Najat (14, F, Djibouti)[11] about the most recent movies she had seen, she responded:

NAJAT: I don't know, I saw *Waiting to Exhale* and I saw what else I saw, I saw *Swimmer*, and I saw *Jumanji*; so wicked, all the movies. I went to *Waiting to Exhale* wid my boyfriend and I was like *men are rude* [laughs].
AWAD: Oh believe me I know I know.
NAJAT: And den he [her boyfriend] was like *no women are rude*. I was like we're like fighting you know and joking around. I was like, and de whole time like [laughs], and den when de woman burns the car, I was like *go girl!* You know and all the women are like *go girl!* you know? And den de men like khhh. I'm like *I'm gonna go get me a pop corn* [laughs].

(individual interview, English)

Najat's response points to two very important phenomena. First, it shows the influence of Black English in the use of *de, den, dat,* and *wicked* as opposed to, respectively, *the, then, that,* and *really, really good* (Smitherman, 2000). Second, it shows that youth bring certain subjectivities to the reading of a text. Indeed, it is these social subjectivities, embedded in history, culture, and memory, that influence what they read and how they read it. Najat's reading of *Waiting to Exhale*, for example, was interpellated by her race and gender identities. She identified with the Black/woman in burning her husband's car and clothes.

In a similar vein, the following is another example (a videotaped moment) demonstrating the impact of Black popular culture on African students' lives and identities. Just before a focus-group interview I had with the boys, *Electric Circus*, a local television music and dance program that plays mostly, if not exclusively, Black music (rap/hip-hop, reggae, soul, and R&B) began. "*Silence!*" one boy exclaimed in French. The boys started to listen attentively to the music and to watch the different fashions of the young people on the program. After the show, the boys' code switched between French, English, and Somali as they exchanged observations on the best music, the best dance, and the cutest girl. Rap and rap music and the corresponding dress were obviously at the top of their list.

These moments of identification point to the process of identity formation which is, in turn, implicated in the linguistic norm to be learned and appropriated. A significant aspect to note about identification is that it works over a period of time and at the subconscious level. Omer (18, M, Ethiopia), in the following excerpt, addresses the different ways in which African youths are influenced by their identification with Black representations.

OMER: Black Canadian youths are influenced by the *Afro-Americans*. You watch for hours, you listen to Black music, you watch Black comedy, *Mr. T.*,[12] the *Rap City*. There you will see singers who dress in particular ways. You see, so.

(individual interview, French)

Similarly, Mukhi (19, M, Djibouti) argued that:

MUKHI: We identify ourselves more with the Blacks of America. But, this is normal; this
is genetic. We can't, since we live in Canada, we can't identify ourselves with Whites
or *country music, you know* [laughs]. We are going to identify ourselves, on the
contrary, with people of our color, who have our life style, you know.

(group interview, French)

Mukhi's identification with Blackness is clearly pronounced, and for him and all the
students I spoke to, this identification which is a pivotal part of their identity formation
is linked to their inability to relate to dominant groups, the public spaces they occupy,
and their cultural capitals and norms. Alternatively, Black popular culture, especially
rap, emerged not only as a site for identification, but also as a space for language learning. However, importantly, since rap and its features were more recurrent in the boys'
narratives than in the girls', this raises the question of the role of gender in the process
of identification. The following excerpts are two of the many occasions on which students performed their investment in Black North America through the re/citation of
rap linguistic styles.[13]

SAM: One two, one two, mic check. A'ait [alright], a'ait, a'ait.

JUMA: This is the rapper, you know wha 'm meaning? You know wha 'm saying?

SAM: Mic mic mic; mic check. A'ait you wonna test it? Ah, I've the microphone you
know; a'ait.

SAM: [laughs] I don't rap man, c'mon give me a break. [laughs] Yo! A'ait a'ait you know,
we just about to finish de tape and all dat. Respect to my main man [pointing to
me]. So, you know, you know wha 'm mean, 'm just represen'in Q7. One love to
Q7 you know wha 'm mean and all my friends back to Q7 ... Stop the tapin boy!

JAMAL: Kim Juma, live! Put the lights on. Wordap. [Students talking in Somali] Peace
out, wardap, where de book. Jamal 'am outa here.

SHAPIR: Yo, this is Shapir. I am trying to say peace to all my Niggaz, all my bitches from
a background that everybody in the house. So, yo, chill out and this is how we
gonna kick it. Bye and with that pie. All right, peace yo.

SAM: A'ait this is Sam represen'in AQA [...] where it's born, represen'in you know wha
'm mean? I wonna say whassup to all my Niggaz, you know, peace and one love.
You know wha 'm mean, Q7 represen'in for ever. Peace! [Rap music]

JAMAL: [as a DJ] Crank it man, coming up. [Rap music]

(group interview, English)

These excerpts are significant for many reasons. First, because they demonstrate the
influence of Black Stylized English, particularly the language of rap: "Respect for my
main man," "represen'in Q7," "kick the free style," "peace out, wardap," "'am outa here,"
"I am trying to say peace to all my Niggaz, all my bitches," "so, yo chill out and this is
how we gonna kick it," "I wonna say whassup to all my Niggaz," "peace and one love."
Second, when Shapir offers "peace to all" his "Niggaz," all his "bitches," he is indeed
repossessing the term *Nigga* (note the spelling),[14] a signifier common in rap/rap
culture. It is common, for example, nowadays, to call a Black friend, especially among

young people, *Nigga* without its traditional racist connotation. However, Shapir is using the sexist language that might exist in rap (Rose, 1991). These forms of sexism have been challenged by female rappers like Eve, Missy Misdemeanor Elliot and TLC and were critiqued by fellow female and male students. For example, Samira (16, F, Djibouti) expressed her dismay at the sexist language found in some rap lyrics:

SAMIRA: OK, *Hip-Hop*, yes I know that everyone likes *Hip-Hop*. They dress in a certain way, no? The songs go well. But, they are really really, they have expressions like *fuck*, *bitches* etc. Sorry, but there is representation.

(group interview, French).

Hassan (17, M, Djibouti) put it this way,

HASSAN: Occasionally, Rap has an inappropriate language for the life in which we live, a world of violence and all that.

(individual interview, French).

For Samy Alim (2007) and Alastair Pennycook (2007), Hassan's use of the word *inappropriate* is discomforting. It describes and reflects what I would call a superficial and heavily media-mediated reading of hip-hop. Hip-hop language is too complex to be brushed as *inappropriate* (Alim, Ibrahim, & Pennycook, 2008).

Nonetheless, in its broader semiological sense, the language of rap was obviously an influential site of identification and language learning for the boys. Depending on their age, the girls, on the other hand, had an ambivalent relationship to rap; though both boys and girls used the same three strategies in learning ESL in general, and BSE in particular, through music: *listening, reading* and *reciting*. Jamal, in the above-cited extract, for instance, was listening to the tunes and lyrics while reading and following the written text. Acting as a DJ, he then repeated not only the performer's words and expressions but also his accent. The girls also used similar strategies to Jamal's. During a picnic organized by a mixed group of males and females, for example, they listened to music while following the written text and reciting it (complete with accents) along with the singer. The girls' choice of music (e.g., Whitney Houston and Toni Braxton) differed in that it was softer than that chosen by the boys and contained mostly romantic themes.

In their relation to hip-hop and rap, the older females (16–18 years old), for the most part, tended to be more eclectic. This was evident in how they dressed and in the language they engaged with and learned. Their clothing was either elegant middle class, partially hip-hop, or traditional, and their learned language was what Nourbese Philip (1991) calls *plain Canadian English*.[15] The younger girls (12–14 years), on the other hand, like the boys, dressed themselves in hip-hop style and performed BSE. Nonetheless, I was able to detect three features of BE in both the older and the younger girls' narratives: the absence of the auxiliary be, BE negative concord, and the distributive be (for further details, see Ibrahim, 1999). Clearly, these young people are living the *hip-hop tension*: celebrating its genesis as a resistant cultural form and critiquing its commercialized, *inappropriate* use and abuse of language (see especially Ibrahim, 2004).

Belonging to What?: Identification, Investment, and Desire

Yet, whether male or female, the youth identification with Blackness is volitional, expressing identity-formation processes and acts of desire. As Amani (16, F, Somalia) contends:

AMANI: We have to wonder why we try to really follow the model of the Americans who are Black? Because *when you search for yourself, search for identification, you search for someone who reflects you, with whom you have something in common.*

(group interview, French; my emphasis)

In my conversation with Mukhi, he expressed similar ideas on the impact of rap (as just one among many other Black popular cultural forms) on his life and others' lives around him:

AWAD: But do you listen to Rap for example? I noticed that there are a number of students who listen to Rap eh? Is...

SAM: It is not just us who listen to Rap, everybody listens to Rap. It is new.

AWAD: But do you think that that influences how you speak, how...

MUKHI: *How we dress, how we speak, how we behave.*

(group interview, English; my emphasis)

These linguistic patterns and dress codes that Mukhi is addressing, on the one hand, are accessed and learned by African youth through Black (and to some extent, American commercial) popular culture and, on the other, as I have already noted, do not require mastery and fluency. Indeed, they are performative acts of desire and identification. Agreeing with both Mukhi and Amani, Hassan argues:

HASSAN: Yes yes, African students are influenced by Rap and Hip-Hop because they want to, yes, they are influenced probably a bit more because it is the desire to belong may be.

AWAD: Belong to what?

HASSAN: To a group, belong to a society, to have a model/fashion [he used the term *un modèle*]; you know, the desire to mark oneself, the desire to make, how do I say it? To be part of a *Rap* society, you see. It is like getting into *rock and roll* or *heavy metal.*

(individual interview, French)

Hence, one may conclude: *one invests where one sees oneself mirrored* (Ibrahim, 1999); an investment that is as much linguistic as it is cultural. Hassan indicated in another context that it would be awkward to see Blackness allied with rock and roll or heavy metal, as these are socially (and commercially) constructed as White music. On the other hand, he argued convincingly that African youths would have every reason to invest in basketball—constructed as a Black sport—but not hockey, for example.

The Return of the Repressed: Race-in-Language

[R]ace works like a language ... That is, there is always, or variously always, a certain sliding of meaning; always a margin not yet encapsulated in language and meaning; always something about race left unsaid; always someone, a constitutive outside, whose very existence the identity of race depends on, and it is absolutely distinct to return from its expel and abject position outside the signifying field, to trouble the dreams of those who are comfortable inside.

(Hall, 1996, transcript)[16]

This chapter is interested in the *sliding of meaning* or the *left unsaid* about race—or better racialization—and how it relates to second language acquisition and ESL. Consistently, I contended, race is left unsaid in the field of second language, either completely obfuscated or couched under *ethnicity*. In the case of Blackness, and given *its expel and abject position* and history in North America (and the Western world in general), I delineated that race was as salient—if not absolutely pivotal—in the process of second language learning. Reviewing the literature and exploring my own research, I walked through the roads taken by African youth in their journey of becoming Black and explored the outcomes of that journey. Rap and hip-hop were identified as influential sites of identification in African students' processes of becoming Black, which in turn affected what and how they learned (e.g., BESL). I have argued that the desire on the part of African youth, particularly the boys, to invest in basketball is analogously no different from their desire to learn BESL. Learning is hence neither aimless nor neutral, nor is it without the politics of identity. As I have shown, a second language learner can have a marginalized linguistic norm as a target, depending on who is learning what, why, and how. I have also discussed how these youth are becoming Blacks, which is a subject-formation project produced by and producing the very process of BESL. To become Black is to become an ethnographer who translates and looks around in an effort to understand what it means to be Black in Canada, for example.

In the course of this translation, importantly, the White gaze is clearly invisible, and so are the technologies of power and domination (Foucault, 1984). The invisible, however, is very real and as I have shown, these technologies permeate the fabric of our psyche, identity, and ways of being and learning (see also Auerbach, 1995). They are the macro mechanisms of power—including race, gender, sexuality, ability, and social class—and we can no longer afford to disregard and keep them outside our second language classrooms (Toohey, 2000). They constitute the axes of our identities—the identities we bring to the classroom, which, in the language of antiracism education (Dei, 1996), is the center of teaching and learning. We need, therefore, to link macro mechanisms of power with micro identity-formation processes, the cultural and the political with the linguistic. Especially in the field of applied linguistics, Pennycook lamented, "there seems to be a loud absence about such connections" (Pennycook, 1998, p. 19). Both as teachers and students, we are part of complex social, economic, and political relations that govern what we teach and learn, and how.

In sum, what I attempted to show in this chapter is the impact of these complex relations, especially race, on our social identities; that is, how they form and transform our subject-or-selfhood which, in turn, influence our language-learning processes and the linguistic norm we populate and eventually learn. In the case of race, we need to return and reposition these racialized subjectivities back into language-learning mechanisms and technologies and link the cultural, the social, the political, the stylistic, with the linguistic. I hope I have done precisely that. Central to this repositioning, however, are notions of identification, desire, and investment. We are yet to desire *the true word* to be spoken, Paulo Freire argued, only then can we desire *the world* differently (1993).

To conclude, for African youth, this chapter raises challenging questions around the modernist, essentialized Black/White dichotomy in North America and the Western world in general. Identity is here impositional, where choices are essentialized by a look, that is, by racially visible features. They may all have *become Black*, but, similar to Bailey's (2000) study, not every African student at MV *wanted* to become Black. On their part, ESL teachers therefore need to be exceptionally mindful of these complex and contradictory desires. They also need to fully grasp the multiethnic, multicultural, and multilingual nature of Blackness itself. For ESL teachers, the following urgent questions pose themselves: knowing these complex desires, what kind of curriculum material and texts should be introduced in an ESL classroom? How do we use these texts in deconstructing the modernist Black/White dichotomy? And above all, knowing what we know in this study, especially the impact of pop culture on the differently raced, sexualized, and gendered identities, are we as ESL teachers ready to make use of pop culture, namely hip-hop, in our classrooms? If so, how? In Paulo Freire's words, finally, how do we envision ourselves as teachers, our students, and our collective world differently using hip-hop as a complexly contradictory yet deeply desired text and music genre? Word up: this issshhhh is here to stay, deal with it! If you can decipher this last sentence, then you are ready to teach hip-hop; otherwise ask your students what it means.

Discussion Questions

1. Now, *what* is the link between race, language, and identity and *how* do these categories intersect?
2. Thinking specifically about race, first, why did Ibrahim erase ~~race~~ and, second, what are the processes and the reference points involved in becoming Black?
3. Describe what the phrase "ethnography of performance" means.
4. Explore the link between identification, desire, investment, and performativity in relation to BESL.

Notes

1. This chapter originally appeared as an article in the *Canadian and International Education Journal*, Vol. 37 (2) and is reprinted here with permission of the editor.
2. According to Silverman (2000, p. 76), suture is "that moment when the subject inserts itself into the symbolic register in the guise of a signifier, and in so doing gains meaning at the expense of being." That is, when something stands-in or takes-the-place-of something or someone, such as my name standing-in for me even in my absence.
3. These are extremely significant features of immigrants' identity-formation processes (Ibrahim, 2001).
4. It is common knowledge that there are more genes shared between than among the races (Back and Solomos, 2000).

5. Alchemy for me brings the metaphor of a laboratory and different chemical elements that give certain reactions and transmutations when put together. In the case of race, the social context is equated to the laboratory and the chemical elements are an expression of the social struggle and the competing definitions of race, whose meaning depends usually on the person signifying it.

6. For Simon and Dippo (1986, p. 195), *critical ethnographic research* is a set of activities situated within a project that seeks and works its way towards social transformation. This project is political as well as pedagogical, and who the researcher is and what his or her racial, gender, and class embodiments are necessarily govern the research questions and findings. The project, then, according to Simon and Dippo, is "an activity determined both by real and present conditions, *and* certain conditions still to come which it is trying to bring into being" (p. 196). The assumption underpinning my project was based on the assertion that Canadian society is "inequitably structured and dominated by a hegemonic culture that suppresses a consideration and understanding of why things are the way they are and what must be done for things to be otherwise" (p. 196).

7. All names are pseudonyms.

8. Staying somewhere to familiarize oneself with the place, its people, and their ways of "being" in that space. In the school, these sites are informal, such as hallways, the schoolyards, the school steps, the cafeteria, and the gymnasium, where the people in them are comfortable enough to speak their minds.

9. Fanon (1967, p. 116) sums up this idea brilliantly in writing about himself as a Black *Antillais* coming to the metropolitan center of Paris:

> I am given no chance, I am overdetermined from without. I am the slave not of the "idea" that others have of me but of my own appearance.... When people like me, they tell me it is in spite of my color. When they dislike me, they point out that it is not because of my color. Either way, I am locked into the infernal circle.

(my emphasis)

10. The subconscious ways in which individuals, given their genealogical history and memory, identify with particular discursive spaces and representations and the way this identification subsequently participates in the social formation of the Subject (identity).

11. Each participant's name is followed by his/her age, gender (F = female, M = male), and country of origin; and each extract is followed by the type of interview (individual or group) and the language in which it was conducted. The following transcription conventions are used:

underlined text	English spoken within French speech or French spoken within English speech
[ ]	Explanation or description of speaker's actions
[...]	Text omitted

12. Mr. T. is an M.C. of a local Canadian rap music TV program called Rap City which airs mostly American rap lyrics.

13. The participants cited in the extracts are Sam (19, M, Djibouti), Juma (19, M, Senegal), Jamal (18, M, Djibouti), and Shapir (17, M, Somalia).

14. To disrupt the racist connotation invoked by the term, *Nigga* with an "a" is used for affinity whereas with "er" for racist purposes (see Smitherman, 2000).

15. Of course my invocation of Philip's notion of "plain English" or what she also calls "flat English" is more poetic than literal. It is an imaginary language that is probably affiliated more with the Canadian Broadcasting Corporation (CBC) and its "plain," non-regionally-identifiable language than with the "actual," regionally different ways of speaking.

16. My transcript of a seminal lecture by Stuart Hall (1996); see also Hall (1997).

References

Alim, S. (2007). "The wig party don't exist in my hood": Knowledge, reality, and education in Hip-Hop Nation. In S. Alim & J. Baugh (Eds.), *Talkin black talk: Language, education, and social change* (pp. 12–23). New York: Teachers College Press.

Alim, S., Ibrahim, A., & Pennycook, A. (2008). *Global linguistic flows: Hip-Hop cultures, youth identities, and the politics of language.* London: Routledge.

Althusser, L. (1971). *Lenin and philosophy.* London: New Left Books.

Amin, N. (1997). Race and the identity of nonnative ESL teacher. *TESOL Quarterly 31,* 580–583.

Auerbach, E. (1995). The politics of ESL classroom: Issues of power in pedagogical choices. In J. Tollefson (Ed.), *Power and inequality in language education* (pp. 110–123). Cambridge: Cambridge University Press.

Back, L., & Solomos, J. (2000). *Theories of race and racism: A reader.* London: Routledge.

Bailey, B. (2000). Language and negotiation of ethnic/racial identity among Dominican Americans. *Language in Society, 29,* 555–582.

Bakhtin, M. (1990). *The dialogic imagination: Four essays* (M. Holquist & C. Emerson, Trans.). Austin, TX: University of Texas Press.

Barthes, R. (1983). *Elements of semiology.* New York: Hill and Wang.

Bourdieu, P. (1991). *Language and symbolic power* (G. Raymond & M. Adamson, Trans.). Cambridge, MA: Harvard University Press.

Butler, J. (1999). *Gender trouble: Feminism and the subversion of identity.* New York: Routledge.

Cox, O. (2000). *Race: A study in social dynamics.* New York: Monthly Review Press.

Cummins, J. (1996). *Negotiating identities: Education for empowerment in a diverse society.* Ontario, CA: California Association for Bilingual Education.

Dei, G. J. S. (1996). *Anti-racism education: Theory and practice.* Halifax, N.S.: Fernwood Publishing.

du Gay, P., Evans, J., & Redman, P. (2000). *Identity: A reader.* London: Sage Publications & The Open University.

Eckert, P., & McConnell-Ginet, S. (1999). New generalization and explanations in language and gender research. *Language in Society, 28,* 185–201.

Essed, P., & Goldberg, D. (2002). *Race critical theories.* Malden, MA: Blackwell Publishers.

Fanon, F. (1967). *Black skin white mask.* New York: Grove Weidenfeld.

Foucault, M. (1984). *The Foucault reader.* Harmondsworth: Penguin.

Freire, P. (1993). *Pedagogy of the oppressed.* New York: Continuum.

Gilroy, P. (2000). *Against race: Imagining political culture beyond the color line.* Cambridge, MA: Belknap Press.

Goldstein, T. (1997). *Two languages at work: Bilingual life on the production floor.* New York: Mouton de Gruyter.

Gumperz, J. (1982). *Language and social identity.* Cambridge: Cambridge University Press.

Hall, J. K., & Eggington, W. G. (2000). *The sociopolitics of English language teaching.* Clevedon, UK: Multilingual Matters.

Hall, S. (1990). Cultural identity and diaspora. In J. Rutherford (Ed.), *Identity, community, culture, difference* (pp. 222–237). London: Lawrence & Wishart.

Hall, S. (1996). *Race: The floating signifier* [videorecording produced, directed, and edited by Sut Jhally]. Northampton, MA: Media Education Foundation.

Hall, S. (1997). *Representation: Cultural representations and signifying practices.* London: Sage Publications.

Hall, S. (2000). Old and new identities, old and new ethnicities. In L. Back and J. Solomos (Eds.), *Theories of race and racism: A reader* (pp. 144–153). London: Routledge.

Heller, M. (with the collaboration of M. Campbell, P. Dalley, & D. Patrick). (1999). *Linguistic minorities and modernity: A sociolinguistic ethnography.* London: Longman.

hooks, b. (1992). *Black looks.* Boston, MA: South End Press.

Ibrahim, A. (1999). Becoming black: Rap and hip hop, race, gender, identity, and the politics of ESL learning. *TESOL Quarterly, 33,* 349–369.

Ibrahim, A. (2000). Identity or identification? A response to some objections. *TESOL Quarterly, 33,* 741–744.

Ibrahim, A. (2001). Race-in-the-gap: Émigrés, identity, identification, and the politics of ESL learning. *Contact, 27*(2), 67–80.

Ibrahim, A. (2004). Operating under erasure: Hip-Hop and the pedagogy of affect(ive). *Journal of Curriculum Theorizing, 20*(1), 113–133.

Ibrahim, A. (2008). The new *flâneur:* Subaltern cultural studies, African youth in Canada, and the semiology of in-betweenness. *Cultural Studies, 22,* 234–253.

Lopez, D., & Espiritu, Y. (1990). Panethnicity in the United States: A theoretical framework. *Ethnic and Racial Studies, 13,* 103–121.

Morgan, B. (1997). Identity and intonation: Linking dynamic process in an ESL classroom. *TESOL Quarterly, 31,* 431–540.

Morgan, B. (1998). *The ESL classroom: Teaching, critical practice, and community development.* Toronto: University of Toronto Press.

Nelson, C. (1999). Sexual identities in ESL: Queer theory and classroom inquiry. *TESOL Quarterly, 33,* 371–391.

Norton, B. (1997). Language and identity. Special issue. *TESOL Quarterly, 31,* 431–450.

Norton, B. (2000). *Identity and language learning: Gender, ethnicity and educational change.* London: Longman.

Omi, M., & Winant, H. (1998). Racial formations. In P. Rothenberg (Ed.), *Race, class, and gender in the United States* (pp. 13–22). New York: St. Martin's Press.

Pennycook, A. (1998). *English and the discourses of colonialism.* London: Routledge.

Pennycook, A. (1999). Special issue: Critical approaches to TESOL. *TESOL Quarterly, 33,* 329–348.

Pennycook, A. (2000). The social politics and the cultural politics of language classroom. In J. K. Hall & W. G. Eggington (Eds.), *The sociopolitics of English language teaching* (pp. 89–103). Clevedon, UK: Multilingual Matters.

Pennycook, A. (2007). *Global Englishes and transcultural flows.* London: Routledge.

Philip, M. N. (1991). *Harriet's daughter.* Toronto: The Women's Press.

Rajchman, J. (1995). *The identity in question.* New York: Routledge.

Rampton, B. (1995). *Crossing: Language and ethnicity among adolescents.* London & New York: Longman.

Rose, T. (1991). "Fear of a black planet": Rap music and black cultural politics in the 1990s. *Journal of Negro Education, 60,* 276–290.

San Juan, Jr., E. (2002). *Racism and cultural studies: Critiques of multiculturalist ideology and the politics of difference.* Durham, NC: Duke University Press.

Silverman, K. (2000). Suture: The cinematic model. In P. du Gay, J. Evans, & P. Redman (Eds.), *Identity: A reader* (pp. 76–86). London: Sage Publications & The Open University.

Simon, R. I., & Dippo, D. (1986). On critical ethnography work. *Anthropology & Education Quarterly, 17,* 195–202.

Smitherman, G. (2000). *Black talk: Words and phrases from the hood to the amen corner.* Boston: Houghton Mifflin.

Talburt, S., & Stewart, M. (1999). What's the subject of study abroad?: Race, gender, and "living culture." *The Modern Language Journal, 83,* 163–175.

Toohey, K. (2000). *Learning English at school: Identity, social relations and classroom practice.* Clevedon, UK: Multilingual Matters.

West, C. (2000). *Race matters.* Boston, MA: Beacon.

Wong, S. (2000). Transforming the politics of schooling in the U.S.: A model for successful academic achievement for language minority students. In J. K. Hall & W. G. Eggington (Eds.), *The sociopolitics of English language teaching* (pp. 117–139). Clevedon, UK: Multilingual Matters.

Woodward, K. (1997). *Identity and difference.* London: Sage Publications & The Open University.

Yon, D. (2000). *Elusive culture: Schooling, race, and identity in global times.* Albany, NY: State University of New York Press.

Part III

Toward a Dialectic of Critically Engaged Praxis

Discussing issues of race in the classroom may not be easy. However, racism underlies various kinds of inequalities, including unequal linguistic hierarchies of power, and influences the lives of learners and teachers in significant ways. Addressing issues of race is essential for teachers who are committed to critically engaged practice for social justice. Part III explores ways in which issues of race are manifested as well as theorized in classroom interactions, instructional texts, curriculum, teacher education, and personal reflections on teaching.

In Chapter 11, "Colorblind Nonaccommodative Denial: Implications for Teachers' Meaning Perspectives Toward their Mexican-American English Learners," Socorro Herrera and Amanda Rodriguez Morales present selected findings from an ethnographic case study that was conducted at a public junior high school in the U.S. southwest with a predominantly Mexican-American student population. Drawing on Jack Mezirow's notion of meaning perspectives that signify one's ways of feeling and acting, the authors detail one major psychological meaning perspective—colorblind nonaccommodative denial (CND), which was shared among teachers in the study. This perspective is discussed in terms of two hallmarks: *colorblindness*, characterized by the statement, "I don't see color, only students"; and *no accommodation*, as seen in teachers' unwillingness to accommodate the needs of Mexican-American students through classroom instruction, structure, or curriculum. Implications for teacher practice and educational policy are explored.

In Chapter 12, "Transforming the Curriculum of NNESTs: Introducing Critical Language Awareness (CLA) in a Teacher Education Program," Carmen Chacón presents an action research project that took place at an English teacher-education program in Venezuela. Aiming to raise student teachers' critical awareness of language and its intersection with race and power, the project introduced CLA through readings and class discussions and encouraged critical reflection of assumptions around issues of power, race, and language. The analysis of journals, class recordings, and a teacher-researcher diary revealed the participants' struggle with their identities as NNESTs and Venezuelans, some of which involved contesting racist discourses not only in English but also in Spanish. Through self-reflection, the participants challenged racist discourses and social inequity. Results suggest that incorporating CLA into the education of NNESTs helps them create a sense of agency and transformation in the search for equity and social justice.

Chapter 13, "Narratives in the Wild: Unpacking Critical Race Theory Methodology for Early Childhood Bilingual Education," addresses race-conscious pedagogy for young

bilingual children of color. Although young children develop ideas of race through interacting with their teacher and peers as well as texts used in the school, racialization of
bilingual children in instructional practices is underexplored. Sara Michael-Luna tackles
this issue through her ethnographic research in a Spanish–English bilingual first-grade
classroom in the United States. Drawing on critical race theory and critical discourse
analysis, she investigates whether children's literature and classroom interactions model
or create space for counter-narratives for children from South America. The data suggest
that texts tend to merely address superficial artifacts, whereas the discussion in Spanish
about Mexican leaders in the classroom enabled students to engage in learning in more
culturally and socially responsive ways. Michael-Luna makes concrete pedagogical suggestions to create space for young multilinguals to construct and resist embedded dominant-culture assumptions about race and language.

In Chapter 14, "Linguicism and Race in the United States: Impact on Teacher Education from Past to Present," Theresa Austin draws on linguicism and critical race theory to
analyze reproduction of racial disadvantage in teacher education. The author examines
how public systems of education in the United States are unsuccessful in educating teachers to reach diverse children. This chapter uses historical policy analysis to show how linguicism dating back to the era of slavery has permeated cross-ethnic encounters in key
moments of reform in U.S. public-education history, and how its legacy continues to
affect teachers who do not grow up speaking so-called Standard English, regardless of
their value to school systems. The author describes the process of developing a teacher-
education program for minority professionals which integrated critical issues of race, language, and politics so that these teachers can serve as agents of change.

In Chapter 15, "Un/Marked Pedagogies: A Dialogue on Race in EFL and ESL Settings," Eve Haque and Brian Morgan engage in a dialogue to examine the possibilities
and limitations of critical multicultural and antiracist pedagogies in the contexts of
Japan and China respectively. The authors discuss a number of key concerns regarding
theory and practice in relation to race and gender in TESOL. By personalizing and contrasting their own entry into the profession, Haque and Morgan illustrate the field's
emerging awareness of differential privileges and constraints based on identity categories of race and gender. Against deterministic sociological theories, the authors end
with an optimistic note by stressing that while they are differently interpellated into the
global field of TESOL, they also retain their creative agentive roles in defining who they
are and can be as teachers.

Finally, in Chapter 16, "Race and Language as Capital in School: A Sociological Template for Language-Education Reform," Allan Luke presents a theoretical explication of
the ways in which race and literacy serve as forms of capital, as defined by Pierre Bourdieu, brought into the contingent social and cultural fields of schools and classrooms.
While drawing on Pierre Bourdieu's theoretical notions of social and cultural fields,
habitus, and capital, Luke argues convincingly for the possibility of different social
actors (e.g., teachers, principals) to actually set and change conditions for students to
use, deploy, and capitalize on the resources (capital) they bring to the school, and thus
the possibility of changing the rules of exchange governing different kinds of capital in
the cultural fields in these social actors' institutions.

11 Colorblind Nonaccommodative Denial

Implications for Teachers' Meaning Perspectives Toward their Mexican-American English Learners

Socorro Herrera and Amanda Rodriguez Morales

Pre-reading Questions

Many parts of the United States are facing an increasing number of immigrant students. Focusing on mostly White teachers at a junior high school, which enrolls predominantly Mexican immigrant students, Socorro Herrera and Amanda R. Morales examine these teachers' belief system. The authors identify the perspective of *colorblind nonaccommodative denial* among these teachers.

- What is a colorblind perspective? How does it affect everyday teaching practices?
- How would teachers justify their not accommodating minority students? What are the educational consequences of nonaccommodation?

Introduction

Improving the learning experiences of culturally and linguistically diverse Mexican-American students in the United States is a complex task critical to the future stability and quality of life in the United States. A recent U.S. Census Bureau report indicates "Hispanics accounted for half of the 2.9 million population growth from 2003 to 2004 and now constitute one-seventh of all people in the United States" (Jelinek, 2005). Conversely, Hispanic Latinas/Latinos constitute the highest dropout rates of any population in the nation, 350,000 per year (Montemayor & Mendoza, 2004). In the last decade, as a proactive approach, researchers and reflective practitioners alike have sought to evaluate, understand, and improve the conditions of schools for culturally and linguistically diverse (CLD) students.

Theory and research has shown that teachers, administrators, and the overall school climate they create play a critical role in the educational success of all students (Baker, 1996; Banks & Lynch, 1986; Benard, 1997; Carr & Klaussen, 1997; Ginorio & Huston, 2001; Johnson, 2002; Palmer, 2003). For better or for worse, the social climate of schools exists as the incubator for attitudes and ways of thinking about race and class that in turn affect teaching and learning (Chang, 2003; Garcia & Van Soest, 1997; Johnson, 2002). For historically oppressed peoples, determining whether discriminatory acts are based on race or socioeconomic status is not always easy. Due to social and historical factors unique to the United States, the oppressed often possess characteristics that make them a target for both. As specified by Helms (1990), "racism is a complex ideology that occurs at individual, cultural, and institutional levels" (p. 4). Because the evidence of its existence in a system is often subtle, the marriage of racism and power proves to be a subversive phenomenon that is difficult to identify and evaluate in school policy and practice (Chang, 2003; Walker, Shafer, & Iiams, 2004). Larson and Ovando (2001) discuss how this is commonly perpetuated in schools: "When inequity has been institutionalized, teachers and administrators no longer have to be biased to continue biased practices; we merely have to do our jobs and maintain the normal practices of the systems we have inherited" (p. 3).

With Mexican Americans being the most demographically relevant population impacting schools today, it is important to evaluate the implications that this dynamic has for their learning, language development, and educational experience (Chen & Goldring, 1992; Contreras & Lee, 1990; Montemayor & Mendoza, 2004; Valencia, 1991). As many researchers have argued, there are few studies that evaluate mainstream teachers' attitudes toward Mexican Americans, and even fewer that focus on how those attitudes and deeply embedded beliefs translate into action regarding second language learners (Chang, 2003; Herrera & Morales, 2005; Johnson, 2002; Kubota, 2004; Walker et al., 2004). These beliefs-in-action shape decisions for programming, curriculum and instruction, and access to opportunities for Mexican-American students.

A distinct avoidance of honest discourse on cultural and linguistic difference perpetuates misconceptions that lead educators to pursue superficial strategies and procedural experiences with racial diversity in an attempt to *lessen* the issues they have with teaching this population. Unfortunately, these types of treatments (e.g., discussion of cultural difference solely within the context of food and festivals) are known to have little impact in fundamentally altering majority teacher and student perceptions or Mexican-American students' performance. Because race impacts both student and teacher identity development, at best these treatments may increase teachers' tolerance of these students (Chang, 2003). They cannot, however, move educators beyond the surface to consider and address the underlying issues of inequity, discrimination, White privilege, and institutional racism that permeate our schools (Nieto, 1995; Youngs & Youngs, 2001).

The chronic failure of educators to address these issues with honesty strongly reflects the need for a specific theoretical framework to examine *why*. This framework would enable insightful descriptions and interpretations of teachers' perspectives that shape not just their discourse but, more importantly, their actions. Therefore, this study is timely by providing one such framework within the context of a psychological meaning perspective. *Colorblind nonaccommodative denial* is a psychological meaning perspective that sheds light on how the schemes *colorblindness* and *no accommodation* impact teaching and learning for CLD students.

The phrase *culturally and linguistically diverse* (CLD) is the most inclusive and descriptive of a student whose culture and/or language differ from the dominant culture or language in his or her social context. The researchers chose to use the term CLD in the place of English-language learner (ELL) to specifically emphasize the needs of those high-risk students in schools who either have been exited out of an ESL program or whose English proficiency scores are just high enough to not qualify for services, monitoring, or support by the school (Buxton, 1999; Chamot & O'Malley, 1994; Escamilla, 1999; New York State Department of Education, 2002).

Theoretical Framework

The term *meaning perspective*, used by Jack Mezirow (1990), refers to the "structure of assumptions within which one's past experience assimilates and transforms new experience" (p. 42). This meaning perspective encompasses a habitual set of expectations providing an orienting frame of reference or perceptual filter that one uses in the interpretation of experience. These interpretations regularly take the form of symbolic models, which are the product of past experiences, and which are projected onto the interpretation of current experience. At the same time, a meaning perspective serves as a tacit belief system for the interpretation and evaluation of the meaning of experience.

More specifically, Mezirow (1991) elaborated on three types of such meaning perspectives: epistemic, sociocultural, and psychological. Epistemic meaning perspectives embody the way we know what we know and the uses that we make of the resultant knowledge. Among the factors that shape our epistemic meaning perspectives, Mezirow (1991, p. 43) lists the following: developmental stage perspectives: cognitive/learning/intelligence styles; sensory learning preferences; scope of awareness; global/detail factors; concrete/abstract thinking; and reflectivity.

Sociocultural meaning perspectives represent our ways of believing, involving social norms, cultural or linguistic codes, and social ideologies. According to Mezirow, some factors that shape this perspective are social norms/roles, cultural/language codes, language/truth games, common sense as cultural system, ethnocentrism, prototype/scripts, and philosophies/theories (1991, p. 43).

The third type, psychological meaning perspectives, reflect one's ways of feeling, involving repressed parental and social prohibitions from childhood that influence adult feelings and behavior. Mezirow has concluded that the following factors shape our psychological meaning perspectives: self-concept; locus of control; tolerance of ambiguity; lost functions; inhibitions; approach/avoidance; and psychological defense mechanisms (1991, p. 43).

Mezirow (1991) believes that our meaning perspectives act as filters on the way we interpret and construe what we experience through our senses. Language and symbolic interaction (communication) personalizes and expands upon these means of interpretation. Additionally, meaning perspectives influence our ways of seeing, our methods of inquiry, and our actions in context. Not surprisingly, "The most significant transformations in learning are transformations of meaning perspectives" (Mezirow, 1991, p. 38). Such transformations enable more discriminating, inclusive, permeable, and integrative meaning perspectives through critical reflection on the taken-for-granted premises and assumptions of our bio-psycho-cultural history, premises and assumptions that are uncritically assimilated throughout our socialization.

According to Mezirow (1991), each of our meaning perspectives can embody several *meaning schemes*. In an important differentiation between the two terms, he clarifies that, "A meaning scheme is the particular knowledge, beliefs, value judgments, and feelings that become articulated in an interpretation" (p. 44). Meaning schemes are the concrete manifestations of our orientation and expectations (meaning perspectives) and translate these general expectations into specific ones that guide our action.

Analysis of teachers' discourse in this ethnographic case study indicated a psychological meaning perspective shared among teachers in their day-to-day interactions with Mexican-American junior high school students. As themes emerged, two major areas of implication for this psychological meaning perspective were evidenced: (1) teacher/faculty decisions for programming and classroom management, and (2) their decisions regarding curriculum and instruction for their students, who are predominantly Mexican-American English learners. This chapter will present an overview, the findings, a discussion, and the implications of this psychological meaning perspective, colorblind nonaccommodative denial, as indicated by teachers' discourse.

Meaning perspectives are, without doubt, a guiding force in interpretation of that which we experience daily. It is important to note that the authors of this piece are both Latinas with meaning perspectives uniquely their own. Herrera is an immigrant whose life, both personal and academic, has been influenced by what it means to be an English-language learner in the United States. Morales's interpretation is through the lens of a biracial Latina who grew up in the rural Midwest as part of the only family of color in her hometown. The authors took a synergistic approach to interpreting the data with an open heart and mind to ensure, to the greatest extent possible, that their own worlds did not cloud their perceptions of the world-views held by the educators participating in this study.

Context of Study

This study focused on how teachers' assumptions and beliefs are translated into professional practice in the context of a public junior high school in the southwestern United States. The major findings of the study emerged from the qualitative research question: What meaning perspectives are indicated by teachers' discourse and action regarding their day-to-day interactions with their Mexican-American junior high school students? From this overarching question, the researchers gained insight into the historical and social context of race relations at this junior high school and the implications they have for their Mexican-American English learners.

According to Mezirow's transformation theory, which served as the substantive framework for the study, a *meaning perspective* functions as a structure of assumptions and a belief system through which we interpret and evaluate experience (Mezirow, 1990, 1991). Among the three types identified by Mezirow, findings from this comprehensive study include five distinct meaning perspectives held by teachers in their daily interactions with students. Two of these meaning perspectives are epistemic in nature, two are sociocultural and one is psychological. In this chapter, the authors focus on the finding related to the psychological meaning perspective—*colorblind nonaccommodative denial*.

Methodology

This research was conceptualized as an ethnographic case study. The design of this study can be summarized in the following design components: (a) development of field relationships; (b) site and sample selection; and (c) data collection and data analysis. Field relationships were developed using ethical strategies for negotiation, exchange, and reciprocity (Jorgensen, 1989). The junior high school chosen for the study will be identified by the pseudonym Valverde. The site for this study is situated within an urban, working-class community in the southwest. The community is comprised of both Mexican Americans who are immigrants and those whose roots are deeply grounded in the community in which they reside. At the time of the study, 75% of the students in the school were of Mexican-American descent, 6% were African American, and 19% were White non-Hispanic, a term used by the district. Some 85% of the student population was considered economically disadvantaged (a term also used by the district) and 13% received special education services.

While the school had an ESL program for recent immigrants identified as ELLs, a majority of the Mexican-American students at Valverde had been exited from ESL or bilingual programs in elementary school or had gained enough English for *basic interpersonal communicative skills* (BICS) prior to entering school to be placed in regular classrooms, even though they came from homes where Spanish was the dominant language (Cummins, 1981). For this reason, the researchers chose to situate the study with content-area teachers in regular classrooms where students' *cognitive academic language proficiency* (CALP) often was not at a level where full participation in classroom activities was possible, given that little or no modification was being made to instruction (Collier, 1995; Cummins, 1981). Given their difference in language and culture and the lack of experience/training held by the teachers who taught them, the researchers found these students to be at great risk (Cummins, 1989; Herrera & Murry, 2005).

The teacher population at Valverde was typical at the state and national level with the staff being over 85% White. The participant group for this study consisted of 36 White teachers and one Latina teacher. Nine of the participants were male and 28 were female. The range of classroom experience was quite broad with one being a first-year teacher and one teacher going on her 37th year in the classroom. The average years-of-experience for the group was 17. This sample was selected as a bounded system and served as the unit of analysis for the study (Chein, 1981).

Participant observations of classroom instruction, individual and group interviews, reflection sessions (researcher-led group discussions of participants' practice), and evaluation of participant-generated records constituted the primary sources of data in this case study (Merriam, 1998). All observation sessions and interviews were audiotaped and videotaped. The recording of field notes taken by the researchers accompanied each session of participant observation. The primary documents collected for evaluation included: critical-incident analyses; concept maps; reaction papers; reflective progress reports; cross-cultural platforms; and daily reflective journals prepared by teachers.

The researchers investigated such artifacts and conducted all data as active observers. The problem addressed by the study was concerned with human meanings and interactions as described from the insider's perspective. Etic coding[1] according to transformation theory, the substantive theoretical framework for this study, initiated data analysis via the constant comparative method (Straus, 1987). These initial and etic codes (e.g., locus of control, approach/avoidance) supported the emic codes[2] (e.g., *I don't see color*), categories, and themes drawn from participants' shared interpretations (Bogdan & Biklen, 1992).

Colorblind Nonaccommodative Denial: Overview

The term *colorblind* has been used to refer to persons who are essentially oblivious to, or choose to overlook, differences (whether perceived as differences of skin color, cultural socialization, or ethnicity) among groups of people regarding the manner in which one or another group is perceived and treated by the dominant group in society. The term colorblind, as used in reference to the psychological meaning perspective identified in this chapter, is consistent with Sleeter's (1995) argument that those persons and institutions that have been described as colorblind are usually also *ethnic-blind* (that is, oblivious to differences among groups of people regarding how members of one or another group perceive themselves in relation to a common, shared historical heritage).

Teachers' discourse in this study not only indicated colorblindness as a denial of biases (the reduction of anxiety by the unconscious exclusion from the mind of intolerable thoughts, feelings, or facts) but also consequent denial (the refusal to recognize, acknowledge, or confront a need, claim, or request) of accommodation in classroom structures or instruction necessary (Nieto, 1992) to meet the particular and often language-based needs of Mexican-American students. Two interrelated meaning schemes indicated the psychological meaning perspective of colorblind nonaccommodative denial—colorblindness and no accommodation. While colorblindness will be described, the second meaning scheme, no accommodation, will be focused on in greater detail.

Findings on Colorblindness

Three patterns in teachers' discourse indicated the meaning scheme of colorblindness. The first is best described by the following phrase: "I don't see color, I see students." According to multiple teachers' discourse in this case study, the majority of teachers at Valverde did not pay attention to such differences (of race) "until someone points them out." Similar comments further indicated that this shared perception could extend to culture as well as color differences. The effort to deny that Mexican-American students brought cultural differences to the school was evident in teachers' discourse, such as this statement made by one of the veterans on staff:

> I have done more reading on issues relating to Mexican-American students ... I have made an increased effort to be more sensitive to students' needs, but again, this is not a Mexican-American issue for me. It is a student issue.
>
> (male Math teacher)

With an emphasis placed on the individual, teachers were able to side-step the experiences, oppression, and disparities felt by those who were assigned membership within a devalued racial/social group (Kubota, 2004).

Second, notions of respect and equality were suggested in the discourse of other teachers. According to some participants, an environment of *respect* between teacher and student is the key to successful practice with student populations such as those at Valverde. One teacher describes her focus in this way:

> I myself emphasize respect in my class everyday and try my best that students respect each other. I respect them, they respect me. They are students to me not Hispanic, Mexican American, White, Black or other. I do not care about the color of their skin, I respect them and they respect me, that is what is important.
>
> (female English teacher)

For her, neither color nor culture were important, only this environment of respect. Statements such as "I do not care about the color of their skin," were commonplace in teacher discourse and illustrated the teachers' desire to remain "colorblind" to students' racial and cultural differences.

Finally, the avoidance of engaged, racial discourse in the classroom was the third factor within the meaning scheme of colorblindness. According to one educator, the *expectation* that teachers should be called upon to acknowledge the cultural heritage (as suggested in those professional development efforts that address awareness-raising among teachers, especially awareness-raising concerning ethnic-blindness and cultural-blindness) is "counter-productive." Three-quarters of the teachers at Valverde considered this to be true especially if the student's heritage is perceived as oppressed. They felt that bringing up such topics would breed an "environment of competition among peoples." Hegemony and sameness were seen as of greatest importance to the teachers as evidenced in the following statement:

> I know that our school is composed of a majority of Mexican American students but I feel that as educators we need to work with all students. I know that we also have to take culture into consideration, but most importantly we also need to remember that we are Americans. And I feel that we are Americans first.
>
> (female Art teacher)

According to this discourse of assimilation, *education* is not an opportunity for diverse peoples to exchange ideas and knowledge through honest critical dialogs; rather, it is the avenue for assimilating CLD students without acknowledging or supporting their cultural differences. Even though the majority of their students were Mexican American, teachers were able to justify their colorblind perspectives on the basis of equality and with a focus on hegemony. By choosing to ignore their Mexican-American students' diverse experiences, these teachers were then able to avoid dealing with difference altogether.

The meaning scheme of colorblindness functions in tandem with the second meaning scheme of no accommodation. When teachers elect to take the stance of colorblindness, their desire and ability to effectively accommodate for the unique needs of Mexican-American students is questionable. From this perspective, they are unable to see the gravity or magnitude of the need for differentiated instruction that accommodates students' varying diversity.

Findings on Nonaccommodation

Study data supports the argument that teachers' colorblind standpoint and lack of accommodation for their students' diverse linguistic, sociocultural, cognitive, and academic needs has negative implications for students' learning and English-language development. The meaning scheme of no accommodation provides further evidence for the identification of a psychological meaning perspective of colorblind nonaccommodative denial shared among the teacher participants in this study.

It should be noted that the term accommodation here denotes the concept of culture-specific accommodation as detailed by Nieto (1992). In brief, culture-specific accommodation would require educators to acknowledge that racial and linguistic differences do matter. This type of accommodation refers to the capacity of schools and teachers to identify and understand schools as socially constructed entities that perpetuate the cultural norms of the majority. This understanding guides reflective practitioners in their efforts to utilize the resources and funds of knowledge that students bring to school (in conjunction with their own biography and socialization). In doing so, educators maximize the students' potential for academic success.

The section to follow will elaborate upon the scheme of no accommodation as evidenced in participant discourse. Many reasons were given for teachers' lack of accommodation. The major themes that surfaced were (a) time, (b) students' low socioeconomic status, and (c) teachers' perception of risk.

Lack of Time as a Rationale for Denial of the Need to Accommodate

Lack of time was a recurrent theme in teachers' discourse that rationalized a denial of accommodation in classroom structure and curriculum to meet the particular needs of Mexican-American students. The following remarks taken from teachers' discourse were typical:

> I believe that once we sit back and ponder we will realize that we "can" have a positive effect on the students and culture of Valverde ... My biggest obstacle in rethinking and restructuring my teaching is time. Planning lessons to meet the needs of Mexican American students does take time and effort.
>
> (female English teacher)

As this excerpt illustrates, the participants often realized the benefits of personal reflection with respect to structural and curricular accommodations necessary to meet the needs of Mexican-American students. Some further acknowledged that such accommodations could have a positive influence on outcomes for these students. Nevertheless, despite these realizations, the lack of time was a recurrent rationale for why such accommodation was not undertaken by teachers within the school. Teachers frequently asserted that time was a restricting factor in their ability to accommodate the needs of Mexican-American students.

Socioeconomic Status of the Student Used against Race-based Accommodation

The perceived socioeconomic status of certain Mexican-American students at Valverde also appeared to influence teachers' denial of the need to accommodate the students' learning. Periodic discussions among participants during reflection sessions surrounded issues of appropriate classroom structures and curriculum for the student population at Valverde. Classroom structures discussed by the researcher as examples meant to prompt group discussion were: (a) the pros and cons of differentiated seating arrangements; (b) the dynamics of project stations as a way to facilitate experiential learning units; and (c) the question of whether order or variety ought to be the benchmark of the classroom routine. Curricular options discussed by the researcher as examples meant to prompt group discussion were: (a) the question of whether certain

English as a second language (ESL) strategies of instruction could be purposively modified for use with any learner having reading difficulties; and (b) the issues of whether struggling junior high school students are ever really challenged by a strict use of basal readers for remediation.

Discourse shared among participants during such sessions indicated a commonly held perception that structural and curricular accommodations specific to Mexican-American students would prove futile since low socioeconomic status, not socialization or linguistic influences, were responsible for their personal and academic problems with the school environment. For example:

> As we look at the culture of our students who are predominately Mexican American, I tend to think that some of the problems are not so much due to culture as much due to low socioeconomic status ... It doesn't matter if they are brown, black, white or whatever, if their economic level is low, the problems would be the same.
>
> (female English teacher)

This teacher's remarks indicated a denial of any color-based, language-based, or culture-based differences in the problems and challenges faced by students at Valverde. The socioeconomic rationale for no accommodation mentioned is one that another teacher struggled to resolve in her mind:

> This [study] has forced me to seriously evaluate my prejudices and to contemplate exactly where those prejudices are directed. I have been determining that, in many ways, prejudices do affect my behavior ... I am forced to accept that a certain socioeconomic group has a lot of negative feelings [i.e., prejudice] directed against it.
>
> (female Social Studies teacher)

This comment taken from a teacher's journal was reflective of how many teachers in this study were just beginning to acknowledge that race or linguistic difference impacted their teaching. This lack of knowledge, which surfaced in the majority of participants' discourse, highlights another deeper issue at hand—fear—and how it relates to some teachers' assumptions about risk-taking and classroom management at Valverde.

Avoidance of Risk-taking as Rationale for Nonaccommodation

Perceived risk-taking was a third significant theme tied to the meaning scheme of no accommodation shared among participants in the study. More specifically, teachers recurrently argued that to accommodate particular needs of Mexican-American students was to risk loss of classroom control. These arguments were to some degree a rationale for teachers' denial of accommodation for students at Valverde.

Participants' discourse placed the primary emphases of education at Valverde on students' strict adherence to rules, a safe environment for students and teachers, students who were on task, and teachers' constant control of both students and classroom environments. Control was a specific emphasis for these teachers, because simply having rules did not necessarily encompass their idea of control. Rather, their idea of control was based on the degree to which their classroom and school environments (as well as those of their fellow teachers) reflected a sense of order.

The following comment from a participant reflected teachers' emphasis on strict *adherence to rules* as an educational goal worthy of attention:

> Are we [schools, educators] supposed to bend the rules to accommodate each and every student? Each student has his problem. Every student needs the rules bent for him or her. I just can't see this! No one bent the rules for me ... Eventually, we all have to follow the rules if we plan to succeed in this society. Eve [one of the course instructors] had to learn to follow rules. She tells me that a teacher bent the rules for her because she was a migrant student. I understand and I am happy that someone helped her out. But the bottom line is that she eventually had to follow the rules set by our society or she wouldn't be the success she is now. Am I being close-minded?
>
> (male Math teacher)

This comment taken from a teacher's reflective journal indicated that the emphasis on rules and authority at Valverde was less focused on Mexican-American students' understanding of the rules and more on whether those students followed those rules to the letter ("the bottom line is that she eventually had to follow the rules"). According to this interpretation, any problems a student might have are less important than the student's need to conform to imposed rules. Participant observation of reflection group discussions and interchanges overall seemed to confirm this mentality.

Other educational emphases at Valverde indicated by teachers' discourse were maintaining a *safe environment* and keeping students *on task*. Teachers saw these as the keys to positive student outcomes. For most of these teachers, their discourse in reflection group sessions indicated that they were less concerned with the safety of the environment from the students' point of view than they were with the safety of that environment from their own perspective. It is arguable that, as seen previously in similar studies in the field, this need for safety was based on some underlying issues of fear and lack of understanding regarding the Mexican-American youth at Valverde (Larson & Ovando, 2001).

According to the discourse of one participant, it is the teacher's job, first and foremost, to get students *on task*, which was often a point of frustration for teachers at Valverde. The teachers' emphasis on keeping students on task correlated directly to their overall apparent need for control and establishing a safe, non-threatening environment for the teachers. For many of these educators, a sense of control (to minimize risk) was best reflected in a classroom and school environment indicative of *order*. In one teacher's reflective journal, she asserted that the maintenance of order in the classroom was essential to a teacher's employment at Valverde, further indicating that these emphases were the product of administrative mandates, not just teachers' shared interpretations of appropriate educational environments for their students.

Analysis of the data indicated recurrent outcomes of the dichotomy between teachers' educational emphases at Valverde (students' strict adherence to rules, safety, time on task, control) and the needs of their Mexican-American students. *Frustration* and *perpetual negativity* among school faculty were two recurrent themes resulting from teachers' lack of flexibility in structural and curricular changes and their unwillingness to risk loss of control. The teachers shared a strong sense of negativity, and their color-blind meaning scheme, which implies the meaning scheme of no accommodation seemed to hinder their critical reflection on the relationship between their educational emphases of control and order and the students' academic performance. Teachers' high levels of frustration with student performance were evident in their discourse from the second and third reflection focus-group meetings and were unmistakable in the following comment: "I hate grading their writing assignments. These [Mexican-American] students cannot write one complete sentence! I get angry, frustrated, and depressed when I grade writing assignments. The most frustrating thing is that students refuse to think!" (female English teacher). This growing frustration necessarily influenced an increasing sense of negativity that became shared among Valverde teachers and was reinforced on a daily basis, from discussions in the hallways, to conversations in the teachers' lounge, to interactions among teachers outside the school itself. Over time, this shared and mutually reinforced negativity became, as it were, self-perpetuating.

Other comments from teachers substantiated this theme of perpetual negativity among school faculty. Nonetheless, while aware of the damaging effects of this negativity, one teacher shared in the following written statement his tentativeness and unwillingness to confront the dynamic:

> If you [other teachers at Valverde] are this negative toward these kids what in the world are you doing here? Do you think these kids don't pick up on your thoughts and feelings? If you don't like/respect these guys, you're certainly not going to get this in return—No wonder you're not happy! (I'd love to relate this to others! Wouldn't dare—but I just don't understand some people!)
>
> (male Physical Education teacher)

Despite the often profoundly negative outcomes of the teachers' skewed educational emphases with their Mexican-American students, their discourse indicated that many were persuaded that accommodating the particular needs of Mexican-American students was not worth the potential risk.

Among the themes found within the schemes of *colorblindness* and *no accommodation*, there was one consistent theme worth noting that was evident in both, and that was *denial*. Many teachers in this case study denied the existence of racial and linguistic difference among their students and the resulting need for accommodation based on their perceived duty to treat all students as individuals. As mentioned previously, this notion of individualism denies the fact that these students are not only a product of socialization in the Mexican-American culture but also the product of the socially constructed identity placed on them in the U.S. school system, and specifically at Valverde. One participant noted:

> Knowing that my classes don't always go the way I want them to [is] because [of] the dynamics of the [Mexican-American] student population rather than because I am a poor teacher makes me realize that I need to give up...
>
> (female English teacher)

This remark taken from a teacher's reflective journal suggested that it is the "dynamics of the student population," not teachers' lack of accommodation or school climate that was at the heart of any problems these students may experience at Valverde. The teachers continued to deny that there existed a direct connection between their beliefs and actions and CLD students' success.

Discussion

This ethnographic case study of teachers' meaning perspectives regarding their day-to-day interactions with Mexican-American junior high students at Valverde resulted in the identification of the two interrelated meaning schemes—colorblindness and no accommodation. Grounded in Mezirow's theoretical framework, the psychological meaning perspective of colorblind nonaccommodative denial indicated that teachers denied the need for accommodation of classroom structure or curriculum to meet the particular needs of their Mexican-American students. Implications for this psychological meaning perspective are evident in all levels of the education endeavor.

Impact on Students

Given the exponential growth of the CLD population in U.S. schools, teachers can no longer stand behind the statement "I don't see color, I treat all my students the same" and then expect the limited number of ESL teachers employed within their schools to deal with those children whose differences cannot be dismissed. Race is central to the way one interprets his or her identity and reality as well as the identity and reality of others (Mezirow, 1991). If educators are looking toward the future and striving to truly educate CLD students effectively, they must begin to explore the role that race and teachers' meaning perspectives toward *the Other* have on identity formation and professional practice in schools.

Teachers' lack of effective cultural competence training regarding CLD students continues to have negative repercussions, often translating into fear, misunderstandings, low expectations, institutional deafness, and labeling. Subsequently, these elements lead to the students' loss of voice and cultural identity, alienation, marginalization, and ultimately a self-fulfilling prophecy (Gay, Dingus, & Jackson, 2003; Hobson-Horton & Owens, 2004; Johnson, 2002; Kubota, 2004; Larson & Ovando, 2001; McLaren & Torres, 1999; Ovando & McLaren, 2000; Palmer, 2003). For ELL students, these practitioner deficits are compounded when teachers also lack training in methods specific to second language acquisition.

Implications for Teachers

This study explored a framework for understanding how teachers' feelings, assumptions, and misconceptions regarding Mexican-American students translate into action and non-action. It also affirms and expounds on previous research that establishes how critical the constant consideration of race and other aspects of diversity in policy, discourse, and practice are for true equitable education of CLD students (Gay, 1993; Nieto, 1995).

Teachers' acknowledgment of cultural and linguistic difference is an important first step in letting go of the colorblind perspective. This, in turn, opens the door for consideration of difference and can result in a willingness to effectively accommodate for those differences. For Nieto (1992), it is the culturally different student who, for too long, has done the accommodating in public school education. This study supports a culturally empathetic and reality-based alternative. As recommended by Nieto, we must take the perspective of mutual accommodation, a perspective in which neither the student nor the teacher expects complete accommodation. The mutual-accommodation argument suggests that culturally competent teachers and CLD students together may best determine the most appropriate strategies and structures compatible with the disposition of each.

As the data in this study would suggest, many of the assumptions and biases that teachers hold regarding Mexican-American students stem from misconceptions. Teachers' fears and anxieties were evident in their emphases on control and maintaining order at all cost. Anxiety connected to what they perceive as a "lack of order" can be mitigated with an understanding of the assumptions and beliefs that drive human interaction within any socially constructed system.

For example, if teachers gain an understanding of the social and historical context of their own identity development alongside the unique biographies of their Mexican-American students, they would be more likely to consider the potential dynamics of their diverse classrooms and effectively accommodate for them. Previous research indicates that this accommodation in turn would have direct, positive consequences for classroom management and student success (Collier & Thomas, 1988, 1989; Garcia, 1995; Gay, 2000; Herrera & Murry, 2005). By creating classroom environments that are low-fear, nurturing, scaffolded, and dynamic, the frustration and perpetual negativity exhibited in the teachers' discourse at Valverde toward Mexican-American students would be alleviated.

Education reform of this kind is only possible when there are opportunities for teachers to critically reflect on their own meaning perspectives. Without critical reflection and ongoing consideration of issues such as oppression, institutional racism, White privilege, and ethnic and linguistic discrimination, teachers seldom prove able to surface and test the culture-bound assumptions (shaped by their experiential and academic backgrounds) embedded in their perspectives. Such assumptions become the unspoken *rules* by which teachers interpret and act within the realm of teaching in a difference-blind institution (Gay, 1993; Herrera, 2005; Larson & Ovando, 2001; Nieto, 1995).

When the teachers and students experience a linguistic and cultural disconnect, the learning environment can become hostile. Critical reflection can provide educators the opportunity to examine the reasons for this disconnect and bring about a shift in teacher meaning perspectives. Through prolonged, in-depth critical reflection, educators may begin to realize that everyone has meaning perspectives (which need evaluating regardless of race, ethnicity, socioeconomic status, language, or gender), and that these perspectives are innately tied to our socialization (Mezirow, 1990, 1991).

Systemic Change in Educating CLD Students—Specifically ELLs

Difference-blindness dissolves the lived experiences and complex realities of CLD groups into an illusion of sameness. When individuals subscribe to this social construct they are engaging in a social and political act that Frankenberg (1993) calls "power evasion." This power evasion position disregards the innate benefits associated with White privilege by claiming that, "we are all the same under the skin" (p. 14). It is suggested that this difference-blind perspective places the responsibility on those people of color to move toward sameness (hegemony) and any failure to do so is their fault (Kubota, 2004).

Because educational institutions are historically a product of socially and culturally privileged individuals and are designed to impart education to the majority population, it is crucial to examine those aspects of schools that are inherently racist and veiled to marginalized groups. The unspoken rules, hidden agendas, ignorance, and coercive relationships of power and privilege that hinder CLD students' access and opportunity are based on long-standing institutionally embedded assumptions/biases. In general, legislators, administrators, and educators make decisions regarding curriculum, instruction, assessment, programming, and student placements every day based on their own meaning perspectives and on the established system, often with little consideration of CLD students' biographies. For this reason, reflective teachers must explore the dynamics of their classroom and their school to determine whether the environments are additive or subtractive for CLD students: Are they conducive for second language development? Do they validate CLD students as legitimate members of the community?

Educators and administrators must develop structures or networks within the school that not only increase access but also support, value, and utilize the experiential and linguistic funds of knowledge that diverse students bring with them if their potential is to be realized. When teachers are given genuine opportunities to critically reflect on their meaning perspectives and apply their new understandings in practice, they can begin to acknowledge the social construct of race by *seeing difference* and all that it implies for CLD students in schools.

As evidenced in this study and the reviewed literature, many of our U.S. educational institutions promote a perspective of difference-blindness. Colleges, universities, and schools commonly overlook the existence of the meaning perspectives that teachers bring with them into their classrooms, where they shape every interaction. In fact, these meaning perspectives are often further *reinforced* in the professional development that both pre-service and in-service teachers receive. As a result of this reinforcement, teachers' skewed and unchallenged perspectives translate into neglect of their students' language and academic needs.

As supporters of critical multiculturalism would assert, effectively teaching a critical consciousness that moves people to impact social change requires the confrontation of racism directly. Critical multiculturalism focuses on deconstructing hegemonic worldviews and engages all learners in the examination of the social, political, and economic implications for race in the development of power and privilege (Kubota, 2004). We must all become concerned with addressing the deeply embedded meaning perspectives and the resulting meaning schemes that are present in teachers' lived experiences.

We must understand the role that examining our own socialization has in the act of teaching, and most importantly, the implications it has for the academic success of CLD students.

Discussion Questions

1. The authors discuss colorblind views held by junior high school teachers in teaching culturally and linguistically diverse (CLD) students. Think about your experience of encountering statements or social practices that reflect colorblindness. What was the context? Who was involved? What were their racial, ethnic, gender, and socioeconomic backgrounds? What effects did colorblindness have on students, parents, curriculum, instruction, or overall school structure?
2. In schools where CLD students are the majority, what kind of expectations do teachers have for these students and their parents? What types of teacher dispositions or educational practices would motivate CLD students to achieve academic excellence? What would help them prepare for their advanced education or future career?
3. The authors advocate mutual accommodation in schools. What are concrete examples of such accommodation? What can teachers do?
4. The authors state that systemic professional development that fosters critical reflection for pre-service and in-service educators is necessary to transform the cultural climate of public schools. Knowing that schools and communities have limited resources, what can change agents within public schools do to impact change (at the classroom, building, and district level)? What about at the program level in colleges of education?

Notes

1. Etic coding: an analysis tool for approaching the data based upon identified concepts or themes defined and outlined within the chosen theoretical framework for a study.
2. Emic codes: those patterns in participant voice or actions within the context of a study from which themes are derived.

References

Baker, R. (1996). Sociological field research with junior high school teachers: The discounting of Mexican American students. *The Journal of Educational Issues of Language Minority Students, 18*, 49–66.

Banks, J. A., & Lynch, J. (Eds.). (1986). *Multicultural education in Western societies.* New York: Praeger.

Benard, B. (1997). *Turning it around for all youth: From risk to resilience.* New York: ERIC Clearinghouse on Urban Education. (ERIC Document Reproduction Service No. ED412309.)

Bogdan, R. C., & Biklen, S. K. (1992). *Qualitative research for education: An introduction to theory and methods* (2nd ed.). Boston, MA: Allyn and Bacon.

Buxton, C. (1999). Designing a model-based methodology for science instruction: Lessons from a bilingual classroom [Electronic version]. *Bilingual Research Journal, 23*(2–3). Retrieved November 12, 2002 from http://brj.asu.edu/v2323/articles/art4.html.

Carr, P. R., & Klaussen, T. R. (1997). Different perceptions of race in education: Racial minority and White teachers. *Canadian Journal of Education, 22*, 67–81.

Chamot, A. U., & O'Malley, J. (1994). *The CALLA handbook: Implementing the cognitive academic language learning approach.* Reading, MA: Addison-Wesley.

Chang, C. Y. (2003, December 1). White privilege, oppression, and racial identity development: implications for supervision. *High Beam Research: Counselor Education and Supervision.* Retrieved July 7, 2005 from www.highbeam.com/library/doc3.asp?DOCID=1G1:112211443&ctr1Info=Round13%.

Chein, I. (1981). An introduction to sampling. In L. H. Kidder (Ed.), *Seltiz, Wrightman and Cook's research methods in social relations* (4th ed., pp. 430–465). New York: Holt, Rinehart, and Winston.

Chen, M., & Goldring, E. (1992, October). *The impact of classroom diversity on teachers' perspectives of their schools as workplaces.* Paper presented at the annual meeting of the University Council for Educational Administration, Minneapolis, MN.

Collier, V. P. (1995). *Acquiring a second language for school.* Washington, DC: National Clearinghouse for Bilingual Education.

Collier, V. P., & Thomas, W. P. (1988). *Acquisition of cognitive-academic second language proficiency: A six-year study.* Paper presented at the annual meeting of the American Educational Research Association, New Orleans, LA.

Collier, V. P., & Thomas, W. P. (1989). How quickly can immigrants become proficient in school English? *Journal of Educational Issues of Language Minority Students, 5*, 26–38.

Contreras, A., & Lee, O. (1990). Differential treatment of students by middle school science teachers: Unintended cultural bias. *Science Education, 74*, 433–444.

Cummins, J. (1981). The role of primary language development in promoting education success for language minority students. In C. F. Leyba (Ed.), *Schooling and language minority students: A theoretical framework* (pp. 3–49). Los Angeles, CA: Evaluation, Dissemination and Assessment Center, CSULA.

Cummins, J. (1989). Language and affect: Bilingual students at home and at school. *Language Arts, 66*, 29–43.

Escamilla, K. (1999). The false dichotomy between ESL and transitional bilingual education programs: Issues that challenge all of us. *Educational Considerations, 26*(2), 1–6.

Frankenberg, R. (1993). *White women race matters: The social construction of whiteness.* Minneapolis, MN: University of Minnesota Press.

Garcia, E. E. (1995). Educating Mexican American students: Past treatment and recent developments in theory, research, policy, and practice. In J. A. Banks & C. A. McGee Banks (Eds.), *Handbook for research on multicultural education* (pp. 372–387). New York: Simon and Schuster Macmillan.

Garcia, B., & Van Soest, D. (1997). Changing perceptions of diversity and oppression: MSW students discuss the effects of a required course. *Journal of Social Work Education, 33*, 19–129.

Gay, G. (1993). Ethnic minorities and educational equality. In J. A. Banks & C. A. McGee Banks (Eds.), *Multicultural education: Issues and perspectives* (pp. 171–194). Needham Heights, MA: Allyn and Bacon.

Gay, G., Dingus, J. E., & Jackson, C. W. (2003, July). The presence and performance of teachers of color in the profession. Unpublished report prepared for the National Collaborative on Diversity in the Teaching Force, Washington, DC.

Ginorio A., & Huston, M. (2001). *Sí, se puede! Yes, we can. Latinas in school.* Washington, DC: American Association of University Women Educational Foundation. (ED 452 330.)

Helms, J. E. (Ed.). (1990). *Black and white racial identity: Theory, research, and practice.* New York: Greenwood Press.

Herrera, S. G. (1995). *Junior high school teachers and the meaning perspectives they hold regarding their Mexican American students: An ethnographic case study.* Unpublished doctoral dissertation, Texas Tech University, Lubbock.

Herrera, S. & Morales, A. (2005, April). *From remediation to acceleration: Recruiting, retaining and graduating future CLD educators.* Paper presented at the annual meeting of the American Education Research Association, Toronto, Ontario.

Herrera, S., & Murry, K. (2005). *Mastering ESL and bilingual methods: Differentiated instruction for culturally and linguistically diverse (CLD) students.* Boston, MA: Pearson.

Hobson-Horton, L. D., & Owens, L. (2004). From freshman to graduate: Recruiting and retaining minority students. *Journal of Hispanic Higher Education, 3,* 86–107.

Jelinek, P. (2005, June 9). Hispanics fastest-growing minority, now one-seventh of U.S. population. *The Santa Fe New Mexican.* Retrieved July 7, 2005 from www.freenewmexican.com/news/28884.html.

Johnson, L. (2002). "My eyes have been opened": Teachers and racial awareness. *Journal of Teacher Education, 53,* 153–167.

Jorgensen, D. L. (1989). *Participant observation: A methodology for human studies.* London: Sage Publications.

Kubota, R. (2004). Critical multiculturalism and second language education. In B. Norton & K. Tooney (Eds.), *Critical pedagogies and language learning* (pp. 30–52). Cambridge: Cambridge University Press.

Larson, C. L., & Ovando, C. J. (2001). *The color of bureaucracy: The politics of equity in multicultural school communities.* Belmont, CA: Wadsworth/Thomson Learning.

McLaren, P., & Torres, R. (1999). Racism and multicultural education: Rethinking "race" and "whiteness" in late capitalism. In S. May (Ed.), *Critical multiculturalism: Rethinking multicultural and antiracist education* (pp. 42–76). London: Falmer Press.

Merriam, S. (1998). *Case study research in education: A qualitative approach* (2nd ed.). San Francisco, CA: Jossey-Bass.

Mezirow, J. (1990). *Fostering critical reflection in adulthood: A guide to transformative and emancipatory learning.* San Francisco, CA: Jossey-Bass.

Mezirow, J. (1991). *Transformative dimensions of adult learning.* San Francisco, CA: Jossey-Bass.

Montemayor, R., & Mendoza, H. (2004). *Right before our eyes: Latinos past, present & future.* Washington, DC: Scholargy Publishing.

New York State Department of Education. (2002). *Key issues in bilingual special education work paper #5.* Retrieved July 10, 2006 from www.vesid.nysed.gov/lsn/bilingual/trainingmodules05rr.pdf.

Nieto, S. (1992). *Affirming diversity: The sociopolitical context of multicultural education.* White Plains, NY: Longman.

Nieto, S. (1995). A history of the education of Puerto Rican students in U.S. mainland schools: Losers, outsiders, or leaders? In J. A. Banks & C. A. McGee Banks (Eds.), *Handbook of research on multicultural education* (pp. 388–411). New York: Macmillan.

Ovando, C. J., & McLaren, P. (2000). *Multiculturalism and bilingual education: Students caught in the crossfire.* Boston, MA: McGraw-Hill.

Palmer, M. T. (2003). *The schooling experience of Latina immigrant high school students.* Unpublished dissertation, University of North Carolina at Chapel Hill.

Sleeter, C. E. (1995). White racism. In F. Schultz (Ed.), *Multicultural Education 95/96* (pp. 70–73). Guilford, CT: Dushkin.

Straus, A. L. (1987). *Qualitative analysis for social scientists.* Cambridge: Cambridge University Press.

Valencia, R. R. (1991). *Chicano school failure and success: Research and policy agendas for the 1990's.* New York: Falmer Press.

Walker, A., Shafer, J., & Iiams, M. (2004). "Not in my classroom": Teacher attitudes towards English language learners in the mainstream classroom. *NABE Journal of Research and Practice, 2*(1), 130–160.

Youngs, C. S., & Youngs, G. A. (2001). Predictors of mainstream teachers' attitudes toward ESL students. *TESOL Quarterly, 35,* 95–118.

12 Transforming the Curriculum of NNESTs

Introducing Critical Language Awareness (CLA) in a Teacher Education Program[1]

Carmen Chacón

Pre-reading Questions

Each country has different racial politics and ideologies. Carmen Chacón investigates how her students in EFL teacher-education courses in Venezuela understand issues of race and racism.

- Due to racial mixing among Whites, Blacks, and Natives, the dominant discourse in Venezuela downplays racial categories, although racial prejudices against dark-skinned people exist. What types of awareness about racism could be developed among Venezuelan teachers?
- How can teacher educators help teachers develop such awareness?

Introduction

Over the past few years there have been shifts in pedagogy that have influenced the training and development of teachers. Research has shown that teachers' knowledge and identity are mediated by multiple discourses (Danielewicz, 2001). Recognizing that teacher identity is culturally mediated demands a shift in the education of English as a foreign language (EFL) teachers that transcends the prescriptive traditional methods. We need an approach that extends beyond description and moves toward a critical pedagogical practice that affirms diversity and combats social injustice and inequity (Kubota & Ward, 2000; Lin, 2004; Norton, 2003; Norton & Toohey, 2004; Pennycook, 1999, 2001).

A critical approach to the education of EFL teachers should address not only the teachers' linguistic knowledge but also the teaching self in its broader sociohistorical context. From this perspective, the education of Nonnative English-Speaking Teachers (NNESTs) demands an emancipatory curriculum that raises teachers' awareness of how language intersects with race, gender, and power (see Freire, 2002, 2004). It is critical for NNESTs to become aware of the fact that language produces and reproduces social inequities. Hence, a critical language awareness (CLA) approach (Fairclough, 1989) involves a praxis that challenges and attempts to change unequal relations in society by having student teachers reflect upon sociohistorical and cultural roots, assumptions, and hidden biases that shape how they see the world and *the other*. Raising "consciousness of how language contributes to the domination of some people by others ... is the first step towards emancipation" (Fairclough, 1989, p. 1). In our globalized world,

English has a hegemonic status as an international lingua franca, creating unequal relations of power between native speakers and nonnative speakers of English. Through their act of teaching English, NNESTs, even as nonnative speakers of English, may unconsciously help reproduce existing educational practices and social inequities through hegemonic cultural discourses that perpetuate domination (Fairclough, 1989).

I call for a curriculum based on praxis "in all its contexts as a constant reciprocal relation between theory and practice" (Pennycook, 2001, p. 3), praxis, as self-reflection that fosters action and alters cultural roots, assumptions, and hidden biases that shape how the individual sees the world and *the other*. This chapter presents the preliminary findings of an ongoing study whose purpose is to empower Venezuelan pre- and in-service English teachers through instruction based on a curriculum that problematizes and deconstructs assumptions and biases hidden in daily discursive practices.

Context of the Study: English Language Teaching (ELT) in Venezuela

The Bolivarian Republic of Venezuela is located at the north of South America with 26,577,423 inhabitants, according to the 2001 Census of Population (OCEI) (Instituto Nacional de Estadística; Institutional Office of Central Statistics). Although Spanish is the official language, the OCEI reports at least 31 indigenous dialects. Venezuela is one of the countries that belong to what Kachru (1992) called the expanding circle where English is taught as the lingua franca that allows access to trade, business, science, and technology in today's globalized world. Thus, in high schools, learning how to understand, speak, read, and write in English is mandatory. The teaching of English is mainly focused on developing communicative competence (Chacón & Alvarez, 2001). Although I do acknowledge the necessity of acquiring communication skills in English for personal and societal benefits, I echo scholars, such as Pennycook (1994, 1999, 2001) and Phillipson (1997), who argue against a purely descriptive and normative view of language teaching as a "neutral" activity isolated from the socioeconomic, historical, cultural, and political forces that interact in a particular society. Elsewhere (Chacón, Alvarez, Brutt-Griffler, & Samimy, 2003), we state, "Our education as EFL teachers emphasized formal linguistics and the need to speak native-like English ... [and to learn] American culture and Standard English" (pp. 143–144). Under this descriptive normative approach, students are uncritically exposed to language that places ELT as an "apolitical" and "transparent" (Freire, 2004; Pennycook, 1994; Phillipson, 1997) activity that legitimates social inequity.

In the next section, I will present my reflective account of language and race relations based on my own learning experience as a graduate student in the United States, and the ways in which my experience impacted my subjectivity and understanding of the role of race and language as a tool to reproduce social injustice.

My Own Story: A Reflective Account of Race Relations

As I have written elsewhere (Chacón, 2006), until a few years ago I was colorblind. However, being *the other* as a Ph.D. student in the United States made me aware that race is a marker of social inequity. As an NNES student in mainstream classes, I felt excluded because my native classmates dominated the discourse; I felt marginalized because my experience as a Latina did not seem to count in discussions centered on the United States. Another instance of exclusion and marginalization within and outside the academic community was my accent; I got used to hearing comments about my accent as a marker of race. These experiences, along with formal instruction and daily intercultural exchanges with colleagues, professors, and members of the community ultimately influenced my way of thinking and enabled me to become aware of race as a social construct that creates power relations.

As a graduate student, I struggled to debunk misconceptions and myths that reproduce inequities in describing *the other* as inferior. Labels such as native/nonnative, standard/nonstandard, and First World/Third World are pervasive terms ingrained in U.S. society and cultivated to give authority to some people over the other. During my doctoral studies from 1998 to 2003, I was intensively engaged with topics related to language, power, and race for the first time in my life. I wrestled with multiple identities that conflicted with my sense of who I am and where I come from. I started questioning my racial affiliation, trying to name my ethnicity from among labels such as White, Jewish American, Caucasian, Asian American, Hispanic, Latino, and so on. In the construction and reconstruction of my subjectivity, I affiliated myself with minorities. As a Latina, a woman, and an NNEST, I consider myself a professional of color who struggles against racial prejudice and discrimination. Although in Venezuela I would be described as White because of my light skin color, I came to the realization that race is not only about skin color but about culture, social status, and power—all concepts historically built through language.

Right after I finished my Ph.D. in 2003, I went back to my home university to teach in the English-teacher-education program. By then, I had already started to rethink and problematize my teaching and praxis. Drawing on feminist and critical epistemologies (Weedon, 1987) as well as on Freirean pedagogy, I initiated a continuous process of questioning my long-held cultural assumptions and pedagogy, which led me to what Freire called *conscientization*. This process has not been easy because it involves uncertainty and a constant struggle with one's multiple and conflicting identities.

In light of theory and my lived experiences, I initiated the transformation of my teaching practice. In this study, I report part of the findings from a larger research project that began with a pilot seminar whose purpose was to have EFL teachers deconstruct their cultural assumptions and biases. That seminar was inspired by Samimy and Brutt-Griffler's (1999) study (see the section entitled "Revisiting the colonial in the postcolonial: Critical praxis for nonnative-English-speaking teachers in a TESOL program") and my own experience as an NNEST (Chacón, 2000), my positionality in TESOL, and my historical *situationality* as an individual from the so-called Third World. Thus, in this chapter, I acknowledge my own biases and personal experiences and world-views as an NNEST, a Venezuelan, a Latina, a learner, a mother, a woman, and a teacher educator who has struggled and keeps struggling with multiple identities, sometimes as an insider and sometimes as *the other*. In the next section, I discuss racialization in Venezuela.

Racialization in Venezuela

During the colonial period, there was an extensive mixture of Spaniards, indigenous people, and Africans in Venezuela as well as in the Caribbean and Central and South

America. Venezuelan society comprised *Peninsulares* (those born in Spain), who had the greatest prestige and power; the *Criollos* (those born in South America of Spanish descent), who occupied a subordinate position; and *Blacks* and *Venezuelan Indians* or *Natives*, who made up the large lower end of the social hierarchy. Researchers (Aranguren, 1997) make the point that relationships during the colonial period were marked by discrimination against Blacks and Natives because of race and social status; their identities and cultural background were denied, and even nowadays, Eurocentrism pervades our history. With regard to Africans, Brito Figueroa (cited in Acosta Saignes, 1985) states that around a quarter of a million of them were brought into the country between 1500 and 1810 as slaves to work in the plantations and replace the indigenous peoples who died from diseases carried to the new world from Europe. Thus, the mixture of Whites, Blacks, and Natives has made distinguishing among racial types difficult.

Consequently, in Venezuela the issue of racialization is quite complex—unlike the case of the United States, in Venezuela public discourses do not openly establish race categories (e.g., African Venezuelan, White, Caucasian). Instead, the discourse of *mestizaje* (mixture of Spaniards, Africans, and indigenous people) prevails as an ideology that—along with the myth of "racial democracy"—serves to reproduce discrimination and social injustice.

Despite the fact that racism is not openly recognized by its institutions, most people in Venezuela hold culturally developed racial prejudices against darker-skinned people. These biases have been learned and reproduced through education (Aranguren, 1997; Montañez, 1993; Quintero, 2003) and the media (Ishibashi, 2004). Quintero (2003) conducted a study in which she examined 96 social-studies textbooks for elementary and high school and the curricula for the teaching of social science—years 1944 to 1968; 1969 to 1984; 1985 to 1997—and she found "constant definitions, symbols, and a system of concepts that discriminate and stereotype indigenous people and Afro Americans contributing to create biases and prejudices against them" (p. 6). Quintero states that the "Afro American is portrayed in the textbooks without history or cultural roots" (p. 12).

The Eurocentric views present in textbooks and in the curricula to teach history in elementary and high school reproduce social inequity and injustice. Thus, not surprisingly, most Venezuelans prefer lighter shades of skin color and straight hair that resemble European ancestors; the more European features one has, the greater one's social privilege and status. Eurocentric views or epistemological racism, as Kubota and Lin (2006) called it, is widely infused in our society, and particularly perpetuated by the media (advertisements, television) and marketing. Racism as discourse and epistemology is part of everyday life, although most people are not aware of, or do not acknowledge, its presence.

According to Montañez (1993), *endorracismo*, or the tendency to reject one's non-white physical features, is a common ideology in Venezuelan society. In other words, people celebrate European ethnic features and try to hide features that resemble African ancestors. Montañez asserts that "the endorracismo is actively and contradictorily reproduced by the Afro Venezuelans themselves" (p. 168).

The preference for *blanca(o)* and *rubia(o)*—i.e., having light skin color, eyes of any nonbrown color (preferably blue or green), and straight hair—is widespread for job positions in TV, magazines, and public places. The *morena(o)*, or brown-tanned person, has brown or black hair that is wavy or curly but not tightly curly, while the *negra(o)* is someone who has the darkest skin, tightly curly hair, and nose and lips that can be broad or not.

Race Ideology and Afro-Venezuelans' Presence

In general, Venezuelans limit the word "race" to mean phenotypic characteristics such as color of skin, hair texture, nose width, and other physical features. These traits, however, are generally used as markers of exclusion and discrimination against darker-skinned people, particularly Afro-Venezuelans and indigenous people. Black is usually associated with pejorative terms such as "ugly," "poor," and "unsophisticated," while blonde and white are related to "beauty." From this perspective, racism is deeply rooted in the daily discourse of the majority who lack racial awareness of such discursive practices and attitudes.

Although racism is not publicly sanctioned and the Constitution states that individuals are to be treated equally without discrimination based on race, sex, creed, or social standing, it is also true that Afro-Venezuelans and indigenous people have been excluded from the national Census since 1873. The most recent Census conducted by the OCEI (2001) recognizes the existence of at least 31 indigenous dialects, but it does not provide data for the number of Afro-Venezuelans and indigenous people who live in the country.

Van Dijk (2003) asserts, "The history of racism in Venezuela is very much alike to the other countries in the Caribbean and Latin America and it can be summarized in a few words: African slavery, blacks' rebellion, natives' oppression" (pp. 180–181). Scholars (van Dijk, 2003; Warren, 2000) recognize the complexity of racism in Latin America, which, as van Dijk states, cannot only be reduced to social inequities or, "antagonism between whites and blacks, the poor and the rich ... racism is more than alive in this Caribbean country" (van Dijk, 2003, p. 180). As this author states, racial discrimination is "alive" despite not being a public topic; on the contrary, discriminatory social practices seem to be so normal that most people ignore them.

When addressing issues of race, scholars tend to emphasize the *mestizaje* ideology, i.e., historically, we are a mixed race, or as some say, a *café con leche* (coffee with milk) society. This ideology is used to justify a race democracy that has become a myth over many years. In the same way, the political discourse reinforces the idea of class division by addressing the agenda to the poor as the excluded, marginalized, and discriminated against. According to Montañez (1993), although class division is central within the Venezuelan society, social inequity cannot be contested unless it is analyzed in light of social practices that intersect with racism.

In spite of the fact that racism has been ignored, it is important to mention that in 1999, an activist movement called Red de Organizaciones Afrovenezolanas (ROA) or Net of Afro-Venezuelan Organizations was established to support Afro-Venezuelans' and indigenous people's rights and to fight racism, xenophobia, and other forms of social discrimination. As the result of the ROA action, for the first time in the history of the country, the government admitted the existence of racism as a social problem (Ishibashi, 2004). ROA representatives went to the Human Rights Commission at OEA in

Washington, DC, to deplore the discriminatory practices of the Venezuelan media against the Afro descendants' community.

Definition of Race

For the purpose of this chapter, race is defined from an anthropological point of view, in its popular conception, as "essentially a cultural invention ... an ideology or world view" (Smedley and Smedley, 2005, pp. 19–20). I echo Kubota and Lin's (2006) argument of race and TESOL where these authors assert that race is socially and historically constructed. According to the authors, the term racism "can be viewed as both discourse and social practice which construct and perpetuate unequal relations of power through inferiorization, a process in which the Other is rendered inferior to the Self" (p. 478). In their discussion, they identify two types of racism: a discourse referring to institutional or structural racism and epistemology—i.e., racism represented by Eurocentric views of Western civilization. In this study, both types of racism will be discussed in the findings. The next section describes the pilot seminar for pre- and in-service teachers, which aimed at transforming the curriculum for preparing NNESTs. Analyzing the teachers' journals, the teacher-researcher's diary, and audio-recordings of class segments, I investigated the participants' perceptions of language, race, and power.

The Seminar: A Strategy Toward Curriculum Transformation

The project took place in the English-teacher-education program at a large university in the western part of Venezuela. The program emphasizes the development of teachers' pedagogical knowledge of teaching and subject-matter knowledge for listening, speaking, reading, and writing in English.

In the fall of 2003, I taught a seminar entitled *Sociopolitical Issues*, which served as a pilot project for the present study. It lasted 10 weeks and met for 2-and-a-half hours every week. I drew on Freirean pedagogy and the work of prominent critical theorists, such as Norton and Toohey (2004), Pennycook (1994, 1999, 2001), Phillipson (1997), and Weedon (1987) to engage participants in critical understanding of hegemonic practices and disempowering colonial discourses that legitimate social inequity. Although these issues have been brought into the TESOL arena over the last decade, NNESTs in foreign-language contexts (e.g., Venezuela) have remained unaware of racial discrimination (e.g., accent and "Standard" English).

The results of the seminar in terms of participants' empowerment led me to propose it as a regular elective seminar to be incorporated into the curriculum of the English-teacher-education program at my home university. The seminar was converted into a 1-year regular course entitled *Psycholinguistics*, which I will describe below.

The Psycholinguistics Course HE5021

In this class, the participants develop critical language awareness (CLA) of issues that intersect with race, language, and power. The course is taught from a critical applied linguistics standpoint as a "way of thinking and doing" (Pennycook, 2001, p. 3); therefore, it focuses on the development of critical reflection that leads to change. The participants are exposed to theories and guided in making connections between the theories and their lived experiences in order to construct conceptual tools to contest racism, resist power, and alter social relations. Course objectives are:

1. To raise the participants' consciousness about the relationship between language, race, and power.
2. To challenge the participants' culturally rooted assumptions and hidden biases in relation to theories and lived experiences.
3. To develop the participants' skills to conduct small research projects and become interested in sociopolitical issues.

The course lasts for 32 weeks with weekly 4-hour meetings, and it is structured in five thematic units:

I. Introduction to psycholinguistics: The nature of human language.
II. Language acquisition: How is a first language acquired? What are the theories of Second Language Acquisition (SLA)?
III. Language and society: Dialects, accents, and Standard English.
IV. World Englishes: Inner, outer, expanding circles. Localized forms of English.
V. Language, race, and ideology: Discourse and ideology. Institutional and individual racism. Stereotypes, prejudices. Race and identity of the NNEST.

Research Questions

Two research questions were addressed in order to investigate the participants' perceptions of language, race, and power:

1. What perceptions of language and race do the participants hold?
2. In what ways do the participants' perceptions of language and race affect their subjectivities?

Course Materials

A course packet with selected writings by scholars (Amin, 1997; Braine, 1999; Kachru, 1992; Lippi-Green, 1997; Tang, 1997) is used to stimulate weekly discussions, online forums, and reflective journals. The films *My Cousin Vinny* and *In America*, a video, and several websites support the topics addressed. The films portray stereotypes and prejudices people hold for *othering*. The teacher-made video presents six English teachers from the United States, Korea, Japan, Guadeloupe, Venezuela, and Croatia, all of whom were Ph.D. students at the university at the time I attended graduate school in the United States. These teachers responded to two questions: What does it mean for you to be an EFL teacher? What difficulties have you experienced as an EFL teacher? As with the films and other resources used, I engage students in discussing the kind of questions Auerbach (1992) suggests: What do you see? Who do you see? What are they doing? (Describe), What is the problem? (Define), Do you ever feel like these teachers?

Like whom? (Relate), What is the root of the problem? Why does it exist? Who created it? (Analyze), What should be done about it? What can you do? (Plan for action.) In addition, I recommend some websites for students to visit, read, react to, and write about for sharing their insights in class later. The NNEST CAUCUS website (see http://nnest.asu.edu) was the most visited, followed by www.redafrovenezolana.com and www.teachersagainstprejudice.org.

Participants

Three groups participated in the study. The pilot seminar on *Sociopolitical Issues* had 28 participants—23 females and 5 males—ranging from 20 to 44 years old. Of these, 19 were in-service EFL teachers, 2 were teacher educators from the program, and 7 were fifth- (i.e., final-) year student teachers from the same program. In the subsequent 2 years, the second and third groups consisted of the fifth-year students enrolled in the *Psycholinguistics* course. The second group comprised 34 participants—22 females and 12 males—ranging from 19 to 36 years old. The third group consisted of 32 partici-pants—14 males and 18 females—ranging from 20 to 26 years old. Except for two males in the third group—one from Taiwan and the other from Rwanda—and two darker skinned males (Enrique and José), all groups shared the same racial background. All spoke Spanish as their mother tongue except the Taiwanese and Rwandan students, who spoke English and were learning Spanish at the time of data collection.

Data Sources

The data were gathered from the participants' journals, the teacher-researcher's diary, and audio-recordings of class segments purposefully selected when hot topics such as racism were discussed. These class segments were later transcribed and analyzed.

Data collection started during the pilot seminar of *Sociopolitical Issues* and contin-ued for 2 consecutive years in the *Psycholinguistics* course which I taught in 2004 and 2005. Besides the participants' journals, I audio-recorded eight classes each year and kept a diary with my insights. To encourage the participants to write freely, the journals were not corrected for accuracy; rather, I urged participants to use them as a safe space to express their voice and keep an ongoing dialogue with me. In addition, I created an online forum for students to elaborate further on the discussion initiated in each class.

Reflective Journals

Journaling has been widely used as an introspective tool to foster critical self-reflection (Bartlett, 1990). In this study, journaling allowed participants to write about critical incidents, beliefs, and feelings they experienced so that they could connect the readings with their lived experiences. To provide ongoing feedback, I responded to and returned journals by the following week. I supported students' responses and challenged them to elaborate more on their new understandings. There were no right or wrong answers to the conflicts/issues they brought up.

Class Discussions

The critical nature of the course was the use of a dialogical conversation that I facilitated by encouraging the participants to openly express their views around the topics addressed. Weekly questions guided the discussion. Small group, pair work, and whole-class discussion were used as strategies to foster the construction and reconstruction of the participants' subjectivities.

Data Analysis

Journals, audio-recordings, forums, and the teacher-researcher diary served to identify the common patterns that emerged from the study. Journal entries were first grouped into categories or themes. Then, through an inductive process of systematic comparison, I read all journals again to sort them out by topic. Throughout the process, I used memos to facilitate data reduction. I also read and reread my own reflections, forums, and audio-recorded transcriptions. After the analysis, the data were displayed on a table to establish the relationships among categories.

Findings

The data collected during the pilot project did not show salient themes with regard to race, rather they helped me readjust the syllabus and redirect the strategies for the *Psycholinguistics* course. During the following 2 years, I focused more on racist discourse embedded in social practices in order to have participants contest racialization in our society as well as discriminatory attitudes and stereotypes against the *other* through a participatory approach that incorporated their experiences (Auerbach, 1992).

In the *Psycholinguistics* course, not only did I address the intersection of power, race, and language in the United States, but also racial prejudices and biases as present in Venezuelans' discursive practices. In addition, I made sure that students felt free to initiate topics and openly talk about discrimination and prejudices they have heard of, seen, or faced in context.

The three major categories that emerged across the data are discussed below. These categories illustrate the participants' perceptions of race relations and the effects that instruction produced on their subjectivities:

1. Awareness of the prevalence of color blindness.
2. Recognition of one's own and others' racist attitudes.
3. Media's influence on biases, racial prejudices, and stereotypes.

1 Awareness of the Prevalence of Color Blindness

As stated previously, race categorization is not common in Venezuela because of the ideology of *mestizaje* that historically has dominated our discourse. Nonetheless, both racism and negative attitudes toward dark-skinned people are present in discursive practices. The problem is that there is no racial consciousness among Venezuelans and even darker-skinned people affirm color blindness. Garcia (2004) asserts:

One of the great problems that we have in the communities of African descent is endo-racism—racism against one's self. The educational system has such a strong effect on our communities that they too deny the existence of racism. Also, they speak of ethnic shame, of their cultural background. I have conducted research in African-Venezuelan communities with people who have the same skin color as I do, who say, "No, no, we are descendants of the Spanish."

(p. 4)

Garcia's words support Montañez's (1993) argument of *endorracismo* as a common characteristic of Venezuelans from the lightest- to the darkest-skinned people. The following excerpts[2] from the participants' journals show their awareness of the hidden nature of racialization and racism as an ordinary practice in everyday life. In their own words, they expressed:

- I think race is not a big problem for us here in Venezuela, but it exists and people tend to be racist somehow. Have you seen watch any black on TV here in Venezuela? Not so many, right? Well, that's an example that not everybody has the same opportunities in this country (Journal, May 25, 2006; Ruby[3]).
- Race does matter but is hidden, and no one accepts it, or we don't know is there, and we keep being racists ... we are used to listening to sayings like *trabajo como un negro para vivir como un blanco* [I work like a black to live like a white] (Journal, May 12, 2006; Rene).
- Racism has been handled in a hidden way. In Venezuela the term race does not categorize a certain human group [nor] implies a social identity. However, the endorracismo is present in our discourse: the white is the symbol of beautiful, pure, and sophisticated while the black is the symbol of poor, impure, and not sophisticated ... descriptive terms for the hair appearance such as straight as opposed to "bad" (tightly curly) hair and references to the nose as profiled against flattened are expressions that have pejorative connotations hiding ethnic biases (Journal, May 17, 2006; Juana).
- We have racial discrimination but it's indirect; many Venezuelans think of blacks as poor without opportunities; some discotheques in Caracas [capital of Venezuela] do not allow access to brown or black people although they're Venezuelans too ... this is racial discrimination ... besides there are jokes and bad expressions to refer to blacks, an unfair situation considering that we are Afro descents and a mixture of races (Journal, May 12, 2006; Maria).
- A form of racism exists in the sense that all that is dark close to black is related with poverty (Journal, May 25, 2006; Nancy).

The above quotations illustrate the participants' acknowledgment that racial inequity exists but it is covert. Some of my students said, "We do not have race problems in the same sense that exists in the U.S.," showing a lack of awareness and justifying discriminatory discursive practices. Nonetheless, both groups of students at the end of the course admitted racialization in Venezuela and recognized that most people are not aware of it. They came to realize that racial issues are reduced to social class.

In addition, data show the participants' unawareness of their historical roots. In the following dialogue in which the class was discussing accent and race, Eduardo showed his lack of awareness of who we are and where we come from.

T: We got into a really hot topic here. So the color is a difference between African Americans and Venezuelans? Right?

EDUARDO: African Americans are really black and Latinos are lighter.

ELIO: We've got a lot of blacks here.

T: [addressing Eduardo] Do we have blacks here in Venezuela? Afro-Venezuelans?

EDUARDO: Here? I don't know any black people here ... the black people, you know are in the coast.

T: Are they Venezuelans?

JENNY: Yeah.

EDUARDO: [no answer]

T: Yes, they are. They are Afro descendants. How about the rest of Venezuelans? Are we African descendants?

EDUARDO: No.

T: Eduardo, you're not sure, or you don't know?

EDUARDO: I'm not sure.

T: Class, what do you think?

ELIO: I met a lot of African descendants. I mean in my hometown ... they migrated from the coast ... I am not sure; probably they're Caribbean ... maybe they arrived from Africa.

Eduardo and Elio's exchanges suggest that the educational system has failed in developing recognition of the value, culture, and history of Venezuelans of African descent. According to Quintero (2003), "the ethnocentrism present in our education as a result of colonialism has not been sufficiently studied and questioned ... which can be interpreted as racist in light of UNESCO's 1978 declaration on cultural diversity" (p. 14).

With regard to the interplay between race and language, the participants were asked to rank different accents in English and Spanish and establish differences and commonalities among the speakers of each accent. Not surprisingly, they ranked "Standard" American and British accent in the first and second place while African American Vernacular English (AAVE) was ranked last. As for Venezuela, the *caraqueño* (the accent of people from Caracas, the capital of the country) was ranked in the first place and that of the *gocho*[4] (the accent of people who come from the Andean Mountains, or where the majority of the participants come from) was ranked last.

The discussion about accent allowed the participants to debunk myths such as nativeness and "Standard" American English and they came to the realization that language is not neutral but carries ideologies. Through a problem-posing approach I posed questions such as: What thoughts come to your mind when you think of African Americans? What thoughts come to your mind when you hear the word *gocho*? Such questioning attempted to dig into students' thinking and have them contest social practices and racist attitudes that exclude *the other*.

2 Recognition of One's Own and Others' Racist Attitudes

Derogatory stereotypes about dark-skinned people, particularly Afro-Venezuelans, are a sign of racial discrimination in a society where there is a covert racism present in daily discursive practices and attitudes (Montañez, 1993). The tendency is to emphasize white ancestors' characteristics and minimize or conceal the African legacy of colonization and slavery. Unlike the United States, where African Americans show pride and a sense of community, Afro-Venezuelans do not affiliate their ethnicity with slavery and colonization. As one student noted, "Ironically, brown people are racist though they are Afro descendants too!" It is worth noting that Afro-Venezuelans have internalized and reproduce the *endorracismo* because they, as the rest of the population who called themselves *mestizos*, reject the African features inherited from ancestors, thereby perpetuating biases and social discrimination (Montañez, 1993).

The majority of the participants recognized that racist comments and jokes victimize those whose skin is nonwhite. They came to realize that racial discrimination exists in Venezuela; the majority of them recognized racist prejudices embedded in their daily attitude and discursive practices in Spanish. The following excerpt from a whole-class discussion illustrates biases against people of color.

T: How about Venezuela? Do we talk about minorities in our country?

OLGA: Yes, indigenous people.

BETTY: Women.

/SS: Nooooo.

T: Who else?

VILMA: Immigrants.

TOMÁS: Some religious groups.

T: Okay. Good. There are not only minorities in the U.S., right? There is also discrimination here.

/SS: In USA there is racism and here too...

BETTY: We don't say it, but it's hard to see a black guy ... you don't want your daughter with a black guy. I'm talking for me but ()

T: Do you agree with Betty? What would you say?

SIMÓN: Yes, because when you see a black guy some people look down on them especially for the color.

ELIO: A guy like Juan?

[Laughs]

JUAN: [interrupting] The other night Elio was driving with me. As we approached some policemen, he told me "Try to hide because the policemen are going to think we are going to steal."

ELIO: Hey, careful with what you say. I said it like a joke...

JUAN: Racism in this country is like a joke, right? I try to understand that is a joke but sometimes is frustrating ... calling me negro ... I know I'm negro, you know ... I've been in Europe and South Africa () nobody called me negro. He's a friend of mine, but why, you know called me suspect. I feel like is a joke but...

ELIO: Yeah, that's really ... That comes from our personality. We Venezuelans ... I can give you my example when I studied in high school my best friend was black so like we used to make fun of him [called him names], the whole year.

T: Why do you think that is so?

ELIO: I don't know, probably because we're racist. Yeah, it's like that.

T: Why is it like that?

ELIO: Somehow, I don't think it's racism. It's our personality … we try to make fun of everything … It's like … I mean…

The above interaction shows cultural biases against dark-skinned individuals. Although Elio refuses to recognize racism and considers instead that racist jokes are part of "personality" among Venezuelans, most participants acknowledged the ideology of colorblind racism embedded in social practices. Pedro, for example, confessed that his father influenced his views on race: "Have I used racist phrases? Yes, I have, and maybe all of us have too. I was raised in a family that discriminates dark people. My father hated darkest-skinned people, and that has some impact on me" (Journal, May 31, 2006). Despite his confession, Pedro acknowledged his struggle when he stated: "I am learning to improve that part of me; the bottom line is yes, we discriminate here, but people have not noticed it yet. Of course that's not good and we have to work on it." Another said, "I grew up experiencing prejudices against blacks. For example, my grandma used pejorative terms and gestures any time she saw a black person on the street or close to her" (Journal, June 16, 2005).

Throughout the course, however, the testimonies in the journals reflect changes in the participants' perceptions of racism and struggles with subjectivity.

- I am not racist; however, last week I watched a movie and there was a black guy, and I thought he was bad, but he wasn't; though I say I consider myself no racist this is an example of racial discrimination I was not aware of before (Journal, May 19, 2005; Marlene).
- Every day, people discriminate just when laughing and saying bad taste jokes against blacks (Journal, April 5, 2005; Julia).
- We tend to be racist; I am racist, but I have to think about the causes. I am unaware of it. I remember one time I was playing with a black kid and I told him, "You're black, you stink" (Journal, May 5, 2006; Samuel).
- I think we contribute to increase discrimination when we laugh at racist jokes or repeat sayings like, "you have to be black" (Journal, May 5, 2005; Sonia).

Like Juan, the other two darker-skinned students described experiencing racial discrimination:

- I am a dark skinned man, and I know what I am talking about because in school I was always excluded from several activities just because of my skin color (Journal, June 16, 2005; Enrique).
- I have faced racism right in my face, but I don't care because I learned to live with it a long time ago (Journal, May 18, 2006; José).

It seems fair to say that the class activities helped the NNES students open their minds to racialization. Though racist discursive practices might still remain in their attitudes and behavior, at least they started a process of concientization to challenge and transform reality.

3 Media's Influence on Biases, Racial Prejudices, and Stereotypes

A number of students became aware of how popular media, particularly movies, ads, consumerism, and fashion coming from what Phillipson (1997) called the Center (e.g., the United States) and reproduced in the local media affected their perceptions of race. Ishibashi (2004) asserts that media in general tends to reinforce Western ethnocentrism or epistemological racism to the detriment of local culture. Colorblindness, which is actually not uncommon among a majority, reproduces race-related social injustice and is constantly reinforced by the media, particularly television and Hollywood movies. The following comments illustrate this type of racism:

- We don't have many black actors, artists, or journalists; most of them are white (Journal, June 2, 2005; Alex).
- I think media has portrayed black people as bad and violent, and for this reason the society rejects blacks. I also think that that manifestation comes from the U.S. People here follow what they see on TV, especially if it comes from the U.S. (Journal, July 6, 2005; Martha).
- People treat you different according to the English "accent" you have, and according to the color of your skin (Journal, May 29, 2006; Jesus).

By the end of each school year, the participants expressed their intention to transform current social practices and their own racist behaviors and showed a commitment to act against racist discourses. One of them said, "It's time to stop those attitudes, as English teachers let's not perpetuate racism" (Sol, June 6, 2005). Moreover, they became aware of bad-taste jokes and recognized prejudices and stereotypes behind the so-called "Venezuelan personality" or "Venezuelan sense of humor." Another expressed, "It's time to stop and not laugh at racist comments and jokes against black people. Our mission as teachers is not perpetuating racism, sexism and so on" (Isabel, July 8, 2005). These last two students' quotations suggest an understanding that racist jokes and expressions are part of an internalized racism they wanted to combat.

The participants' change in perceptions led them to choose issues related to language and race to be researched and presented as their final projects:

- Influence of Reggaeton[5] songs on primary school students.
- Sexism in some TV commercials in Spanish.
- Latino stereotypes shown on the TV series That 70s Show and C.S.I.
- Racial stereotypes as portrayed in the movie Crash.
- Can you lose your foreign accent? Do you really want to?
- Perceptions of Standard English among teachers and students at Los Andes University.

The projects showed students' progress in terms of change of attitudes and assumptions of *othering* as a result of instruction. It is important to notice that changes occur over the long term and are impossible to quantify in the classroom; however, students' projects and comments indicate that they had altered their world-views and opened their minds to issues of racialization.

The following examples taken from students' self-reflections suggest a deeper understanding of hegemonic practices that discriminate against *the other* and perpetuate inequity. Lisa expressed:

> People in Venezuela are racist ... As teachers, we must scrutinize ourselves, and if we are racists, we must reflect on it and try to change our attitudes; we need to accept diversity and people as they are ... we can teach our students not to be racist ... It does not matter the color, religion, race etc., you are; the important thing is YOU as a human being.
>
> (Journal, June 18, 2006; Lisa)

Mary, another student wrote, "I understand the need of implementing new ways to fight racism in our educational system. If we do, we will be improving the life quality of many children in our country" (June 19, 2006). Mila also contested the apparent non-racialism when she stated:

> We see racism in schools from teachers to students and vice versa and students to students, so as teachers, we need to reflect on it and try to learn how to face situations where racism is present and how to teach students to respect the other avoiding discrimination. I think the important thing to change racism is to start changing ourselves and, then, we can hope people change.
>
> (Journal, June 25, 2006; Mila)

The participants' struggle led them to rethink and reflect upon their long-held beliefs and assumptions. One of them said:

> The social issues we have studied such as racism and accent created a conflict in my mind ... [the issues] suppose the ability or disposition to change, which is not easy ... Now, I am conscious about racism, accent, proficiency and many other related issues, but the important thing is to incorporate it in my professional life, and I'm trying ... this is worthless if we do not include it on our daily practice; of course, it is not easy.
>
> (Journal, June 29, 2006)

In addition, the participants deconstructed long-held assumptions such as Standard English and the superiority of native speakers over nonnative speakers and challenged their own preconceptions hidden in discursive practices. In the same way, they positioned themselves as NNES student teachers who, rather than searching for native-like pronunciation, shifted to intelligibility and developed a self-awareness of language as a marker of racism. One student wrote:

> Kahakua[6] is a perfect example of discrimination, but some ignorant people in Spanish countries love and prefer those who have a British or American accent. That is an example of how accent affects people's lives, and this kind of discrimination is in people's minds, and if people keep thinking this way racism is not going to disappear.

Another mentioned, "I insist on saying that our role goes beyond being just the English instructor as to what can we do to end racism? I am not sure we can end it, but we must work on it."

Through a conscientization process they debunked the myth of language neutrality. The following excerpts illustrate an increasing awareness of the intersection of race and language:

- Now, I could say that I wouldn't prefer a native speaker teacher because I'm more conscious and critical about the meaning of nativeness; definitively, the concept of a native speaker reflects more than physical appearance (Journal, May 23, 2006; Deisy).
- It is a sad reality that here in Venezuela and other places around the world many proficient English teachers are excluded and discriminated because of accent, physical appearance, and other factors that intersect with language and race (Journal, May 22, 2006; Maria).
- I guess we have to ask ourselves what role we play being a nonnative English teacher? How can we overcome the stereotypes that most students have? Where do we place ourselves as English teachers in a non-English-speaking country? What's more important here to respond to these questions is that race and identity are very powerful in ELT, and that's something we have to be aware of in our country (Journal, May 16, 2005; Marina).
- There are many connections between race and language we have been discussing a lot in classes; race is not only related to physical characteristics but also to the place you come from (Journal, June 29, 2006; Bertha).

Conclusion

English-teacher-education programs can become sites of resistance to contest inequity and help NNESTs to construct and reconstruct their identities as TESOL professionals. This study suggests that it is possible to develop a sense of agency for transformative action by incorporating into the curriculum not only the skills to acquire language intelligibility, but also critical self-reflection, or conscientization so that NNESTs gain empowerment and legitimacy. Such transformation of the curriculum involves a struggle with multiple subjectivities and a continuous challenge to question our role as English teachers within the sociopolitical and historical forces that surround us.

In the light of my personal experience of change, I am aware that altering one's world-views and constructing and reconstructing one's subjectivity is painful and conflicting. This is not a linear process. Thus, as students are faced with issues of identity change, I, in dialogic conversation, try not to impose my own world-views; rather I listen to them and pose questions to help them position as *the other*.

Assuming language from a critical perspective is not easy for my students. They wrestle with conflicting views and resistance. Most of them, like me, have been educated under Structuralism, learning English from a neutral standpoint centered upon the acquisition of communicative competence. Hence, unlearning long-held assumptions around language as a neutral activity is an uneven process that takes time.

This action research study shows that although each participant's level of reflection varied, in general they seemed to expand their understanding of racism. Most were capable of demonstrating a self-awareness of racist discursive practices present in their everyday life. Despite the pilot group's resistance to acknowledging racial discrimination in their own milieu, the last two groups debunked and recognized racist practices and attitudes ingrained in their everyday discourse; most of them questioned long-held beliefs they had not unveiled before.

As a teacher educator, I am committed to the process of transforming prescriptive pedagogy into praxis and calling into question sociopolitical and historical forces that regulate social relations. I am committed to engaging students, co-workers, and loved ones in self-reflection to combat racism that devalues *the other*. This study has implications for English-teacher-education programs in foreign contexts, where generally ELT emphasizes formal linguistics and teaching as apolitical and neutral. As findings indicate, a critical inquiry into the education of NNESTs helps them break down hegemonic discourses toward the construction and reconstruction of NNES students' identities as TESOL professionals. It is crucial to transform the NNESTs' curriculum into a praxis that engages them in questioning and problematizing their individual presence in the world as racialized beings and their relation with history and culture (Freire, 2004).

Discussion Questions

1. The author argues that even nonnative speakers of English who teach English as a foreign language could "unconsciously help reproduce existing educational practices and social inequities through hegemonic cultural discourses that perpetuate domination" of English. Think about some concrete examples of how this could be manifested in various instructional practices.

2. The author describes the racial demographics of Venezuela. Choose a country you are familiar with and investigate (1) racial or ethnic diversity (types of racial or ethnic groups and their populations); (2) a history of racial diversity; (3) public discourses and policies on diversity (e.g., discriminatory, anti-discriminatory, color-blind); and (4) people's attitudes toward different racial or ethnic groups.

3. The author mentions the tendency of Afro-Venezuelans to deny racism and even devalue their own ethnic and racial identity. Why are such perceptions produced and perpetuated? What are the consequences? Are there any other examples of oppressed people's denial of their own oppression?

4 Take an example of a class (either teacher education or second language) and explore how you could conduct a type of action research that is similar to what the author did. How would you collect data from the students about their views on racialization, racism, and culture? How would you improve the instruction based on the data?

Notes

1. Two different versions of this chapter were presented at the 39th Annual Convention of TESOL 2005 and the 41st Annual TESOL Convention 2007.

2. The testimonies taken from the journals are presented here as originally written in English.

3. Names are pseudonyms.
4. The term *gocho* has a pejorative connotation meaning not intelligent, stupid.
5. *Reggaeton* (also spelled *Reguetón* in Spanish) blends Jamaican musical influences of reggae and dancehall with those of Latin America. Some *Reggaeton* lyrics are offensive to women, and the musical form is associated with a dance with explicit sexual overtones.
6. Kahakua is a name that appears in *The myth of non-accent* (Lippi-Green, 1997, p. 44).

References

Acosta Saignes, M. (1985). Procedencia de los Africanos. In J. Salvat (Ed.), *Conocer a Venezuela Historia 2 Procedencia de los africanos y población actual* [Knowing Venezuela history 2: Origin of Africans and current population] (pp. 123–169). Caracas, Venezuela: Salvat editores Venezolana.

Amin, N. (1997). Race and identity of the nonnative ESL teacher. *TESOL Quarterly, 31*, 80–583.

Aranguren, C. (1997). *La enseñanza de la historia en la escuela básica* [The teaching of history in basic education]. Mérida, Venezuela: Consejo de publicaciones Universidad de los Andes.

Auerbach, E. R. (1992). *Making meaning making change. Participatory curriculum development for ESL literacy.* McHenry, IL: Center of Applied Linguistics.

Bartlett, L. (1990). Teacher development through reflective teaching. In J. C. Richards & D. Nunan (Eds.), *Second language teacher education* (pp. 202–214). Cambridge: Cambridge University Press.

Braine, G. (Ed.). (1999). *Non-native educators in English language teaching.* Mahwah, NJ: Lawrence Erlbaum Associates.

Chacón, C. (2000). Reflections from the classroom: Empowering NNESTs. *NNEST Newsletter, 2*(2), 11.

Chacón, C. (2006). My journey into racial awareness. In A. Curtis & M. Romney (Eds.). *Color, race, and English language teaching: Shades of meaning* (pp. 49–63). Mahwah, NJ: Lawrence Erlbaum Associates.

Chacón, C., & Alvarez, L. (2001, February). *Critical pedagogy and empowerment in teacher education.* Paper presented at the 35th TESOL annual convention, St. Louis, MO.

Chacón, C., Alvarez, L., Brutt-Griffler, J., & Samimy, K. (2003). Dialogue around revisiting the colonial in the postcolonial: Critical praxis for nonnative-English-speaking teachers in a TESOL program. In J. Sharkey & K. E. Johnson (Eds.), *The TESOL quarterly dialogues: Rethinking issues of language, culture, and power* (pp. 141–150). Alexandria, VA: TESOL.

Danielewicz, J. (2001). *Teaching selves: Identity, pedagogy, and teacher education.* Albany, NY: State University of New York Press.

Fairclough, N. (1989). *Language and power.* London: Longman.

Freire, P. (2002). *Pedagogy of the oppressed.* New York: Continuum.

Freire, P. (2004). *Pedagogy of indignation.* Boulder, CO: Paradigm Publishers.

Garcia, C. (2004, January 21). *Chucho Garcia Interview: Racism and racial divides in Venezuela.* Retrieved June 18, 2005 from www.venezuelanalysis.com/articlesphp?artno=1091.

Instituto Nacional de Estadística (OCEI). (2005). Republica Bolivariana de Venezuela. Retrieved July 20, 2006 from www.ine.gov.ve.

Ishibashi, J. (2004). Hacia una apertura del debate sobre el racismo en Venezuela: Exclusión y inclusión de la persona "negra" in the media [Towards an opening about the debate of racism in Venezuela: Exclusion and inclusion of the black person in the media]. Colección Monografías # 4, Universidad Central de Venezuela, Caracas. Retrieved July 31, 2006 from www.globalcult.org.ve/monografias.htm.

Kachru, B. B. (Ed.). (1992). *The other tongue.* Chicago, IL: University of Illinois Press.

Kubota, R., & Lin, A. (2006). Race and TESOL: Introduction to concepts and theories. *TESOL Quarterly, 40,* 471–493.

Kubota, R., & Ward, L. (2000). Exploring linguistic diversity through World Englishes. *English Journal, 89*(6), 80–86.

Launer, D. (Producer), & Lynn, J. (Director). (1992). *My cousin Vinny* [Motion Picture]. United States: Twentieth Century Fox.

Lin, A. M. Y. (2004). Introducing a critical pedagogical curriculum: A feminist reflexive account. In B. Norton & K. Toohey (Eds.), *Critical pedagogies and language learning* (pp. 271–290). Cambridge: Cambridge University Press.

Lippi-Green, R. (1997). *English with an accent: Language, ideology, and discrimination in the United States.* New York: Routledge.

Montañez, L. (1993). *El racismo oculto en una sociedad no racista.* [The hidden racism in a nonracist society]. Caracas, Venezuela: Fondo Editorial Tropykos.

Norton, B. (2003, May). *Language teacher education as critical practice.* Paper presented at the Third International Conference on Language Teacher Education, University of Minnesota, MN.

Norton, B., & Toohey, K. (Eds.). (2004). *Critical pedagogies and language learning.* Cambridge: Cambridge University Press.

OCEI. (2001). Oficina Central de Estadística e Informatica [Central Office of Statistics and Computer Science of the Bolivarian Republic of Venezuela]. Retrieved May 6, 2005 from www.ocei. gov.ve/demografica/censopoblacionvivienda.asp.

Pennycook, A. (1994). *The cultural politics of English as an international language.* New York: Longman.

Pennycook, A. (1999). Introduction: Critical approaches to TESOL. *TESOL Quarterly, 33,* 329–348.

Pennycook, A. (2001). *Critical applied linguistics: A critical introduction.* Mahwah, NJ: Lawrence Erlbaum Associates.

Phillipson, R. (1997). *Linguistic imperialism.* New York: Oxford University Press.

Quintero, M. P. (2003). Racismo, etnocentrismo occidental y educación. El caso Venezuela [Racism, western ethnocentrism, and education. Case Venezuela]. *Acción Pedagógica, 12*(1), 4–15.

Red de Organizaciones Afrovenezolanas (ROA) [Net of Afro Venezuelan Organizations]. Retrieved May 1, 2005 from www.redafrovenezolana.com.

Samimy, K., & Brutt-Griffler, J. (1999). Revisiting the colonial in the postcolonial: Critical praxis for non-native-English-speaking teachers in a TESOL program. *TESOL Quarterly, 33,* 413–431.

Sheridan, J. (Producer/Director). (2002). *In America* [Motion Picture]. United States: Twentieth Century Fox.

Smedley, A., & Smedley, B. D. (2005). Race as biology is fiction, racism as a social problem is real: Anthropological and historical perspectives on the social construction of race. *American Psychologist, 60,* 16–26.

Tang, C. (1997). The identity of the Nonnative ESL teacher: on the power and status of nonnative ESL teachers. *TESOL Quarterly, 31,* 577–580.

van Dijk, T. A. (2003). *Dominación étnica y racismo discursivo en España y América Latina* [Ethnic domination and racist discourse in Spain and Latin America]. Barcelona: Editorial Gedisa.

Warren, J. W. (2000). Masters in the field: White talk, white privilege, white biases. In F. W. Twine & J. W. Warren (Eds.), *Racing research, researching race: Methodological dilemmas in critical race* (pp. 135–164). New York: New York University Press.

Weedon, C. (1987). *Feminist practice and poststructuralist theory.* Oxford: Blackwell.

13 Narratives in the Wild

Unpacking Critical Race Theory Methodology for Early Childhood Bilingual Education

Sara Michael-Luna

Pre-reading Questions

Children develop their identities from an early age. Nonetheless, research on young children and racial and ethnic identities has not been conducted extensively. Sara Michael-Luna examines how texts for children and classroom interactions might influence minority bilingual children's identity development in the United Sates.

- What are characteristics of books about and for minority children? What topics and contents tend to appear?
- How would a teacher address issues of racial/ethnic issues in a bilingual classroom?

Introduction

> "I've seen it [racism] many times and have tried to fix many things myself, but I haven't taken it back to the kids."
>
> (Tom, bilingual teacher narrative, October 5, 2003)

Tom, a Mexican-American bilingual teacher, reflected on the racism he and his students experienced in a small bilingual program within a larger English-dominant school and community. During the course of our 2-year Teacher-Researcher Collaborative ethnographic research, both Tom and I transformed our assumptions about race and racism through our experiences working with young bilingual students. Tom's statement reflects that movement from early childhood multilingual learners as passive recipients or victims of racism to students as active agents of change. This movement was made possible by a reconsideration of classroom practices and research methodology regarding spaces for students' construction of their identity and the social construction of who they are and what they can do within the confines of the schooling context.

Young children create meaning and come to understand who they are and what they can do by participating with others in "culturally organized routine practices" (Graue & Walsh, 1998, p. 52). But what happens to young multilinguals of color when the organized routine practices of school are embedded with racialized assumptions, essentializations, and dominant-culture norms (Ladson-Billings & Tate, 1995)? To date, Critical Race Theory, Early Childhood Education, and Second Language Acquisition research have not directly addressed both the ability level of young children (Bredekamp & Copple, 1997) and the embedded assumptions of race in the dominant discourse of schooling (Ladson-Billings, 1999). The dominant culture and the dominant discourse of schooling in the United States are complex and dynamic ways of enacting values, beliefs, and norms which signify a participant as being a certain kind of person (Gee, 1996; Foucault, 1972). Historically, these discourses are products of white, monolingual, and middle-class males and are directly related to hierarchical structure and distribution of power in society (Gee, 1999).

I frame an appropriate approach to data collection and analysis around concepts of racial and linguistic identity construction of early childhood multilinguals. I draw from empirical evidence on Spanish-speaking children in the United States. First, I review Critical Race Theory (Ladson-Billings & Tate, 1995) as a theoretical lens for analysis of race in educational practice. Second, I present considerations of race research for early childhood education contexts and multilingual learners. Given the parameters discussed in the first and second sections, the third section discusses a three-step methodology for unpacking the racial, cultural, and linguistic identity construction of young bilinguals. Specifically, I suggest that a close analysis of children's literature for the tenets of Critical Race Theory should accompany a change in traditional classroom practice to model and create space for counter-narratives. Fourth, I exemplify how this three-step methodology was used to uncover the tenets of Critical Race Theory in the texts and contexts of early childhood education in a 2-year ethnographic study. Finally, I make suggestions for pedagogic and research strategies to create space for young multilinguals to give voice to, construct, and resist embedded dominant-culture assumptions about race and language. These contextual narratives, or *narratives in the wild*, illuminate the multiple spaces in the school context for age- and language-relevant *counter-narratives* (Matsuda, 1995). I argue that these *narratives in the wild* serve as a means of reconstructing the dominant discourse of schooling to include and accommodate more students (Solórzano & Delgado Bernal, 2001).

Theoretical Framing

Critical Race Theory and Education

Does race really matter? While much educational research has been dedicated to examining how immigrant status, socioeconomic status (SES), national origin, and language have contributed to a dynamic and complex construction of learner identity, institutional norms, and dominant-discourse assumptions (Gee, 1996), very few studies have examined the role that race plays in young children's learner identity construction. Educational research has spent the last decade attempting to explain how and why race is an important part of older students' educational experience. Much research has focused on how racially embedded practices, curriculum, and texts have served to alienate, silence, and *other* many ethnically and racially diverse learners in secondary school (Ladson-Billings & Tate, 1995; DeCuir & Dixson, 2004; Duncan, 2002; Fine, 1991; Alim, 2005). This section will define Critical Race Theory and examine the methodology suggested when using Critical Race Theory as a tool of analysis.

Founded in the 1970s as a part of a movement by progressive legal scholars, Critical Race Theory was introduced into educational research as a theoretical lens to interrogate education policy and practice as tools of racial oppression (Ladson-Billings & Tate, 1995; Ladson-Billings, 1999). With the understanding that racism is an "endemic facet of life in our society and that neutrality, objectivity, colorblindness and meritocracy are all questionable constructs" (Pizzaro, 1998, p. 62), Critical Race Theory is used to challenge the meritocracy of the dominant discourse (Gee, 1996) and the perception that racism is an individual act. Critical Race Theory also puts forward four additional understandings: (1) Racism is a permanent and (often) invisible part of the legal, educational, and other systems in the United States (Bell, 1992, 1995); (2) The White race maintains the highest or dominant status and has been legally treated as *property* (Harris, 1995); (3) There must be a convergence of interests with the dominant race, or White race, for (basic civil) rights to be granted to people of color (Bell, 1980); (4) Liberalism or traditional understandings of multiculturalism primarily benefit the White race, or dominant race (Crenshaw, 1988; Kubota, 2004). The use of Critical Race Theory by legal scholars has been to "work toward the elimination of racism as part of a larger goal of elimination all forms of subordination" (Matsuda, 1991, p. 1331, cited in Solórzano & Yosso, 2001, p. 472). In educational contexts, Critical Race Theory has been used as a way to make visible the embedded racial assumptions in text, context, and practice. These assumptions are unmasked through nondominant stories and counter-stories reflection on school experience (see DeCuir & Dixson, 2004; Duncan, 2002; Fine, 1991; Ladson-Billings & Tate, 1995).

Matsuda (1995) proposes an empirical method for uncovering these understandings called *counter-storytelling* (Matsuda, 1995). Counter-storytelling uses narrative-inquiry techniques to give voice to people of color and their experiences with systemic racism. Counter-storytelling told in "outgroups" (Delgado, 2000, p. 61) serves to counter the stories told by dominant groups. In education, these dominant-group stories are embedded in texts, curriculum, and pedagogy. The dominant group or ingroup's stories "remind it of its identity in relation to outgroups, and provide it with a form of shared reality in which its own superior position is seen as natural" (Delgado, 2000, p. 60). Counter-storytelling works to unveil the mask of neutrality, endowing the tellers with agency to contest the status quo.

Critical Race Theory in education has focused exclusively on the experience and construction of race for adolescents and adults. Counter-storytelling is reflective of this demographic and has been used as a data source for exploring the tenets of Critical Race Theory within educational contexts (Alim, 2005; DeCuir & Dixson, 2004; Duncan, 2002; Fine, 1991; Ladson-Billings & Tate, 1995; Solórzano & Yosso, 2001). The counter-narratives produced during formal and informal interviews are culturally and socially appropriate forms of *talking back* to a racist system for adults and adolescents who have the abilities to reflect on and produce these types of stories during interviews. However, with young children, interviews are not always a productive space to negotiate meanings around race, language, and ethnicity. In the next section, I will examine what previous research on race and young children has suggested.

Literature Review

Early Childhood Education, Language, and Race

How do young children understand race and ethnicity? As early as the 1920s, psychologists have explored children's perceptions of race and ethnicity (Lasker, 1929; Horowitz, 1936) and found that young white (Anglo) children consistently choose racially similar peers and groups to othered (African American) peers and groups. Follow-up studies identified African American children also choosing Anglo peers over African American peers (Spencer & Horowitz, 1973; Spencer, 1982) suggesting that the African American children misidentified themselves as Anglos (Aboud, 1977). In addition to an exclusive focus on a black–white racial binary, these studies drew heavily upon developmental psychology and experimental methods to examine children's perceptions of race. This research emphasizes the development of a linear developmentally appropriate model of racial attitudes among young children (Bigler & Liben, 1993) and assumes a deficit model of cognition.

The developmental work on children's understandings of race does not take into consideration the social contexts in which the young child is apprentice to, negotiates, and constructs its understandings. Activity Theory (Vygotsky, 1978) and Social Constructionism (Gergen, 1985) perspectives on early childhood suggest that children construct knowledge through social interactions within their communities of practice (Lave & Wenger, 1991), which include families, school, and playgroups. These relationships present socially complex perspectives on race, language, socioeconomic status, culture, immigrant status, national origin, and identity which are mediated during moment-to-moment interaction (Graue & Walsh, 1998). As young children negotiate multiple perspectives on race, language, and ethnicity in their different environments, they are constantly adapting, opposing, and negotiating these understandings on a moment-to-moment basis. By focusing on contextual interaction as the site of knowledge production, the locus of meaning making is moved from the individual student, as suggested by developmental theory, to the context and interactions of the student. These relationships in context can only be examined using a long-term ethnographic approach in which moment-to-moment interactions are analyzed for changing understandings of race, language, and ethnicity.

Unfortunately, few research studies in early childhood use race as a lens through which to examine interaction, preferring to discuss ethnicities (Holmes, 1995) or not to examine race at all. The daunting task of examining perceptions of race by young children through social interaction has only been done by Van Ausdale and Feagin (2001), who specifically examine how the social interactions of young children in an early childhood classroom shape children's perspectives on race and racism through a year-long ethnographic study. Their research emphasizes the role that the racist social structure within the United States plays in children's understandings of the differences among racial groups (p. 196). Additionally, Van Ausdale and Feagin's (2001) research critiques prior research on early childhood education and race for emphasizing the individuality of our pseudo merit-based society in which each participant's success and failure is blamed solely on their individual choices:

The social toolbox is wide open and ready for children to use as their skills develop. When the nature of everyday discourse and practice is laden with racial-ethnic meanings, children, too, will make much practical use of that discourse in everyday life.

(p. 196)

Although bilingual children were represented in their study, Van Ausdale and Feagin (2001) did not take into consideration first language narratives in context of bilingual children as a site of analysis for the tenets of Critical Race Theory.

Much of early childhood research has also glossed over the importance of English-language learners (ELLs) or multilinguals in their investigations into children's understandings of who they are and what they can be (Hawkins, 2005). While each of these ethnographic studies contributes to a fuller understanding of how ELL identity forms during early elementary school, specifically drawing on immigrant status, SES, and language production, the research did not (1) examine native language interactions of the ELLs, nor (2) examine how the ELLs understood race and ethnicity. Race is an ignored part of young children's complex and dynamic learner identities; thus, a race lens brings nuance to previous research by highlighting an additional factor. At the same time, race is a complex construct which is contextually bound as well as linked to immigrant status, language, SES, and culture.

Second language acquisition research in early childhood contexts presents many challenges to the traditional site of analysis for Critical Race Theory tenets—counter-stories. A first consideration is the language of analysis. When examining narrative identity construction and negotiations with young multilinguals, researchers should weigh native and nonnative language production differently. As a language learner, perceptions of the world change, based on the embedded social constructs and norms that are evident in the language used (Holland & Quinn, 1987). When young children are asked to produce or interact using a language they are learning, their responses and interactions are limited by their language level. Research examining young multilingual learners for understandings of race should consider both native language and second (or nonnative) language interactions. Previous research has only analyzed second language interactions. A method of research must take into consideration first language interactions of multilingual students.

Additionally, the narratives and counter-storytelling traditionally used by Critical Race Theory educational researchers do not take into consideration the ability levels of young children.

Asking children why they are doing things, explanations they do not give in their normal interactions, is like asking a fish about water. First you need to explain what water is and remind her that it is there. What the fish then has to say about water may be interesting, but it has as much to do with your question and its setup as it does with the fish's experience with water.

(Graue & Walsh, 1998, p. 43)

Formal question-and-answer formats about abstract concepts such as race, language, and culture are difficult for young children to discuss. Young children's answers to formal interview questions give a momentary glimpse into their temporal construction of reality (Hawkins, 2005). Interviews can provide a space for counter-narratives in adults or adolescents (DeCuir & Dixson, 2004; Alim, 2005); however, due to the developmental level of many children in early childhood, these interviews are not the optimal situation in which children can express their perspectives. Previous research on bilinguals' understandings of race in early childhood contexts found that children did not use this space to construct alternative realities to the dominant discourse (Michael-Luna, 2005). Even when interviewed in their home language, young multilinguals did not produce counter-stories or narratives but instead answered questions in school-appropriate fashion. Therefore, a second consideration of a method should examine children's narratives in context. Such spaces might include the moment-to-moment interactions around texts within the confines of the school day.

Finally, a research method to uncover the tenets of Critical Race Theory should consider the educational context of young children. Part of the goal of Critical Race Theory is to unveil the mask of neutrality on the dominant discourses. In early childhood contexts, the dominant discourse is a part not only of pedagogy (Heath, 1982) but also children's literature (Michael-Luna & Canagarajah, 2007; Nathenson-Mejia & Escamilla, 2003). When analyzing young children's understandings of race, researchers and teachers must also consider the environmental factors in and with which the child interacts.

Method

Exploring how racially diverse young bilinguals interact and examining the texts present in their classroom environment can be especially salient in exposing and critiquing the tenets of Critical Race Theory. One way to do this is to analyze moment-to-moment interactions and texts using critical discourse analysis (Gee, 1999). This analysis tool involves:

> Asking questions about how language, at a given time and place, is used to construe the aspects of the situation network as realized at that time and place and how the aspects of the situation network simultaneously give meaning to that language.
>
> (p. 92)

Reflecting the earlier discussion on the importance of contexts, situation networks are systems which include signs, social activities, materials, social *goods*, and cultural knowledge (Gee, 1999). By examining the texts and the moment-to-moment interactions in a classroom, one can examine not only how systemic racism is reproduced at the local level, but also how young children construct, resist, and negotiate this system. Data which can reflect the local construction of race for young bilinguals includes texts used during instruction and video-taped moment-to-moment interaction. The following section suggests a series of questions developed during a 2-year ethnographic study of a bilingual first grade. The questions can be used by both teachers and researchers to analyze texts and contexts for tenets of Critical Race Theory.

The tenets of Critical Race Theory are an endemic facet of children's literature and reading materials. Critical Race Theory suggests that traditional understandings of multiculturalism serve to benefit the dominant, White race and this can be especially true of multicultural texts. However, uncovering this invisible, systemic racism can be a challenge. Even when characters in children's texts appear to physically resemble children of color, the underlying message (or moral) of the story may run counter to the students' home norms and understandings. When examining a text for Critical Race Theory tenets, teachers and researchers might ask the following questions:

1. What do the characters look like?
2. What do the characters value? What is the moral of the story?
3. Who makes decisions? Who has the power to decide?
4. Are any characters portrayed negatively?
   a.   What makes the character *bad*?
   b.   Who gets *hurt* and who does not?
5. What is considered *common sense*?
6. What languages are used? How? Why?
7. What are the direct/indirect statements made about race, SES, geological location, and power/intelligence?
8. Do students of color see themselves in one of the characters?
9. Do the books serve to introduce a superficial artifact of *difference*?
10. Are dominant-culture models embodied in *othered* characters?

These questions can be enacted when the teacher selects a book or when a research conducts a critical discourse analysis (Gee, 1999) of a text.

Examining the texts that students encounter in classroom settings can help to uncover how *ingroups* (Delgado, 2000) use narratives to make the subordination of people of color seem "natural." However, unmasking these assumptions is only part of the task; Critical Race Theory also calls for people of color to tell their own narratives or counter-narratives. As discussed in the previous section, this may not be developmentally appropriate for young bilinguals as they do not have the narrative resources or interviewing skills necessary. Therefore, researchers and teachers might consider introducing and modeling counter-storytelling strategies in the students' first language and creating space in the classroom for students to tell their own stories. In our study, we used the following two-pronged strategy:

1. Introduce texts and contexts that contained "counter-narratives" on cultural-historical figures such as Cesar Chavez, Diego Rivera, and Frida Khalo (see Appendix A).
2. Create space during calendar time and read-alouds for students to ask questions, negotiate meaning, and tell stories.

During our 2-year ethnographic study, the narratives the young bilinguals told were (1) in their home language; (2) related values, norms, and cultural models relevant to them; and (3) assisted the teacher and researcher in understanding how a young child *saw* his/her world (Michael-Luna, 2005). These stories ranged from eating pizza at Chunky Cheese, to retelling popular movie plots, to relating superstitions (Michael-Luna, 2005). By creating this space in the classroom discourse for narratives, the teacher and researcher gain a deeper understanding of how the students understand who they are and what they are capable of; the students' families, communities, and school experience; and also what academic knowledge became a part of the students' discourse.

Additionally, the teacher and researcher developed a specific way to critique the classroom practice for evidence of oppressive dominant-culture norms and values. After video-taping and transcribing student interaction during calendar time and read-alouds, the moment-to-moment interaction was analyzed using the following questions:

1. Were Spanish speakers' (specifically Mexican or South American) values, norms, language, race(s), and ways of knowing represented in the context, text, and pedagogy?

    a. If yes, were they presented in a positive way?

2. Were there global or local Mexican-origin leaders who were directly involved with either the theme or content-area topic taught?

    a. If yes, were the students empowered through activating prior schema on Mexican-origin leaders?

    b. If yes, were the leaders depicted positively as models of agents of change?

An analysis of moment-to-moment interaction during calendar time or around texts can give multiple insights into young children's construction of race, ethnicity, and language, as well as uncover how the pedagogy, curriculum, and texts help construct who they are and what they can be. Each of the questions above suggests not only race but also SES, immigrant status, national origin, and language as factors to consider in book selection. The following section demonstrates how this method uncovered the tenets of Critical Race Theory during a 2-year ethnographic study of a bilingual first grade.

Context and Participants

The data presented here are part of a 2-year ethnographic study and examined the question: How does language used by teachers, students, and texts within literacy events contribute to shaping a learner identity for students in a first-grade bilingual (Spanish–English) classroom? During the ethnographic observations, video-tapes were made of the 136 hours of classroom interactions. The video-tapes were submitted to a multi-modal analysis (Kress & Van Leeuwen, 2001), linguistic transcription (Ochs, 1979), and a critical discourse analysis (Gee, 1999). After examining issues of race during the pilot study (Michael-Luna, 2005), the teacher and researcher began to consider how to create a classroom environment where race, ethnicity, and language were topics reflected upon by the teacher and researcher and were presented in an open manner to the students. Ultimately, the researcher and teacher developed a set of questions and strategies around the tenets of Critical Race Theory during teacher-researcher collaborative interviews (Hawkins & Legler, 2004). The moment-to-moment interactions as well as texts in the classroom were analyzed using these questions.

The site of the research is a Spanish–English bilingual first-grade classroom in a large urban elementary school, Lakeland Elementary. All names and places are pseudonyms.

Lakeland Elementary is located in a medium-sized U.S. city in the Upper Midwest called Midland. At the time of the study, Lakeland Elementary had a population of 640 students and served grades K–5. Of the 108 first-grade students, 26 were African American, 24 Hispanic, 7 Asian, and 51 White. The data presented here is from the 2003–2004 school year.

During 2003–2004, the focal classroom was a bilingual first grade with 12 students (seven males and five females). Ten of the children were born in Mexico and immigrated to the United States with their parents. One female child was from Uruguay, and one male was from Argentina. All of the children spoke Spanish as their primary language among themselves at school and at home with their parents. The children were socially constructed as nonwhite by the teacher, researcher, and school staff. The children had dark skin and strong indigenous features.

The teacher, Tom, is a 35-year-old male who is of Mexican-German heritage. The teacher had taught for 4 years in the Midland school district, and 8 years in total. While he grew up in a bilingual/bicultural Spanish–English home, the teacher's formal schooling was all in English. He is often socially constructed as white and has light olive skin and blue eyes. The researcher is a middle-class Anglo-American who learned Spanish as a second language as an adult.

Findings and Discussion

Text Analysis

The books on the shelves of a typical first grade include characters of different ethnic, racial, and linguistic backgrounds in a variety of environments. However, on analysis many of these books focus on the superficial artifacts of a nondominant discourse life such as food, clothing, and shelter while imposing dominant-cultural norms on the characters of color. Because the visible parts of the text appear to represent "the other," the embedded cultural norms lead to an invisibility of the colonization of nondominant culture, language, and races. Teachers choosing to present culturally relevant (Ladson-Billings, 1994) texts to their students must consider not only the race of the characters and topic of a book, but must examine the deeper values and norms represented through these characters. One such book which was used before the teacher-research collaboration conceived a method of critique and analysis was *Tortillas, Tortillas*.

Tortillas, Tortillas is a part of a series of graded readers described as "multicultural" by the publisher. The text was in English and used as part of the English as a Second Language (ESL) literacy guided-reading group by the teacher. A deep analysis of the text uncovered both positive ways that the text was "culturally relevant" (Ladson-Billings, 1994) as well as ways that the text held some of the tenets of Critical Race Theory.

The topic of *Tortillas, Tortillas*, a Mexican-American family preparing tortillas, appears to be culturally relevant to Mexican immigrant students:

> Tortillas, tortillas.
> We eat crisp ones
> And soft ones.

Tortillas, tortillas.
We eat them in a bowl of milk.
We eat them covered with honey.

The text describes the types of tortillas a family makes and eats. The accompanying pictures present an indigenous-Mexican family working together in a kitchen to make and eat the tortillas. The critical discourse analysis (Gee, 1999) suggested that the characters and their actions are familiar to the focal students and held the values of family interdependence. Additionally, an extended family was portrayed. These two norms help support the cultural values of the students rather than assimilate the nondominant characters into dominant-culture norms of nuclear family and independence.

Additionally, because *Tortillas, Tortillas* is a descriptive text, it fits previous researchers' findings that Spanish-speaking children may not narrate sequences of events as frequently as their U.S., Canadian, Japanese, or African American peers (McCabe, 1997). Instead, their narratives focus on descriptive information usually related to family and personal relationships (Cazden, 1986; Silva & McCabe, 1996). The narrative structure, in addition to the theme of describing and evaluating, presents a culturally familiar narrative type despite the unfamiliar language (English).

However, when analyzing the text with a Critical Race Theory lens, several of the tenets are clearly at play: the text serves as an ingroup narrative by presenting a superficial view of Mexican culture by focusing on food. The message that it sends is that indigenous Mexican-origin people make tortillas together. This in no way critiques or threatens dominant-culture norms; rather it highlights superficial differences (Lillis, personal communication, February 26, 2006). Critical Race Theory suggests that the convergence of interest lies in the fact that immigrant, subordinate cultures and people of color are: (1) portrayed as preparers of food (a low-paying, low-prestige job and characters can be constructed as not taking advantage of the merit-based society); (2) contributing superficial (food) items to the dominant culture (thus not threatening or challenging social structure, norms, values, or institutions); and (3) the story is told in a way that appears "natural" that these people of color would act in this way.

The majority of multicultural books which were analyzed over our 2-year ethnography focused on the superficial artifacts of life such as food, clothing, or shelter. Larger themes such as the social structure and function of the family unit were found to be the dominant culture superimposed on characters of color. Themes of efficiency and independence were found in several guided-reading books termed multicultural by the publisher. Many of these books were in Spanish and presented very young characters of color eating breakfast, getting ready for school, or waking up in the morning without the assistance or support of other family members. The students in Tom's class reacted very negatively to these norms or attempted to reconstruct the norms using their cultural models (Michael-Luna, 2005). When considering the Critical Race Theory tenets, the interest convergence lies here by saying it is all right for the other to give new and interesting food (clothing or shelter) to the dominant culture, but the foundational morals and systemic structures, such as family units, classroom practice, and historical perspectives, are not different from hegemonic dominant culture. The age-old addum appears natural—the United States is a *melting pot* where the larger social structures of immigrant cultures melt away and do not threaten the dominant status of the white, monolingual, middle-class, hegemonic culture.

Many early childhood multicultural texts show how people of color and the ethnically othered are folded into the dominant culture. These texts do not present a true exploration of the home culture of ethnic, linguistic, and racial minorities. The use of this type of multicultural children's literature that cites superficial differences serves to (1) mask the colonization of people of color's cultural norms and values with dominant-culture norms; (2) secure the status of the dominant culture by trivializing, essentializing, and exoticizing the other (Kubota, 2004); (3) emphasize the role of individual choice versus systemic racism. The counter-stories which superficially appear in these multicultural readers actually serve the dominant race by imposing dominant-culture values and norms on the other. A culturally relevant pedagogy (Ladson-Billings, 1994) begins by setting a curriculum and context in which students of color can engage with texts that represent relevant social structures and understandings.

Interaction

Pedagogic practice around read-alouds and guided reading in early elementary school often do not leave space for students to *talk back* to the dominant-discourse norms, values, and ways of knowing that colonize children's literature characters who, in superficial ways, represent them. Research has examined question–response patterns among teachers and students and found that teachers ask questions to which they already know the answer (Gee, 1996; Gutierrez, 1994). Often, these are yes/no or short-answer questions. There are very few times during the school day where students are allowed space and time to talk about their real-life experience in relation to the topic presented in a text (Gee, 1996). Culturally relevant pedagogy (Ladson-Billings, 1994) suggests that teachers should recruit techniques and methods, such as prolonged schema activation or creating space for student narratives, that fit the local cultural models of their students. By creating space for students to connect to text, context, and knowledge, teachers "assure each student of his or her individual importance" (Ladson-Billings, 1994, p. 66), thus legitimizing their voice and experience within the dominant discourse of school. Ladson-Billings' (1994) assertions regarding student voice and narratives reorganize CRT's methodology (Matsuda, 1995) in an appropriate form for classroom interaction. Thus, when considering ways for the students to *talk back* or *have a voice*, teachers and researchers should consider creating space in the classroom practice for student narratives.

One such narrative encounter happened after the students had read stories about Martin Luther King, Jr. and Cesar Chavez. After our pilot study had revealed how a weekly reader on Martin Luther King, Jr. served to alienate the students (Michael-Luna, 2005), the teacher took special care in presenting counter-narrative models of Cesar Chavez, Frida Kahlo, and Diego Rivera. In the following excerpt from morning calendar time, the students apply this knowledge to a discussion on Earth Day (see Appendix B for transcription key and Appendix C for translation):

1   TOM (T): Y también, saben quién nos ayudaba mucho con la tierra? Para cuidar la

2   tierra mejor? [Maria, Eli, Dan hands up]. Huh-huh [nods to Maria]
3   MARIA: César Chávez
4   T: César Chávez. Muy Bien. Cómo?
5   LEO: <u>Eso es</u>
6   T: <u>Cómo?</u>
7   LEO: Yo también lo iba a decir
8   T: Oh, sí? Sí?
9   LINDA: Yo lo dije porque porque él es muy imporante.
10   T: Porque él es muy importante, sí sí.
11   LEO: Maestro, Maestro. Quién es más importante: César Chávez o Martin <u>Luther</u>
12   <u>King?</u>
13   DAN: <u>Martin Luther King</u>.
14   ELI: <u>Los dos//</u>
15   T: <u>//Los dos. Sí es cierto;</u> los dos. Porque los dos lucharon por la libertad, verdad?
16   ELI: Maestro. Porque unidad es más fuerte, verdad?
17   T: [Nods yes] [Loud speaker interrupts].
18   ELI: Los dos ayudan a la gente a <u>tener más fuerza</u>
19   LEO: <u>Todos esos</u>, todos esos … fueron los que ayudaron a todas las personas; ellos.
20   T: Ok. Es cierto. Porque él estaba ayudando … um … Antes usaban muchas cosas
21   para para las uvas y para las plantas para que no vienen los los insectos para
22   comerselos. Y él estaba ayudando para cambiar los leyes, verdad? Para que no
23   tengan esas cosas. Son malas para la tierra, sí?
24   SS: Sí

While the weekly reader text had photos of young people of color planting trees and picking up garbage, the leaders profiled on the poster were older and white. Tom was careful to ask questions that would prompt students to apply their prior knowledge of a Mexican-origin leader (lines 1–4). Tom then allowed space for the students to apply their prior knowledge (lines 5–10) and, finally, space for the student to ask the question (lines 11–13) "Who is more important, Cesar Chavez or Martin Luther King, Jr.?" Upon post-lesson reflection, the teacher voiced his surprise, "I really didn't think they had put those two people together" (April 2003, interview). The teacher left space for the students to voice their opinions (line 15) and then the teacher confirms Eli's answer (line 16) and explains why "because they both fought for liberty, right?" Eli explains why she believes the actions of Cesar Chavez and Martin Luther King, Jr. were important, "because unity is stronger, right?" (line 18). Eli's and Leo's interactions in their first language give voice to both the prior knowledge about civil-rights leaders and the cultural norms within the civil-rights struggle—strength through unity. Tom confirms their statements (lines 15, 17, 20) and further explains how Cesar Chavez's work against pesticide use (lines 20–24) specifically dealt with the Earth Day theme. By creating space in the question–answer protocol, Tom enacted a culturally relevant model of interaction for his students to activate prior knowledge regarding a Mexican leader, Cesar Chavez. While the text of the lesson presented a dominant-discourse view on Earth Day, Tom created space for his students to relate prior knowledge that could activate a sense of cultural, racial, and language pride. Unlike the text *Tortillas, Tortillas*, in which the students' voice, values, and norms were co-opted by the dominant discourse, Tom's students voiced culturally relevant connections to Earth Day which were ignored by the dominant discourse.

The counter-stories read and retold orally to the students about Cesar Chavez became a theme throughout the school year. Students were often heard singing the chorus of a Cesar Chavez protest song: "Si se Puede" (February 23, 2003; April 27, 2003). Tom noted that his students:

> will have to face many challenges and struggles as immigrants to this country ... Racism and cultural misunderstandings are prevalent at our school and the community. I feel orgullo (pride) that I am offering my students the tools and knowledge that they will need to overcome the challenges of being an immigrant. I also challenge them to be leaders that affect change on the world around us. I have introduced to them leaders from around the world who have changed the world we live in, many of which were Latino.
>
> (Teacher journal, December 4, 2003).

The teacher's intentional focus on Cesar Chavez as well as several other prominent Mexican figures, such as Diego Rivera's involvement in the labor movement and Frida Khalo's perspectives on feminism, came from an intentional shift in his thinking (October 9, 2003; December 14, 2003; December 19, 2003). While Critical Race Theory suggests that Whiteness is a property in the larger society, the teacher attempted to make being Latino a valuable property in his localized classroom practice. Tom states,

> all the racism I have seen at school ... has been so: bad. I have a really hard time with it and I'm 35. They're seven or six ... They need those tools (pride and unity) to be able to handle this.
>
> (Interview, April 28, 2004)

He saw racism as a permanent part of his students' current and future lives and he decided to arm his students with the tools of "pride" and "unity" to combat current and future social problems which arose around race, language, immigrant status, and socioeconomic status (teacher interview, April 28, 2004). By including Mexican and South American-origin leaders in his curriculum, the teacher tried to show his students how Latinos were active agents of change, and made visible the role of Latinos of color in society.

Conclusion

While authors, publishing companies, and classroom teachers have worked at placing multicultural books in the hands of young readers, culturally, linguistically, and racially embedded assumptions are still prevalent in K–3 children's literature as well as early childhood pedagogic practices. The series of questions to interrogate texts for tenets of Critical Race Theory and the strategy to model and create space for young bilinguals to voice their questions, concerns, and resistance to embedded racial and cultural assumptions presented in this chapter can help to unmask these hegemonic ingroup narratives. For early childhood classroom teachers and second language acquisition researchers the following challenges exist:

- Increase awareness of the social construction of race of both self and other in early childhood educational environments where bilinguals are present.
- Understand the ways different Critical Race Theory tenets can play out in early childhood educational classroom texts, pedagogies, curriculum, and moment-to-moment interactions.
- Make time and space for children to tell stories in their native language during calendar time and guided reading.
- Allow children to explore ideas of race in the language they choose, even in ESL classrooms, as having children reply to questions or prompts by adults in a second language may cause *mimicking* or *joining* (Canagarajah, 1999) the dominant-discursive assumptions.
- Provide young children with models of counter-narratives by people of color.
- Provide safe spaces for children to be exposed to and allowed to discuss children's literature that positively focuses on racial, cultural, and ethnic differences.
- Examine how bilinguals understand their racial and ethnic identity construction within the dominant discourse of schooling through analysis of moment-to-moment interaction.

Considering how the tenets of Critical Race Theory can play out in early childhood contexts for bilinguals is a challenge ready to be met. A reconsideration of how to approach data collection and analysis as well as classroom practice should consider three steps: (1) a close analysis of children's (multicultural) literature used in classrooms; (2) modeling counter-narratives for young bilinguals; and (3) creating space in classroom practice for bilingual students to question, construct, and critique their racial and linguistic identities. In this way, embedded racial assumptions can be exposed and countered in developmentally and linguistically appropriate ways for young bilinguals.

Discussion Questions

1. The author mentions the challenge of eliciting personal views from young children through interviews. Observe young children and see how their understanding of race, ethnicity, gender, and class is manifested in their verbal and nonverbal interactions.
2. Using the 10 questions that are based on the tenets of Critical Race Theory (CRT), choose a children's book and analyze it.
3. The author discusses the usefulness of counter-storytelling in exposing racialized experiences. Have a conversation with your colleague(s) or student(s) who have a different racial/ethnic background from yours and listen to their experiences of racial discrimination or their pride in their racial/ethnic heritage.
4. In the conclusion, the author lists suggestions for second language teachers of young children. One is to "provide safe spaces for children to be exposed to and allowed to

discuss children's literature that positively focuses on racial, cultural, and ethnic differences." Think about a concrete reading material to use and develop classroom
strategies or lesson plans.

Appendix A

- Cesar Chavez (1927–1993) was a Mexican-American labor activist who was the
  leader of the United Farm Workers. He is noted for his tireless work on migrant
  farm-worker conditions. His work lead to the banning of several harmful pesticides.
- Diego Rivera (1886–1957) was a Mexican artist who specialized in painting murals
  on labor movements and workers' rights.
- Frida Kahlo (1907–1954) was a Mexican artist known for depicting indigenous
  Mexican culture in her paintings as well as her feminist perspectives.

Appendix B

Transcription key:
Italics   Spanish Language
( )   Description of nonverbal action
(pause) Pause of 5 seconds or less
(long pause)   Pause of 5 seconds or more
:   Long sound

Appendix C

English translation:

TOM (T): And also, do you know who else help us with the land? To take care of the
     land better? [Maria, Eli, Dan hands up]. Huh-huh [nods to Maria].
MARIA: Cesar Chavez
T: Cesar Chavez Very good. How? Do you remember it?
LEO: This is
T: How?
LEO: I also was going to say that.
T: Oh yes? Yes?
LINDA: I said it because because he is very important.
T: Because he is very important, yes yes.
LEO: Teacher, teacher. Who is more important: Cesar Chavez or Martin Luther King?
DAN: Martin Luther King?
ELI: The two//
T: The two. Yes, it's certain; the two. Because the two fought for liberty, right?
ELI: Teacher. Because unity is stronger, true?
T: [nods yes] [Loud speaker interrupts]
ELI: The two helped the people to have more strength.
LEO: All of them ... They helped all of the people. Them [pointing to Earth Day
     poster].

T: Ok. It is true. Because he had helped ... um ... before they used a lot of things for for the grapes and for the plants that didn't let the insects live so that they could eat them [the plants]. And he was helping to change the laws, right? So that they didn't have those things. The bad things for the earth, yes?

SS: Yes.

References

Aboud, F. (1977). Interest in ethic information: A cross-cultural developmental study. *Canadian Journal of Behavioral Science, 9*, 134–146.

Alim, H. S. (2005). Critical language awareness in the United States: Revisiting issues and revising pedagogies in a resegregated society. *Educational Researcher, 34*(7), 24–31.

Bell, D. (1980). Brown v. Board of Education and the interest convergence dilemma. *Harvard Law Review, 93*, 518–533.

Bell, D. (1992). *Faces at the bottom of the well: The permanence of racism.* New York: Basic Books.

Bell, D. (1995). Racial realism. In K. Crenshaw, N. Gotanda, G. Peller, & K. Thomas (Eds.), *Critical race theory: The key writings that formed the movement* (1st ed., pp. 302–312). New York: The New Press.

Bigler, R., & Liben, L. (1993). A cognitive-developmental approach to racial stereotyping and reconstructive memory in Euro-American children. *Child Development, 64*, 1507–1518.

Bredekamp, S., & Copple, C. (Eds.). (1997). *Developmentally appropriate practice in early childhood programs.* Washington, DC: National Association for the Education of Young Children.

Canagarajah, A. S. (1999). *Resisting linguistic imperialism in English teaching.* Oxford: Oxford University Press.

Cazden, C. (1986). Teachers as language advocates for children. In P. Riggs & D. S. Enright (Eds.), *Children and ESL: Integrating perspectives* (1st ed., pp. 206–222). Washington, DC: TESOL.

Crenshaw, K. (1988). Race, reform, and re-entrenchment: Transformation and legitimation in anti-discrimination law. *Harvard Law Review, 101*, 1331–1387.

DeCuir, J., & Dixson, A. (2004). "So when it comes out, they aren't that surprised that it is there": Using critical race theory as a tool of analysis of race and racism in education. *Educational Researcher, 33*(5), 26–31.

Delgado, R. (2000). Storytelling for oppositionists and others: A plea for narrative. In R. Delgado & J. Stefancic (Eds.), *Critical race theory: An introduction* (1st ed., pp. 60–74). New York: New York University Press.

Duncan, G. (2002). Beyond love: A critical race ethnography of the schooling of adolescent black males. *Equity and Excellence in Education, 35*, 131–143.

Fine, M. (1991). *Framing dropouts: Notes on the politics of an urban public high school.* Albany, NY: State University of New York Press.

Foucault, M. (1972). *The archaeology of knowledge & the discourse on language.* New York: Pantheon Books.

Gee, J. P. (1996). *Social linguistics and literacies: Ideology in discourses.* Bristol, PA: Taylor & Francis.

Gee, J. P. (1999). *An introduction to discourse analysis: Theory and method.* New York: Routledge.

Gergen, K. (1985). The social constructionist movement in modern psychology. *American Psychologist, 40*, 266–275.

Graue, M. E., & Walsh, D. J. (1998). *Studying children in context: Theories, methods, and ethics.* Thousand Oaks, CA: Sage.

Gutierrez, K. (1994). How talk, context and script shape contexts for learning: A cross-case comparison of journal sharing. *Linguistics and Education, 5*, 335–365.

Harris, C. I. (1995). Whiteness as property. In K. Crenshaw, N. Gotanda, G. Peller, & K. Thomas (Eds.), *Critical race theory: The key writings that formed the movement* (1st ed., pp. 357–383). New York: The New Press.

Hawkins, M. (2005). Becoming a student: Identity work and academic literacies in early schooling. *TESOL Quarterly, 39*, 59–82.

Hawkins, M., & Legler, L. (2004). Reflections on the impact of teacher/researcher collaboration. *TESOL Quarterly, 38*, 339–343.

Heath, S. B. (1982). *Ways with words: Language, life, and work in communities and classrooms.* Cambridge: Cambridge University Press.

Holland, D. C., & Quinn, N. (1987). *Cultural models in language and thought.* New York: Cambridge University Press.

Holmes, R. (1995). *How young children perceive race.* Thousand Oaks, CA: Sage.

Horowitz, E. (1936). The development of attitudes toward the Negro. *Archives of psychology, 194.* [Cited in Van Ausdale, D., & Feagin, J. R. (2001). *The first r: How children learn race and racism.* Lanham, MD: Rowman & Littlefield.]

Kress, G., & van Leeuwen, T. (2001). *Multimodal discourse: The modes and media of contemporary communication.* London: Oxford University Press.

Kubota, R. (2004). Critical multiculturalism and second language education. In B. Norton & K. Toohey (Eds.), *Critical pedagogies and language learning* (pp. 30–52). New York: Cambridge University Press.

Ladson-Billings, G. (1994). *The Dreamkeepers: Successful teachers of African American children.* San Francisco: Jossey-Bass Publishers.

Ladson-Billings, G. (1995). Toward a theory of culturally relevant pedagogy. *American Educational Research Journal, 32*, 465–491.

Ladson-Billings, G. (1999). Just what is critical race theory, and what's it doing in a *nice* field like education? In L. Parker, D. Deyhle, & S. Villenas (Eds.), *Race is … race isn't: Critical race theory and qualitative studies in education* (pp. 7–30). Boulder, CO: Westview Press.

Ladson-Billings, G., & Tate, B. (1995). Toward a critical race theory of education. *Teachers College Record, 97*, 47–68.

Lasker, B. (1929). *Race attitudes in children.* New York: Holt, Rinehart and Winston.

Lave, J., & Wenger, E. (1991). *Situated learning: Legitimate peripheral participation.* Cambridge: Cambridge University Press.

Matsuda, M. (1991). Voices of America: Accent, antidiscrimination law and jurisprudence for the last reconstruction. *Yale Law Journal, 100*, 1329–1407.

Matsuda, M. (1995). Looking to the bottom: Critical legal studies and reparations. In K. Crenshaw, N. Gotanda, G. Peller, & K. Thomas (Eds.), *Critical race theory: The key writings that formed the movement* (pp. 63–79). New York: The New Press.

McCabe, A. (1997). Cultural background and storytelling: A review and implications for schooling. *The Elementary School Journal, 97*, 453–473.

Michael-Luna, S. (2005). *Exploring the language and literacy development of "native bilingual speakers": Collaborative research in a first grade classroom.* Unpublished Dissertation, University of Wisconsin-Madison.

Michael-Luna, S., & Canagarajah, A. (2007) Multilingual academic literacies: Pedagogical foundations for code meshing in higher education. *Journal of Applied Linguistics, 4*, 55–77.

Nathenson-Mejia, S., & Escamilla, K. (2003). Connecting with Latino children: Bridging gaps with children's literature. *Bilingual Research Journal, 27*, 25–49.

Ochs, E. (1979). Transcription as theory. In E. Ochs & B. Schieffelin (Eds), *Developmental pragmatics.* St. Louis, MO: Academic Press.

Pizzaro, M. (1998). "Chicana/o power!" Epistemology and methodology for social justice and empowerment in Chicana/o communities. In L. Parker, D. Deyhle, S. Villenas, & K. Nebecker

(Eds.), Special issue: Critical race theory and qualitative research in education. *International Journal of Qualitative Studies in Education, 11*, 57–80.

Silva, M., & McCabe, A. (1996). Vignettes of the continuous and family ties: Some Latino American traditions. In A. McCabe (Ed.), *Chameleon readers: Teaching children to appreciate all kinds of good stories* (pp. 116–136). New York: McGraw-Hill.

Solórzano, D. G., & Delgado Bernal, D. (2001). Examining transformational resistance through a critical race and LatCrit theory framework: Chicana and Chicano students in an urban context. *Urban Education, 36*, 308–342.

Solórzano, D. G., & Yosso, T. (2001). Critical race and LatCrit theory and method: Counterstorytelling. *Qualitative Studies in Education, 14*, 471–495.

Spencer, M. (1982). Preschool children's social cognition and cultural cognition: A cognitive developmental interpretation of race dissonance findings. *Journal of Psychology, 112*, 275–296.

Spencer, M., & Horowitz, F. (1973). Effects of systemic social and token reinforcement on the modification of racial and color concept attitudes in black and white preschool children. *Developmental Psychology, 9*, 246–254.

Van Ausdale, D., & Feagin, J. R. (2001). *The first r: How children learn race and racism*. Lanham, MD: Rowman & Littlefield.

Vygotsky, L. (1978). *Mind in society: The development of higher psychological processes*. Cambridge, MA: Harvard University Press.

14 Linguicism and Race in the United States

Impact on Teacher Education from Past to Present

Theresa Austin[1]

Pre-reading Questions

Periodic education reforms change teachers' status and their language use in education. These changes often devalue nondominant varieties of a language.

- How do changing laws and policies impact who become teachers and teacher educators?
- How have educational reforms in your area impacted teachers' ability to serve linguistically diverse populations? Which language and literacy instructional practices have become racialized?
- Linguicism often becomes a normative regulatory practice to control those who aspire to be teachers. What consequences might this regulation have on the wider community?

Introduction

How did public systems of education become entrenched in replicating systems that are unsuccessful in educating teachers to reach diverse children? Why are so few teachers in the United States members of diverse ethnic groups, particularly African American? How has linguicism become deeply embedded in educational policy? This chapter uses historical policy analysis to demonstrate how linguicism dating back to slave times has permeated cross-ethnic encounters in key moments of reform in U.S. public education history, and how its legacy continues to affect teachers who did not grow up speaking Standard English (SE), regardless of their value to school systems.

The demographic profile in the United States of who become teachers and who educates teachers reveals a predictable profile dominated by Whites born in the United States (Cochran-Smith & Zeichner, 2005). Additionally, educational reforms have produced sets of institutional practices that have also been complicit in excluding teachers for whom SE is a second dialect or language.

In considering the patterns of educational reforms that have reduced the numbers of teachers from nondominant groups, I pay particular attention to the impact on language educators because this group profoundly affects social views of nondominant communities' language resources in relation to SE. Although my examples come from contexts separated considerably by time and place, I show how the thread of linguicism that runs through all of them is indicative of a deep-seated problem within American culture concerning language and national identity. Thus I look at two historical periods of major education reforms, post-Civil War Reconstruction[2] and Civil Rights-era desegregation,[3] as well as educational reform and its impact on bilingual teachers in local school districts in Massachusetts. Against this background, I describe a recent site of struggle in teacher education in response to language inequities, and provide a basis for theorizing and researching the complexities of race and language in classroom learning and teaching.

I draw on Critical Race Theory, critical multiculturalism, and sociolinguistics to analyze the social reality of race in teacher education. I give primacy especially to lived experiences in first-person accounts, and other primary sources including interviews with current teachers, archived slave narratives, and secondary sources to build warrants for my analysis.

Critical Race Theory and Linguicism

Critical Race Theory (CRT) offers a postmodern perspective on race and racism in public institutions using various epistemologies that converge to question neutrality and objectivity with regard to how race functions in the United States. From a long tradition in legal studies (Matsuda, Lawrence, Delgado, & Crenshaw, 1993; Bell, 1995) to a proliferating body of scholarship in education (Ladson-Billings, 1999; Solórzano & Yosso, 2001; Yosso, 2006), CRT has uncovered institutional practices and policies that have privileged members of dominant groups and undermined social justice. While acknowledging that social formations such as race, ethnicity, class, gender, and sexual orientation intersect with race in particular manifestations of injustice, CRT foregrounds race through historical and interdisciplinary perspectives, often analyzing data collected from the primary experiences of those whose lives are directly impacted by racism but otherwise silenced and ignored.

Although various forms of criticism have been leveled at the limitations of CRT, my own epistemological stance within CRT is on the persistent imposition of linguicism in historical education policy and the practices authorized by the U.S. federal law, No Child Left Behind, that have led to limiting language teachers for whom SE is a second dialect or language. Skutnabb-Kangas (1988, p. 13) defines linguicism as "ideologies, structures, and practices which are used to legitimate, effectuate, regulate, and reproduce an unequal division of power and resources (both material and immaterial) between groups which are defined on the basis of language." Hence, linguicism is a form of social discrimination that privileges one language variety over another (Skutnabb-Kangas & Phillipson, 1990).

African American Teachers during Education Reforms in Reconstruction and Desegregation

Starting this inquiry with the end of slavery and the urgent need for preparing teachers for instructing African Americans, the link between linguicism and race emerges clearly in education reforms during Reconstruction. Major ideological differences existed between and among White and African American educators that influenced the preparation of teachers, the curricular exclusion of African American English (AAE), and inclusion of languages other than English.

Existing Language and Literacy in African American Communities

Under the forceful prohibition against using African languages *and* against becoming literate in English, extant narratives show that AAE developed because of a need to communicate across languages within a slave society. While eliminating the slaves' use of African languages was successful—for, unlike European immigrants' languages, "no indigenous African language survived the Atlantic crossing" (Baugh, 2001, p. 285)— AAE grew into a powerful mode of insider communication to overcome the surveillance of slave overseers.

Although deep southern states such as Georgia and South Carolina already had slave codes in the 1740s to prevent the education of slaves, and North Carolina and Missouri followed suit in the 19th century, clandestine teaching of literacy by African American freedmen (Ullman, 1972) and sympathetic Whites continued (Anderson, 1988; Gundaker, 2007). Furthermore, some slaves taught themselves by whatever means possible (Anderson, 1988).

Because slave literacy in the South posed a grave threat to most Whites, it remained largely hidden within the slave community, often being taught in churches rather than schools. In the South, then, the church was not only the prime social institution where racism was challenged through the struggle for literacy, it also became a bastion for literacy and the use of AAE (Fairclough, 2007; Richardson, 2003), both of which became a form of social capital (Mitchell, 2008). Thus, both literacy and a tradition of teaching within African American communities commenced prior to Emancipation.

Post-Civil War Reforms—Questioning of Qualifications of African American Teachers

The post-Civil War Reconstruction era brought the massive spread of public and private education for emancipated slaves. Between 1861 and 1866 at least 500 "Native schools" were founded and maintained by ex-slaves, bearing testimony to their appreciation of literacy (Anderson, 1988, p. 7). Yet how were these schools to be run? Few Whites could imagine futures as teachers in African American communities. Who would decide what to include in the curriculum? How would schools deal with varieties of AAE that had become normative in their communities? Wouldn't Whites seek to maintain their privileges by preserving SE superiority toward AAE language and literacy practices? During the early post-Civil War period between 1865 and 1870, linguicism played a significant role in teacher responses to each of these questions.

During the early post-Civil War period between 1865 and 1870, the Freedman's Bureau oversaw the welfare of newly freed African Americans. Both teachers and texts in the new Black public schools during Reconstruction generally came from New England (Fairclough, 2007), and the primers—written in SE—emphasized order, morality, middle-class values, and forgiveness of southern Whites.

During Reconstruction, African Americans self-monitored their participation in education based on color and language. African American teachers were not always accepted by African Americans to work in their new public schools. In 1870, Virginia school super-intendent R. M. Manly reported that communities of primarily freeborn Blacks were often "unwilling to accept a teacher born in bondage, unless of a very light complexion" (Morris, 1981, p. 109). In Louisiana, where elite, freed, biracial professional Blacks had a legal tradition of education prior to Emancipation, there were cases where newly freed-men's children were excluded from schools based on skin color (Morris, 1981).

Further, many of the former southern Black teachers were not considered qualified, and educated Whites were typically considered more prepared. Part of this prejudice was language-based. In response, private organizations, many of them religious, quickly inducted many southern-born African Americans into teaching. Furthermore, Chris-tian churches provided church space, and wealthy White landowners donated land and supplies, while local Black communities contributed food, land, and supplies to supple-ment meager teacher salaries. In contrast, public educational institutions never pro-vided adequate support to attract sufficient African American teachers to rural schools.

Combined, these factors led to the nation's first shortage of Black teachers. The core problem was that the government opened the way to educating newly freedmen without establishing teacher-education programs that could produce sufficient teachers from their own communities. Some areas precipitously hired African Americans as teachers regardless of their lack of preparation, creating a perception of them as second class. In 1866, an Alabama superintendent, Charles Buckley, declared, "It is our policy to convert colored pupils into teachers as fast as possible. It is cheaper if not so beneficial, and it has good effects in many ways" (Morris, 1981, p. 91). Similarly in Georgia, the bureau's superintendent, Col. John Lewis, responded to a complaint about Black teachers doing more harm than good by stating, "Some have aided because we could do no better & because we wished to get them to do *something* and arouse an interest in the school-work" (Morris, 1981, p. 91). In 1867, being a southern Black teacher carried implications of being underprepared and inferior, regardless that both newly emancipated and non-enslaved Black populations who graduated from private schools were highly qualified.

What has been largely overlooked throughout this discriminatory view of Black teachers, however, was the issue of language. From the moment formal education began, rural Black communities felt a tenuous relationship with schooling, for the lan-guage of school influenced the community symbolically and ideologically. The rele-vance and significance of becoming literate, beginning with New England primers, often conflicted with the need for survival as a community. Furthermore, rural African American teachers faced criticism within their own communities:

> While blacks understood the value of education, many found the language of education strange and forbidding. Ministers attuned their language to their church members, who were poorly educated, often illiterate, and responsive to eloquence rather than erudition. Teachers by contrast, communicated in an entirely different way. They sought to change the way blacks spoke, thought, and behaved – to raise blacks to their level and encourage them to adopt different values. Whereas the church emphasized the unity between the minister and congregation exemplified by the "call and response" pattern of the preacher's sermon, the school stressed the separation of the teacher from the community.
>
> (Fairclough, 2007, p. 19)

This internalized racism through linguicism is thus explained by Lippi-Green (1997, p. 66):

> When persons who speak languages which are devalued and stigmatized consent to the standard language ideology, they become complicit in its propagation against themselves, their own interests and identities. Many are caught in a vacuum: When an individual cannot find any social acceptance for her language outside her own speech communities, she may come to denigrate her own language, even while she continues to use it.

Undoubtedly these conflicts attenuated rural teachers' investments in teaching for improvement of rural conditions and for higher education, that is, high school. Despite political and educational barriers,[4] efforts to recruit Blacks into teacher education continued to increase during Reconstruction, creating a situation where teaching became one of the major professional careers open to Blacks, particularly ministers, women, and those who were free prior to the Civil War. The Freedman's Bureau, benevolent societies, and institutions of higher learning provided funding to educate Black teachers until the mid-1870s.

However, the idea of successful Black education faced deep cultural opposition within society as a whole. Possibilities of Blacks having more education than their local White counterparts provoked fear among Whites who supported Black education in the South.[5] A particularly effective counter-strategy was to deny or strictly limit state tax revenues to support public schools in Black communities, leading to substandard facilities, teaching materials, and the like.

Post-Reconstruction Debates over Curriculum

From the 1880s into the early 20th century, national debates over the curriculum were concerned with *pragmatic* learning and *liberal humanistic* learning. For African American communities dependent on public education, these debates had significant repercussions for the future teacher education of Blacks, affecting both class and gender.[6] The General Education Board, consisting of White Southern philanthropists, was an influential funder of Black teacher education for the South. In their view, a single model of teacher education was deemed suitable: eliminating "Latin, Greek, etc., to say nothing of piano music and the like, they should teach agriculture and related industries with constant and growing appreciation of the education values in such courses" (Anderson, 1988, p. 134).

Accordingly, public schools in many rural southern Black communities removed classical languages. Yet, these subjects were still offered to White high school students in more privileged urban communities. Teacher-education institutions aligned with this ideology were formed to implement this policy. In sum, these institutions stressed vocational and industrial training, producing "semi-skilled labor while satisfying the prevailing public moral sense" (Silver, 1973, p. 25). In essence, Black teachers were taught subjects that related to their gender: culinary and millinery arts for women; carpentry, shoemaking, and such for men. A central goal of education was for Blacks to know their station in life as subordinate to Whites.

In contrast, there were some who followed the W. E. Du Bois school of thought (Anderson, 1988), which championed liberal arts education and leadership and included the study of classical languages. But in reality few public schools maintained the same curriculum for Blacks and Whites, and the tradition of offering Greek and Latin instruction, highly regarded symbols of advanced education and a precursor to the legal and medical professions, was rarely included in rural public schools in Black communities. In Tennessee, Secretary of State Samuel Smith "offered one black principal five hundred dollars to add industrial education," thereby pushing out Latin (Fairclough, 2007, p. 249). In general, southern Whites continued to object to the emancipating effects of a classical education because of its perceived ability to produce leaders. During the progressive era in the early 20th century, the governor of Georgia stated: "I do not believe in the higher education of the darky. He should be taught the trades, but when he is taught the fine arts he gets educated above his caste and it makes him unhappy" (National Park Service, 2000, p. 28). Or, as the governor of Mississippi (1904–1908), James K. J. Vardaman, declared, "This education is ruining our negroes. They are demanding equality" (Franklin, 1976, p. 81).

Teachers who provided education commensurate with White schools undermined the subservient station of Blacks as projected by Whites and thereby threatened White supremacy. Under such intense political pressure to delimit what African Americans should learn, rural teachers in public schools tended to follow the Hampton–Washington line wherein the learning of foreign languages became far removed from their *industrial education* curriculum for self-help. In a setting where the goal of education was to prepare workers to know their place, the emancipatory symbolic power of learning classical languages became solidified as the cultural property of elites. By 1900, with less than "one college graduate for every 3,600 blacks—0.027 percent of the black population" (Fairclough, 2007, p. 149), few would be eligible to enter the field of language education. The low rate of college entry, combined with the exclusion of African Americans from the Modern Language Association (founded in 1883) and the National Council of Teachers of English (founded in 1911), meant few Blacks were among the shapers of language education. Meanwhile, exclusion and segregation took its toll on the entry of teachers of color into leadership positions in world language and English departments. By 1937 the Association of Teachers of English in Negro Colleges was formed and eventually evolved to include foreign-language teachers in 1940, changing its name to the Association of Teachers of Language in Negro Colleges. In 1949, it changed its name once again to the College Language Association to include members from predominately White institutions (Buncombe, 1987). This organization continues to provide vital leadership today in teacher education and curriculum.

Thus in the aftermath of Reconstruction and continuing segregation, linguicism prevailed even in foreign-language study within the African American community, and those who did study and teach languages were systematically excluded from professional organizations, fostering a second-tier status with their White peers.

Brown Versus the Board of Education—Desegregation and its Effects on Teachers

When Federal statutes affirmed that *separate but equal* was indeed unequal and unconstitutional in the watershed case of Brown v. Board of Education in 1954, the arguments drew on explicit contexts of intentional racism that could be named, specifically overt segregation of human and material resources evident in unequal funding of schools serving Blacks, assignments to dilapidated buildings, use of out-of-date textbooks, and so forth. However, Southern desegregation reforms also resulted in many Black teachers and administrators losing their positions, as all-Black high schools were often the first to be closed down or turned into elementary schools (White, 2004; Franklin & Savage, 2004). Black teachers at those schools were dismissed or reassigned to middle and elementary schools. Such demotions and firings induced many teachers to private schools, many newly formed to retain Black control over community education.

African American teacher supervisors who had been prepared through the alliance of philanthropists and Southern progressives were also dismissed. One teacher-education program, funded through the Jeanes Fund, had been functioning since 1907 and was devoted to creating a special corps of Black school teachers (Jones, 1937; Smith, 1997). Many were sent to traditionally Black colleges such as Tuskegee and Hampton Institutes for in-service training and became equipped with the latest technologies of pedagogy, albeit mostly limited to industrial education: farming, gardening, sewing, cooking, etc. These Jeanes teachers then became the teacher educators of large numbers of newly inducted Black teachers. Recognizing the need for mentorship, they organized summer institutes for professional development and traveled within states observing lessons and providing demonstrations. In light of reduced southern state funding of Black schools, these teachers also helped to raise money for school programs, and encouraged parents, teachers, and students to work together (Botsch, 1997).

With desegregation this resource was lost, because "having black Jeanes teachers supervise White teachers would have been awkward at the time and would not have been acceptable" (Botsch, 1997; web page). The Jeanes Supervisor program ended in 1968, a casualty of funding lost in the wake of the desegregation reform policy.

Public education's failure to serve a large number of African Americans and produce any significant numbers of teachers led to prominent debates which focused on recognizing language rights for children who speak languages other than English as a form of civil rights in 1974 in Lau v. Nichols. To overcome language barriers that obstructed equal participation of African American students (Wiley, 1996), language rights were again asserted in 1979 when linguists testified against the Ann Arbor, Michigan, Board of Education under the Equal Opportunities Act. In that ruling, the Ann Arbor School District was directed to use the home language of Black children during instruction for Standard English. This decision failed to point out an underlying problem of linguicism that cannot be resolved with mere technical information on language variation. Teachers need to understand and creatively use their understandings of linguistic difference to be effective in promoting academic literacy.

In 1996, AAE was championed by Black educators but was met with large public resistance in Oakland, California. This resistance appeared from prominent Black leaders, such as Jesse Jackson and Maya Angelou. This debate pitted activist teachers and administrators, eager to improve provisions for African American youth struggling with school-based literacy, against the federal government. It was argued that the principle of equal opportunity required states to accommodate learners whose primary language was different from English, a second language to many AAE speakers. However, with few exceptions, there was little support for the Oakland School Board's action that positioned AAE as a legitimate language variety in schools (see Perry & Delpit, 1998, for further details). The public lack of support was not only for AAE but also for curriculum and texts in AAE. Adger (1997) states that materials created for AAE users were never used (Feigenbaum, 1970; Wolfram, Adger, & Christian, 1999). Thus, efforts to revalue AAE as education reform produced simultaneous responses of rejection and acceptance in both dominant *and* nondominant sectors, motivated by the general perception that using AAE was an inadequate response to address the inequity of services. The two responses—criticism of instructional efforts perceived to be negligent in preparing learners with the skills of the dominant language (Delpit, 1998) and acceptance of using nondominant ethnolinguistic resources in schools (Smitherman 1977; Baugh, 1998; Bell, 1995; Jordan, 1988)—produced conflicting responses to the question of what literacy-instruction strategies would raise the academic achievement of AAE speakers.

Even today many educators still view AAE from a deficit perspective despite sociolinguistic evidence (Labov, 1972; Smitherman, 1977; Mufwene, Rickford, Bailey, & Baugh, 1998; Rickford & Rickford, 2000) that innovative practices using key features in AAE build academic language registers in the dominant language (Lee, 2005; Labov & Baker, 2001; Makoni, Smitherman, Ball, & Spears, 2003). Similarly, reforms for including bilingual learning have failed to fully prepare teachers to recognize the complexity of learning academic literacies when students bring different varieties of language and cultural resources into schools. The interests of the dominant ideology that one variety is the only acceptable variety in school are maintained through this ironic convergence on language policy in schools.

Recently, judges and legislators in Arizona and Florida have echoed the same conservative arguments in response to the use of Spanish. According to these sources, using a language other than Standard English creates a "ghetto" (Mujica, 2003; Gingrich, 2007). The repeated appearance of this discourse represents a perspective that not only privileges the dominant language but also ignores the exclusionary practices within institutions that conceptualize the notion of *ghetto* on the basis of nondominant-language usage, effectively demonizing minority-language-speaking groups as *other*. Ignoring the structural inequities that maintain exclusionary practices, this discourse falsely blames individual language use for creating economic disparities.

The dearth of teachers from nondominant linguistic backgrounds is a direct result of this situation. Different racial experiences generate different investments and positioning in education.[7] We can apply this principle to language use as well, for the perception of authority in Standard English, particularly in schools, likewise generates critical positioning in relation to language, which in turn leads to particular language policies in society. Thus, linguicism in U.S. language policy has racial overtones. When powerful social institutions construct policy based on linguicism, differences of culture, language, and race function as categories that lead to inequitable treatment along the same lines. This is evident in the racial disparity between those who bring nondominant-language resources to school and those who speak *normal*. The relative absence of racially nondominant teachers in the teaching profession stems from this background.

The reform of desegregation in fact led to a loss of teaching jobs for African Americans because providing access to a similar curriculum or the same schools did not include the imperative to eliminate prevailing racist hiring or teaching practices. Not only were the teaching jobs for Blacks in traditional Black schools protected but also Black teachers were rarely allowed to move up to a position of supervisor over Whites.

Massachusetts Reform in 2003 and Linguicism

When Massachusetts' Question 2 initiative was implemented in the fall of 2003, specifications for ELL teacher licensure had not been finalized, which meant that very few new teachers were qualified to teach English-language learners. Nonetheless, a concerted effort was well under way by many district superintendents to eliminate many bilingual teachers who had been on licensure waivers or who were tenured. To ensure that superintendents implemented the new statute, the Commissioner of the Board of Education, David Driscoll, issued a memorandum in August 2003 requiring superintendents to verify that teachers of all subjects were fluent in English. The memo specified several paths that superintendents could take and several delegated the task of administering the assessment to their school principals or assistant principals. Some school officials used their personal sense of spoken-English ability as the standard upon which Question 2 empowered them to eliminate bilingual teachers, nearly all of whom were nonnative English speakers and non-Whites.

For example, in Springfield, Holyoke, and Lowell, Massachusetts, bilingual teachers were subjected to an oral English-language test (SPEAK) and the Oral Proficiency Interview (OPI). Results from these tests removed nearly all nonnative speakers from teaching positions. Rather than questioning the tests' validity as indicators of the teachers' actual use of English or, more importantly, of their teaching ability,[8] the districts chose to dismiss these teachers ostensibly because their scores did not meet the cut-off score criteria, the equivalent of 85% correct, a level higher than the scores required on the State's licensure test for entering teachers in foreign languages (MTEL, Foreign Languages). Thus, monolingual, unaccented spoken English became a requirement for continuation of employment, guaranteeing elimination of almost all those who learned English as an adult.

In these same districts, a temporary strategy of repositioning bilingual teachers as co-teachers or having them demoted to paraprofessionals was also implemented. Simultaneously, many monolingual, native-English-speaking teachers without ESL training became responsible for educating emergent bilingual children with whom they could not communicate. One Springfield teacher I interviewed exclaimed:

> I don't know how to help these Somali kids. We just let them sit and watch but they don't know what's going on and we can't help them much because they don't speak English and we don't have anyone who speaks their language.

This, in turn, produced disengagement from learning. Qualifications for licensure and tenure to teach at a certain grade level were suddenly redefined such that one had to be a native speaker of English to teach. In-service training on behavior management became many districts' response to controlling classroom learning. In middle and high schools, suspension and expulsion rates became a pressure valve that pushed students with "behavior" issues out of schooling, nondominant students being over-represented in these cases. Even more disappointing was the response of the teachers' union, the

Massachusetts Federation of Teachers, which did little to support bilingual teachers who were dismissed besides providing mini-courses to improve the employed bilingual teachers' ability to use English.

For teachers whose native language is not English or who received a significant part of their education outside the United States, their particular variety of English-language usage frequently encountered significant barriers to professional careers in the public school system. However, there has been no accountability measures put in place for monolingual teachers whose variety of English is dominant and who do not know other varieties in order to aid the students who do not speak Standard English.

Theorizing Linguicism and Race under Reform—Macro Discourses that Re-emerge

Each period of reform was ostensibly designed to help those whose interests had been adversely served by judicial decrees, legal statutes, and educational policies. Essentially, they claimed to benefit underserved populations while at the same time they created a need for teachers from the dominant group. While each reform did generate a change that potentially could improve the status of nondominant teachers and language students, each also had consequences that undermined local teachers, minority teachers, and grass-roots efforts in public education. Across time the issues of linguicism and race co-occurred repeatedly to reduce the numbers of nondominant teachers in the field.

The periodic nature of reforms creates an ever-changing professional landscape with shifting sanctions and controls that affect the most vulnerable. Typically this process has been dominated by creation and enforcement of top-down pedagogical change generated in the context of managed responses to political, historical, and economic crises. These typically require a method of population control through testing, ideology, and licensure, all of which are tied to funding resources. Given the general instability that is characteristic of reform, there is a need to position language teacher educators to ethically assess vulnerabilities of teacher candidates and to critically address the relationship of the goals of systemic reforms to the effect of the implementation of such reforms on under-represented teachers. In recent years, at the University of Massachusetts, we have seen a steady decrease in enrolment from under-represented populations applying to teacher-education programs.

As normative controls are part of any educational system, language teacher educators of the dominant group have a responsibility to not only recognize their privilege but also develop institutional responsiveness to the racial realities of classrooms. As language teacher educators we need to be particularly vigilant in preparing teachers to instruct *other* people's children by maintaining a critical stance toward the consistent *failures* of education to meet the needs of students without distancing any one group from their sociohistorical context.

Language teachers can identify structural issues in their own schools, beginning with assessment procedures and instruments used to label and categorize English-language learners (Gebhard, Harman, & Seger, 2007). Consistent failures are spaces to question sociopolitical and historical influences operating through language and literacy practices in that particular context. Who are the racial groups of teachers/learners who receive awards/incentives? How are their practices with language more often legitimated in contrast with those who are more often disenfranchised? How do systems of disenfranchisement work via routines that go unquestioned, as compared to those that encourage successful, sanctioned, active participation? Linguicism's interface with race is visible here through students' differential consequences for learning language.

A Program for Resisting Linguicism

Clearly, preparing teachers to be successful with linguistically and culturally diverse learners warrants a program that includes an examination of how linguicism mediates not only racially differentiated access to a rigorous education but also access to graduation and higher education. During the reforms affecting bilingual teachers, at the University of Massachusetts, Amherst, we began a special program for non-traditional undergraduates. This program prepared a cohort of future bilingual teachers for employment in local school districts.

In 2001, during the time of Question 2 when many bilingual teachers were dismissed, our concentration in Language, Literacy, and Culture in the School of Education received one of the last Title VII federal grants. Through this grant several initiatives were created. I directed one to launch a new cohort of bilingual teachers on a path toward licensure. Inaugurated as the Interdisciplinary Inquiry into Linguistically and Culturally Diverse Bachelor of General Studies (BGS), the goals of the interdisciplinary curriculum were:

1. To provide an academically rigorous undergraduate program to prepare a cohort of 20–25 bilingual paraprofessionals to obtain a BGS degree concentrating on disciplinary inquiries that would enable them to effectively teach English-language learners at the elementary school level.
2. To increase the number of highly qualified educators by removing several known barriers to professional licensure.
3. To increase the number and articulation of outreach efforts by colleges into underserved local communities in ways that build local capacity to solve social, cultural, economic, and political problems, specifically through disciplinary inquiries that are sensitive to the needs and cultures of underserved populations.
4. To help paraprofessionals further their educational and professional aspirations through higher education and help them build networks of university support to be drawn upon for their own students' future advancement (School of Education, University of Massachusetts, Amherst, 2006).

Understanding that nearly 90% of American teachers and teacher-education students (Lara, 1994; Ladson-Billings, 1999; Ladson-Billings & Tate, 1995; Zumwalt & Craig, 2005) are White middle-class women from backgrounds vastly dissimilar to the growing diverse urban populations they are teaching, we sought to recruit students from areas of the highest concentration of bilingual paraprofessionals. By making a requirement of bilingualism, the recruited population was predictably dominated by Spanish-speakers, totaling 21 participants: one Afro-Brazilian, one Mexican, one Franco-American, one Polish-American, and 17 Puerto Ricans. All but one were female and most were from working- to middle-class backgrounds employed as (1) para-educators, (2) Headstart teachers, or (3) staff members in schools, community educational centers, or social welfare agencies.

Our curriculum was designed to meet both the Massachusetts Department of Education's criteria for elementary teacher licensure at the preliminary level, a university degree in a disciplinary area, and also the university's requirements for conferral of a Bachelor degree. The 60-credit program was designed to position the students as highly skilled professionals and included courses in sociology, geosciences, language, linguistics, literatures, mathematics, communication, theater, Latin American Studies, African American studies, human development, and education (critical academic literacy, writing for professional development, multicultural children's literature, bilingualism in society, and ESL methods).

These courses provided opportunities for future teachers to engage in inquiries inside and outside their communities. Similar to Jeanes teachers during segregation, all participants would work together with diverse institutions within communities. However, unlike Jeanes teachers who were constricted by segregation, our program would help participants forge new links and build their participation in new communities across racial boundaries. Thus, as the courses progressed, our curriculum began with inquiries rooted in their own lived experiences, an examination of how their own migration affected their family life, and their community's political and economic development. Later courses involved progressively wider circles of inquiry affecting communities larger than those in which they lived. For example, in their communications course, students examined how Spanish-speaking communities nationally and locally were affected by systems of mass-media representations of Latinos. They explored regional public displays of Latino art and television programs, and learned to critically analyze mass-media commercialization of *Latinidad*, as a representation of being *Latino*. In their geography courses, students documented how their communities' environment had been affected across time through climatic and historical land formations. Included here was the theme of how demographic changes impacted these formations and a cultural *sense of place*. In one noteworthy inquiry, a student examined public recycling efforts in the city of Holyoke by taking the initiative to interview city officials and local business leaders. She discovered that public participation was uneven, revealing a pattern of little effort in the areas highly settled by Latinos. Her study prompted city officials to investigate further.

Through BGS courses, local research drawing on disciplinary ways of *reading and writing the world* were used to create knowledge that was often shared later at public forums, conferences, and teacher-education seminars with wider public audiences.[9] In each inquiry, students used disciplinary concepts and tools to collect both primary and secondary sources of data, analyze them, and present results to both professional and lay audiences across racial and ethnic boundaries. This activity cycle required intensive writing in English and computer skills, as well as multimodal and multilingual presentational skills, new to many of the mature learners.

Recruitment of Interdisciplinary and Racially Diverse Faculty

The program recruited 23 university faculty members from education, humanities and fine arts, behavioral and social sciences, geosciences, and math. While all faculty taught in English, 17 were bilingual, including those who could instruct either in English or Spanish as well as those who could understand but not instruct in Spanish. Of the remaining six, four were monolingual and two had working knowledge of a language other than Spanish. There were seven Whites, four African Americans, 10 Latinos, and two of dual racial heritage. The diverse racial background and strong ideological support for bilingualism, marks this program as the most diverse and supportive in preparing future teachers who are bilingual in my 12-year experience at this institution.

Reciprocal Relations Between Schools, the University, and Community Organizations

Another program feature was collaboration between NGOs and community centers which, in addition to school districts, granted us access to classroom space and resources. This provided the university an extended presence in spaces that were non-traditional, allowing schools and community organizations to share material and human resources.

Formative Assessment of Instruction and Learning

Over 3 years, faculty and students together discussed how to support specific learners and their development of academic literacies. This third program characteristic involved direct engagement with an analysis of systems of oppression. In addition to racism, our program included disciplinary subjects and recurrent analyses of patriarchy, sexism, and classism. Students critically examined immigrant patterns using oral histories, interviews, and *testimonios* or first-person narratives bearing witness, Latino representation in the media, teaching methods of ESL, African American history as one of the histories not included in dominant U.S. history texts, and sociological mapping of neighborhood community organizations.

The program was supportive of direct discussions about race, immigration, and language diversity in education because of their relevance to community development. Participants were particularly successful in drawing on their own lives and skills which at times meant challenging their most cherished ideas about community, Spanish and English languages, literacy, and education in order to face social, political, linguistic, health, and ecological issues impacting their communities. Recurrent opportunities to use and analyze their own languages allowed productive dialog over what is needed to build academic performance. Additionally, these students worked on fund-raising for local radio programming and community-based organizations and contributed original oral histories to their local library.

This group represents the largest bilingual cohort to have graduated from the University since the passage of Question 2. Of 17 total graduates, 11 graduated with honors and four are enrolled in graduate studies. One has won an award as an outstanding nontraditional student in Continuing Education. With the exception of two, all are teaching in some capacity as early childhood educators, paraprofessionals, or teachers in elementary and middle schools. Many are currently preparing themselves for the Massachusetts Tests for Educator Licensure (MTEL). However, linguistic discrimination continues; one graduate has found that it has kept her from getting a position as a classroom teacher, despite the fact that she is frequently called on to substitute teach (see research by Flippo & Canniff, 2003). In other words, knowledge of linguistics, knowledge of methods of teaching and learning academic subject matter, and research skills still did not prevent her from being targeted as unqualified based on her accent. She has not given up and has applied for other positions within the district.

Directions for Theorizing and Research

The brief selective historical review demonstrates that reform movements through the use of linguicism have often impacted nondominant teachers and learners in ways that made them vulnerable to being positioned as inferior. In both the African American case and the bilingual-teacher case, multiple-legislated education reforms periodically have removed culturally and linguistically diverse teachers and students from public education in the name of being responsive to a limited definition of educational needs. Despite good intentions, reforms typically create a need based on historical injustice and promise solutions generally permeated by linguicism. There is a pattern of removing access to primary language or literacy, and a questioning of the values of existing community resources in language and literacy practices. Thus many education reforms supplant primary-language resources with a focus on academic English in service of nondominant students, but they fail to provide advanced language study in either their first or second language. This effectively reduces learners' success in secondary and post-secondary education, both of which are a sine qua non for becoming teachers. Simultaneously, in-service teachers from these communities are regarded as "less than qualified," leading to the recruitment of "better" teachers from privileged backgrounds with tertiary education.

Through various reform movements, linguicism has become naturalized to perpetuate notions of inferiority in culturally and linguistically diverse teachers and students. Today this ideological stance about language is still the means by which resources are used to stratify nondominant and dominant groups, in particular ESL and foreign-language learning (Shuck, 2006). Although more students are engaged in foreign-language learning in the United States and some foreign-language teachers do come from non-White backgrounds, generally most do not. The few nondominant teachers that do succeed endure institutional pressures in ways that are not widely documented in the language-education field (see for example Lin, Kubota, Motha, Wang, & Wong, 2006; Kubota, 2002).

In addition to economic factors that draw highly educated bilinguals away from teaching, the historical legacy of excluding language-minority teachers and the current opposition to bilingual education also contribute to the lack of teachers from nondominant groups. Learning of foreign languages in privileged secondary-education settings may indeed lead to their graduates becoming bilingual, but because of traditional prejudice toward variety-speaking or nonnative-speaking teachers, with few exceptions the preponderance of teachers and students in such programs are White. Society regards this kind of bilingualism as an achievement through schooling, and it is no surprise that those who thus succeed through tertiary education are White. In contrast, students growing up in homes where English is not the primary spoken language and who thus also have the potential to be bilingual and biliterate instead receive the impression that their *other* language is either irrelevant or pernicious because it negatively impacts their acquisition of English. A by-product of this is the discriminatory way that world languages are treated in our educational system. To a great extent White, American-born bilingual graduates pursue careers as language teachers relatively easily, whereas students whose first language is a variety of English or a language other than English will find numerous institutional barriers to that same career.

Educational policies that restrict bilingual programs in primary schools and do not provide advanced classes in secondary schools for those with strong non-English language literacies significantly reduce the possibilities for nondominant groups to develop advanced literacies in both their primary language and English as a second language. This problem is exacerbated by many teachers who do not have adequate preparation to educate bilingual or dialect learners and are not required to demonstrate their ability to succeed with them. Older ESL students are acutely vulnerable to dropping out of secondary school because of limited academic skills in English and limited opportunities for academic learning in their mother tongue. Thus their potential for entering university to become teachers is also diminished. If bilingual learners' needs are not met, we will undoubtedly have fewer successful teachers who are bilingual.

Consider at the same time that many teachers of English as a second language in the United States need to grasp the language needs and expectations of their students both locally in multilingual communities and in the context of transnational migration. The language of the learners' peers, of their teachers, and of their textbooks all compete as targets of the learners' attention in class while a full range of other options await learners in their communities, in the media, and on the Internet sites they may frequent. Yet teachers who do not understand learners' needs to use these language varieties will fail to support their struggle to participate as members in a racially and ethnically diverse community of English users where social meanings are conveyed through many Englishes and where other languages continue to be a major part of their lives in multilingual contexts.

Given the U.S. legacy of historically entrenched linguicism, we have yet to overcome racism's effect on addressing issues of race in language classrooms. This is particularly true when multiple races are in contact and teachers and administrators have to address an ever-widening gap of achievement between those well-served and those historically underserved while struggling over continually limited resources. Particularly with rising university education costs, a smaller pool of African American and other nondominant-group university graduates causes fiercer competition for their recruitment into teacher education.

In rethinking history's lessons, we can assume that reforms may obscure the intent and effect of racist actions. Therefore not all racist acts are clearly apparent or readily perceived by dominant groups, though their consequences often directly affect nondominant groups. U.S. teachers from nondominant languages may still struggle to learn formal academic varieties (Guerrero, 1997) and yet many have been socialized to value dominant varieties. This perpetuates an expectation of one language variety in schools and a lack of personnel available to help children value both first and second languages. The historical purging of culturally and linguistically diverse students from academic institutions is evidence that educational reforms have not produced more teachers knowledgeable about these varieties or who can be successful in responding to the ethnolinguistic struggles facing dialect learners or second language learners. Both policies and practices need to be examined to discern how racism manifests itself through sanctioned language use, literate practices, and allocation of resources across racial groups. Effects are also felt at the post-secondary level where a National Education Association (2008, p. 6) report indicates a growing under-representation of non-dominant faculty, well below projected population growth.

Language and literacy teachers are implicated and therefore ethically responsible for examining how racism may be deeply embedded in their daily routines and assumptions that push certain students out of schooling. Recruitment efforts, reciprocal community/school/university relationships, and formative assessment on learning and mentoring are all sites where attention to impact on different racial groups can detect where reforms have produced racialized consequences.

Discussion Questions

1. The author argues that educational reforms have often reduced the number of teachers knowledgeable about minority students and their communities, perpetuating racialized linguicism. What are some contemporary debates shaping your position on diverse language varieties in your classroom, school, or course? What are the effects of these debates on other teachers?
2. Educational reforms can ostracize the most vulnerable populations. When nondominant teachers are excluded because of linguicism and racism, valuable resources and skills are also lost. How does this matter to the teacher, students, school, and community?
3. The author illustrates how legal mandates, professional associations, and charitable organizations exert ideological influences on administrators' and teachers' responses to linguicism. In what concrete policies or practices today is there evidence of these at your site?
4. Within your profession, how could students' language varieties and racial backgrounds be valued and advocated in curriculum and instruction?

Notes

1. I gratefully acknowledge critical feedback from Christopher Tinson, Sonia Nieto, and Fatima Pirbhai-Illich.
2. This period is recognized as post-Civil War when southern states were reorganized and reintegrated into the Union, 1865–1877.
3. Often the 1954 Supreme Court Decision in Brown vs. Board of Education is seen as the beginning of de jure desegregation. The 1960s saw the rise of African American Civil Rights Movement and, as a result, in the 1970s courts were active legislating desegregation plans to ensure compliance.
4. However entrenched this perception was among White communities, as well as some Black communities, other Black communities demanded Black teachers. At times these demands were thwarted by White leaders and at other times these were acquiesced to. Reasons for not allowing Blacks to teach Blacks ranged from not having the proper "southern disposition" of holding Whites as superior, to not having the discretion to withhold treating Blacks as equals to Whites, to lacking proper English, to lacking adequate preparation. Some, despite their superior qualifications to White teachers, were deemed not acceptable because of their insistence on being given treatment equal to that of White teachers.

5. According to Franklin and Moss (1994), "In 1869 there were 9,503 teachers in schools for former slaves in the South. Although some of the teachers were Southerners, a majority of whites came from the North" (p. 230).
6. Note that private and religious normal schools largely maintained their academic orientation and included classical languages.
7. Compare with Omi and Winant (1986), who define racialization as assigning racial meaning to the previously unclassified difference.
8. See technical guide of SPEAK for inappropriate use and Johnson (2001).
9. For other events in which participants informed larger communities, see www.umass.edu/accela/bgs-events.htm.

References

Adger, C. (1997). Issues and implications of English dialects for teaching English as a second language. *TESOL Professional Papers no. 3.* Alexandria, VA: TESOL.

Anderson, J. D. (1988). *The education of Blacks in the South, 1860–1935.* Chapel Hill, NC: University of North Carolina Press.

Baugh, J. (1998). Linguistics, education, and the law: Educational reform for African American language minority students. In S. S. Mufwene, J. R. Rickford, G. Bailey, & J. Baugh et. al. (Eds.), *African-American English: Structure, history, and use* (pp. 282–301). London: Routledge.

Baugh, J. (2001). Coming full circle: Some circumstances pertaining to low literacy achievement among African Americans. In J. Harris, A. Kamhi, & K. Pollock (Eds.), *Literacy in African American communities* (pp. 277–288). Mahwah, NJ: Lawrence Erlbaum Associates.

Bell, D. A. (1995). Serving two masters: Integration ideals and client interests in school desegregation litigation. In K. Crenshaw, N. Gotanda, G. Peller, & K. Thomas (Eds.), *Critical race theory: The key writings that formed the movement* (pp. 5–20). New York: New Press.

Botsch, C. S. (1997). The Jeanes Supervisors. Retrieved August 20, 2004 from www.usca.edu/aasc/jeanes.htm.

Buncombe, M. H. (1987). Legacy from the past, agenda for the future: The College Language Association, 1937–87. *College Language Association Journal, 31,* 1–11.

Cochran-Smith, M., & Zeichner, K. M. (2005). *Studying teacher education: The report of the AERA panel on research and teacher education.* Mahwah, NJ: Lawrence Erlbaum Associates.

Delpit, L. (1998). What should teachers do? Ebonics and culturally responsive instruction. In T. Perry & L. Delpit (Eds.), *The real Ebonics debate* (pp. 17–26). Boston, MA: Beacon.

Dittmer, J. (1977). *Black Georgia in the progressive era, 1900–1920.* Urbana, IL: University of Illinois Press.

Fairclough, A. (2007). *A class of their own.* Cambridge, MA: Belknap Press.

Feigenbaum, I. (1970). *The use of nonstandard English in teaching standard.* In R. Fasold & R. Shuy (Eds.), *Teaching standard English in the inner city* (pp. 87–104). Washington, DC: Center for Applied Linguistics.

Flippo, R., & Canniff, J. (2003). Who is *not* teaching our children? The paradox of the Massachusetts Tests for Educator Licensure. *Multicultural Perspectives, 5*(2), 40–45.

Franklin, J. H. (1976). *Racial equality in America.* Columbia: University of Missouri Press.

Franklin, J. H., & Moss, A. (1994). *From slavery to freedom. A history of African Americans.* New York: McGraw-Hill.

Franklin, V. P., & Savage, C. J. (Eds.). (2004). *Cultural capital and Black education: African American communities and the funding of Black schooling, 1865 to the present.* Greenwich, CT: Information Age Publishing.

Gebhard, M., Harman, R., & Seger, W. (2007). Reclaiming recess in urban schools: The potential of systemic functional linguistics for ELLs and their teachers. *Language Arts, 84,* 419–430.

Gingrich, N. (2007). Speech to the National Federation of Republican Women, April 2003. Retrieved April 6, 2007 from www.cnn.com/video/#/video/politics/2007/04/02/franken.gingrich.spanish.cnn.

Guerrero, M. (1997). Spanish academic language proficiency: The case of bilingual education teachers in the U.S. *Bilingual Research Journal, 21*(1), 25–43.

Gundaker, G. (2007). Hidden education among African Americans during slavery. *Teachers College Record, 109*, 1591–1612.

Hatchett, M. Matilda, Interviewer: Samuel S. Taylor. (1979). Collected by the Federal Writers Project, Works Progress Administration, Arkansas. In George P. Rawick (Ed.), *The American slave: A composite autobiography* (pp. 195–201). Westport, CT: Greenwood Press.

Johnson, M. (2001). *The art of non conversation. A reexamination of the validity of the oral proficiency interview*. New Haven, CT: Yale University Press.

Jones, L. G. E. (1937). *The Jeanes Teacher in the United States 1908–1933*. Chapel Hill, NC: University of North Carolina Press.

Jordan, D. F. (1988). Rights and claims of indigenous people: Education and the reclaiming of identity. The case of the Canadian Natives, the Sami and Australian Aborigines. In T. Skutnabb-Kangas & J. Cummins (Eds.), *Minority education: From shame to struggle* (pp. 189–222). Clevedon, UK: Multilingual Matters.

Kubota, R. (2002). The author responds: (Un)Raveling racism in a nice field like TESOL. *TESOL Quarterly, 36*, 84–92.

Labov, W. (1972). *Language in the inner city: Studies in the Black English vernacular*. Philadelphia, PA: University of Pennsylvania Press.

Labov, W., & Baker, B. (2001). Linguistic component. African American Literacy and Culture Project. Retrieved November 29, 2007 from www.ling.upenn.edu/~wlabov/FinalReport.htm.

Ladson-Billings, G. (1999). Just what is critical race theory and what's it doing in a *nice* field like education? In L. Parker, D. Deyhle, & S. Villenas (Eds.), *Race is … race isn't: Critical race theory and qualitative studies in education* (pp. 7–30). Boulder, CO: Westview.

Ladson-Billings, G., & Tate, W. F. (1995). Towards a critical race theory of education. *Teachers College Record, 97*, 47–68.

Lara, J. (1994). *State data collection and monitoring procedures regarding overrepresentation of minority students in special education* [US Department of Education, Office of Special Programs Contract No. HS92015001]. Washington, DC: National Association of State Directors.

Lee, C. D. (2005). Double voiced discourse: African-American vernacular English as resource in cultural modeling classrooms. In A. Ball & S. W. Freedman (Eds.), *New literacies for new times: Bakhtinian perspectives on language, literacy, and learning for the 21st century* (pp. 281–384). New York: Cambridge University Press.

Lin, A., Kubota, R., Motha, S., Wang, W., & Wong, S. (2006). Theorizing experiences of Asian women faculty in second- and foreign-language teacher education. In G. Li & G. H. Beckett (Eds.), *"Strangers" of the academy: Asian women scholars in higher education* (pp. 56–82). Sterling, VA: Stylus.

Lippi-Green, R. (1997). *English with an accent: Language, ideology, and discrimination in the United States*. New York: Routledge.

Makoni, S., Smitherman, G., Ball, A., & Spears, A. (Eds.) (2003). *Black linguistics: Language, society, and politics in Africa and the Americas*. New York: Routledge.

Matsuda, M. J., Lawrence, C. R., Delgado, R., & Crenshaw, K. W. (1993). *Words that wound: Critical race theory, assaultive speech, and the First Amendment*. Boulder, CO: Westview.

Mitchell, A. B. (2008). Self-emancipation and slavery: An examination of the African American's quest for literacy and freedom. *The Journal of Pan African Studies, 2*(5), 78–99.

Morris, R. (1981). *Reading, 'riting and reconstruction: The education of freedmen in the South, 1861–1870*. Chicago, IL: University of Chicago Press.

Mufwene, S., Rickford, J., Bailey, G., & Baugh, J. (Eds.). (1998). *African American Vernacular English.* New York: Routledge.

Mujica, M. E. (2003). We are individuals, not categories. Washington, January 23, *New York Times* Letters to the Editor. Retrieved January 25, 2003 from http://query.nytimes.com/gst/fullpage. html?res=9504E3DC1239F934A15752C0A9659C8B63.

National Education Association. (2008). Women/Minorities. *Advocate, 25*(5), 5–6.

National Park Service. (2000). *Racial desegregation in public education in the U.S.* Washington: U.S. Department of the Interior. Retrieved February 5, 2009 from www.nps.gov/history/nhl/ Themes/Education%20Deseg.pdf.

Omi, M., & Winant, H. (1986). *Racial formation in the United States: From the 1960s to the 1980s.* New York: Routledge.

Perry, T., & Delpit, L. (1998). *The real Ebonics debate.* Boston, MA: Beacon Press.

Richardson, E. (2003). *African-American literacies.* New York: Routledge.

Rickford, J., & Rickford, R. (2000). *Spoken soul: The story of Black English.* New York: Wiley.

School of Education, University of Massachusetts, Amherst. (2006). Access to critical content and English language acquisition. Retrieved January 15, 2008 from www.umass.edu/accela/bgs-goals.htm.

Shuck, G. (2006). Racializing the nonnative English speaker. *Journal of Language, Identity, and Education, 5,* 259–276.

Silver, C. B. (1973). *Black teachers in urban schools. The case of Washington, D.C.* New York: Praeger.

Skutnabb-Kangas, T. (1988). Multilingualism and the education of minority children. In T. Skutnabb-Kangas & J. Cummins (Eds.), *Minority education: From shame to struggle* (pp. 9–44). Clevedon, UK: Multilingual Matters.

Skutnabb-Kangas, T., & Phillipson, R. (1990). Linguicism: A tool for analyzing linguistic inequality and promoting linguistic human rights. *International Journal of Group Tensions, 20,* 109–122.

Smith, A. B. (1997). *Forgotten foundations: The role of Jeanes Teachers in Black education.* New York: Vantage Press.

Smitherman, G. (1977). *Talkin and testifyin: The language of Black America.* Boston, MA: Houghton Mifflin.

Solórzano, D. G., & Yosso, T. J. (2001). From racial stereotyping and deficit discourse toward a critical race theory in teacher education. *Multicultural Education, 9,* 2–8.

Ullman, V. (1972). *Martin R. Delany: The beginnings of Black Nationalism.* Boston, MA: Beacon Press.

White, M. (2004). Paradise lost?: Teachers' perspectives on the use of cultural capital in the segregated schools of New Orleans, Louisiana. In V. P. Franklin & C. J. Savage (Eds.), *Cultural capital and Black education: African American communities and the funding of Black Schooling, 1865 to the present* (pp. 143–158). Greenwich, CT: Information Age Publishing.

Wiley, T. G. (1996). *Literacy and language diversity in the United States.* CAL and McHenry, IL: Delta System.

Wolfram, W., Adger, C. T., & Christian, D. (1999). *Dialects in schools and communities.* Mahwah, NJ: Erlbaum Associates.

Yosso, T. J. (2006). *Critical race counterstories along the Chicana/Chicano educational pipeline.* New York: Routledge.

Zumwalt, K., & Craig, E. (2005). Teachers' characteristics: Research on the demographic profile. In M. Cochran-Smith & K. M. Zeichner (Eds.), *Studying teacher education: The report of the AERA panel on research and teacher education* (pp. 111–156). Mahwah, NJ: Lawrence Erlbaum Associates.

15 Un/Marked Pedagogies

A Dialogue on Race in EFL and ESL Settings

Eve Haque and Brian Morgan

Pre-reading Questions

The current global circuits of capital and the legacy of colonial histories produce both an instrumental need and a cosmopolitan desire for English which is embedded within a racialized imaginary of English speakers and learners. In this chapter, the two authors utilize a dialogical approach to examine the possibilities and limitations of critical multicultural and antiracist pedagogies based on both authors' experiences of teaching English as a Foreign Language in Asia and English as a Second Language in Canada.

- What do the notions of "marked" and "unmarked" mean within the field of linguistics? How might they be related to a discussion of race and identity?
- In which ways are the contexts of EFL and ESL teaching similar and/or different? How might these similarities or differences influence the teaching of issues around racial identity, particularly in settings in which you are familiar?

Introduction

The purpose of this dialogue is to examine the possibilities and limitations of critical multicultural and antiracist pedagogies in the context of our past and current sites of pedagogical practice. Given that current global circuits of capital and the legacy of colonial histories produce both an instrumental need and a cosmopolitan desire for English which is embedded within a racialized imaginary of English speakers and learners, we hope to foreground and unpack a number of our key concerns regarding theory and practice in relation to race and gender in TESOL. The narrative structure we have utilized is intended to facilitate an increased awareness of several conceptual issues pertinent to our topic: (1) by personalizing and contrasting our own entry into the profession, we hope to illustrate the field's emerging awareness of differential privileges and constraints based on identity categories of race and gender; (2) at the same time, we want to consider the ways in which we exceed and transgress the overdetermined categories ascribed to us, and how we negotiate, often in unique ways, the rigid and regulative boundaries of these identity categories. Using Stuart Hall's idea of *articulation*, Judith Butler's notion of *performance*, and Diana Fuss' complications of *identity* and *identification*, we attempt to map out how we are differently interpellated into the global field of TESOL as at the same time we retain our creative agentive roles in defining who we are and can be as teachers.

It is worth mentioning that the process and structure of our dialogue itself is a reflection of our self-defining agency. As with many colleagues in other universities, the current demands of teaching, research, and administration make it difficult to pursue the kind of sustained co-reflection we have undertaken. Though we spoke on the phone about general points to consider, once we began to commit these ideas to print, neither one of us was certain how the other would respond, or which kernels of thought (i.e. specific theories, experiences) would become, in turn, focal points and conceptual shifts in the written exchange to come. Though a great deal of stylistic predetermination and conformity goes into the making of any academic text, much of what unfolds below can be characterized as genuinely *interactive*—a dialogue in which prior beliefs are reassessed and potentially changed as a result of the exchange taking place. Of course, the guiding voices of the editors are a welcome component of the final text we present below.

Brian Morgan

I'd like to start this dialogue on race in TESOL reflecting on several insights and blind-spots that are deeply rooted in my personal and professional experiences over the years. There was a time early in my career when I would have been reluctant to have this conversation. I would have thought, "Why bother? I'm not black, and I don't have the right to speak about or for such experiences, or their relevance for second language education." It's true that as a white, male teacher with ingrained middle-class sensibilities, I lack an "authentic" voice forged through the pain of racial taunts and exclusion. My silence in this regard, however, could also be seen as a failure to look beyond crude instances of discrimination and grasp the complex, systemic underpinnings that perpetuate the problem—a perspective I've come to recognize through conversations with colleagues and my readings of a growing body of vital research, especially pertaining to TESOL (Amin, 1999; Ibrahim, 2003; Kubota & Lin, 2006). This is a key point that I'm sure we will discuss further and one that is reflected in our title. That is, even those such as myself who are racially "unmarked" and whose participation in systems of social injustice are largely hidden from view, are still implicated in their reproduction. As Robin Lakoff (2000) notes, "if you're a member of the dominant group, your attributes are invisible, as your role in making things the way they are is not noticeable" (p. 53).

For those of us who acknowledge such membership, Lakoff's observation reminds us that we are, in many ways, invisible to ourselves. Still, in small and big ways, we all retain the capacity or agency to learn about and challenge the status quo, especially through our teaching practices. Gloria Ladson-Billings (2001), for example, describes how notions of "whiteness" are taken for granted in education. Most white, middle-class teachers, she notes, have never experienced being a visible or political minority, and they are often unaware of how race, class, and gender have influenced their circumstances or perspectives. In order to develop "cultural competence," according to Ladson-Billings, white teachers need to learn about their own identities and privileges in order to deal with the kinds of systemic barriers that their minority students face.

Self-realization, on Ladson-Billings' terms, is no straightforward matter, however. In my own case, growing up as a Jew in Regina didn't feel particularly privileging, not with the schoolyard taunts and embarrassment of having to attend Hebrew school while other kids got to play. Also, growing up through the late 1960s and early 1970s, I remember watching the civil rights marches on television and the race riots in major U.S. cities that followed the assassination of Martin Luther King. Many of us assumed, somewhat smugly, that racism was a white-on-black problem exclusive to American society. Certainly not in Regina, where the blacks we encountered were almost exclusively African American football players there to play with the Saskatchewan Roughriders, hence exotic heroes in our youthful eyes. In one respect, this was the biggest blind-spot of all in that racism was all around us in our relationship to the aboriginal and Métis peoples of Saskatchewan. Segregated from our upper- and middle-class neighbourhoods, mostly invisible in our school curricula, the few places and moments of aboriginal–white contact served to promote our common stereotypes of alcohol abuse, unemployment, broken homes, and violence. To reiterate Lakoff's point, we had no idea of our "role in making things the way they are"—no lessons on the systematic dispossession of aboriginal lands to facilitate white settlement on the prairies or of the residential school system designed to assimilate/obliterate indigenous cultures and languages (see, e.g., Warnock, 2004, chapter 7).

Perhaps these are the kinds of reflections that are necessary in developing "cultural competence" in our interactions with minority students. Yet, the pedagogical challenge I see as I look back on my own life is that there are many complexities involved, indeed, many racisms rooted in particular places and histories. What are your thoughts and memories on this point?

Eve Haque

Born to South Asian immigrant parents in Ottawa, and brought up in a similar era, I also lived a daily contradiction where the schooled narratives of our national history, that racism was a white-on-black problem exclusive to American society, were inconsistent with my family's lived reality. These whitewashed histories were the foundations of my earlier school curriculum built on what Dei (2000) calls the "historic and continuing depriviledging and marginalizing of subordinate voices in the conventional processes of knowledge production … in Euro American contexts" (p. 112). The late 1970s and early 1980s saw the emergence of a strengthening discourse about Canada as a multicultural nation. However, this celebratory official state discourse did little to supplant the white settler hegemony of the nation (Bannerji, 2000; Walcott, 2003); rather, racist exclusion was shifted more perniciously from biological onto cultural and linguistic categories (Haque, 2005). It is out of this context that I came to English-language teaching in 1992, when, having graduated from my undergraduate degree a year earlier and finding myself in a Canadian job market considerably enfeebled by the rise of neoliberal economic practices characteristic of the era, I did what many of my peers did and looked abroad for work, any kind of work. I think it is important to acknowledge that it is the globalizing force of neoliberal economic regimes (Hardt & Negri, 2000) which has sustained and reinvigorated the symbolic capital of the English language, creating an expanding EFL job market for the unemployable of the "inner circle" countries (Kachru, 1992). It is precisely within this iteration of globalization, with its genealogical links to Anglo colonial expansion, that I was able to parlay my native speaker of English linguistic capital into a well-paid job teaching English in Japan.

In 1992, I went off on the Japan Exchange and Teaching Programme (JET), now one of the largest international cultural and educational exchanges of its kind in the world with a current annual budget of approximately U.S.$500 million and participants in Japan numbering over 5,000 per year (McConnell, 2000). Created as a response to international criticisms of Japan's economic and cultural insularity, the JET programme was presented at the Reagan–Nakasone summit in 1986 which was convened primarily to discuss the massive trade imbalance between Japan and the United States (Lai, 1999; McConnell, 2000). Thus, JET's beginnings are clearly rooted in global economic imperatives which explain its stress on cultural exchange and "internationalization," as well as a programme design that emphasizes the hiring of "native" speakers of English from "inner circle" countries with no requirement for second language teaching experience—or any teaching experience—at all. In this era, it was precisely these circuits of economic and cultural exchange that provided domestically unemployable Canadian university graduates, as "native" speakers of English, the opportunities for fashioning cosmopolitan identities as mobile members of the high-end international-migrant labour market.

Brian Morgan

Your insights on the "bigger picture" shed light on my own first steps into the English-language teaching field. With a Bachelor degree in anthropology and ethnomusicology, I was one of the "unemployable Canadian university graduates" you mention, part of a growing surplus labour force of educated baby boomers displaced by the inequality and stagnation wrought by Reaganomics, Thatcherism, and our own Mulroney's "free trade" embrace in the 1980s. Yet globally, as you point out, these same neoliberal "reforms" created the opportunity for me to become a "high-end" employee in the "expanding circle," a privilege conferred upon me because of my "inner circle" birthright (i.e. the "right" accent, cultural background, and skin pigmentation). In terms of mobility, I was already deeply enthralled with the idea of becoming a worldly cosmopolitan of sorts, having already spent 2 years (1979–1980; 1983–1984) backpacking and working in various parts of Europe and Africa. So, when the Master of Norman Bethune College at York University asked me if I wanted to go to China and teach English at the Sichuan Foreign Language Institute in Chongqing (Toronto's "sister city" at the time), it was an easy decision to make.

China was also coming out of an extended period of isolation, but the reasons were as much geopolitical as they were cultural. Unlike Japan, the post-Maoist government of Deng Xiao Ping was acutely sensitive to its lack of economic clout and its diminished technological and military power in a world of increasing global integration and competition. English instruction was seen as a key component of Deng's Four Modernizations (i.e. science and technology, agriculture, industry, and the military) and structured in ways that might accelerate China's global prestige and power. The "Preparatory Department," in which I taught an intensive 1-year English for Academics Programme (EAP), reflected these developments. Most of my students were experienced professors, primarily in the applied sciences and funded by the government to spend 1 year abroad as visiting scholars/researchers in university departments of their specialization.

Even though a TESOL certificate was not required at the Institute (and most of the foreign teachers of English didn't have one) I was grateful that the Master of Bethune College had arranged for me to study TESOL at George Brown College the year prior to my arrival. Still, in many ways, I was woefully unprepared to teach these experienced and mostly older academics and professionals in the preparatory programme. I was also very conscious of the fact that I was earning ten times the salary of my more qualified Chinese colleagues in the same EAP programme. Of course, they were too polite to ever criticize this inequity or my often-demonstrated linguistic and intercultural shortcomings on the job. One example I still recall was my initial surprise at the types of L2 errors I found in my first needs analyses of student writing samples at the beginning of the term. I was frustrated by what I perceived to be errors in English that would be indicative of lower-level competence (e.g. subject–verb agreement, verb tense usage, word-formation rules/suffix use) and not advanced language learners as the university had led me to believe. Over time, I came to realize that I had misjudged what were, for the most part, "surface" errors. Most of these students were indeed "advanced" and quite capable of highly complex academic reasoning in English. With help from my bilingual Chinese colleagues, I started to learn more about the kinds of contrastive, lexicogrammatical challenges particular to Chinese learners of English. Clearly, there was a sharp learning curve ahead of me.

In retrospect, I can only wonder at the frames of reference used by my Chinese colleagues to evaluate the mostly white, mostly monolingual, mostly unqualified and overpaid "foreign experts" suddenly in their midst after many years of self-reliance and insularity. To what extent did they equate our whiteness with the ownership of English and the cultural capital, worldly power, and affluence that might arise from and hence justify our presence? Or alternatively, was our presence viewed as a sell-out of the revolution, yet another reckless imposition on the people? It is hard to say, though we were definitely a visible anomaly wherever we went. During my year in Chongqing (1988–1989) there were probably fewer than 100 foreign residents in a city of over 25 million people. Whenever we went on day-trips, especially to the countryside, the Institute would insist on accompanying us as large crowds would gather to stare at us and follow us around sometimes to our discomfort. Coming from Canada, where whiteness is unmarked and taken for granted, these visits to the Sichuan countryside were unusual experiences for me, and I couldn't help but wonder what collective meanings and historical memories my racialized self evoked in these settings. How was your racialized identity taken up in Japan, and specifically on the JET programme?

Eve Haque

Even with the strong emphasis on hiring mainly "inner-circle" country participants, the various levels of JET programme administration knew that this was not a monolithic category that would ensure the ideal straight, white, blond and blue-eyed American male JET participant desired by most cities, towns, and villages in Japan. McConnell (2000) details how the central administration dealt with local communities' requests for only white JET participants through "hairyo" or *special care/consideration* which would rarely place non-white JET participants in rural areas, preferring instead to place them in larger centres with other JET participants, and in high schools where the students would be more mature. Given the mandatory requirement for an undergraduate degree, the pool of participants was already skewed away from poorer communities of colour towards a mainly middle-class white participant pool, and the detailed application form and interview process at the Japanese embassy of each participant country meant that a first-order filtering process was already in place, which probably also had similar skewing effects along racial lines. It is within this context that in July 1992, I arrived as the first JET participant in a small rural village of 6,000 in one of the mountainous prefectures of Japan.

The administration of the JET programme is a giant, complex bureaucracy involving municipal to national levels of government, which means that there is a long lead time until the actual arrival of the JET participant in the community to which they have been assigned. This meant that months before my arrival, my incredibly detailed application form (with picture) had been circulated through the town hall and published almost in its entirety in the local town paper. Therefore, the arrival of a non-white, female JET participant evinced little overt shock; however, people still wanted to stare, touch, and talk to me as I made my daily way through the town, and in the first few weeks of my arrival, whenever I got lost, people would give me detailed directions home as everyone knew exactly where I lived. Given the funding structures of the JET programme, I was the town's JET and this sense of ownership was a point of conflicted pride for the board of education, which was my direct employer, as having a JET was a mark of the town's level of "internationalization," but not having the ideal white male American JET, as did the neighbouring village, meant some loss of face. However, as well as attending all the local elementary and junior high schools, I was dutifully trotted out for all local events including festivals, visits from international dignitaries, and other community activities. Overall, my primary function was not so much to teach English as it was to model a digestible international "otherness" in the nation's larger pedagogical project for moulding the next, more internationally minded generation of Japanese citizens. Therefore, within the context of JET, this meant a continual recital of my "authentic" Canadian biography at all events and school visits; an authenticity which was confirmed by my passport and my English-speaking "nativeness." There was never any declared interest in my visible "Indianness," even though I was a direct living contradiction of the idealized English-speaking subject of JET, and to this day, it is still not clear to me if this silence was as a result of proscriptions from the central bureaucracy (which produced pages and pages of instructions for local authorities in the handling of JET participants) or a refusal, perhaps even inability, to deal with the complexities of my Canadian identity. Caught in the EFL setting between an inauthentic visibility and authentic practice of language, I am also aware that this inability to deal with the complexity of my Canadian identity was not only a result of the Japanese government's desires for the JET programme playing out at a local level, but also the Canadian state's ongoing complicity in maintaining and promoting a fictive history of white settler nationhood internationally, even as it celebrates an under-resourced and overstated official multiculturalism domestically. Although my 2-year experience on the JET programme introduced me in only a very cursory way to the field of English-language teaching, it did outline the very clear geopolitical flows of the practices of English-language teaching that frame and racialize the multibillion-dollar industry within which we are all, in different ways, interpellated. These interpellations are difficult to specify and name, as they vary and are contingent on the particularities of each context.

One among several incidents during my time on JET revealed the particular complications of naming a particular formulation of race, gender, and nationality as the axes of exclusion in Japan. Once, on a day-trip to a local tourist destination, my repeatedly thwarted attempts to rent a bicycle at a series of bicycle shops led me to the local city hall and a request to meet with an officer of their international division. When the local head of the international division arrived, I explained who I was and my experience of what I named as racial discrimination at the bicycle shops and my disappointment at the disjuncture between the promise of their widely disseminated tourist literature, and my personal experience of being repeatedly denied this opportunity despite the overtly visible availability of rental bicycles at the various shops. The head of the international division explained to me that this incident was probably the result of the fact that there were many Brazilians living and working in the factories on the outskirts of the city and that these shop owners had stereotypical fears about theft by the Brazilians and that they had probably mistaken me for one of the workers. He also assured me that these practices were completely against the law and were not tolerated by the city. He clearly had an understanding of how racial discrimination was a factor not only in my bicycle-rental incident but also in the economic organization of the city, and he assured me that if I would just wait patiently, he would deal with the problem. When he returned about 20 minutes later, I was taken down to the entrance and he proudly produced a woman's bicycle from the trunk of his car and he said that his wife would be honoured to lend her bicycle to a Canadian English teacher for my enjoyment that day. Perhaps naively, I had expected that as a relatively senior employee of city hall, he had seen my complaint as an opportunity for intervention into the discriminatory policies of bicycle rental in the city and had gone off to make this explicit to the shop owners, but clearly this was not the case. Instead, he had focused on the task of making sure that the international English teacher from the neighbouring town had an enjoyable tourist day visit. What could I do? I took the bicycle, the proffered maps and brochures and bicycled off as the members of the international division waved goodbye. In this incident, it is difficult to pin down how any specific identity I was named or possessed was the reason for how this incident unfolded. Rather, specific historical processes which bring Brazilians—many of them of mixed Japanese descent—to Japan to work in lowly regarded factory jobs and, as outlined above, particular histories of colonialism and capitalism which endow English teaching with sufficient social capital in the present to create official municipal government jobs for JET participants, interlock with processes of racialization, nationality, and gender in ways that orchestrate exclusion and opportunity which elude simple naming as a fixed identity. Instead, these identities are contingent upon time, place, and subject position of the interlocutors.

Brian Morgan

Reflecting on your bicycle incident, I'd like to expand on your point regarding the geopolitics of ELT and how we are differentially interpellated within what is an ever-expanding multibillion-dollar industry. Your JET experience of complexity—caught "between an inauthentic visibility and authentic practice of language"—struck me as significant especially because it was a racialized tension or contradiction I never felt in China. Instead, I took my visible "authenticity" as a professional responsibility, not realizing the extent to which the colour of my skin provided me with credibility; that is, as a "real" Canadian in sound and appearance, it was a condition of my employment to dispense the cultural and linguistic capital of which I was in natural possession. Towards this end, I would need to replace the "archaic" and "inefficient" language pedagogies traditionally favoured by my Chinese hosts with the "state-of-the-art" ELT methods and materials, of which my recent TESOL training comprised. In this respect I was truly "interpellated" (cf. Althusser, 1971)—"hailed" or "summoned" as a "bona fide" English native speaker to perform an "authentic" role/function in relation to a neocolonial ideology—the taken-for-granted superiority, progressivism, and scientificity claimed for West-based TESOL (see, e.g., Ramanathan & Morgan, 2009) and one that justified my Chinese employment and relative affluence in the global ELT hierarchy. Fortunately, over a short period of time, I came to meet many competent EFL speakers schooled in traditional Chinese language-learning techniques. For the remainder of my stay, I began to seek out more of a balance between local approaches and the ones that made up my prior repertoire. More importantly, I started to take a more critical and investigative look at the geopolitics of my professional training—how it is that particular ELT technologies/commodities such as Communicative Language Teaching (CLT) or learner-centredness, as examples, become discursively constructed as state-of-the-art "truths" applicable anywhere and at any time, pressuring teachers and administrators to abandon locally appropriate methods and materials and invest scarce resources that ultimately enrich West-based publishers and foreign consultants.

Regarding this last point, another relevant and complementary theoretical concept is Stuart Hall's (1996) notion of *articulation*, how within contingent moments and places, seemingly discrete or previously disconnected elements of social organization/differentiation are correlated and/or transposed through external contact or conquest (e.g., colonialism) setting into motion new modes of stratification, in part realized through the distribution and control of language policies and practices. Ramanathan's (2005) book is an excellent example in that she traces the postcolonial continuities of lower-caste (Dalit) marginalization in Gujarat, India, through institutional policies and commonsense ideologies that restrict vernacular-medium Dalit students from entering English-medium colleges and gaining access to the higher-order literacy skills in English deemed necessary for social mobility. Articulation, in this sense, is a powerful conceptual tool for understanding the sociohistorical conditions underpinning the commensensical authority assigned white EFL teachers from the "inner circle." But it is also a way of illuminating *emergent* articulations of race and power that are somewhat intrinsic to specific fields such as ELT. One of the best examples I can think of comes from the late Nuzhat Amin, a friend of ours, whose critical insights on race and gender in ELT will be sorely missed. I remember reading Nuzhat's (Amin, 1999) accounts of being consistently challenged by some students who saw her race, gender, and Pakistani variety of English as evidence of professional illegitimacy. As a preventative measure, she describes the extra preparation time required to demonstrate her professionalism. I was particularly struck by the racialized double-standard involved, particularly from my current vantage point as a language-teacher educator and curriculum consultant in TESOL. What I might take for granted as indicative of the "good teacher"—e.g. the humanistic, rapport-building response of "I'm not sure," or "I don't know and will look it up"—would be much less of an option for colleagues like Nuzhat. Indeed, it would be most reasonable from her perspective to shy away from the very types of learner-centred pedagogies that are promoted and valued universally in the literature. An articulated perspective draws attention to systematic formations and colour-blind forms of racism within particular fields and institutions. Inspired by Nuzhat's work, an articulated view draws attention to the contingent ways in which the presumed neutrality and utility of particular practices (e.g., CLT or learner-centredness) become, instead, "marked" pedagogies with dangerous implications for teachers deemed "other"—in *both* EFL and ESL settings.

Eve Haque

I think that your comments point compellingly to the complexities of how teachers such as you, me, and Nuzhat, all of us who did our final degrees at the same institution and therefore are at least on paper similarly qualified, can be positioned and taken up so differently in the pedagogical project of teaching English. As you have outlined, Hall's theory of articulation is a way to understand how history, race, and standardization of language come together as practices of power in how we come to be taken up so differently in our English teaching endeavours; however, I am also interested in the various ways in which we have had to learn to negotiate these sometimes dangerous and often bemusing straits. If I think of teaching in English in Canada, for example, I know our jobs both as ESL teachers and particularly as TESOL teacher trainers are powerfully regulated through the national framework of liberal multiculturalism, yet, while we have been constrained by this context, we have also found our own ways of pushing and operating within the boundaries of these limits.

The discourse of official Canadian multiculturalism has marked racialized subjects like Nuzhat and me as Other to the nation and obscured your particular history of difference through the elisions of skin colour in a white settler nation. However, we have found ways to exercise our agency within the classroom and among our colleagues in order—in the case of Nuzhat and myself—to reclaim our expertise, albeit sometimes as an ongoing project. As you stated earlier, in Amin (1999), Nuzhat writes how the humanizing teaching methodologies lauded by most of her white colleagues served only to mark her as inexpert, but I also know that she was able to use her sense of humour, sharp intellect, and her quick intuition about people in ways that made her an incredibly popular and respected teacher with her students and colleagues. Although not marked by "nonnative" accent, when at the head of a class, I also occupy a position of inauthenticity which requires me to continually reclaim my expertise and qualifications in order to be taken up as the legitimate teacher in the class. This is not a unique experience as most women and racialized teachers, including myself, have, particularly in the North American university classroom, a long and familiar history of being asked when the real professor will arrive, of being challenged often about their knowledge base and, within some disciplines, have been accused of advocating partial and "biased" points of view when attempting to disrupt Eurocentric and patriarchal assumptions in our teaching. In TESOL, the legitimate teacher of English is constituted through the ideologies that frame who is a legitimate speaker of English and, in the classroom, this exclusion is compounded by intersecting gendered and raced historical constructions of who is and can be "expert," scientific or "objective." It is these durable constructions of the teacher/professor that require negotiation, disruption, and reclamation through our particular performances both within the classroom and among our colleagues.

In her theorization of the performance of gender identity, Butler (1993) outlines how the performative constitutes the identity it is purported to be, but does so within a rigid and regulatory framework. Furthermore, Butler (1997) writes, the iterability of the performative provides the possibility of agency from the margins in order to expropriate and resignify the rigidity of dominant discourses. Butler's work is a useful way to think about how the dominant constructions of legitimate classroom authority are negotiated and resignified by racialized bodies. I have realized that both in and out of the classroom, I am involved in a set of performances that, although constrained by the regulatory framework of racialized and gendered notions of academic expertise, I deploy to interrupt my students' expectations of who I am. These are never set routines, rather they are variable performances used to startle, cajole, and discipline in order to resignify who I am and who can be a teacher.

Brian Morgan

I really like your point that the discursive framework of official Canadian multiculturalism contains both constraints and opportunities for the kinds of interventions around teacher identity that you and Nuzhat were able to achieve. This also reminds me of the importance of considering how and when such opportunities arise—what broader contexts and flows, tensions and contradictions, permeate classrooms and create productive openings for "disruptive" meaning-making. Neo-liberalism, again, can be cited as a contributing factor as national governments give up effective control over their own globalized economies, on the one hand, yet for electoral purposes, find themselves compelled to promote the continuity of the nation-state as a viable instrument of policy, on the other. Similar tensions emerge as countries like Canada increasingly compete in a global marketplace of ideas, "re-traditionalizing" and "re-branding" themselves in selective ways (e.g., liberal multiculturalism) that appeal to particular international audiences (i.e., non-White, skilled workers, and investors), on the one hand, while attempting to shore up the internal fragility of the imagined nation, its originary narratives and idealized citizens (i.e. the White settler origins of Canada), on the other. To reiterate, such "contradictions"—or new articulations of the global and local (cf. *glocalization*, Robertson, 1995; Lin, Wang, Akamatsu, & Riazi, 2002) and of the past and present—create opportunities for transformative identity work on the part of teachers positioned as "inexpert" or "inauthentic" in ESL and TESOL, but also for those of us assigned privileged membership in the visible and audible "mainstream."

In this regard, we both agree that Butler's theory of performativity has important pedagogical potential for teacher agency in TESOL. Elsewhere, I have explored this possibility and Simon's (1995) associated conceptualization of "image-text," through a notion of "teacher identity as pedagogy" (Morgan, 2004; Varghese, Morgan, Johnston, & Johnson, 2005). As teachers we are always partially or wholly unaware of how students "read" our performances within the regulatory frameworks of our professional and personal lives. By gaining bits of insight into these situated and co-constructed meanings, we can "re-play" the identity cards dealt us in strategic and creative ways, in new combinations and sequences that provocatively disrupt ascribed patterns, beliefs, and stereotypes—and, perhaps most important, in ways that encourage critical reflection rather than reactive resistance.

In my own case, "identity as pedagogy" has meant seeking out ways of discovering and harnessing the contingent authenticity and authority conferred by identity discourses and deploying them in transformative ways less available to visible "minority" teachers. I emphasize a notion of contingency, provisionality, and of individual agency here. For example, in the Chinese community centre in which I taught ESL for 10 years, it was not just a case of being male or white, or speaking the language of colonial and global economic power in a class dominated by recent immigrants from Hong Kong. It was all of these in combination and in *actualization*—the moment the "subject-in-discourse" simultaneously realizes and potentially transposes his or her positioning through the insertion of *personalized* meanings, which you clearly describe in your own situation and by way of the re-signification and re-constitution inherent in Butler's performative framework. So, in my case, it was *also* the fact that I had lived and taught in China, visited Hong Kong and knew the names of major neighbourhoods, spoke a bit of Mandarin in class, sang Chinese folk songs at special events sponsored by the community centre, went out for dim sum, ordering my favourite dishes in Cantonese, or the fact that L1 use was valued and integrated in language learning and that Chinese themes and issues were often central to ESL syllabus design—all of these cumulatively shaped the mostly positive "image-text" I projected and allowed me to say and do "disruptive" things that otherwise might not be permitted or taken seriously (e.g., model and promote a different kind of masculinity, one that included childcare, housework, cooking, and a secondary role to my wife with regard to financial decision-making; Morgan, 2004).

Canadian inter-ethnic, interracial relations were also a focus of my performative interventions in this class. For many of my students, the relative homogeneity of their previous lives in China has not been altered in any substantial way upon arrival in Toronto, a city in which almost all of the cultural and linguistic elements of home have been faithfully re-produced. From what I observed, many reasons—simple and complex—help explain this intentional lack of contact. Clearly, fear of racial and ethnic Others was present and sometimes expressed in class. Also, the fact that many of my students were seniors contributed to a kind of intercultural lethargy—a reluctance to break old habits and patterns of interpersonal contact, particularly through English (even though my class was the "advanced" class at the centre). Underpinning all such responses was a strong sense of cultural pride—at times, excessively chauvinistic—in the achievements of Chinese-Canadians and the global stature of the People's Republic of China.

I saw my "image-text" and the contingent prestige I had in the eyes of these students as a means of addressing this social insularity, and I often tried to perform my identity in ways that promoted a kind of cultural and racial equivalencing in class. So, when students asked me if or when I was going back to China, I would say that I hoped to go back to Africa as well, where I had travelled for 4 months in the early 1980s. Or, when students asked me if Chinese food was my favourite, I would talk about my equal preference for Indian or Ethiopian cuisine. Or, when we talked about our plans for the upcoming weekend, I might talk about local events I was going to attend: an aboriginal festival, an African music concert, the Caribana Festival, or the annual Gay Pride parade, and so on. I would also talk about friends and colleagues who were aboriginal, or gay, or from the Caribbean. For my students, these were lived experiences and contacts that they had never had. The fact that I valued them made them seem less exotic and something worth checking out in their new Toronto lives.

These ways of *texting* my identity helped me introduce language units around several topics that were particularly challenging for this group of students in the context of inter-ethnic, interracial relations. One example was a unit on the internment of Japanese-Canadians during the Second World War, an official act of racial discrimination for which a recent Canadian government apology and financial compensation invoke mixed feelings among many Chinese-Canadians, based on their collective memory of Japan's invasion and brutal occupation of China during the 1930s and 1940s. Another important unit was organized around an article I brought into class called "Cracking the Colour Code" (Jones, 2000), an article describing the discrimination perceived and experienced by Black youths in a suburban mall specializing in Chinese products and services. Certainly, both units had moments of tension, and the extent to which each student accepted or resisted the intertextual meanings generated in class is uncertain. As teachers, we cannot change elements of identity through the same causally direct methods we might use to change an aspect of L2 pronunciation, grammar, or vocabulary use. Still, I think that we need to consider ways of formalizing and presenting these types of identity pedagogies to new teachers in TESOL, especially an awareness of the "marked" and "unmarked" constraints/opportunities each of us must address in our work.

Eve Haque

Your important discussion about "identity pedagogies" brings us back to the centrality of "identity" to our dialogue. If we have had to think through the complexities of our variable identities as teachers in TESOL and TESOL teacher training, it has been because the issue of identity, both ours and our students', lies at the heart of our experiences. However, it is important to have a careful analysis of identity since this issue has entered and taken root in the field of TESOL with great fanfare and has become to some extent the explanatory endpoint for many of our colleagues and subsequently our students, particularly those enrolled in TESOL programs. I think that Diana Fuss's (1995) writings about identity and the processes of identification can provide possible direction in framing some of our thinking in this area. If, as Fuss explains, "identity is identification come to light" then "as a psychical mechanism that produces self-recognition … identification inhabits, organizes, instantiates identity" (1995, p. 2). She continues, "Yet, at the very same time that identification sets into motion the complicated dynamic of recognition and misrecognition that brings a sense of identity into being, it also immediately calls that identity into question," and remains a process that "keeps identity at a distance, that prevents identity from ever approximating the status of an ontological given, even as it makes possible the formation of an *illusion* of identity as immediate, secure and totalizable" (p. 2). It is this complex relation between the processes of identification and the production and disruption of stable ontological identity/s that I believe must continually be at the forefront of our analysis and pedagogy if we are to move beyond the continual replay of essentialist explanations based on an ongoing project of delineating fixed identity categories.

Brian Morgan

When I think of the students I've had in our TESOL programme, I wonder how we might draw them into an awareness of the identity/identification complexities you raise based on Fuss's work. Or, in other words, how might they engage with their own emerging identities as TESOL professionals, many of whom enter this field with a well-intentioned desire to challenge racism and other forms of discrimination through pedagogy?

Eve Haque

I think that this is an important question for our pedagogy since, in many cases, fossilized notions on identity have become the essentialist equivalence of culturalist explanations of difference, and for many of our students, both in the TESOL programme and those pursuing questions of language and learning at the graduate level, their research has become about mapping out bounded notions of identity as if prescriptions for effective language learning can then be extrapolated by "knowing exactly who the learners are." So, for example, our students spend a lot of time interviewing, observing, and studying learners to find out how they "identify," be it as "second-generation Iranian-Canadian," "first-generation Japanese-Peruvian" or "Indo-Trinidadian" and so on as if these identities can be distilled into these fixed collocations and subsequently provide a template for the effective teaching and learning of language. Furthermore, language learners who identify as second-generation "Iranian-Canadian" are in the very process of identification restricted by the vocabulary of the nation-state that produces by the very incommensurability of Iranian to Canadian the awkward collocation of "second-generation-Iranian Canadian" in order to capture the complexity of these learners' lives. Similarly, your, my and Nuzhat's various teaching experiences cannot be explained simply through a distillation of our fixed "different identities" as if they were simple explanatory formulae with predictive power across variable teaching contexts. Therefore, it is precisely these reifications of identity, and identity as explanation, that we need to disrupt in our teaching as this brief dialogue on our various teaching experiences points so clearly to the instability and iterability of identity across place and time. Ultimately, even though "Identification names the entry of history and culture into the subject, a subject that must bear the traces of each and every encounter with the external world" (Fuss, 1995, p. 3), this history is not a totalizing and ontological limit; rather, our performance of pedagogy ensures that this process of identification is also always in negotiation across spatial and temporal boundaries.

Discussion Questions

1. In your opinion, do aspects of racial identity inform ESL/EFL students' judgements of a "legitimate" or "authentic" teacher? If so, what implications arise for teacher–student interactions and syllabus design?

2. Given the constraints and limitations of naming and fixing identity positions across teaching contexts, how can teachers in both ESL and EFL sites strategically perform their identities in order to negotiate challenges presented in the classroom?

3. In an ELT setting in which you are familiar, discuss how you might strategically "perform" or "text" your identity in ways that might challenge students' stereotypes and assumptions around race and language use.

4. In what ways, according to Ladson-Billings, is whiteness taken for granted in education? Can you think of examples more specific to the field of second/foreign-language education?

References

Althusser, L. (1971). Ideology and ideological state apparatuses. In *Lenin and Philosophy and Other Essays* (trans. B. Brewster) (pp. 131-187). New York: Monthly Review Press.

Amin, N. (1999). Minority women teachers of ESL: Negotiating White English. In G. Braine (Ed.), *Non-native educators in English language teaching* (pp. 93–104). Mahwah, NJ: Lawrence Erlbaum Associates.

Bannerji, H. (2000). *The dark side of the nation: Essays on multiculturalism, nationalism and gender.* Toronto: Canadian Scholars' Press.

Butler, J. (1993). *Bodies that matter.* London: Routledge.

Butler, J. (1997). *Excitable speech.* London: Routledge.

Dei, G. J. S. (2000). Rethinking the role of indigenous knowledges in the academy. *International Journal of Inclusive Education, 4*(2), 111–132.

Fuss, D. (1995). *Identification papers.* New York: Routledge.

Hall, S. (1996). On postmodernism and articulation: An interview with Stuart Hall. In D. Morley & K.-H. Chen (Eds.), *Stuart Hall: Critical dialogues in cultural studies* (pp. 131–150). New York: Routledge.

Haque, E. (2005). *"Multiculturalism within a bilingual framework": Language and the racial ordering of difference and belonging in Canada.* Unpublished doctoral Dissertation, University of Toronto.

Hardt, M., & Negri, A. (2000). *Empire.* Cambridge, MA: Harvard University Press.

Jones, V. C. (2000, March 30–April 5). Cracking the colour code. *Now Magazine, 19*(11), 18–19, 30.

Ibrahim, A. (2003). "Whassup, homeboy?" Joining the African diaspora: Black English as a symbolic site of identification and language learning. In S. Makoni, G. Smitherman, A. Ball, & A. Spears (Eds.), *Black linguistics: Language, society and politics in Africa and the Americas* (pp. 169–185). London: Routledge.

Kachru, B. B. (1992). *The other tongue: English across cultures* (2nd ed.). Chicago, IL: University of Illinois Press.

Kubota, R., & Lin, A. (Eds.). (2006). Race and TESOL. *TESOL Quarterly [Special issue], 40*(3).

Ladson-Billings, G. (2001). Teaching and cultural competence: What does it take to be a successful teacher? *Rethinking Schools, 15*(4) 16–17.

Lakoff, R. (2000). *The language war.* Berkeley, CA: University of California Press.

Lai, M.-L. (1999). Jet and net: A comparison of native-speaking English teachers' schemes in Japan and Hong Kong. *Language, Culture and Curriculum, 12*(3), 215–228.

Lin, A., Wang, W., Akamatsu, N., & Riazi, A. M. (2002). Appropriating English, expanding identities, and re-visioning the field: From TESOL to teaching English for glocalized communication (TEGCOM). *Journal of Language, Identity, and Education, 1,* 295–316.

McConnell, D. L. (2000). *Importing diversity: Inside Japan's JET program.* Berkeley, CA: University of California Press.

Morgan, B. (2004). Teacher identity as pedagogy: Towards a field-internal conceptualisation in bilingual and second language education. *International Journal of Bilingual Education and Bilingualism, 7,* 172–188.

Ramanathan, V. (2005). *The English-Vernacular divide: Postcolonial language politics and practice.* Clevedon, UK: Multilingual Matters.

Ramanathan, V., & Morgan, B. (2009). Global warning? West-based TESOL, class-blindness and the challenge for critical pedagogies. In F. Sharifian (Ed.), *English as an international language: Perspectives and pedagogical issues* (pp. 153–168). Clevedon, UK: Multilingual Matters.

Robertson, R. (1995). Glocalization: Time-space and homogeneity-heterogeneity. In M. Featherstone, S. Lash, & R. Robertson (Eds.), *Global modernities* (pp. 25–44). London: Sage.

Simon, R. I. (1995). Face to face with alterity: Postmodern Jewish identity and the eros of pedagogy. In J. Gallop (Ed.), *Pedagogy: The question of impersonation* (pp. 90–105). Bloomington, IA: University of Indiana Press.

Varghese, M., Morgan, B., Johnston, B., & Johnson, K. (2005). Theorizing language teacher identity: Three perspectives and beyond. *Journal of Language, Identity, and Education, 4,* 21–44.

Walcott, R. (2003). *Black like who? Writing Black Canada.* Toronto: Insomiac Press.

Warnock, J. W. (2004). *Saskatchewan: The roots of discontent and protest.* Montreal: Black Rose Books.

16 Race and Language as Capital in School

A Sociological Template for Language-Education Reform

Allan Luke

Pre-reading Questions

This chapter provides a theoretical explication of the ways in which race, language, and literacy constitute capital in school. The author proposes a template for transforming school and classroom structures so that students' knowledge and skills are equitably exchanged into valued resources and power. Before reading this chapter, reflect on your own experience and think about the following questions:

- Have you had the experience of being treated as *other* in a school or social institution?
- Did this treatment have *high stakes* in influencing your life chances and pathways?
- Did your experience shape your current attitudes and practices?

> The most brutal social relations of force are always simultaneously symbolic relations. And acts of submission and obedience are cognitive acts which as such involve cognitive structures, forms of categories of perception, principles of vision and division. Social agents construct the social world through cognitive structures that may be applied to all things of the world and in particular social structures ... The cognitive structures are historically constituted forms ... which means we can trace their social genesis. State Nobility.
>
> (Bourdieu, 1998a, p. 53)

The Educational Problem

The narrative structures around race, power, and speaking position have historically been written from the margins of power—from diasporic positions produced by histories of displacement, migration, and cultural and economic marginalization. But it is a different task to document the experience of the symbolic and physical violence of racism, as First Nations, African Americans, migrants in all countries, Jewish people and Palestinians, and postcolonial people of colour have done for centuries. From the treatises of W. E. B. Dubois, to narratives of writers like James Baldwin and Franz Fanon, Sally Morgan and Amitav Ghosh, we see the common theme of unbridled and deliberate, systematic yet gratuitous violence spanning diverse and often incomparable peoples, places, and times. Even where it has been suppressed from official archives and histories, the experience of racism represented in oral tale and music, story and memoir, literature and cinema, poetry and art is visceral and ugly. It is not a figment of discourse or political correctness. It is materially and phenomenally real for those who have experienced it. It remains in the body, in memory and behaviour. For those who have not experienced it, it is often beyond comprehension.

Though we know its colour and its sources in our own times, in our own places and histories, it is not the exclusive domain of any particular dominant class or colour of male patriarchs. Even within this century, and at this moment, it is occurring not just white upon black and brown, but yellow upon white, black upon black, and so on. Racism appears to know no sociological and geographical bounds, operating across different state formations, political ideologies and economies, operating within heterogeneous cultural communities as well as across them. But as a raw act of power, racism historically is connected with the assertion of power by class and cultural elites, by male patriarchy upon marginalized *Others*. Women have been participants and, indeed, everyday discrimination on the basis of race and language occurs *within* marginalized and diasporic communities. There are few exemptions on offer here. But not all racist moments or acts have co-equal force, material or bodily effect. And historically the locus of control for the large-scale and systematic assertion of racism has rested with ruling-class men in power.

Understanding racism requires that we not see it as simply a particular form of ubiquitous human evil, the product of fascist and patriarchal psychopathology, even where this is demonstrably the case. To disrupt and foreclose it, to deter and preclude it, we need to see racism as a practice of power, as an exercise of human judgement and action, an act of *discrimination*—however vulgar, however irrational and rationalized—within social fields where capital, value, and worth are evaluated and exchanged. Such an analysis can augment our educational efforts to change hearts and minds—something that those of colour have fought to do in white-dominated societies—with attempts to alter those social fields, to critique and to supplant the institutional structures, categories and taxonomies, and practical technologies that sustain them. This requires that we unpack its structures and practices. We can then situate and understand the partiality and limits of any particular educational intervention and approach, instead of wasting our energies and resources fighting over a *correct* institutional strategy, or abandoning in frustration particular pedagogic or curriculum approaches because they did not appear to work in particular cultural and social contexts. Strategic responses to sociologically and culturally complex, nonsynchronous phenomena (McCarthy, 1997) must by definition be multilayered and simultaneous.

For over three decades, those educators committed to education for equity and social justice have used race, ethnicity, class, and gender as variables in explaining the unequal and stratified production and reproduction of knowledge, skill, and disposition. The chapters in this volume highlight the role of language as a key variable in the production of educational equality and inequality. In classical quantitative research, factor and regression analysis demonstrate that these variables have differential yet combinatory effects upon the production of conventional educational achievement outcomes (OECD, 2005). We can begin the case for an antiracist, linguistically fair approach to education from this strong empirical evidence that race, class, gender, and language count. But how they are made to count, and the mechanisms of racism, sexism, and exclusionary language education practices bear closer theoretical scrutiny.

Educational institutions are sociologically contingent, mediated and structured by their location within political economy, secular and non-secular ideology, cultural history, and place. But as well, they are structured and mediated by their human subjects, often idiosyncratically and eccentrically. The practices of racism and marginalization have particular coherent *logics of practice*: explanatory schema, taxonomies, operating procedures, even sciences, that explain why, how, and to what end particular tribes, communities, and ethnicities count as less than fully human against an unmarked normative version of *Man*. But they also are characterized by degrees of volatility and unpredictability: human subjects tinker with, manipulate, bend, and undermine rules in face-to-face exchanges.

What follows are general theoretical terms for describing the nexus of race and language, class, gender, sexuality in the habitus. Using Bourdieu's (1990) model of habitus, capital, and social fields, my aim is to situate race and language as forms of capital brought into the contingent social and cultural fields of schools and classrooms. Race and language as forms of capital never have absolute, universal, or guaranteed value, either generative or pejorative. They are key but not mutually exclusive or determinate. They are readable and interpretable elements of habitus brought to social fields of educational institutions. Institutions may indeed be racist. This may be asserted through overt exclusion from educational provision, peer bullying, authoritarian pedagogy, hegemonic curriculum content, face-to-face exclusion in classroom exchange, labelling and tracking, the legislation of linguistic monoculture, and so forth. We well know how racism can be built into the discourse and institutional structures of schools, universities and other educational systems, and that it is enacted in face-to-face interactional exchanges.

My own view is that the relationships of race, gender, and class—and their semiotic representations and decodings in cultural practice and linguistic form—are sociologically contingent configurations. Each individual habitus constitutes a set of resources and representation, some acquired willingly, some historical and genealogical and, quite literally, genetic characteristics (e.g., skin colour, phenotype, physical appearance). These are reassembled to constitute one's capital brought to educational institutions, to social fields. The human subjects in authority assign distinction and, through pedagogy, curriculum, and evaluation, set out conditions for the transformation of capital into value. This entails the exercise of recognition and misrecognition, categorization and discrimination: "forms of categories of perception, principles of vision and division," in Bourdieu's (1998a, p. 53) words.

My case here is that the array of approaches adopted over the past four decades—including but not limited to compensatory education, progressive education, curriculum revisionism, antiracist pedagogy, bilingual education, community schooling, culturally appropriate pedagogy, indigenous pedagogy, critical literacy, and radical pedagogy—all constitute historically legitimate and reasoned strategies. Yet each in turn tends to focus on a specific and major element of what tends to be a larger, more comprehensive, historically durable and unyielding logic of practice. This is particularly the case in those modern societies and corporate entities that demonstrate the capacity to diachronically evolve, repressively tolerating diversity and difference to maintain the privilege and power of class and gendered, racial, and linguistic elites.

At the least, we need to understand which strands and elements of the problem we can alter with which pedagogical approaches, how each of these educational strategies is necessarily partial and contingent—even as we acknowledge the thresholds and limits of educational interventions in societies and communities whose economies and institutions practice racism and linguistic discrimination with relative impunity.

Race and Language in Social Fields

To parse the logic of educational discrimination on the basis of race and language requires that we begin by acknowledging that *race* itself is a Eurocentric construction, historically evolved as a term and category to scientifically demonstrate the superiority of Anglo/European cultures in the context of colonialism, slavery, and genocide (cf. Darder & Torres, 2004). This is not to say that other societies did not have comparable nomenclature of naming and vilifying ethnic and phenotypical Others, as Kam Louie's (2002) history of Chinese constructions of Western masculinity demonstrates. We can also begin with a recognition of the universal right to the language of one's community (Hymes, 1996), despite the historical enlistment of science and political ideology to claim the intrinsic superiority of one language over another, again enlisted in the service of colonialism (Pennycook, 2007). The systematic destruction and desecration of language communities has been both a means for and an artefact of historical and contemporary domination, marginalization, and exclusion (Phillipson, 2008).

But note the term *discrimination* in the first sentence above, as in the common terminology of racial or gender or linguistic discrimination. Discrimination entails judgement and evaluation, or the exercise of *taste*. Bourdieu's (2007) analysis of French society moves beyond the classical structuralist definitions of class in terms of socioeconomic status and role. It augments classical Marxist analysis of class as indexical of relationships to ownership and control of the means of production. While not discarding these, Bourdieu points to the embodied competences of human subjects as the products of social class, specifically in their acquired and exercised tastes. Judgements around cultural and linguistic style are part of the tastes that constitute one's class disposition.

In Bourdieu's (1977) early fieldwork with the Kabyle, distinction and class are indexed in kinship and style (e.g., culinary, household practice) and in systems of exchange of value in everyday community and family life. Habitus is taken in much of the educational literature to refer to one's acquired cultural capital and total sociocultural disposition (Albright & Luke, 2008). But it also entails cultural schemata, structured categorizations and scripts (Holland & Cole, 1995; Bourdieu, 1998b). These constitute logics of practice, guides and categories for action, agency and everyday decisions. Consider race, gender, and language in these terms, not just as resources that human subjects bring to bear in social fields, but also as categorical distinctions schematically applied by human subjects in construing and assigning value in everyday exchange. Simply, human subjects are racialized, gendered, and classed in discourse taxonomies that are deployed, however consciously and deliberately, by other human subjects. *Racializing practices*—that is, the use of categorical distinction in the assignment of arbitrary value to the habitus (cf. Omi, 1994)—are undertaken both by objects of power (e.g., students, learners, the racial "other") and by those who relationally exercise power (e.g., teachers, administrators, community elders), though obviously not with equivalent institutional force.

One's habitus moves across participation in overlapping social fields (school and classroom, community group, church and mosque, gang, workplace, university, language school, corporation). The school constitutes a social field and a linguistic market (Mey, 1986) where prior competence, fluency, accent and dialectal variation, and indeed colour, kinship and ethnic affiliation, and race may be made to count in different ways. The habitus consists of race and language—but these are never freestanding. Habitus also comprises a complex combinatory blend of embodied durable resources including gender, kinship, sexual orientation, knowledge, and skill, along with acquired resources including credentials and artefacts, social networks and affiliations, convertible wealth, religious affiliation, and so forth.

Within any given social field, these forms of capital are evaluated by others who possess the symbolic power to set (and perhaps negotiate) the terms of exchange. In this way, the field and its authoritative agents set rules for the realization, valuation, exchange, and transformation of capital. In the school, this can lead to entry or exclusion, further access to linguistic goods, further training, promotion or demotion, levels of participation, and so forth. Recognition and evaluation of student capital is what teachers do—both deliberately through developmental diagnostic observation and less overtly, through tacit assumptions about students' linguistic capacities on the basis of other visible forms of capital or through assumptions that level of fluency in a given language enables or disenables developmental access to another target language. Teachers read and interpret bodily dispositions (Luke, 1992).

This valuation—a *minting* process of symbolic recognition of capital—is undertaken by other human subjects in positions of authority (e.g., teachers, employers, bureaucrats, bosses). Here distinction and judgement may foreground or background language and race as principal or key discourse categories in judgement. This depends on the degrees of flexibility of the rules of exchange of the social field in question, and the relative agency and available anticipatory schemata, which can be idiosyncratic, asserted by those with authority. School rules, clinical ascertainment and diagnostic grids, testing and examination regimes, accountability systems, funding policies, and administrative guidelines grant teachers and administrators varying degrees of local autonomy and flexibility in judgement. These are enabling and constraining contextual conditions for the exercise of schematic discrimination by those in authority.[1] In terms of race and language, this can entail both "recognition" and "misrecognition" of cultural and linguistic resources brought to the field (Bourdieu & Passeron, 1990, p. 31), replete with assumptions, presuppositions, and stereotypes about what particular cultural and linguistic resources enable and disenable.

Race/ethnicity, gender, class, sexual preference, and linguistic performance constitute key, though not exhaustive, elements of embodied cultural capital. As such, they are differentially recognized and misrecognized, and exchanged for value in the multiple and overlapping social fields that people traverse. The rules of exchange within the fields are to varying degrees rigid and flexible, durable and transient. Each instance of the assignation of value in any institutional or social or community field has the potential for bending rules and elaborating schemata, what Bourdieu (1998a, p. 15) refers to as agentive "position-takings" (*prises de position*) in the face of structural forces of "positioning." And there are potential moments of agency not just for the person whose capital is put into play for exchange, but for those in positions of power who assert and regulate the rules for exchange. That is, through resistance, remaking or recombining and representing one's capital, an individual can attempt to alter the patterns and practices of judgement in a social field. Refusal to participate or surface compliance are principal options. But equally, for those asserting judgement in exchange—teachers, administrators, counsellors, psychologists, judges, businessmen, community elders— there is the potential for them to alter, shift, and bend conventions and systems of exchange.

Essentialism, Multiplicity, Habitus

In education, important theory on race and language through the 1980s and 1990s has been dominated by both African American and U.S. cultural- and linguistic-minority writers and, internationally, by the writings of postcolonial subjects writing either as migrants or intellectuals in former colonial states (e.g., Fine, Weiss, Pruitt, & Wong, 2004). Notably in the Subaltern Group and in recent African American and Latino writing, the connections between race, gender, and class were highlighted as a tripartite explanation of contemporary categories of marginalization (Spivak, 2006). With the rise of historical focus on gay and lesbian rights, and the concomitant emergence of queer theory, sexual preference has augmented these categories (e.g., Kumashiro, 2001). There are contending and potentially divisive hierarchies of misery tabled by historically marginalized communities, as each asserts its educational, linguistic, and indeed, human rights. Disputes between and among Indigenous communities, feminists, white antiracists, antipoverty activists, radical socialist educators, between African American and Hispanic communities, between and within migrant and second language communities have arisen over the prioritization of strategy, over the allocation of resources, over shared political strategy and struggle. These reflect profound differences in histories and experiences of oppression and domination, even where communities have suffered at the hands of common and identifiable elites and are seeking to establish inclusive social coalitions.

Dialogue between racially and linguistically disenfranchised communities continues. But dissensus can set the grounds for a classic *divide-and-rule* situation—where valuable political solidarity and strategic potential are lost because of the inability to agree on a common front about what is to be done. It is complicated further by issues of eco-sustainability, which qualify any claim that education for social justice can aim for a better and more equitable division of the spoils of an infinitely expanding and ecologically voracious corporate capitalism. Redistributive justice (Fraser, 1997) cannot entail the more equitable distribution of inequitably and destructively acquired value and resources. And given emergent understandings of the complex local push/pull effects of global flows, gains in one site by a marginalized community can readily translate into catastrophic loss elsewhere.

Yet attempts to forge new coalitions against power risk the hierarchical ranking of claims about who has been most aggrieved, contending essentialist claims about originary exploitation—a comparative victimology. The underlying assumption is that hierarchies of oppression can form the basis for priorities for emancipation. But the complexity of contemporary racism and oppression is that it operates across and in combinatory categories: that is, that difference within difference (Luke & Luke, 1999), heterogeneity and multiplicity are objects of power as often as singular identification might be. The force of racism may be exercised with subtle, nuanced categorical distinctions and qualifications as frequently as it might excise all members of a particular community or history from value and recognition (Matsuda, Lawrence, Delgado, & Crenshaw, 1993).

In the last two decades, poststructuralist feminists provided the template of *multiple subjectivity* to explain the combinatory blends of identity, affiliation, and disposition that human subjects develop. Postcolonial theorists speak of *hybrid* subjectivity, of blended and heterogeneous identities that embody the lived experience of residual and emergent, colonial and postcolonial, Indigenous and non-Indigenous culture and language (e.g., Ang, 2000). This is an anti-essentialist proposition: against the notion that people have singular and defining identities or resources with essential, generalizable, and population-specific characteristics. The concept of multiple subjectivity suggests that people are simultaneously and differentially positioned by discourse and practice—and that identity is an amalgam of different characteristics (Norton, 2000). In more recent work on social identity, the argument has been put that we strategically deploy different *selves*. And in recent work on new economies and cultures, it has been argued that people strategically assemble and deploy different versions of the self from available discursive, semiotic, and representational resources (Gee, 2000).

These notions of multiplicity and hybridity compound our traditional understandings of race and racism, which are derived from work over a century that bears witness to deliberate and brutal slavery, genocide, and linguicide. These historical phenomena were premised on two essentialist beliefs: (1) that there were inextricable phenotypical, genetic, and structural isomorphisms between race and one's intrinsic human characteristics, virtues, and value; and (2) that race, culture, identity, affiliation, and nation could be assembled by the state in homologous and singular correspondence (Hall, 1993). This essentialism has been used both as a discourse strategy to massify, rule and, in instances, eradicate whole communities and cultures. At the same time, *strategic essentialism*—that is, the claim of shared historical origin and unity for political and cultural purposes—has been reclaimed in defiant attempts to reassert cultural and linguistic solidarity by threatened peoples in the face of racist power.

Individuals' and groups' differential identities are constructed in and through discourse. The critical multiculturalist and pedagogic notions of "voice" refer to those repressed histories, memories, and experiences of diasporic and marginalized people. The notion of *heteroglossia* derives not just from Bakhtin (1982) but also from Voloshinov's (2006) early conceptualization of every speech act and dialogic exchange revoicing and invoking intertextually prior class struggles and exchanges. Weaving across these different concepts of positioning are the sociological dialectics of structure/agency, of interpellation of language and discourse and its relative power to impose discipline and power upon human subjects as against human subjects' capacities to resist, exercise, and assert discipline and power. This potential for rule-bending and schema-elaborating agency includes not just those racialized objects of power, but the agency of those (like teachers) who stand in some position of epistemological authority, official authorization and potential authoritarianism in these social fields.

Though much of the work of social fields is done through discourse, the world is not solely a construction of discourse. Discourse is, *inter alia*, a making visible of those "cognitive structures, forms of categories of perception, principles of vision and division" (Bourdieu, 1988a, p. 53; cf. Van Dijk, 1993). And not all discourses have coequal or significant effects upon species being, upon human subjects, upon material conditions or, indeed, upon our capacities to generate further discourse (Luke, 2004). Some discourses kill people, take away their livelihood, others humiliate, others marginalize and shame. Some modes and plays of *differance* make a difference in people's lives, others simply do not matter much. In this way, the ubiquitous poststructuralist observation that we can account fully for the world through discourse, or rather for the world's partiality and continually deferred (in discourse) meaning, is at worst glib and at best partial. It is particularly unhelpful for those who find that some of their phenotypical features, their gender or sexuality, their language and accent are not chosen, not wholly malleable through discourse, however their relative value may be assigned by others through discourse categories. And it is at best a footnote for those who are the objects of discourse and physical violence that trivializes, marginalizes, and shames them.

Further, the very concept of multiple subjectivities also has its problems: offering a human subject who is assembled and reassembled longitudinally through discourse and practical inscriptions without foundational basis. The concept of habitus offers a means for describing the tension between multiple positionings and identities, on the one hand, and a foundational basis of kinship and culture, gender and sexuality, on the other—without recourse to a priori essentialist claims about *all Latinos, all women, all Chinese, all Aborigines*, and so forth.

While habitus may be multiple and overlaid, elements are not of our choice and remain durably across our lives. If we are black in a white- or yellow-dominated culture, if we are women in a patriarchal system, if we are youth who speak in nonstandard dialects or accents—that structure of the habitus is durable. As ethnomethodologists claim, it may be construed through discourse and thereby *made* and *remade* in everyday talk (McHoul, 2001)—yet it remains a semiotic presence which is embodied prior to and within discourse exchange that cannot be elided or undone. We can willfully hide it, alter it, redesign and garnish it by degrees. Yet whether it should or is made to count or not, it does not simply appear or go away as readily as might clothing or credential, or even accent and paralinguistic gesture. And no matter how many other acquired overlays of institutional, material, social, and economic capital we acquire and develop, elements of habitus are omnipresent.

This is not to take a cultural-essentialist or genetic-determinist position, or to assume that the discourses and practices of primary socialization cannot be reshaped malleably in early cultural and linguistic socializations. But all the discourse overlays and constructions in the world will not undo the social facticity of being white in a culture where yellow is the unmarked norm, or black in a white-dominated culture, or female in male-governed institutions. No cultural communities or social formations are without hierarchical discrimination and value, without an indexicality of an unmarked (typically patriarchal) norm and a marked other (Beteille, 2002).

Significant forms of capital can be acquired later in life: cultural practices and disciplines are performed and reperformed, languages can be learned, accents can be altered, elaborated disciplinary and institutional codes can be mastered, schemata and scripts acquired and elaborated, credentials won, taste shifted. But those embodied dispositions, like their affiliated cultural and experiential and historical memories, remain. How and in what ways they can be modulated, withheld, or played as trumps or jokers in fields of exchange and language games (Luke & Luke, 1998) marks out agentive action. But they occur in the context of structural positionings within the field, via taxonomic and hierarchical classifications of value assigned (modified and perhaps even waived) by convention and by ruling class, patriarchy authority (or by surrogates acting on behalf of that authority) within the field.

Value is contingent on the field: race, gender, and language, as other forms of capital, are read and interpreted by participants in the field. Different value will be assigned to habitus via discourse exchange in specific social fields, and subfields within institutions, communities, families, societies. In this regard, the value assigned to habitus is an artefact of discrimination in discourse (and might be assigned differently as a social field changes). But it is also the biosocial fact that our bodies, and the linguistic capacity of those bodies, have some irrevocable characteristics that remain, no matter how many discourse or stylistic designs we may overlay over those bodies. The postmodern assumption that the human subject is wholly malleable, that face and body can be styled to assume an invented identity runs into the problems of the durability of one's internal schemata. The body does indeed remember. We remain, in many ways, products of kinship and blood. And our cultural and linguistic production, much of which is physical in both performance and outward appearance, is given, at the very least until the formal institutions of school, state, corporation, religion begin their work of longitudinally reshaping performance.

But this is not to speak of a fixed determination via kinship, biology, or primary socialization. It is simply to acknowledge that there are foundational principles, embodied, culturally and linguistically generated and situated, which all subsequent learning, linguistic acquisition and development, literacy and textual competence are based upon, build from, and sit in longitudinal, reflexive relationship to. Linguistically derived epistemological categories and an intuitive sense of lexico-syntactic function from one's first language and affiliated cultural practices remain, however modified and augmented.[2] But this, the overlaid and durable, shaping and shaped disposition each of us brings to a given field, does not preclude deliberate remaking of the habitus or agentive action within particular social fields—"position-takings" in anticipation of and in response to the "positioning" that occurs through structural distinctions and categories of discourse that constitute rules of exchange within fields (Bourdieu, 1998a, pp. 6–7).

An understanding of the relationships between race and ethnicity, language and discourse requires that we contend with issues of multiplicity and durability at once, without recourse to essentialism and determinism. The premise here is: though they may be differentially asserted and valued in different social fields, human subjects bring complex (and idiosyncratic) combinations of gender and sexuality, class disposition, colour and race, ethnic affiliation and identity, and linguistic competence to bear in social fields. Race is but one element. Language is but one element. Different social fields, often overlapping and not discrete, have in place conventions and rules of exchange that differentially value these forms of capital. Race might count in this particular field, in this particular political economy and cultural/institutional milieu. But it might be combined as a criterion of value by another form of embodied capital valued in the social field, say, gender and credential.[3]

So what we are, and how we agentively foreground different elements of our own dispositions in a social field (a classroom, a boardroom, a workplace, a mosque or church) entails discourse in the broadest sense. The very categories and *namings* with which we present ourselves and are valued have histories in discourse and language. But that discourse and language itself is produced by embodied subjects, by human agents with durable, embodied capital, augmented by and in cases overwritten by other forms of acquired and transformed capital—via this process of valuation and exchange embedded in the structures of social fields.

The Practical Problem Sociologically Reframed

For the last four decades, there has been compelling empirical evidence, both quantitative and qualitative, that mainstream schooling systems in the United States, Canada, Australia, New Zealand, the United Kingdom, and many European states systematically discriminate against children from racially and linguistically "different" populations.

The historical explanations for differential engagement, participation, achievement, and outcomes vary, including: de jure and de facto school segregation, cultural and linguistic deficit, limited home literacy resources, culturally alienating classroom exchange structures, exclusionary and alienating curriculum content, early tracking and streaming, inequitable school funding, poor teacher quality, face-to-face classroom prejudice, and, more recently, socially induced neuropsychological disorders. These explanations all remain in play in current research and policy.

The educational responses have been various. The legacy of both Frankfurt School and Birmingham cultural studies has been to focus on the racism and linguistic discrimination as dominant ideological formations, a critique of corporate media and curricula and to call for revisionist critique of mainstream curriculum and instruction as systematically excluding minority knowledge, competence, language, and approaches to learning. African American, Latino, Asian-American and Indigenous writers have called for a systematic recovery of *voice* in history, literature, art, and the textual representation of everyday social and economic reality (e.g., Nieto, Bode, Kang, & Raible, 2007). The legacy of feminist poststructuralist models has been a focus upon silences and exclusions in classrooms and curriculum. The focus on discourse has led to close analysis of the patterns of face-to-face exclusion and marginalization of speakers, the exercise of classroom forms of discrimination, and the differential representation and valuing of linguistic and textual forms, knowledge, and experience (e.g., Luke, Kale, Singh, Hill, & Daliri, 1995). The response has been to argue for more inclusive modes of pedagogy, ranging from dialogical models (e.g., Wong, 2005), to critical approaches to language and text (Norton & Toohey, 2004), to forms of culturally appropriate pedagogy (Ladson-Billings, 2005).

The educational response, then, centres on the politics of recognition, with calls for a general shift in school discourse to accommodate diverse ways of knowing and cultural interactional patterns. This entails: (1) voice and inclusion of repressed texts, discourses, and histories in curriculum representation; (2) inclusive and purposive engagement with diverse languages and discourses (bilingual education, critical ESL, critical foreign-language study); (3) expansion of school knowledge to include Indigenous, traditional, and migrant epistemologies and intellectual fields; (4) more equitable, inclusive, and democratic forms of classroom talk (critical pedagogy); (5) alteration of cultural patterns of interaction (culturally appropriate pedagogy); (6) explicit engagement with issues of racism and all forms of discrimination (antiracist education, citizenship education, intercultural studies). Each has a different focus on the habitus and its potential for agency in the field of the school, stressing the alteration of:

- *learner habitus*: remaking of student habitus prior to and in initial encounters with the field;
- *language of the field*: alteration or augmentation of the dominant *lingua franca* of the school field;
- *regulation of the field*: systematic alteration of interactional codes of the school as a field of exchange to accommodate those of diverse learners;
- *knowledge in the field*: systematic inclusion of the alternative and revisionist school knowledge as a change in the "value" and discourse of the field;
- *discrimination in social fields*: explicit analysis of the racist, sexist, class-based and other discriminatory rules of regulation of school fields and other institutions;
- *teacher habitus*: alteration of teacher habitus, introducing new schemata for "discrimination" of student habitus and capacity at any of the pedagogic and curricular approaches noted above.

In what follows, I provide brief glosses on each family of approaches, treating them as institutional strategies that attempt to alter or shift relationships of exchange and value within school fields. My aim here is to unpack their assumptions about habitus, capital, and field, rather than to query whether they are educationally appropriate or effective in any specific school or classroom, community or system.

Learner Habitus

The remaking of student habitus features in those models of compensatory education that entail the systemic early introduction of linguistic and cultural knowledge and practice that is seen as requisite to mainstream school achievement. This varies from preschool early-intervention programmes that focus on the introduction of dominant linguistic knowledge, knowledge of print, familiarity with interactional patterns of school and mainstream culture. Longstanding early childhood programmes (e.g., "Headstart") attempt to remediate student *lack* or *deficit*, variously construed as material, cognitive, linguistic, or cultural. A similar assumption is found in those progressive humanist early childhood philosophies that are promoting middle-class, mainstream cultural approaches to play and social relations as an unmarked norm of psychosocial development. Deficit models feature prominently in early literacy debates. Many advocates of scripted direct instruction in phonics for minority and second language children work from the assumption that student habitus needs to be systematically altered through early intervention to accommodate the print practices of schooling (Luke & Luke, 2001).

Early systematic English as a Second Language instruction further attempts to enable the transition to English (or other dominant language) of instruction. Typically it is premised on the assumption that the mainstream instructional framing and knowledge content and classification are valid and, with transitional accommodation for language of instruction, can remain unchanged. Their varying ideological intents aside, the shared assumption of these models is that the habitus of the learner needs to be systematically modified at entry to enable her to develop mainstream forms of cultural capital, as defined in existing systems of curriculum, pedagogy, and assessment. The rules of exchange and value in the social field of the school and classroom remain beyond criticism.

Language of the Field

Bilingual education alters the lingua franca of pedagogy and curriculum, shifting what counts in the linguistic market of the school. In contrast with compensatory models, it begins with an explicit recognition of the learner's pre-existing linguistic habitus as having value in the home, cultural community and, indeed, other affiliated social fields. The approaches here range from transitional bilingual programmes, to language-maintenance programmes, to attempts at culturally reciprocal *two-way* education that focus specifically on bilingual exchange and intercultural understandings. The approaches vary in the degrees to which they recognize and grant exchange value in pre-existing linguistic competence other than that of the medium of instruction. Discussing the possibilities for language education in South Africa and Bolivia, for example, Hornberger (2002) outlines a model of bilingual and biliterate education that takes two or more languages as co-equal cultural and pedagogic resources.

While these bilingual approaches move away from a deficit model of the habitus, they do so by degrees upon different assumptions about the need to alter the rules of value of the social field. Transitional bilingual education recognizes the developmental and cultural value of L1 but assumes that the purpose of the bilingual education is to prepare the student for English-medium instruction and social life. As in compensatory models, the dominant criterion of value in the field remains English, albeit with a recognition of the need for educational support to ensure access and use to the dominant language.

Language maintenance or *additive* approaches are premised on the assumption that L1 requires instructional support and educational recognition to preclude language loss and shift to dominant L2. That is, it recognizes the value of existing linguistic habitus as an end in itself, rather than as a means to L2 and affiliated mainstream educational experience. This entails more explicit recognition of the potential of L1 for application to domains of knowledge within the school field. Further, additive models have the potential for altering the regulative rules of the field insofar as L1 is explored as a medium for altering the discourses of schooling.

Two-way bilingual and bicultural education, featuring in some Australian and New Zealand Indigenous contexts, argues for reciprocal setting of the conditions for exchange, with valuation and exchange of multiple linguistic and cultural artefacts and practices (e.g., Malcolm et al., 1999; cf. McNaughton, 2002). As in Hornberger's (2002) models of bilingual and biliterate education, there is an attempt to alter the rules of recognition of the habitus, the interactional frameworks guiding exchange, and the dominant knowledge contents and structures of the curriculum.

Regulation of the Field

A correlative focus is on changing the regulative rules of exchange within the class-room, shifting the structures of pedagogic action and how knowledge is interactionally framed through turn-taking and exchange structures, topic nomination and choice, kinship and age/authority/status relations. Some models of culturally appropriate ped-agogy focus on spatial organization and on paralinguistics (e.g., *face*, eye contact, gesture). Here the focus is on altering the social interactional and sociolinguistic exchange to better match those cultural practices and interactional patterns brought to school. The focus is on altering the rules of exchange within the field to accommodate diversity of student habitus. In some instances, its aim is the more effective transition to mainstream curriculum outcomes, as in the use of culturally appropriate patterns in reading instruction (e.g., Au & Mason, 1983). Where this is the case, as in compensa-tory ESL education, the recognition of difference in learner habitus is seen as a means towards conventional achievement as determined by existing rules of the field. In other instances, it entails an attempt to expand and alter the cultural knowledge that is made to count in the field, focusing on incorporating the languages and practices, epistemol-ogies and local stocks of knowledge of learners and their communities.

Knowledge in the Field

This entails an alteration of the structures and knowledge valued in the social field of the school and classroom. Curriculum entails a selective tradition of knowledge (Apple, 1990): that is, a canonical set of cultural, social, and political selections of what will be valued in the field from what is, in theory at least, an infinite range of possible social fields and disciplines, texts and discourses, knowledges and possible worlds. Work in critical multiculturalism, critical race theory, queer theory, and feminist theory stresses the need for a more inclusive curriculum, one that includes standpoints and epistemol-ogies, voices, histories, memories and experiences, cultural genres, aesthetic forms and modalities of expression of those who have been marginalized from mainstream schooling, and, more generally, dominant systems of cultural representation. This revi-sionist approach to curriculum is based on principles of *recognitive justice* (Fraser, 1997)—that the elimination of misrepresentation of communities' and cultures' histo-ries and their recognition in official knowledge will have the effect of altering the rules of value in the school. In this regard, it entails both the inclusion of minority *voices* in schooling—and can extend to the critique of conventional formations of knowledge and ideology, epistemologies and disciplines, cultures and practices that currently are made to count.

Discrimination in Social Fields

Critical pedagogy, approaches to critical literacy and antiracist education offer varied pedagogic approaches. They share a focus on making the regulatory rules of the field of the school itself, and those of other significant social fields (politics and the state, work-places, community and religious organizations) the objects of critical analysis. In socio-logical terms, these pedagogic approaches are further attempts to "objectify the objectification" (Ladwig, 1996, p. 56), by making transparent the rules of recognition, discrimination, and exchange in dominant institutions. These bids to *read the world* (Freire, 1987) might entail, for instance, working with students to identify how racial or linguistic discrimination works, where and in whose interests (Milovich, Luke, Luke, Land, & Mills, 2001), analysing the conditions of production and reception for particular discriminatory texts and discourses (Fairclough, 1990), or engaging with a critical analysis of the rules of exchange and value in social fields of work, media, civic, and community life (Luke, 2000).

Teacher Habitus

There is a strong and ongoing focus in teacher education on the development of teachers who are able to recognize and capitalize upon linguistic and cultural diversity. There is ample research that demonstrates how teachers' cultural-deficit models, entailing a misrecognition of student habitus, contribute to educational inequality (Comber & Kamler, 2004). Teacher habitus, as argued, entails embodied cultural disposition and taste, and salient schemata and scripts for reading and engaging with student habitus. Attempts to change teacher habitus occur in teacher training and specialized professional-development programmes: these range from antiracist and antisexist programmes, to training with developmental diagnostic tools that recognize diversity, to engagement with many of the pedagogic and curriculum strategies noted above (Luke & Goldstein, 2006). The assumption here is that teachers can be trained to position-take in social fields in fair and equitable ways, using their discrimination even in those fields that have histories and structures that are based on the misrecognition and inequitable exchange of students' cultural capital.

A Sociological Template for Whole-School Language-Education Reform

We can put to the side for a moment hairsplitting arguments in legislatures, courts, and the media over whether this or that constitutes racism, an apology, or genocide (Luke, 1997; cf. Moreton-Robinson, 2004). There is overwhelming evidence—scientific, experiential, historical, narrative—that modern schooling is a sophisticated institutional technology for social reproduction, the stratification of knowledge and discourse resources, wealth and capital, power and force along the fault lines of race and gender, social class, and culture.

But the moral consensus among members of linguistic- and cultural-minority groups who have experienced racism and sexism does not begin to resolve the complex issues around educational strategy. It is all too easy for us to agree on the need for fair and equitable approaches to schooling and language education. It is even easier to embrace the broad egalitarian goals of empowerment and social justice for those communities and student bodies who have been educationally marginalized.

But the road of school reform has been full of potholes, detours, and blind alleys—and along the way, we often find the abandoned vehicles of those educators who have preceded us. We also encounter other travellers who believe, often with good reason and evidence, that their distinctive map and journey are the only viable ones. Simply, our preferred approaches and solutions to the challenge of equitable education are based on different descriptive analyses of the problem.

I have here offered a cautionary but enabling map of the sociological terrain. The first lesson is about the limits of the school as a social field. Students live in and move across a range of community, economic, and social institutions before, during, and after their formal schooling. Many of these domains remain exclusionary and discriminatory, precluding the use and extension of their educationally acquired capital. In this regard, the mobility of students across social fields cannot be seen to be *caused* directly by their level of skill, knowledge, or educational credential. Rather it is contingent upon the systems of objectification and rules of exchange of other fields. In this regard, the assumption that English, or genres, or phonics, or critical literacy vest students with durable, portable, and universally valuable power is a spurious one (Luke, 1996). For power is always contingent upon whether the structures and authorities of social fields set out the conditions where it can be recognized and used for gainful purposes.

Further, governments and the private sector have shown a remarkable penchant for providing community conditions for the dysfunctional and uncoordinated availability. In Aboriginal and Torres Strait Islander communities, historically this has entailed the scattered, sporadic deployment of resources: a health policy push for hospitals and nurses this year, a press for curriculum reform around phonics in another, a new model of community policing one decade, a collaboration around community employment and private-sector jobs the next (Luke, Land, Kolatsis, Christie, & Noblett, 2002). While all of these might be of value in themselves, whole communities are left unable to convert and mobilize educationally acquired skills and knowledge, *sans* healthy living conditions, proper housing, generative social and community relations, meaningful and productive work. In North American urban settings, calls for educational reform often sit within contexts where the same state authorities and corporate advocates have failed to develop viable economic development, where community social capital is the object of active disinvestment, and where political franchise is precluded. *Language-in-education policy and practice therefore needs to sit as a subset of larger community-based social and economic policy.*

That said, schools can make a difference. Following Bourdieu, I have argued that we can begin from an understanding of how race and language—and gender, sexual orientation, and difference more generally—are made to count in the social fields of the school and society. The habitus is a complex amalgam of received and acquired dispositions, woven and rewoven together in ways that make essentialist and unitary claims about race and gender and social class as freestanding, universal phenomena at best contingent and, at worst, misleading. How student habitus is mis/recognized, evaluated, exchanged, and, potentially, transformed is sociologically contingent. That is, it depends upon the structured and structuring rules of exchange in the field, and the relative agency and realized exercise of power of those whose human authority the field relies upon. As teachers, teacher educators, administrators, curriculum developers, educational bureaucrats, and public intellectuals, we have within our grasp the everyday possibilities of setting up fair and equitable rules and procedures for the evidence-based recognition of students' capital, and for establishing enabling conditions via curriculum, pedagogy, and assessment for the optimal valuing, exchange, and conversion of these complex forms of capital into a normative model of new human subjects: multilingual, transcultural subjects who remain grounded and engaged with their communities and cultures.

Children develop a sum total of dispositions across a life time, across multiple, nonsynchronous social fields of families, communities, religions, the state, and other key institutions. As an ideal type in modern democratic societies, the school's responsibility—though always qualified and quarantined in effect and force—is to enable the gainful and agentive, fair and transparent conversion of this habitus into one that enables a meaningful, gainful, and agentive pathway to community cultures, to civic participation, to productive and meaningful labour. Despite attempts to change this historical mission to a grossly oversimplified market model, and in the face of the continued proliferation of patently racist and socially unjust social and economic structures and institutions—schooling remains a means for redress, for equity, and for change.

Constrained by policy contexts and the localized cadences of school reform, attempts to redress current conditions are often piecemeal: teachers' attempts at innovation and change are met with scepticism by others; principals often can only push through or finance a single approach; state departments committed to reform are often frustrated by the limits of their own bureaucratic capacity at programme development and implementation; policy-funding regimes often target student groups by a single category of habitus. A sociological model provides us with a definitional threshold on the limits of purely race and language-based categorization and ascertainment and funding strategies. Given the complexity and multiplicity of the habitus, single categorizations of students for funding, "treatment," remediation and intervention can misrecognize sources of exclusion and misdirect valuable resources.

Contra determinist readings of Bourdieu, those in power, those who are engaged in structural positioning, also have agency: the agency to disrupt hierarchical exchanges of value, the agency to make exceptional cases, the agency to be rule bound by various degrees, the agency to challenge and alter the discourses of law. The position-taking, agentive possibilities within a social field can be exercised not only by the object of racialized power, who can resist, but by those with power. Whether this demonstration is overt—as in sovereign benign pardon and exception—or covert, via a subtle bending of a rule, it is an everyday assertion of agency. But to massify power—even ruling-class, patriarchal power—as absolute and never bending ignores the very contingencies of modern rule and law. Modern rule and law is by definition never literal, but always interpretive and elastic. In this way, unlike the customary exchange systems of gifting and bartering, modernist institutions have a range of capacities for being nonracist, nonsexist and nondiscriminatory. They have legal and juridical rationale, won through legislation, for exception and exemption. The result can be construed as substantive or token. The simple fact is that teachers and principals, counsellors and clinicians every day have the capacity to alter the fields of exchange.

What would a whole-school approach to equity and social justice for linguistic- and cultural-minority students look like? There is a series of practical implications of the Bourdieu model for curriculum and pedagogy, assessment and accountability issues in schools. My own view is that the school would operate from a sociological logic of practice, intervening to shift the field at the different structural pressure points I have described in this chapter. It would:

- *Accurately and fairly recognize and evaluate the cultural capital that students bring to school*: This would entail a much more detailed understanding and engagement with student habitus beginning with systematic, face-to-face developmental diagnostic procedures that would evaluate students' competence in their community languages, engage with their "stocks of knowledge" (Moll, Amanti, Neff, & Gonzalez, 1992, p. 132) and repertoires of practice gained in community (McNaughton, 2002). The aim would be to identify and validate cultural scripts and schemata, skills, knowledges, and practices, in order to set the optimal conditions for transformation and conversion of these into a substantially modified and augmented version of school knowledge. A principled, culturally and linguistically sensitive, sociologically grounded *evidence-based teaching* would supplant deficit thinking (Darling-Hammond & Bransford, 2004).

- *Change the lingua franca of the school field*: Depending upon community and student aspirations, it would provide a balanced programme of English as a Second Language and/or bilingual programmes for transitional bilinguals to enhance their English (or other mainstream language competence) in ways that do not directly contribute to language loss. It would weigh and consider the local viability and value of appropriately resourced approaches to bilingual and biliterate education (Hornberger, 2002).

- *Change the regulative rules of interaction in the school field*: This would entail teachers developing pedagogic strategies that complement and reflect student cultural and community practices of exchange and gifting, paralinguistics and gesture and turn-taking. Culturally appropriate pedagogy would be one of a rich range of pedagogic repertoires that would include traditional didactic, constructivist, and critical pedagogies as these are suited to the acquisition and practice of different kinds and levels of knowledge (Luke, 2007).

- *Revise the curriculum*: This would entail the revision of curriculum to include both community and mainstream, alternative and dominant curriculum fields and knowledges. Minority voices, histories, and world-views would be included. There would be a direct but analytic engagement with new media and cultural forms. A critical approach to curriculum and pedagogy would enable students to compare and contrast these knowledges for evaluation and analysis. But such a critical stance would not entail an ad hoc discarding of conventional scientific and canonical cultural knowledge requisite for participation in mainstream education and economy (Young, 2008)—and it would articulate to a mastery of dominant technologies of discourse, field knowledge, and inscription (Escobar, Fernandez, Guevara-Niebla, & Freire, 1994).

- *Critique social fields*: the critical component of the programme would engage students with a broad analysis of how social fields discriminate, their rules of exchange, and who they historically have included and excluded. The aim would be to make the discriminatory technologies that students will face transparent and available for naming and analysis. In critical-literacy studies, for example, this entails an understanding of how texts work in specific social institutions; that is, how a media report is constructed by specific lexicogrammatical conventions, by particular historical authors, with particular intents and audiences. In sciences and social sciences, it would entail an analysis of how they operate as social fields, with particular criteria of access, rules of value and exchange.

- *Remake teacher habitus*: As Freire (2005) argued, the teacher can become a learner of student habitus, community culture, and community language. But this is not to understate or undermine the significant role in enhanced teacher expertise in socially grounded developmental diagnostic capacity, use of assessment data, field knowledge, L1 to L2 transition, and affiliated pedagogic repertoire. As an established epistemic authority and elder in the social field of the school, teachers require evidence-based discrimination about student learning as against operating from staffroom folklore, received wisdom and commonsense assumptions about the capacities of particular language groups and communities. The approaches noted above will require enhanced professional technical knowledge and professional expertise, and cannot be sustained solely by principled belief in justice and equality.

One of the cul-de-sacs of language-education research has been its tendency to prioritize one form of capital as "making a difference" when, in fact, they are always deployed *in situ* (in a definable social field), and as part of a larger amalgam (the habitus' array of different modes of capital). How these are symbolically valued, how they are transformed in everyday practice depends largely upon the rules and practices of exchange in schools and classrooms. A combined, multiple-strategy approach is needed.

I have here advanced a template for what an equitable classroom, curriculum, and school should entail. The school's responsibility is to establish equitable and transparent rules of exchange that enable the student to transform their existing cultural capital into educationally acquired value, that is, knowledge and skill (embodied capital), educational and cultural artefacts and performances (material capital), and credentials (institutional capital). This is the challenge for all teachers and systems. When these exchanges are misaligned, arbitrary, and nontransparent, the evidence is found in those who have achieved credentials without demonstrated work, those whose artefacts apparently exceed their acquired competence and skill, and those whose obvious skill and knowledge does not convert into value. An equitable and just classroom would set out clear, effective, and enabling spaces and contexts, interactional patterns, and practices for the conversion and exchange of capital.

Schools are by definition dynamic but clearly circumscribed social fields. As such, they are limited in their capacity to *preserve* languages and cultures, should this be their intent, nor is their historical mission the simple recognition and acceptance of student habitus. Simply making schools more relevant and attuned to local communities and habitus can be self-annulling (Luke & Carrington, 2002). Teaching and learning are always about extending human development and potential, about moving students from the known to the new, about elaborating and extending existing cultural schemata and scripts, constructing and inventing new knowledge, new cultural practices and novel applications of existing ones. In this regard, the grounded recognition of student habitus, the validation and inclusion of community and minority knowledge, the use of community stocks of knowledge and expertise are not ends in themselves. They potentially enable the transformation and conversion of capital into value, expertise and, indeed, cultural practices and wisdom that did not exist for that individual and community before.

A Postscript

As theoretical as this chapter might be, it actually started as an autobiographical reflection on race, but for the usual reasons, this proved more difficult than *doing theory*. Perhaps at another time—but there is standpoint at work here.

This has been a sociological reflection about race and power—written from my experience of it as a variously racialized, class-located, Chinese male—and now middle-class academic working in a white-dominated society. This is not an archetypal story of the alterior, minority male in white-dominated societies nor a model minority narrative. I have lived across several and multiple life worlds, marked by differing combinatory historical relations of race, gender, class, and location: in Australia, Asia, and North America—never self-same, but shifting in status, with differential value attributed to my subjectivity (Asian, American, Chinese-American, Asian-American, Canadian, Asian-Canadian, Australian, Han Chinese, Cantonese, heterosexual male, poor student, good student, senior bureaucrat, ruling class, middle class, doctorally certified, North-American-accented English speaker). This is both a privileged and corrosive position of seeing and experiencing power from both sides: both its benign and productive moments, and its centralist negative, destructive force, both as racialized object of power and unmarked ruling subject asserting power, both as outsider and insider.

Racism is an act of power, a form of symbolic and physical violence. I have lived and written about race as position, as alterity, as Other, as object of power, violence, and exclusion. Made through our own historical trajectories, many of us working in language and education, TESOL, literacy, and related fields have worked as visible minorities. In the face of the social facts of social, economic, and cultural reproduction in education, we have sided, with various strategies and political investments, with the Other, whether we have been marked by self-same colour and difference or not. But this siding brings with it an optics, a view from the histories of colonialism, patriarchy, and domination that we set out to oppose and redress. Much of our work on the everyday experiences, institutional machinery, and discourse and material structures that exclude those of difference, has been premised on a one-dimensional theorization of racism, sexism, and other forms of exclusionary blindness, standpoint, and miscategorization. This is the historical irony: we have understood racism from the standpoint of marked, racialized subjects—not from the standpoint of unmarked racists. This may be where literature fails us, offering nothing other than stereotypes of racists. For I am not certain that white, male power in white-dominated societies has a capable self-understanding.

For me this changed substantially first when I moved for several years into a life world, a political economy, institutional context, and a system of cultural and linguistic exchange where I was admitted to a centre, where I was not racially other but rather racially dominant, the unmarked normative male that theorists of gender and whiteness refer to. The combinatory capital I brought to this field—flawed but good enough to gain admission—was mixed and only enabled me access to being able to see and understand certain elements of its logics of practice. I spoke English but not Mandarin. So my sense of the field I worked in is, admittedly and necessarily, limited—I understood perhaps a third of what I saw and heard. Nonetheless, this was an experience of *crossing* in optics, standpoint and embodied context from margin to centre (and back again).

This has left me either a cosmopolitan subject of mixed pedigree, at times quite cognizant of the various kinds of difference (mine and others) at play in everyday life and in professional/academic work, and at times quite naive and confounded. I am not, as one senior white rationalist scholar put it to me many years ago, so multiple as to be simply confused. At the time, I explained to him that the many personas and identities we bear are not a problem unless we are absolutely wedded to an essentialist unity of self, position, and deed. It was his problem and not mine. It occurred to me later that his self-understanding as a rational male in a white-dominant culture was wholly unproblematic: he need not give it a second thought.

Nor am I naive or sufficiently unmarked to believe in, to paraphrase another white male, critical-rationalist colleague, the "universal good in all people" through these experiences of crossing. Having seen power and racism from both sides—as object and as subject—that universal virtue is at best elusive. I have sat in boardrooms and staff-rooms sometimes silent and thereby complicit, regardless of my strategic rationalizations. More often than not, when speaking out or *acting on behalf* of others, I have asserted and at the same time expended and relinquished insider power and credibility. This is the case in those cultures where the saving of face is paramount and in those cultures that purport to value being upfront.

To see racism, sexism, social class, and linguistic discrimination from the vantage point of those who exercise power against others is unsettling. Yet it was my "defective" habitus, not fully culturally and linguistically suited for rule, but admitted variously by virtue of race, institutional and/or cultural capital, that enabled me to *see* racism and patriarchy at work. I could step outside it as it occurred, hear my own words and others echo around the table. As Bourdieu (1990) notes, where the habitus is matched optimally to systems of value and rules of exchange, the legitimacy of these systems and rules appears seamless, natural, and untroubled. And for many participants, it is not racism or sexism at all. It is just the way things are done.

These experiences continually unsettle and disturb my own understandings of race and language, difference and diversity. Each of our own racialized and gendered lives is an ongoing work in progress. But there is agency in both how we respond to racism, and in the ways that those in authority in social fields assert or choose not to assert it. Just as we need to continue critical work on where racism and sexism are asserted, upon whom and by whom, how and to what ends, we need to attend to instances where they are precluded, broken, and effectively stopped. To do so, we too need to consider the Other, no matter how confounding and difficult a task that might be. The biggest test of my own commitment to social justice as a teacher has not been teaching the oppressed or about the oppressed—nor in recounting and reconciling tales of where I and my family have been objects of racism and sexism. It has been teaching equitably students who are racist, some who were verbally abusive to me outside school. The biggest tests of my own work as a government bureaucrat and university administrator were what to do as part of a corporate and collegial body that was *othering* people of colour and difference.

Discussion Questions

1. How will you deal with the *others* in your classroom (e.g., marginalized students in terms of race, gender, sexual identity, social class, etc.)? Should they be seen as *others*

in the first place? How can you undo this *seeing*? And how can you help your students or colleagues undo this *seeing*?

2. What kinds of sociological, demographic, cultural, and linguistic evidence do you have on your students, their lives, and communities? Based on this evidence, what kinds of capital do they have or not have, and what kinds have currency in the cultural fields in your institution?

3. How can you set conditions for your students to use, deploy, and capitalize on these resources (capital)? That is, how can you (in whatever capacity) contribute to changing the rules of exchange governing different kinds of capital in the cultural fields in your institution?

Acknowledgement

Thanks to Carmen Luke, James Ladwig, Jo Carr, Aileen Moreton-Robinson, and Victor Hart for discussion of these ideas; to Courtney Cazden and Nancy Hornberger for their editorial suggestions; and to the editors for their patience and support.

Notes

1. This does not apply exclusively to the assertion of racism or linguistic marginalization by and through rule systems. The relative agency of discrimination and taste may be asserted by a racist teacher flying under the legal-juridical radar of official anti-discrimination laws—or it could rest in the hands of an antiracist teacher flouting or subverting racist institutional rules.

2. Following the psychoanalytic feminist claim that the paleosymbolic experience prior to entry into language remains in body and memory (Kristeva, 1983), I would argue that the initially acquired "namings" and functions have developmental and longitudinal salience.

3. Consider, for instance, a recent *Economist* ("Nearer to overcoming", 2008) study that found that African American women with postgraduate credentials earn substantially more than their white counterparts, while those with first degrees and without degrees earn less.

References

Albright, J., & Luke, A. (Eds.). (2008). *Pierre Bourdieu and literacy education.* New York: Routledge.

Ang, I. (2000). *On not speaking Chinese.* London: Routledge.

Apple, M. W. (1990). *Ideology and curriculum* (2nd ed.). New York: Routledge.

Au, K. H., & Mason, J. M. (1983). Cultural congruence in classroom participation structures: Achieving a balance of rights. *Discourse Processes, 6,* 145–167.

Bakhtin, M. (1982). *The dialogic imagination* (V. Liapunov & K. Brostrom, Trans.). Austin, TX: University of Texas Press.

Beteille, A. (2002). Inequality and equality. In T. Ingold (Ed.), *Companion encyclopedia of anthropology* (pp. 1010–1039). London: Routledge.

Bourdieu, P. (1977). *Outline of a theory of practice* (R. Nice, Trans.). Cambridge: Cambridge University Press.

Bourdieu, P. (1990). *The logic of practice* (R. Nice, Trans.). Oxford: Polity Press.

Bourdieu, P. (1998a). *State nobility* (R. Nice, Trans.). Oxford: Polity Press.

Bourdieu, P. (1998b). *Practical reason* (R. Johnson, Trans.). Palo Alto, CA: Stanford University Press.

Bourdieu, P. (2007). *Distinction* (R. Nice, Trans.). Cambridge, MA: Harvard University Press.

Bourdieu, P., & Passeron, J. C. (1990). *Reproduction in education, society and culture* (2nd ed.). Beverley Hills, CA: Sage.

Comber, B., & Kamler, B. (2004). Getting out of deficit: Pedagogies of reconnection. *Teaching Education, 15*(3), 293–310.

Darder, A., & Torres, R. (2004). *After race.* New York: New York University Press.

Darling-Hammond, L., & Bransford, J. (Eds.). (2004). *Preparing teachers for a changing world.* San Francisco, CA: Jossey Bass.

Escobar, M., Fernandez, A., Guevara-Niebla, G., & Freire, P. (1994). *Paulo Freire on higher education.* Albany, NY: State University of New York Press.

Fairclough, N. (Ed.). (1990) *Language and power.* London: Longman.

Fine, M., Weiss, L., Pruitt, L. P., & Wong, L. M. (Eds.). (2004). *Off white: Readings on power, privilege and resistance.* New York: Routledge.

Fraser, N. (1997). *Justice interruptus.* New York: Routledge.

Freire, P. (1987). *Literacy: Reading the word and the world.* London: Routledge.

Freire, P. (2005). *Education for critical consciousness.* London: Continuum.

Gee, J. P. (2000). Identity as an analytic for research in education. *Review of Research in Education, 20,* 99–125.

Hall, S. (1993). Culture, community, nation. *Cultural Studies, 7,* 349–363.

Holland, D., & Cole, M. (1995). Between discourse and schema: Reformulating a cultural-historical approach to culture and mind. *Anthropology and Education Quarterly, 26,* 1–16.

Hornberger, N. H. (2002). Multilingual language policies and the continua of biliteracy: An ecological approach. *Language Policy, 1,* 27–51.

Hymes, D. (1996). *Ethnography, linguistics, narrative inequality.* London: Taylor & Francis.

Kristeva, J. (1983). *The Kristeva reader.* New York: Columbia University Press.

Kumashiro, K. (Ed.). (2001). *Troubling intersections of race and sexuality.* New York: Rowman & Littlefield.

Ladson-Billings, G. (2005). *Culturally relevant teaching.* Mahwah, NJ: Lawrence Erlbaum Associates.

Ladwig, J. (1996). *Academic distinctions.* New York: Routledge.

Louie, K. (2002). *Theorising Chinese masculinity.* Cambridge: Cambridge University Press.

Luke, A. (1992). The body literate: Discourse and inscription in early literacy instruction. *Linguistics and Education, 4,* 107–129.

Luke, A. (1996). Genres of power: Literacy education and the production of capital. In R. Hasan & G. Williams (Eds.), *Literacy in society* (pp. 308–338). London: Longman.

Luke, A. (1997). The material effects of the word: Apologies, stolen children and public discourse. *Discourse, 18,* 343–368.

Luke, A. (2000). Critical literacy in Australia: A matter of standpoint and context. *Journal of Adolescent and Adult Literacy, 43,* 448–461.

Luke, A. (2004). Notes on the future of critical discourse studies. *Critical Discourse Studies, 1,* 149–152.

Luke, A. (2007). Pedagogy as gift. In J. Albright & A. Luke (Eds.), *Pierre Bourdieu and literacy education* (pp. 67–91). New York: Routledge.

Luke, A., & Carrington, V. (2002). Globalisation, literacy, curriculum practice. In R. Fisher, M. Lewis, & G. Brooks (Eds.), *Language and literacy in action* (pp. 231–250). London: Routledge/Falmer.

Luke, A., & Goldstein, T. (2006). Building intercultural capital: A response to Rogers, Marshall and Tyson. *Reading Research Quarterly, 41,* 202–224.

Luke, A., Kale, J., Singh, M., Hill, T., & Daliri, F. (1995). Talking difference: Discourses on aboriginality in grade one classrooms. In D. Corson & A. Hargreaves (Eds.), *Power and discourse in educational organisations* (pp. 184–193). Creskill, NJ; Toronto: Hampton Press and Ontario Institute for Studies in Education Press.

Luke, A., Land, R., Kolatsis, A., Christie, P., & Noblett, G. (2002). *Standard Australian English and language for Queensland Aboriginal and Torres Strait Islander students.* Brisbane, Australia: Queensland Indigenous Education Consultative Body. Retrieved July 3, 2008 from http://cli. ed.qut.edu.au/documents/Standard_Australian/ESL_report.pdf.

Luke, A., & Luke, C. (2001). Adolescence lost/Childhood regained. On early intervention and the emergence of the techno-subject. *Journal of Early Childhood Literacy, 1*(1), 91–120.

Luke, C., & Luke, A. (1998). Interracial families: Difference within difference. *Ethnic and Racial Studies, 21,* 728–733.

Luke, C., & Luke, A. (1999). Theorising interracial families and hybrid identity: An Australian perspective. *Educational Theory, 49,* 223–250.

Malcolm, I., Haig, Y., Konigsberg, P., Rochecouste, J., Collard, G., Hill, A., et al. (1999). *Towards more user-friendly education for speakers of Aboriginal English.* Perth, WA: Education Department of Western Australia.

Matsuda, M., Lawrence, C. R., Delgado, R., & Crenshaw, K. W. (1993). *Words that wound: Critical race theory, assaultive speech and the first amendment.* Boulder, CO: Westview Press.

McCarthy, C. (1997). *The uses of culture: Education and the uses of ethnic affiliation.* New York: Routledge.

McHoul, A. (2001). *How to analyse talk in institutional settings.* New York: Continuum.

McNaughton, S. (2002). *Meeting of minds.* Auckland, New Zealand: Learning Media.

Mey, J. (1986). *Whose language?* Amsterdam: John Benjamins.

Milovich, I., Luke, A., Luke, C., Land, R., & Mills, M. (2001). *Moving forward: students and teachers against racism.* Melbourne, Vict.: Eleanor Curtain Publishers.

Moll, L. C., Amanti, C., Neff, D., & Gonzalez, N. (1992). Funds of knowledge for teaching. *Theory into Practice, 31*(2), 132–141.

Moreton-Robinson, A. (Ed.). (2004). *Whitening race.* Canberra, ACT: Australian Aboriginal Press.

"Nearer to overcoming" (2008). *The Economist,* May 8, 2008. Retrieved July 4, 2008 from www. economist.com/world/na/displaystory.cfm?story_id=11326407.

Nieto, S., Bode, P., Kang, E., & Raible, J. (2007). Identity, community, and diversity: Retheorizing multicultural curriculum for the postmodern era. In Michael Connelly, Ming Fang He, & JoAnn Phillion (Eds.), *Sage handbook of curriculum and instruction* (pp. 176–197). Thousand Oaks, CA: Sage.

Norton, B. (2000). *Identity and language learning.* London: Pearson.

Norton, B., & Toohey, K. (Eds.). (2004). *Critical pedagogies and language learning.* Cambridge: Cambridge University Press.

OECD (Organisation for Economic Co-operation and Development). (2005). *School factors related to quality and equity.* Paris: OECD.

Omi, M. (1994). *Racial formation in the United States.* New York: Routledge.

Pennycook, A. (2007). *English and the discourses of colonialism.* London: Routledge.

Phillipson, R. (2008). The linguistic imperialism of neoliberal empire. *Critical Inquiry in Language Studies, 4,* 1–43.

Spivak, G. (2006). *In other words.* London: Routledge.

Van Dijk, T. A. (1993). *Elite discourse and racism.* London: Sage.

Voloshinov, V. I. (2006). *Marxism and the philosophy of language* (L. Matejka & I. Titunik, trans.). Cambridge, MA: Harvard University Press.

Wong, S. (2005). *Dialogic approaches to TESOL: Where the ginkgo tree grows.* Mahwah, NJ: Lawrence Erlbaum Associates.

Young, M. F. D. (2008). From constructivism to realism in the sociology of the curriculum. *Review of Research in Education, 32,* 1–28.

Contributors

Theresa Austin, University of Massachusetts, Amherst, United States

Francis Bangou, University of Ottawa, Canada

Carmen Chacón, University of Los Andes Táchira, Venezuela

Ana Christina DaSilva Iddings, University of Arizona, United States

Constance Ellwood, University of Melbourne, Australia

Rachel A. Grant, George Mason University, United States

Eve Haque, York University, Canada

Socorro Herrera, Kansas State University, United States

Awad Ibrahim, University of Ottawa, Canada

Ji-Yeon O. Jo, University of North Carolina at Chapel Hill, United States

Laurie Katz, The Ohio State University, United States

Ryuko Kubota, University of British Columbia, Canada

Incho Lee, Pennsylvania State University-Harrisburg, United States

Tonda Liggett, Washington State University Vancouver, United States

Angel Lin, City University of Hong Kong, Hong Kong

Allan Luke, Queensland University of Technology, Brisbane, Australia

Sherry Marx, Utah State University, United States

Sara Michael-Luna, Rutgers, The State University of New Jersey, United States

Brian Morgan, York University, Canada

Lan Hue Quach, University of North Carolina at Charlotte, United States

Amanda Rodriguez Morales, Kansas State University, United States

Cosette Taylor-Mendes, University of Manitoba, Canada

Luis Urrieta, Jr., University of Texas at Austin, United States

Shelley Wong, George Mason University, United States

Index